D0640119

PARTY OF ONE

The Selected Writings

of

CLIFTON FADIMAN

Party of One

The Selected Writings

of

CLIFTON FADIMAN

Cleveland New York

The World Publishing Company

Library of Congress catalog card number: 55-5284

First edition

———————

ACKNOWLEDGMENTS

FOR PERMISSION to include the following, grateful acknowledgment is made to Simon and Schuster, Inc., New York: introduction to Abner Dean's *What Am I Doing Here?*; introduction to the Inner Sanctum Edition of Dickens' *Pickwick Papers;* introduction (in part) to the Inner Sanctum Edition of Tolstoy's *War and Peace;* sections of the introduction to *Reading I've Liked.*

For permission to include sections from "In Praise of E. B. White" (herein retitled "A Traveler in Reality") grateful acknowledgment is made to The New York Times Book Review.

For permission to include the following, grateful acknowledgment is made to Random House, Inc., New York: introduction (in part) to *Great Stories of Science Fiction;* introduction to the Modern Library edition of Sinclair Lewis' *Dodsworth;* introduction to *The Short Stories of Henry James;* note on "The Beast in the Jungle" from *The Short Stories of Henry James;* introduction to the Modern Library edition of Henry James' *Washington Square;* a note on "The Altar of the Dead" from *The Short Stories of Henry James.*

For permission to include the following, grateful acknowledgment is made to George Macy, New York: introduction to the Limited Editions Club edition of Melville's *Moby Dick;* introduction to the Heritage Press edition of Mark Twain's *Huckleberry Finn;* material from the Foreword to the Readers Club edition of Leonard Ehrlich's *God's Angry Man.*

For permission to include the introduction to *The Collected Writings of Ambrose Bierce* grateful acknowledgment is made to The Citadel Press, New York.

For permission to include "The Decline of Attention" (in altered form) grateful acknowledgment is made to The Saturday Review, New York.

For permission to include the following, grateful acknowledgment is made to the Curtis Publishing Company and Holiday magazine: a review of William Faulkner's *Requiem for a Nun;*

5

"Reflections on Musical Comedy"; "No Knights in Minnesota"; "Conversation"; "Judy and Juan"; "Mother Goose"; "Emlyn Williams, Charles Laughton, and the Art of Reading Aloud"; "Clowns, Humorists, Comics"; part of the essay here entitled "The Wild Child"; "Fadiman's Law of Optimum Improvement"; part of the essay here entitled "Books for Children"; "Plain Thoughts on Fancy Language"; "An Experiment in Teaching"; "Some Passing Remarks on Passing Remarks"; "I Nominate for the Pulitzer Prize—"; "Pillow Books"; "Fanfare for Fireworks, Fawkes, and the Fifth"; "The Voice of the Dodo"; "Ladies and Gentlemen, Your Host—"; "A Gentle Dirge for the Familiar Essay"; section from the essay herein entitled "Prefatory and Retrospective"; "The Maze in the Snow"; "How Pleasant to Know Mr. Lear!"

For permission to include "The Wolfe at the Door" grateful acknowledgment is made to C. H. Hood & Co., Inc., New York.

For permission to include various parts of reviews of William Faulkner's *The Sound and the Fury, As I Lay Dying,* and *Sanctuary* grateful acknowledgment is made to The Nation, New York.

For permission to include the following, grateful acknowledgment is made to The New Yorker, New York: various items in "From My Notebooks"; "G. K. C."; "She Did Not Know How To Be Famous"; sections of "Gertrude Stein"; sections of "William Faulkner"; "How to Attract the Attention of a Schrafft's Hostess"; sections of "A Period Sample: Three Reviews of John O'Hara."

For permission to reprint material from book reviews originally published in the Book-of-the-Month-Club News grateful acknowledgment is made to the Book-of-the-Month Club, Inc., New York.

FOR *Annalee*

Contents

Contents

PARTY OF ONE

Prefatory and Retrospective

◇◇

Prefatory and Retrospective

1. ON BEING FIFTY

To DIVIDE one's life by years is of course to tumble into a trap set by our own arithmetic. The calendar consents to carry on its dull wall-existence by the arbitrary timetable we have drawn up in consultation with those permanent commuters, Earth and Sun. But we, unlike trees, need grow no annual rings. I do not wish to boast but—I am a continuum.

Yet, continuum or no continuum, for many men there is one year that often stands apart: one's fiftieth. I, my friends, am fifty.

At fifty, face to face with physiology, I concede sheepishly that I am mortal. This is the year in which I catch myself turning into a low-level philosopher and reflecting, however ineptly, on first and last things. This year I start that baffled, intermittent self-review only my last breath can sum up. This is the year I begin to talk to myself, having previously been too busy to make my acquaintance. It is, in Arnold Toynbee's phrase, a time of Withdrawal-and-Return. It is watershed year.

This is the year when ordinary men, such as the writer, admit at last to having spent half a century trying to pour a quart into a pint pot. Many of my exact contemporaries seem to be wearing an inward, stocktaking look. I recognize it. They too are making a secret assay of the limits of their being. For good or ill, we have charted our coast line, sounded our Dogger Bank shallows or Tuscarora Deeps. We

15

are what at birth (more likely eons before our birth) lay in us to become. Life is far from over, but we know both what we can do with it and what it has done with us. Or we should.

I do not speak of those exceptional men who have an onion genius for peeling off old and exposing new layers of personality. Nor do I speak of those stubborn heroes whose talent for obtuseness enables them to avoid self-measurement, or who use as their yardsticks power or possessions— yardsticks subject, one fears, to a kind of zero-limited Fitzgerald contraction. I speak of ordinary men, Thoreau's quietly desperate men, and I claim that at fifty, though they may never admit it in public, they generally know pretty well who and what they are.

All this is not as lugubrious as it may sound. I rather like being fifty. For one thing I revel in the probability that I will not in the future make very much more of a fool of myself than I already have. At twenty I knew I would amass the great American fortune. At thirty I knew I would write the great American novel. At forty I knew I would become a Socrates for sagacity. At fifty I know better. I know I shall end my days semieducated and semisolvent, leaving behind me an untidy paper trail of forgettable prose. To have snatched even this much ragged wisdom from the fifty-headed Cerberus of my life is no small matter. Some have fared farther and learned less.

Part of knowing who you are is knowing what you want. It is not easy to know what you want. I speak of the unrepeatable you, the unmultipliable you, not the carbon-copy, serial-number you which wants what it is told to want. The shelves of our odd twentieth-century world are crammed like a dime store with plausible objects and experiences, and we excited children rush up and down its aisles, infinite choice about us, infinite greed within us. Do you not remark a thousand geniuses of accumulation to ten geniuses of rejection?

At fifty, one should begin to know what to throw away. To men of fifty I suggest, now is the time to travel light. Carry airplane emotional luggage. Self-respect weighs less than self-pride, sifted memory less than confused anticipation, a few friends less than a file of contacts.

Moreover, do not be ashamed of your disencumberment. At fifty, if I obey the laws of my country, of morality and of courtesy, I have earned the right to be the self I have spent so much time uncovering.

I am, for example, no longer embarrassed to confess that at fifty I take but a cursory interest in current events. Things are interesting but I suspect not quite as interesting as the news criers make out. On the whole I prefer my history strained through the filters of the minds of historians rather than served up by the ticker bubbling with pinpoint carbonation.

Having at least dabbled my toes in the wide, wide sea of business and affairs and concluded that I would be but an indifferent swimmer, I now hope to spend a fair portion of the rest of my time voyaging among the doubtless narrower waters inside my skull, with no expectation of sensational discoveries. Quietism? The indictment no longer frightens me as once it did. I recognize the bogy for what it is: an eight-letter word hurled by those who, because they are so vigorously contemporary, would deny others the right to become outmoded. The quietist has at least this value: he provides a fixed point from which the activist may measure his own velocity. It is, of course, the activist who makes the world move. But it is still uncertain whether on balance he makes it move forward or backward. He may even make it fly apart.

The quietist contributes little except the occasional feeling that for a moment the world is standing still. Do not dismiss this feeling. It can be delightful.

At fifty I can afford to look my neighbor firmly in the eye and tell him that baseball bores me; that I think intellectuals are often valuable and patriotic citizens; that I no longer find any use for more than two suits of clothes; that a household with books in it is almost always more interesting than one with none; that most expensive fountain pens aren't worth the ink they dribble; that I will never write really well but judge it quite worth-while to spend the next twenty years trying to do so; that I think E. M. Forster, Joyce Cary, and Thornton Wilder more interesting novelists than William Faulkner and Ernest Hemingway; that I have chalked up about 100,000 air-miles and think that will do me; that the average house built thirty years ago is better than the average house built yesterday; that either colleges and universities should devote themselves solely to education or that we as a people should declare ourselves uninterested in education, both courses being honest and justifiable; that motor traffic in New York City should be limited to commercial vehicles, doctors' cars, and automobiles necessary for governmental and municipal services; and that I salute my neighbor no less warmly should he hold the contrary of any or all of these notions.

I could not have written the foregoing paragraph so easily at forty, much less thirty. That at fifty I can write it, without bellicosity and with no wish to convert others, is a small solid satisfaction.

To be able to live, at ease but without complacency, with one's prejudices is good. To be able to live, with regret but without shame or agony, with one's limitations is still better. Now at fifty I know I shall never understand much of the world of nature or cast more than a myopic eye on its felicities; never grasp machinery more complex than a can opener; never be or even act or look like a man of the world; never play tennis even as poorly as I did at thirty; never use the language as neatly as a well-born, well-educated Englishman; never have the ease, the charm, the grace of movement of those who have been sure of themselves from the cradle; never command that constant flow of specific instance which marks the concrete rather than the abstract mind; never have the magnificent courage of those who take chances and always elect to draw, with or without success, to an inside straight.

Yes, at fifty the blood cools. But the mind clears. In youth and early middle age competition is the thing, and a good thing too, for it tests one's powers. In retrospect some of it may seem wasteful. As we look back the objects of competition appear to have shed some of their magic. But was it really wasteful? Partly we compete to gain something. But partly competition is also a mode of self-exploration as much as a technique for acquiring goods.

At fifty, however, the results of the self-exploration should be more or less apparent. We should know who we are. We should compare ourselves—a niggling occupation—less frequently with others, having learned to live quietly with our success or failure. It is then that the real competition begins, not with the rival across the street but with the rival inside ourselves. For now we know whom and what we admire. These persons or ideas are merely the external forms projected by our ideal self, who has for years been overlaid by the smother of competition. Now we can begin a new game with a subtler opponent, the person we would like to be. Never quite matching him, we have the pleasure of feeling that at least the struggle is for real and not illusory stakes.

To know what we are may well take half a century. To develop that which we now know is well worth the rest of one's life.

At thirty, one should measure others, at fifty one's self, at seventy mankind.

2. FIGURES IN THE CARPET

At fifty then, or in its vicinity, one has gained the right to try to make sense of one's self. Often that is one's sole victory. Perhaps the other objects of our striving—security, recognition, achievement—should be framed in those curled accents of doubt, quotation marks. If it were not so, attaining these objects should make one feel whole. That this is rarely the case our most probing literature, from Henry Thoreau to John Marquand, continuously bears witness. The difference between our literature and that, for example, of pre-Revolutionary Russia lies here: the American hero finds troubling or even embarrassing the urge to examine the meaning of his life, whereas for the Russian hero it is as natural as breathing. Both kinds of literature are sound, bearing within themselves the kernel of growth. Only a literature like that of Soviet Russia, where the meaning of life is laid down in a dictionary, is dead, a corpse jerked into a semblance of activity by the galvanic pile of state authority.

All very easy to say, and hardly novel. The trick remains —to find the figure in one's own carpet. Here we collide with the biologist's facer: How examine an organism in the laboratory when that organism is changed by the very conditions of the examination? We can look at another man's life and make a fair fist at saying what it is about. Look at your own. It shimmers like a silverfish and is as suddenly not there.

To see ourselves we have to use a reflecting mirror, art. A man may learn more about himself from Hamlet's introspection than from his own, and the (perhaps deceptive) appeal of great music does not lie in the beauty of its sound so much as in its seeming to echo faintly our own deep muffled vibrations. Artists may fail in their first intention, which is to reveal themselves, and succeed in what was hardly their object —to reveal everyone else.

Nevertheless, remembering always Socrates' words about the unexamined life, we persist in our spiritual field geology, hoping always to come upon an outcropping of the truth, or, at worst, a fault.

What I think I have found out about myself may be mildly interesting for this reason only: that many Americans involved in one or more of my trades seem to show figures in their carpets not unlike my own. Or so I fancy.

The life of competition produces mainly two kinds of men: job-men and career-men. Both are captive, owning a common master, competition itself. But the career-men, who make or own or partly own businesses, a fruit stand or General Motors, breathe a larger air of freedom than do the job-men. The job-men, who work for others, are, whatever their income, of a lower order—not as total beings, of course, but as competitive beings.

I am a job-man, formed by nature for the salariat.

But of this species I am a particular, if common, variety. I am a job-changer. Most bank presidents have become bank presidents by persisting in working in banks. But most novelists I know, and even more rabbity types, such as essayists and book-reviewers, are natural job-changers. They have done scores of different things, rarely any supremely well.

That is my case. Like most men ill-suited either to business or bohemianism, I have a low boredom threshold and cannot fix for long on the delights of either accumulation or irresponsibility. The consequence is that I have had no career. Instead I have held down, until my antagonist calmly arose and threw me, a fairly large number of jobs. Each time I took one of these jobs—librarianship, tutoring, magazine selling, nurse-companioning, camp-counselling, translating, writing semifake biographies of businessmen, editing, publishing, journalism, reviewing, teaching, lecturing, radio, television, anthologizing, platform-reading, book-club-judging, movie-advising, dealing in first editions, or waiting on table—I thought my motive was to earn a living. It is one of the comic delusions of the sentimental American working middle-class male that he does it for the wife and kiddies. If he cared to poke about in his unconscious he might often discover that he acquired the wife and kiddies so that he might have a socially respectable excuse for acquiring the jobs. And he acquired the jobs, in my own case as in the case of many others, partly to keep himself alive but just as much to test himself against life. I have never listened to the studio audio-engineer with his "Testing-one-two-three-four-testing" without a sense that I had just overheard my biography.

It is another delusion to suppose that we earn a living by a series of accidents, catching opportunities as they whiz by. Our country is too magnificently various, too generous in its gifts, for this to be entirely true. We pick and choose without knowing it. Only the semicentenarian has gained enough perspective to see that this is so.

I can now detect, even in my own pocket assortment of small trades, some elements of the antirandom.

We are all Walter Mittys, of course, but I think American men mittier (women, as more rational, are excluded from this rhinestone generalization) than those of other stocks. Mr. Mitty was content to dream of being a heroic bomberpilot and such popular avatars. I have always dreamed, among other things, of being a scholar, perhaps even a college professor. These callings seem to my mind far more exciting than the most glamorous of Mr. Mitty's secret lives, involving as they do the never-ending risk of working amid ideas, which are *really* dangerous. The airman at most kills himself, but a bad idea can kill tens of millions. It has done so and is doing so.

I do not have enough brains to be a scholar—I mean a good scholar—and that's about all there is to it. But I can now see that the Mitty in me has in part dictated my life. My Mitty, at turn after turn, has urged me toward activities that have resulted in my becoming a kind of hemi-demi-semi-professor, or perhaps only a hemi-demi-semi-quasi-professor. For about a quarter of a century I have been one of that small, unimpressive army of American communicators who act as middlemen of thought and opinion. (I have also engaged in several televisionary enterprises that did not impinge on thought or opinion in any way. One must live. So—I speak as a married man and father of three—must five.)

I have been a kind of pitchman-professor, selling ideas, often other men's, at marked-down figures, which are easier to pay than the full price of complete intellectual concentration. I do not apologize for this. It is the best I and my many peers can do. And I am convinced the job is necessary.

In our country the effects of universal literacy are as yet not entirely clear. We would seem to have eliminated the mental torpor of the traditional Old World peasant class, and in a sense we have done so. Even the hill-billy wants to start a band and end his days a hill-william, lording it in a stucco palace in the high country back of Hollywood. But in another sense (see the essay in this book, "The Decline of Attention") we have substituted a new, streamlined torpor for the old-fashioned one. It doesn't look like torpor at all. The lovely girl cheer-leaders who decorate the pages of our picture magazines are alert, shining-eyed, beaver-busy. But our educators, who are doing their best, are not quite sure that the content of the cheer-leading mind is much denser than that of the mind of a fourteenth-century goose-girl. The goose-girl, believing in God, had at least some connection with large ideas.

At times it would appear that the effect of universal literacy has been simply to produce universal literates, and to stop there. But this is a crass overstatement. It would be truer to say that at the moment we are producing a large class (large in comparison with former ages) of highly educated citizens, and a much larger class of formally instructed but undereducated citizens. What we do not seem to be producing in adequate quantity is a large class of fairly well-educated citizens. The gap between a Norbert Wiener and a (fill in a name of your own choice) is slowly widening, despite the fact that our *institutions* of education—school, press, publishing house, museum, symphony orchestra—are more efficiently organized than anywhere else on the face of the globe.

To reduce this gap, to re-create and nourish the kind of middle-brow public that in another century used to read and listen to, let us say, Emerson, the popularizer has been invented. At his best—take, for example, *Life's* remarkable science and natural history articles—he is extremely useful. He mediates between a formed body of thought and a rather formless, shifting body of readers. It is not only that he assuages the mental hungers of a group that feels alienated or even repelled by more difficult material, such as most modern poetry, philosophy, criticism, and even certain kinds of vanguard fiction. It is also that he acts as a solid floor preventing too many members of this group from falling into the sub-cellar of the comics and the soap opera. Call him a stopgap, if you wish, but admit that there is a gap and that he is a stopper.

If the subcellar exists, so does the airy and remote garret in which, far above the living quarters, dwells our highly educated class. This too is increasing in numbers; but as it does so it increases also in subtlety, refinement, and remoteness. Feeling itself outside the main stream of American opinion, it chooses what appears to be the only course open to it, that is, to intensify, with a certain stoic, unconcessive pride, its sense of its own insulated identity. High-level literary criticism becomes more and more learned, makes more and more delicate distinctions, forges more and more passionately its own private closed language—and moves further and further away from the mass of moderately educated Americans who, still respecting the things of the mind, feel cut off from first-class intellectual leadership. The same thing is happening in poetry, in philosophy, and in other areas of thought. We are developing a magnificent mandarin class and a less magnificent mental-coolie class. If the intermediate class is starved out a most unhealthy state of affairs will result.

For some years people such as myself—not well educated but frankly amorous of education—have been trying to use every available medium of communication as a means of closing the gap and ministering to a beleaguered audience that is in danger of becoming the Forgotten Public. We have not done this out of "social consciousness" or any nobility of soul. We have done it in part because it is the only way we know to make an honest living and in part because it provides a most enjoyable and interesting occupation.

As I write this, for example, I am engaged in running a

radio show called "Conversation." It attempts, using the
talents of three good talkers plus my M.C. self (see the essay
in this book, "Ladies and Gentlemen, Your Host—") to revive an obsolescent art, that of civilized, noncontroversial,
discursive, nonpatronizing talk. We try, though not too
sweatily, to entertain; but, between you and me and don't
tell anybody, whatever modest value the program has is
basically educational. Nothing we say deserves to be treasured in the memory. But merely to dramatize once a week
the *idea* of mental play, in a period unduly suspicious of that
idea, has to my mind educational merit.

The response of the public would seem to bear me out. The
letters come from intelligent but not highly educated citizens,
few of them apparently very young, who feel that most radio
and television fare offers them little. Their words breathe an
atmosphere of wistfulness, as if they had been too long confined on a mental island, and were overjoyed at a glimpse of
any rescuing sail. This audience—the radio and TV critics
have been saying it for years—exists, is capable of development, and is even eager to buy sponsored products. But
(there are several noble exceptions to this stricture) it is
neglected or fed phony artiness.

"Conversation," on its particular level, is one example of
the mental brokerage business I have for years been engaged
in, just as this book, on its particular level, offers another
example. Both blend the pitchman and the would-be professor, a weird combination that only the wonderful flexibility
of our fluctuating culture would permit and even encourage.

3. ABOUT THIS BOOK

One of the sections in this book is headed "Lead-Ins." But
the word might well apply to the entire volume, excluding
the pieces on Gertrude Stein and William Faulkner. (These
are private exits.) The rest, except for a few bits of foolery,
are all samples of the work of a professional Master of Ceremonies, engaged this time in introducing ideas rather than
people.

Some of these pieces deal with cartoonists, scientists, conversationalists, actors, comedians, musical comedy, the radio
and television trades, teaching, the inspiration business, education, pyrotechny, technology, language, and deathbed remarks. A few are autobiographical. The remainder have to do
with writers and books and represent what may be called my
critical moments.

These latter are not, I suppose, literary criticism, and offer
little to the professional student of literature. As I look back
upon them I see that they are humble attempts to revive
another obsolescent form of discourse: talk about books that
is intended for that elusive personage, the general reader.
Their real intention is seduction. I am trying, as did a master
like Matthew Arnold, not to draw nice literary distinctions
but to communicate, by any means open to me, the love and
enjoyment of literature, whether it be science fiction or
Henry James. Thus I have not hesitated to grant myself what
Swinburne called "the noble pleasure of praising." (See the
section "Admirations.")

In France this sort of thing is called *causerie*. I have attempted to introduce into these literary pieces something of
the actual tone of talk, though not, I hope, that of chit-chat.
The masters whom I most revere—Hazlitt, for example—

were in beautiful command of this tone and by its use persuaded their audiences to creative reading. I am not ashamed to say that I have tried to do as well as I can what they did perfectly, in the full consciousness that I was practicing an art rather outmoded today. (See "A Gentle Dirge for the Familiar Essay.")

In his recent *The Languages of Criticism and the Structure of Poetry*, Professor R. S. Crane distinguishes three kinds of critics. The first, whom we shall call A, is an applier of a system. He measures literature by a single yardstick—Jeffersonian liberalism or Kierkegaard existentialism or Soviet Marxism. The second, familiarly known as B, practices "scientific" criticism. He is rigorously analytical. He studies the work of art as a whole, particularly its structure, as Aristotle studied the structure of Greek tragedy. He is "disinterested," as of course A is not. Professor Crane himself is a B. Then there's C. He's not disinterested either. He practices "literary journalism . . . that takes the form of cultivated *causerie,* after the manner of Hazlitt, Sainte-Beuve, Matthew Arnold and their many descendants."

It requires stricter application to become A or B than to become C, more learning, perhaps even greater moral conscientiousness. Yet the odd fact is that in our own country A's and B's are increasing in number, C's are lessening. I can name you ten brilliant A's or B's to one Edmund Wilson or Gilbert Highet or John Mason Brown.

Why should this be so? The answer is involved with the question of the nature of the audience. Whether he be a conservative Anglo-Catholic, like T. S. Eliot, or a Southern agrarian, like Allen Tate, critic A has an audience. Each of these schools has its scholars and, as with schools of fish, these tend to keep together for mutual support. Critic B has an audience too, made up of like-minded specialists or jealous competitors, usually college and university scholars.

But C, working within neither a sect nor an academy, is never quite sure who his audience is or indeed whether he has any. Sainte-Beuve, Hazlitt, Emerson, Arnold had no trouble in finding an audience of moderately cultivated men and women who were neither sectarians nor specialists. Our friend C is a character wistfully in search of this audience. It is his uncertainty, among other things, that prevents him from multiplying.

Then there is science. Let us admit that at least in our own country science kings it over the realm of intellectual discourse, as philosophy did in the thirteenth century. Thus all other faculties, often unconsciously, try to catch some of the divinity that hedges the king. System-critic A can legitimately claim for his doctrine an inner coherence and clarity that are also the mark of scientific statement. Analytical critic B can claim, plausibly enough, that his methods imitate the rigor of modern philosophical, linguistic, or even physical and chemical inquiry. Both A and B, along with King Science, scorn subjectivity. Both, as does science, develop a private language, often departing widely from vernacular English. Thus both seem well adapted to an environment whose climate is set by science.

But poor old C, floundering along with his nineteenth-century, pretechnological, slovenly habits, has no world-view, no key to fit all locks, no "tools," no infallible methods of inquiry, nothing but perceptiveness and love and an old-fashioned idea that criticism itself should be a work of literary art, no less than the matter criticized. In all these respects he is nonscientific or even antiscientific. Thus in a scientific age his tenure is infirm, his self-confidence tottery.

There are fashions in feelings no less than in hats and hair-dos. The efforts of C spring from a feeling that appear to be losing currency. That feeling is a simple one: the love of literature. Many brilliant critics today are profoundly *interested* in literature; there has never, I wager, been a time in which more critics were more *learned* in literature; but the signs that they *love* literature are harder to discern. Or if they do love it they seem unable to transmit their passion to others. Perhaps they are ashamed to confess so innocent an emotion. Or perhaps above all things they aspire to be contemporary—and ours is not a time pervaded by the emotions of love and admiration.

I have dared to say a kind word for C because if I were a critic I should like to be like him.

Of the papers that follow, those that are literary in nature are of the B variety. They are designed to introduce the reader to certain works of art. I do not think originality is their forte. I do think enthusiasm and reasonable clarity of statement may be claimed for them. In all cases I have tried to deal with books not as studiable texts (though that is often a good way to deal with them) but as organisms as lively and vascular as the men who made them were or are.

They represent a fair sampling of the pre-fiftieth year production of a working journalist. All have been published before, usually in a somewhat different form, for I have shortened or expanded here and there. A few are still in print as introductions; the great majority have been salvaged from out-of-print material or from the files of magazines. Though many inelegancies of style doubtless remain, I have excised as many as I could detect. A few topical references have been deleted, and I have not dated the essays. These pieces are good, bad, or indifferent irrespective of their time of composition. A few have a mild "historical" value (those on

Faulkner, O'Hara, and Gertrude Stein) and in these cases chronological signposts have been set up.

The book opens with some jottings from the kind of notebook every essayist keeps. I have included them (together with a few scissorings from reviews) because I thought it might interest the reader to note, in a miniature and unfinished form, the run-of-the-mine material that later on is often developed into longer and more elaborate articles.

CLIFTON FADIMAN

November 22, 1954

From My Notebooks

A man in love with a book is like a man in love with a woman: he is not truly happy until he has introduced her to all his friends and forced them to admire her qualities. This often turns him into a crashing bore and even more frequently loses him the woman.

It is notable that the doctrine of the omnipotence of love has often been proclaimed by the most sorry-looking females, such as George Sand, Mme. de Staël, and Elizabeth Barrett Browning.

I am appalled when I consider how many more good books I have read than Plato did. My old professor, Dean Woodbridge, was fond of saying that one advantage the Greeks had over us is that they couldn't read the Greeks.

I know many men of the highest social utility to whom daily living is merely a baffling interruption to thought. Such men should be spotted early by competent thinker-scouts, as baseball scouts watch the bush leagues. They should be protected by law from the time-wasting bother of the crude experience which is the very stuff of life to the rest of us.

"Only Connect." Civilization is the record of man's efforts to find objects of the preposition *with*.

The century to come will force us to redefine democracy. The rule of the majority? Rather, making the majority fit to rule.

The formula for Utopia on earth remains always the same: to make a necessity of virtue.

Liquor is not a necessity. It is a means of momentarily side-stepping necessity.

A good memory is one trained to forget the trivial.

The movie cartoon reconstructs the animistic world of our forefathers where everything lives, is dangerous, or must be placated.

New York City dwellers delighted in the great snowfall of 1947 precisely because *nothing worked*. We could not live without the jungle of pipes and cables under the asphalt; but they, except in rare instances, preclude the miracle of snow. The great snowfall threw us back for a few hours into a preindustrial America, in which everything quietly, softly, magically slowed down.

What is a romantic? One who, when life is too banal or too lazy to manufacture tragedy for him, creates it artificially, thus getting himself into the hot water he himself has boiled. Out of his maladjustments, noble or base, the practicing romantic constructs an ideal which human nature manages without difficulty to make quite unattainable. Then, in his endeavor to attain it, he is forced into a career of tragic excitement. The same mechanism produces the poetry of John Keats and the Peace Ship of Henry Ford. The one thing it does not produce is a dull life.

Our times do not encourage the literature of digression. There are many incoherent writers, few discursive ones;

many to ask whither we are drifting, few to drift. What was once the art of irrelevance has now become the act of impertinence, and all our Sternes are Steins. This is matter for mourning, for while any fool can weary you by sticking to a single point, only an ingenious madman can entertain you by saltation amid a thousand points. The self-centered mind cannot rival in interest the mind that is, in a sense, continually beside itself. I am thinking, of course, only of those cases in which real eccentricity is married to equally real intellectual power, producing, as in *Tristram Shandy,* a masterpiece of the roundabout.

The Renaissance is the Circean isle of world history. There are certain writers who have but to touch on its seductive coasts to be lost to reality for ever; and though the Renaissance Circe does not precisely transform them into swine, she has certainly succeeded in turning a good many into bores. More pink-and-purple slush, I wager, has been written about the Italian Renaissance than about any other comparable period in history. For years it has been the happy hunting ground of the glamour-boys and the glamour-girls, from Winckelmann through Pater and Symonds down to Rachel Annand Taylor. The future still holds the historian with a head hard enough to stress certain obvious facts: that the Renaissance culture-men (excluding real geniuses like Michelangelo and Leonardo) were most of them feeble bores; that the great *condottieri* and ducal conquerors, no matter how nobly they now bestride Verrocchio's bronze horses, were in essence the Owney Maddens and Little Augies of their day; and that, if you seek a symbol, the Medicean three balls make a far more sensible one than the Borgian poison cup.

There are certain subjects—alas, too few—that lend themselves only with the greatest difficulty to dull treatment. I have never, for example, read a really uninteresting book about bees or ants—and, more particularly, I have never read an uninteresting book about mountain-climbing. Mountaineering is author-proof as *Hamlet* is said to be actor-proof. I have never been able to work out a plausible explanation of this fact (if it be a fact); perhaps the reason is somehow connected with the circumstance that stories of mountaineering combine the maximum of physical and emotional suspense with something one can only call spiritual exaltation. Mountaineering is neither as gross as mere sport nor as moving as religion; partaking of both, it is something troublingly in between. Hence, for the most part, it has been the avocation of noble, or at least imaginative minds. The greatest mountain-climbers have been fine men, and many of them have been fine writers.

It was both an original and an educational thing for the late Dr. Hans Zinsser to write, in his *Rats, Lice and History,* a biography of the typhus bacillus. It now only remains for the bacillus to write a biography of man. "What a creature is man," muses the bacillus. "As far as I can see, he lives always in the utmost squalor and poverty, amid rats and lice. I see him always dying needlessly of famine, engaged in fruitless war with his own kind, neglecting his children and aged dependents. Where the results of his base passions are most apparent, in jails, in encampments, on battlefields and fighting ships, there I encounter him most frequently. He is a bestial being, similar in all his habits to the rat on which we feed, and worthy only of extermination. It is a law of Nietzsche for the lower parasites to be destroyed by the higher. Brother bacilli, to arms."

We living are a meager handful whose pathways briefly intersect in a flash of time, before we join the larger population of The Dead. Are we not but the rim, the outer edge, transiently illumined, of the world's people, the little passing as against the great passed? We choose to believe that we alone exist and that we exist alone, just as we choose to call the thin crust beneath our feet "the earth," ignoring the enormous, deep-extending mass under it. That the dead are alive in us, logic, psychology, and genetics agree. But how few of us feel it to be true! Tacitly we throttle in ourselves the sense of the dead—or relegate that sense to what we may not improperly call the dead files, to our imagined hells and heavens, Valhallas, and Happy Hunting Grounds.

By letting the dead die we have killed a certain part of the life in us. Our worship of the "career," of "achievement," of the measurable, the boundable in human experience is helping to wither in us that piety of the imagination which springs from an awareness of our links with the past. Marcus Aurelius, who was a mature man, began his book by making grave obeisance to those, many of them dead, who had formed his mind—his tutors and friends and family. Arnold Toynbee, shaped in a similarly classic mold, does the same in the preface to the seventh volume of *A Study of History*. How many of the bright children of all ages who in the past twenty-five years have offered us their autobiographies would think of thus beginning their narratives?

Note on Sex Differences. It is a sweltering day in Manhattan. Sweating, I climb into a cab. Its windows, I find, are closed tight—a Turkish bath would be cooler. I swear, open the windows, wonder for a furious second whether the previous occupant could have been an imbecile (doubtful) or perhaps an incubator baby with cab fare in its pocket (improbable). I realize that it must have been a woman, anxious about her hair. As long as hideous incidents of this sort recur, so long will the War Between the Sexes continue to rage.

The Invisible. The most apparent thing about us is that we live amid the unapparent. How tiny are the five ports of our senses set against the vast mysterious coastline of the invisible. The past and the future—the two countries in which we mainly live—are invisible. Our minds, which make us men, are unseen by us. We live on a gigantic sphere of which only a pinpoint is sensible to us at any moment. Our very bodies, which seem so palpable, are for the most part invisible: two and a half billion unseen worlds, each with its red racing ocean, its branching strata of bone, its strange islands and archipelagoes, its flora and fauna, its gulf streams and bays and rivers, its millions of microscopic living beings —all in a darkness sealed to our eyes from birth to death. All children should be given a sense of the invisible. At an early age take your child into a dark room, insert a flashlight into your mouth, show him the bony caverns of the skull weirdly lit in the reddish glow. It will do more for him than television.

The Private Life. Among certain African tribes the conception of privacy does not exist. All live together. What can you expect, we say. After all they're primitives.

How about our civilized selves? Not only is privacy in decline but we greet with amiable ridicule, as if they were the work of cranks, most efforts to defend its rights. Though one of the most admired of men, Charles Lindbergh when he smashed the camera of an overzealous photographer aroused considerable criticism.

The candid interviewer, the Fuller Brush man, the telephone pollster, the gossip columnist, the bought-and-sold sucker list, the wired dinner-music, the unordered merchandise in the morning mail, the adman's use of the second person plural (*Know Your French Provincial!*), the televised wedding, the juke box in front of your soda-counter seat, the TV set in your bar, the radio in your bus, the jet plane over your rooftop, the charity solicitor on the telephone, the tapped wire, the portable radio at the football game, the alert photographer at the busy street corner, the loud-speaker in the train, even the picture window and Dr. Buchman's public confessional and the couch of the psychiatrist: we accept these without demur.

In 1910, except in backward countries such as Russia, the world was virtually passportless. Today the papers are more important than the man; what is public is essential.

Is it possible that the world-wide unpopularity of privacy is to be explained not by the historian but by the anthropologist? Our increasing reliance on the picture as against the written word begins to look like an involved regression to the age of the hieroglyphic and the cave drawing. May not our gradual relinquishment of the private life be an involved regression to the state of the African primitive? Human history, some think, is cyclic. Are we regressing on a higher level, transporting with us our magnificent civilized baggage, re-creating a kind of pre-neolithic culture tricked out as the atomic age? Does not the monitoring eye of Orwell's *1984* make for the ant-heap conception of life that seems so natural and happy to the African primitive?

For about 3,500 years we have been working hard and painfully at the task of becoming private individuals. Perhaps the strain is beginning to tell. Perhaps we are beginning

unconsciously to hunger for a thousand years or so of rest on
the vast bosom of anonymity, in the great glass house of the
tribe.

A Note on Classics. Our superiority over the primitive
Greeks is debatable, but one advantage we *do* have. They
had no classics; we have three thousand years of them to look
back upon—a time-vista more beautiful by far than any the
duller dimensions of space have to offer. And the odd part of
it is that the classic we are surest of is the one that came
spang at the beginning: Homer. So true is this that for three
millennia Homer has fixed for us our notions of what a classic
should be. Ever since, contemplating any supremely great
book, our eyes travel beyond it to where in the distance the
shield of Achilles shines.

The greater number of books we judge to be classics share
with Homer this quality of beginningness. Most of them are
great starters. A few, like Dante, intoning the last incantations of the Middle Ages, are finishers. But starters or finishers they all are, and mostly starters: Homer starting European literature, Virgil starting the literature of nationality,
Huckleberry Finn starting Ernest Hemingway, Shakespeare
starting commentators. Many first-class works stand in the
middle of a process; but not a classic, which is too proud to
say anything but the first word or the last. That is one reason
why classics remain interesting. First and last words are so
often the crucial ones.

A great book may be open or it may be closed. Anyone
who wishes to take a little trouble can enjoy Homer. The
fact that only a small proportion of human beings has ever
taken the trouble to take the trouble is beside the point.
Homer, like Mallory's mountains, is there, permanently laid
on, like water or gas, or any other public utility. He is open.

There are other great books that are closed. Joyce, for example. Joyce is a far subtler writer than Fielding; but *Tom
Jones* is a classic because it is an open book. *Ulysses* will
never become a classic because it is closed, except to a highly
literate minority. It is private property. *Tom Jones* is public
domain.

Another odd thing about classics is that when their authors
are writing them, they don't know what they're doing. Do
not be misled by the boasts of poets. "Not marble, nor the
gilded monuments of princes, shall outlive this powerful
rhyme" was melodious whistling in the dark. Shakespeare
knew he was good but it is only we who know how good he
is. Indeed we might even say that the lower the level of the
work of art, the more closely the artist can estimate its
chances of duration. Mickey Spillane knows just about how
long his masterpieces will last, whereas poor old Homer
didn't even know he was writing one. A vast infusion of unconsciousness permeates the creative efforts of even the most
deliberate writer who produces a classic. He is always building better than he knows.

A classic is written now and created three hundred years
later.

Admirations

No Knights in Minnesota

A FEW YEARS ago, in Rome, a city separated by several universes from Zenith and Gopher Prairie, Sinclair Lewis died. Had he lived till February 7, 1955, he would have been 70 years old. I do not suppose the eager youngsters whose godlings are Kafka and Faulkner think much or well of Lewis these days. Only my own uneasy Middle Generation, forbidden to be "modern" and reluctant to be mellow, still wears him in its heart's core. Let posterity yank him up or pull him down, to us he remains the wonderful wizard of Sauk who freed us from the thrall of dullness. Lewis himself knew that this act of liberation was his main job. Indeed, he is explicit about it. In a revealing collection* of odd bits and pieces of his nonfiction journalism he says: "I have never been a propagandist for anything, nor against anything save dullness."

Once, I am told, the conversation turning to which dead authors had most influenced which living ones, Lewis jerked out, "With me it was Sir Thomas Malory." He went on, "As a kid my favorite reading was Howard Pyle's King Arthur stories, based on Malory. Well, when I grew up—I found there were no knights in Minnesota." No knights in Minnesota . . . the phrase is a little looking-glass and in it, if you look closely, you may see the faces of Carol Kennicott and

---

* *The Man from Main Street,* edited, with an introduction, by Harry E. Maule and Melville H. Cane.

47

Babbitt and Dodsworth and a red-headed Yale undergraduate who began his literary career with Tennysonian verse. In a foreword to his *Collected Short Stories* he remarked of himself that "he who has been labeled a 'satirist' and a 'realist' is actually a romantic medievalist of the most incurable sort." Never did he quite get over his disappointment at discovering that his country, however magnificent and fascinating, was vowed to other quests than that of the Holy Grail and that all the magic casements opened on Main Street.

Disappointment, yes; but it must have been a creative disappointment. It spurred him on to write his novels, good or bad. Also it helped to ease into being the quirky personality, all fizz and fire, that, I think, forms one of his three claims to the attention of the future. The other two claims are apparent. More than any other novelist he called into question the adman's version of American life, based and quite properly on the fear of looking into a mirror. Second, possibly in Dodsworth but surely in Babbitt, he created a universally recognizable national type—that is, someone in whom we can see a little bit of every one of us.

It is the third claim, Lewis's personality, that is apt, if not rescued, to slide into limbo. In this connection, I understand that his literary executors have entrusted to the distinguished literary critic Mark Schorer the task of writing the official biography. Mr. Schorer is an erudite fellow and, to judge from his writings, a man of rectitude. Whatever he turns out is bound to be intelligent, rich in social and literary analysis, and full as to fact. But I hope too it will give us the whole cantankerous and lovable man himself, as Boswell gave us Johnson. For this we need a biographer who knew Lewis well, drank with him, laughed with him, quarreled with him; and who in addition is at least touched with that easy disregard of mere respectability which was the habitual gesture

of Lewis's mind. The late Carl Van Doren might have Bos-
wellized Lewis. Among the living my choice would be John
Gunther, who should, as a matter of fact, be compelled by
law to set down his recollections. I hope Mr. Schorer is the
kind of human being capable of an inner sympathy with
Lewis's qualities, whether admirable or outrageous.

At first blush such questions may appear to be of merely
"literary" interest, but actually I think little matters of this
sort may well involve all of us, and for a simple reason. The
memory of a salient personality is a national treasure, to be
guarded and preserved with far more care than we devote to
the Washington Monument or even Fort Knox. We can ill
afford to forgo our pipe-and-slippers intimacy with Lincoln,
Mark Twain, Thoreau, or any outstanding American who,
in addition to being able or successful or important, was also
a miracle of personality. It is not that such intimacy "teaches"
us anything, but that it *gives* us something, it enhances our
own feeling of life. Our knowledge of just how interesting
Lincoln was makes all of us just the barest fraction more
interesting ourselves. We are nourished not only on the deeds
of outsize men but on their laughter, their oddities, and even,
if these should happen to be sufficiently extraordinary, their
foibles.

In a collection* of rather businesslike letters to (and also
from) his publishers, letters full of the go of the young literary man on the confident make, I came across this judgment
of Sinclair Lewis on another writer: "He lacks a passionate
reaction to daily life." A passionate reaction to daily life was,
except perhaps toward the twilight-colored end, precisely
what Lewis had. Often ill-balanced, brash, unreflective, he
would rather have been found dead than half-alive. He be-

---

* *From Main Street to Stockholm: Letters of Sinclair Lewis 1919-1930*,
edited and with an introduction by Harrison Smith.

haved as though not merely his books but his whole wiry frame and mobile mind were sworn to the destruction of dullness. If, to strike a spark from the sullen anvil of the commonplace, gaiety was needed, he would be gay; if wildness, he would be wild; if rudeness, he would be rude. He may have looked an unromantic figure, "a Yorkshire yeoman farmer" (as he once put it) "with none of the farmer's strength and horsey dash" but he talked and acted like a Mercutio from the prairies.

One of the ways in which we can step up the sense of life in ourselves and in others is through impersonation. The love of the impersonator lies at the root of the deep pleasure we draw from great clowns such as Chaplin, Danny Kaye, or Groucho Marx, all of whom possess the power of turning magically into somebody other than themselves, and this not in the formal manner of the actor, but with a weird, startling spontaneity that somehow touches the very heart of humor. This ability Sinclair Lewis had, and the ideal future biographer will do well to stress it, for it explains much of his genius. Lewis himself often pooh-poohed his talent for mimicry as a mere parlor trick, and it is of course true that one of its springs was garden-variety exhibitionism. But it was more than that. It welled up out of a lust to defeat dullness —to defeat it, among other ways, by the extension or multiplication of personality.

Stories about Lewis the impersonator are legion. Let me recall a few.

Lewis and Carl Van Doren were once traveling together through the Midwest when into the Pullman compartment came a stranger who introduced himself amiably as a small-town doctor. Lewis at once introduced Van Doren as *another* small-town doctor. Not in the least fazed, Van Doren introduced Lewis as a doctor too—a horse-doctor. The next

two hours passed in animated shoptalk with Lewis assuming
to perfection the style of a drawling, hard-bitten local vet
who had spent his life curing glanders, administering clysters,
and forcing large doses of laxative down equine throats. A
good time was voted by all.

Once Lewis, staying in a hotel that boasted a swimming
pool, heard that the latter was at the moment occupied by a
contingent of policemen who were using the hotel as a convention headquarters. Lewis promptly descended to the pool,
somehow secured admittance, took off his clothes, jumped in,
introduced himself as Patrolman So-and-so, and spent a
happy hour exchanging professional anecdotes with two hundred nude cops. By dinnertime they were all buddies. Everybody clambered out. The policemen got into their uniforms.
Lewis got into his sack suit. He grinned at his colleagues—
and made a quick beeline for his room.

I remember spending one evening with Red (this was before he went on a spree of sobriety) in the course of which
he got himself into a state of considerable illumination. As
a matter of fact he grew pretty obstreperous and I, rather a
novice in these situations, didn't quite know what to do with
him. He wouldn't go to bed, he out-reasoned me in my attempts to reason with him, he pigheadedly refused to pass
out, and I felt a certain impropriety in a young sprig of a
book reviewer clunking a Nobel Prize winner on the head
with a baseball bat. Desperate, and figuring that a little civilized conversation might calm him down or tire him out or
something, I phoned a mutual friend and blandly proposed
that he invite us over. He hesitated, then assented, adding
that he was entertaining some old family friends and hoped
Red was feeling well. I replied truthfully that Red was feeling fine.

We reached the house (by this time Red was a veritable

Vesuvius of uninhibited monologue) to find that the guests included two highly respectable ladies in their seventies, one of them our friend's mother-in-law. Aghast, I was about to drag Red out and if necessary abandon him at the street corner. I should have known better. Lewis paid no heed to the rest of the company. He headed straight for the old ladies, kissed their hands, paid them the most elegantly worded compliments, told them witty anecdotes, and in general, without the least grind of gears, transformed himself instantaneously into a charming, worldly beau of the 1890's. The old ladies succumbed to him without a murmur, Red enjoyed himself vastly, I sat and trembled without ceasing until it was time for us to make our adieux, I in a state of near-coma, Lewis with a happy blend of arch tenderness and the most high-toned consideration.

In this ability to enhance himself by disguising himself— always to serve the ends of comedy—Lewis resembled his literary hero, Dickens. His admiration for Dickens, as a matter of fact, forms one of the deepest springs of his nature and supplies still another useful clue for our future ideal biographer. In their careers and talents the two were startlingly alike. Indeed, though far inferior as an artist, Lewis is nevertheless the nearest thing to the English master our country has yet produced. In one important detail they diverged: Dickens' genius deepened as he grew older, Lewis's weakened after *Dodsworth*.

In other respects they present many interesting parallels. Both were restless, feverishly addicted to travel, driven by a constant inner dissatisfaction. Both possessed extraordinary creative energy, marred by sentimentality, moralizing, and flawed taste. Both were exhibitionists, both wanted to be actors, both were mad for stage and platform. Humor, fantastic exaggeration, and burning social indignation mark the work of both. Both were fond of conviviality, both remained inward solitaries. Both came of modest backgrounds, essentially provincial, both rose to paramountcy in their fields. Both were extremely close to their audiences, both were *popular* artists, both were superb journalists, both almost from the inception of their careers had absolute self-confidence. When the whole story is told it will be found, I believe, that the sexual patterns of both men were similar and led them to somewhat similar experiences. Both were great talkers, great clowns, great enlargers of the sense of life in all who were privileged to encounter them.

Many decades must pass before a final judgment can be handed down on Sinclair Lewis. Meanwhile there is the sentence he wrote for his own pretended obituary, putting the words in the mouth of one of his truest and stanchest companions: "This was a good workman and a good friend, who could still laugh when the world had almost worried itself out of the power of laughter."

A Traveler in Reality

It has been remarked that the superior American writer often becomes famous, wealthy, influential, even more skillful, but only rarely becomes mature. Maturity still makes us uneasy. Many of our writers find growing up not merely difficult but socially unrewarding. Those who do insist on developing whether their readers like it or not are freaks.

E. B. White is a freak.

The statement will embarrass Mr. White, who not only writes as if he were a modest man but actually is one. It may arouse skepticism in others, including those who admire Mr. White for certain qualities that are delightful but relatively unimportant. He has the charm of a dozen Irishmen. He is a master of light verse. His sketches of country living are humorous and poetical. He is fey. He is whimsical. He is funny. Because he is these things there is some danger of his being considered a minor writer.

In using the basso profundo word major I run some risk of alienating people, including the subject of this essay. Nevertheless, E. B. White is a major writer. He is a major writer because his ideas and sentiments are large and basic and because, within the limitations of his chosen style and form, he writes about them perfectly.

In the early years of the *New Yorker* magazine E. B. White contributed excellent light verse and various prose oddments. For about ten years prior to 1938 he wrote or rewrote the

54

first page (Notes and Comment) each week. For several
years thereafter he wrote small essays for *Harper's* magazine
under the heading One Man's Meat, and is now back on
Notes and Comment again. He has published a couple of
books of light verse; *Quo Vadimus* (amusing sketches); *Is
Sex Necessary?* (with James Thurber), still funny and reasonably wise; *Every Day Is Saturday*, a collection of the *New
Yorker* pieces; *One Man's Meat*, mainly from the pages of
Harper's, and, more recently, a best-selling collection of some
of his finest magazine work, *The Second Tree from the Corner.* During the years covered by the publication of these
frail-appearing volumes he has grown from a paragrapher to
a writer, from a light-fingered original humorist to a light-
giving original thinker.

I do not mean that you will find much that is "new" in him.
I mean only that his mind naturally works from origins. His
most casual remarks, and most of them are casual, come out
of a sense not only of where man is but of what he started
from. They are almost always based, though rarely explicitly,
on an original—that is, fundamental—proposition which
mankind when it is rational accepts as true. I have been casting about for a good short example of this kind of thinking
and believe I will start with this one:

> Clubs, fraternities, nations—these are the beloved barriers
> in the way of a workable world; these will have to surrender
> some of their rights and some of their ribs. A "fraternity" is
> the antithesis of *fraternity*. The first (that is, the order or
> organization) is predicated on the idea of exclusion; the sec-
> ond (that is, the abstract thing) is based on a feeling of total
> equality. Anyone who remembers back to his fraternity days
> at college recalls the enthusiasts in his group, the rabid mem-
> bers, both old and young, who were obsessed with the mys-
> tical charm of membership in their particular order. They

were usually men who were incapable of genuine brotherhood or at least unaware of its implications. Fraternity begins when the exclusion formula is found to be distasteful. The effect of any organization of a social and brotherly nature is to strengthen rather than to diminish the lines which divide people into classes; the effect of states and nations is the same, and eventually these lines will have to be softened; these powers will have to be generalized. It is written on the wall that this is so. I'm not inventing it, I'm just copying it off the wall.

This is original reflection. It goes back to an original abstract idea accepted by mankind when mankind is thinking rationally—the idea of fraternity. It demonstrates that college fraternities represent the opposite of this idea. The plain fact of the matter is that, if all college men could think, the mere attentive reading by them of Mr. White's half-dozen sentences would result in the immediate abolition of all fraternities.

Mr. White is a useful writer because he is an abstract thinker who does not write abstractly. His base is always a generalization, which is what makes him more than a journalist; but the development is always concrete. Here is an example: In October, 1940, he wrote a semi-joshing, semi-indignant piece on the design of the American motorcar. In the course of it he said, "The ultimate goal of automobile designers is to produce a car into whose driving seat the operator will sink without a trace." After enlarging on that nice (and true) point he went on to state: "The public's passive acceptance of this strange vehicle is disheartening, as is the acceptance by other peoples of the strange modern governments which are destroying them in a dulcet fashion. I think there will some day be an awakening of a rude sort, just as there will some day inevitably be a union of democracies, after many millions have died for the treacherous design of nationalism."

Now the parallel between the design of the motorcar and the "treacherous design of nationalism" is more than a piece of wit. In the first place it is based on a true relationship: in both cases "the operator will sink without a trace." But underlying Mr. White's concrete statements are certain unmentioned abstract ideas: first, that liberty is a good; second, that passive acceptance, as against rational reflection, is an evil.

Philosophy is a calm vision of the whole, journalism an excited perception of the part. Mr. White once wrote that he liked the radio comments of the late Hendrik Willem Van Loon on the day's events "because he has made them seem like a part of a whole, not like an isolated moment in time." This is profoundly true, and it is just as true that if radio commentators in general dared to talk about the events of the day as part of a whole the network officials would be bewildered.

One of the results of having a vision of the whole is that Mr. White is forced to see the part for exactly what it is. If it is part of something big he sees that. (Remember the comment on college fraternities.) If it is part of something little he sees that. If the part is so small as to be almost nothing he cannot help seeing that too.

In July, 1938, he wrote, "It must have been two years ago that I attended a television demonstration at which it was shown beyond reasonable doubt that a person sitting in one room could observe the nonsense in another." Note that Mr. White does not say that it is not pleasant to observe nonsense. On the contrary, he knows, as we all do, that nonsense may be very pleasant, indeed, and interesting, and even necessary. But nonsense is small. The implication of the sentence is that television is small. It is small when it relays the contortions of a blues singer twenty feet into another room. It is exactly as small when it relays the antics of diplomats ten thousand miles if the antics say no more than does the blues singer. Mr. White has his eye on the ends; the networks have their eye on the means.

Mr. White, even in his very early days, never lost sight of the fact that the accumulator, living under whatever system of government, has set a yoke upon his own back. I offer two diverting samples (but all Mr. White's diversions, remember, seek rather than escape the center). 'Way back in the *New Yorker* of May 26, 1928, he printed this small quip:

> A life insurance man told us of a remarkable business migration which took place in Madison Square recently. He said that one division of the Metropolitan Life moved en masse from one building to another, across the connecting bridge. At 2:30 the one hundred clerks ceased work and got up from their desks. At 2:41 the first desk was upended by a porter. At 3:35 the whole works had been transferred to the other building and electricians were installing the telephones. At 3:36 the clerks sat down and took up their duties. "And didn't any of the clerks escape?" we asked. But it was the wrong question.

It was, of course, the right question. It is we who have been giving the wrong answers.

Which leads to another brief entry, of May 13, 1933:

> Mr. Edward A. Filene, the merchant of New England, told the alumni of Columbia University that we all want the same thing. "We all want some arrangement by which more people will be enabled to buy more things." Do we? That is a fair question to ask, because the cumulative goal of "more things" has remained almost unchallenged in all the long palaver of industrial recovery. A little research among the writings of another New Englander, who long ago turned

out a passable essay on economy, reveals a more amusing, possibly a more sound, ideal. "The mass of men," he wrote, "lead lives of quiet desperation." And then, you will recall, he told of being present at the auction of a deacon's effects and of noticing, among the innumerable odds and ends representing the accumulation of a lifetime of endeavor, a dried tapeworm.

Thoreau remembered the tapeworm; White remembers the tapeworm; most of the rest of us merely manufacture the tapeworm.

He who remembers the tapeworm is the valuable commentator on our life. When Knute Rockne died, for instance, the nation gave way to an orgasm of grief, and President Hoover sent a eulogistic message. Mr. White (this was in 1931) uttered the one piercing comment on this national event. He said of it that Knute Rockne "was in the big money, and that was why Hoover happened to know about him." He then said the proper and human thing: "We see nothing wrong in the President's expressing grief over the loss of a beloved football coach," but, he went on, "from a diplomatic angle it seems to leave out certain other deceased members of college faculties, men who worked with undergraduates in groups other than groups of eleven. In our unofficial capacity, therefore, we take this opportunity to express the nation's grief in the death of all the other upright members of college faculties who died during the past year. We are sorry we don't know their names."

The point about Mr. White's attitude is that it is the attitude of a realist. His whimsical remarks are not sweet, though they are sweetly put; each one grasps a truth, holds it fast, exhibits it for all to see. His wit is realistic, his humor is realistic and, of course, his fantasy is realistic. It is, for example, the stock market reports that are fantastic, whereas it is Mr. White who is realistic in saying, "If a man wants to buy wheat, let him buy wheat and let the wheat be delivered to his door."

The spur of Mr. White's realism is the fact that he has the eye of a poet, a poet being a man who sees through things. Having the eye of a poet he is intensely aware of the unreality of our taken-for-granted environment. He is aware of the millions of substitutes for things, the millions of substitutes for ideas, the millions of substitutes for emotions, the millions of substitutes for human beings. Out of this awareness the sweet and bitter of his prose continually wells.

Perhaps I can make this clear by a personal reminiscence. In the course of an average American day the following minor things happened to me:

1. I received a bill for my quarterly dues from the American Federation of Radio and Television Artists. But I am not a radio or television "artist," and neither are 99.9 per cent of my colleagues "artists." I am a radio and television worker, my perfectly honorable status being that of employe.

2. I lunched with an amiable publisher, a valued friend, who suggested to me four ideas for books which he said would prove popular. They would have, too; but it never once occurred to him that a book should come out of a writer's mind and heart rather than out of a publisher's inventive powers.

3. I noticed an advertisement for toffee showing two American soldiers, candy bar in hand, riding hell-for-leather in a jeep. The caption read: "When the going gets tough, it's Blank's Toffee." The writer of the advertisement and the readers of it were unaware that the statement is mad.

4. A placard in a hotel lobby attracted my attention. It informed me that a well-known band was returning to entertain the hotel's clientele "by command." It is obvious that

nobody had commanded the engagement of the band, and even if anybody had, the band would not play better or worse for that reason.

5. Returning home, I found a letter from the alumni committee of my alma mater, urging me to contribute money. The money was to be used for seven clearly listed purposes. Not one of these purposes had to do with the proper education of young men, although my college was founded for that purpose and, so far as I can see, should not be used for any other.

I have drawn up this list of items (selecting these five from a much larger day's bag) to indicate that, for the most part, we live in a world whose connection with reality is of the frailest. The average man, one of whom is speaking to you, functions on a level, observes on a level, entertains himself on a level, noticeably remote from what is real. It is not that we lie to each other; it is that we think we are speaking truth. This is a kind of lunacy.

The restaurant that calls attention to its "world-famous apple pie" is not dishonest. It is merely unconsciously confessing its alienation from the obsolescent world of reality where words have checkable meanings.

The *New York Times* once refused to run an ad for the movie *Scandal in Paris*. The ad's headline ran: "The Whole Town's Talking About *Scandal in Paris*." The *Times* took the position that this was not literally true; and of course it wasn't. The point, however, is only secondarily involved with literal truth. The really disturbing thing is that the writer of the ad may not have known he was lying. Exaggeration had long since become his reality.

The Hollywood press agent who walked into the office of a network press department and inquired, "Say, do you want a real humanitarian gimmick?" was innocent of cynicism.

In his particular world of unreality—but unreality that works —no disharmony exists between the idea of humanitarianism and the idea of a gimmick.

It is our accepted, conventional, respectable lunacy that Mr. White sees and writes about, as did Swift and every other important satirist that ever lived. White is untouched by it. He sheds it as a duck's back does water. Week after week he reports to us, lightly and seriously, his travels in the Country of Reality, that native land from which we are in temporary semi-exile and for whose simplicities and solidities we feel a troubled, a wistful homesickness. But E. B. White is always At Home.

I Nominate for the
Pulitzer Prize—

In 1931 the London *Times Literary Supplement* remarked of Ogden Nash's first book, "Neat ideas marred by careless rhyming." In 1949—the *Times* having changed—it commented, "He has a Democritean streak which entitles him to the respect due to a philosopher, albeit a laughing one." This would seem to lend color to the theory (albeit an ungenerous one) that if you want to catch an Englishman in the act of enjoying the point of a joke, come back 18 years later. "Careless" is, of course, the *mot injuste* for the rhymes of Ogden Nash. Any dullard can match "June" and "moon." It needs an ear as highly trained as a piano tuner's to fashion lines like

> *O Kangaroo, O Kangaroo,*
> *Be grateful that you're in the zoo,*
> *And not transmuted by a boomerang*
> *To zestful, tangy Kangaroo meringue.*

Indeed a *really* careless rhyme Mr. Nash will not forgive, even if it be Tennyson's. He makes a certain Mr. Bogardus say that

> "Any man who would rhyme 'onward' with 'six hundred' didn't deserve any affidavits at all."

Back in 1931, however, the English reviewer may have innocently assumed Mr. Nash to be but the latest in a long line of earnest American provincial rhymers. He may have

63

had in mind, for instance, J. Gordon Coogler who achieved at least the immortality of Bartlett when in 1897, among other couplets that cheer but not inebriate, he wrote:

> *Alas! for the South, for her books have grown fewer—*
> *She was never much given to literature.*

Or he may have been thinking of Mrs. Julia A. Moore (1847– 1920) whose collection of determined verse, *The Sweet Singer of Michigan,* was revived in 1928, only three years before the Nash début. As a matter of fact, Nash did start out as a parodist of the Coogler-Moore school but soon realized the folly of giving up to parody what was meant for mankind.

As part of mankind I now rise to thank Ogden Nash for benefits received. He is over 50, he is a grandfather, he has been with the firm a long time, and he deserves a testimonial watch or something. For 25 years his verse has been heard in the land. His published books total 13, his poems surely over a thousand. More widely quoted than Longfellow (what young mother has not reflected that a little talcum is always walcum?), better-loved than Whittier, more judiciously patriotic than Whitman, he has over these worthies the further advantage of having no beard.

Despite which, the Messrs. Anon who award the Pulitzer prizes every May have never tossed one Nash-ward. The reasons are not far to seek. As a poet Nash works under two disadvantages: he is a humorist, and he is easy to understand. I herewith suggest that neither of these disabilities should continue to prevent his receiving the honors due him.

The Pulitzer Prize has been four times and with fourfold justice awarded to Robert Frost. One of the reasons surely is that Mr. Frost has shown us what new and beautiful things can be done with the language. So has Mr. Nash.

For one thing his English is fluid. His vocabulary is as

multipositional as that of classical Latin or even of Chinese.
Syntax is deliberately fractured so that, when reset, it may
be all the stronger:

> *And when my horse is in that center,*
> *The hooks I hang upon are tenter.*

Or

> *To actually see an actual marine monster*
> *Is one of the things that do before I die I wonster.*

A poet who can do this enlarges the frontiers of our language. That alone entitles him to the consideration of the
Pulitzer jury.

I am serious. No technical regulation bars our greatest
living master of light verse from getting the prize. If there
is a bar, it is laid only across the judges' minds. Somehow a
"light verse" writer must be inferior, a popular poet untouch-
able. Yet Horace wrote light verse, and so did Herrick, Goldsmith, Pope, Burns, Byron, Chesterton, and Kipling. These
classic masters, all popular in their day, are respectably dead.
But Nash is impertinently alive. While he is engaged in gradually overcoming this handicap, we might consider his ac-
complishment to date.

First, Nash is no mere oddity. A large part of his work continues (though on his own terms) a solid tradition, restating,
in a way acceptable to his time and place, the stuff of "serious" poetry. Here, for example, are the opening and closing
lines of a famous sonnet we were forced to learn at school:

> *The world is too much with us; late and soon,*
> *Getting and spending, we lay waste our powers:*
> *Little we see in Nature that is ours;*
> *We have given our hearts away, a sordid boon!*

. . . .

............*Great God! I'd rather be*
A Pagan suckled in a creed outworn;
So might I, standing on this pleasant lea,
Have glimpses that would make me less forlorn;
Have sight of Proteus rising from the sea;
Or hear old Triton blow his wreathèd horn.

And here are a few stanzas from Nash:

In far Tibet
There live a lama,
He got no poppa,
Got no momma,

He got no wife,
He got no chillun,
Got no use
For penicillun,

He got no soap,
He got no opera,
He don't know Irium
From copra.
....
He got no teeth,
He got no gums,
Don't eat no Spam,
Don't need no Tums.
....
Indeed, the
Ignorant Have-Not
Don't even know
What he don't got.

If you will mind
The Philco, comma,
I think I'll go
And join that lama.

Now Wordsworth, if Mr. Nash will forgive me, is the greater poet—but not with respect to these two poems. Emotionally the poems are of equal value; that is to say, Wordsworth was talking as effectively to his audience as Nash is talking to his. Both poets are making the same wistful comment on modern competitive life. But Wordsworth's lines, however beautiful, do not reach most of us; Nash's, however bantering, do. Both men are serious, because they are making a serious statement; but Nash is funny as well as serious. Wordsworth's Triton was as meaningful to his audience as Nash's Tums are to his. The water in the well has changed; the same truth glimmers at its bottom.

The advance of old age, the isolation of the human being, married love, Spring, the out-of-jointness of the time—these staples of orthodox poetry are the staples of Nash's heterodox rhymes.

However, what brings Nash home to our hearts is not his restatement of the familiar matter of poetry but his statement of the familiar matter of daily living. Wordsworth talked about introducing into poetry "familiar matter of today" but, whatever one may think of his face, his finest verse is not in the least homely. Nash actually does what Wordsworth thought he was doing. He writes about what we share—the common cold rather than the uncommon Highland lass.

Now for the most part "serious" poetry is not built to work well with such typical Nash themes as tipping, vacations, paying taxes, dinner parties, motoring, shaving, shopping, dogs, gossiping, hobbies, gadgets, shower baths, entertaining small boys, and chewing celery. Shakespeare must have known that Hamlet spent more time washing himself or eating breakfast than he did brooding over his old man. But breakfast and blank verse cannot mate. Hence such material is usually left to the light versifier—and the light versifier usually does little with it beyond expressing conventional jocularity in conventional meter.

Nash's achievement lies in saying nontrivial things about trivia, and saying them perfectly. His subject matter is endless, for it is human nature—not human nature on the heights or in the depths, but human nature caught square in the middle, often in undignified positions. He deals with the ten thousand diurnalities that are a closed book to Keats and Shelley: enjoying railway trains, liking or disliking animals, complaining about the weather, dreading the first of the month, reducing the waistline, suffering children's parties—the small-scale crises that make up 90 per cent of petty living, not the large-scale crises that make up 90 per cent of portentous literature. Nash is a true household poet in that he really understands the joys and sorrows of domestic life. He does not, like the folksy household poet, sentimentalize them. He is always the understanding host, never the unwelcome Guest.

Domestic life, however, has taken an odd turn in our era. To that era catastrophiles have given various labels: the Age of Unreason, the Atomic Age, the Age of Longing, the Age of Anxiety. But my guess is that in 50 years none of these labels will be found sticking to the bottle. The average hard-pressed citizen, who lives from hour to hour by dint of an unending succession of stratagems, may well come to think of our time as the Age of Friction. He is less disturbed by the prospect of joining the cosmos by courtesy of the hydrogen bomb than he is by the prospect of removing several needless yards of Cellophane from ordinary objects in the course of an average working day.

The drawback of an age in which more things and more experiences are available to more people is that we have more things and more experiences to think about when what we really want to do is to relapse into the normal human condition of occasionally not thinking much about anything. An added and related source of friction is that our techniques of communication are constantly piling up these things and experiences on the doorstep of our attention. Irritator and irritatee are in continuous touch with each other. Years ago, for example, before the hearth was replaced by an assemblage of vacuum tubes permanently surrounded by an expert mechanic, a man could pass from play pen to Paradise without once encountering a parlor game. Today the miracle of television has made him a nervous participant in a nonstop series of 16-inch charades.

Or take advertising. We could not do without it, and would not want to, for it makes modern distribution possible. And yet, says Nash,

> *I think that I shall never see*
> *A billboard lovely as a tree.*
> *Indeed, unless the billboards fall,*
> *I'll never see a tree at all.*

Nash is the laureate of the Age of Friction. In a verse form often fittingly bumpy (actually a great deal of his output is in regular meter) and with the aid of a dazzling assortment of puns, syntactical distortions, and word coinages, he points out that most improvements in daily living entail a tiny irritation tax. Once in a while the tax may even become confiscatory. Nash reminds us:

> *Consider the auk;*
> *Becoming extinct because he forgot how to fly and could*
> *   only walk.*
> *Consider the man who may well become extinct*
> *Because he forgot how to walk and learned how to fly*
> *   before he thinked.*

Nash's central theme is simply the difficulty involved in what is turning out to be a full-time job nowadays—just being human. Somewhere he refers to our era as "opened by mistake"—a feeling even the bravest among us have at moments experienced. And which of us on December 31, amid the confetti and the popping corks, has not echoed in his heart of hearts Nash's immortal couplet:

> *Hark, it's midnight, children dear.*
> *Duck! Here comes another year!*

Yet, despite parsley, people who say "Bobby Burns," testimonial banquets, the impossibility of remaining anonymous in a hotel, and guests who stay late and then suggest that everybody go out in the kitchen and scramble eggs—despite these pebbles in the shoe of twentieth-century man, no bitter indignation lacerates Nash's heart. As with all humorists worthy of the name, irony always wins out over ire. His verse is tonic. More than that, it is, in its own unimposing way, major, as the cynic-sadness of Dorothy Parker or the acerbity of Hoffenstein could never be.

> *Humanity must continue to follow the sun around*
> *And accept the eternal run-around.*
> *Well, and if that be the case, why come on humanity!*
> *So long as it is our fate to be irked all our life let us just*
> *keep our heads up and take our irking with insouci-*
> *ant urbanity.*

And so, ladies and gentlemen, I hope that during some appropriately merry month of May Mr. Ogden Nash will wake up in the morning and be Pulitsurprised.

Abner Dean's Naked Little Man

MUCH AS he hates to admit it, the life of the average man (which means virtually all of us) tends to assume the form of a longish doze, interrupted by fits and starts of bewildered semi-alertness. We invent a hundred ways of heading off self-awareness to one that may force us to ask ourselves who the devil we are. You cannot turn on your TV set or unfold your newspaper without being offered all the answers. But where shall we turn if we wish to be asked the questions?

The question-askers are usually of two kinds. There are, first, the men of religion, the prophets, of whom only a few exist in any generation, and to whom, since the Reformation, we have decided to pay respect in lieu of attention. Then there are the artists, among whom we should include, of course, all true scientists, educators, and philosophers. On occasion we still listen to them. They are the ones who rowel us out of our sleep. They are the magnificent cockleburs of the human race.

Abner Dean is such a cocklebur. He disquiets us. He unsettles us. He takes us by the scruff of our unconscious and drops us all squealing right into the middle of his astonishing pictures. He asks us questions and makes us ask ourselves questions.

Is life like making the 5:15, in which every commuter is meaningless? Or is it more like wandering in a wood in which every tree is a mystery? Am I complete because I have a pocketbook, a Social Security number, a last will and testament? Or have I lost something I cannot put a name to? I am elated because I possess electric switches, clocks and watches, pants with zippers, clutchless automobiles, telephones, TV sets, and a civil servant in gray who brings me newspapers and magazines telling me I should acquire more electric switches, pants with zippers, etc. Am I a fool in my elation? Or do I really have reality reduced to a dial system? Do I know my way around? Or don't I?

Abner Dean's naked little man wanders about among other naked men and women, full of good will, curiosity, and fatuity. He gets into jams, but is always pretty certain that something can be done about them. He's proud of the idiot contraptions he's assembled. He's always forgotten something, he's always looking for something. He tries hard to conform; that is to say, he preserves a bland detachment among the lunacies that strew his path. Then in maniac glee he breaks out of the design and throws the shoe of his questionings into the machinery. He will stumble, he will fall, he will be beaten, he will be blindfolded, he will be disappointed. He will survive.

It is pointless to try to "explain" Abner Dean. His pictures are trick mirrors in which we catch sight of those absurd fragments of ourselves that we never see in the smooth glass of habit. Formulae for the art of Abner Dean are irrelevant. What is important is the fact that it jolts us into lightning awareness of our own pathos, our own plight, our own unending laughableness.

The naked wanderings of his eternally bemused, eternally hopeful hero trace an interesting pattern, full of fuguelike ingenious echoes and returns. The macabre alternates with the wistful, the hero leaps from exaltation to self-reproach, he holds the truth in his hand—no, he has lost it. Love is the answer—or isn't it? A hundred stray, flying strands of the inner life are woven into this visible odyssey of a latter-day Everyman.

The urge to call Abner Dean bats will be strong. But that is only because we have so large a vested interest in being "normal" that we panic easily when the investment is threatened. We have always tried and always will try to laugh down those who question the value of this investment. But, sooner or later, such is their charm, such the subtle appeal they make to that repressed part of ourselves which knows that we are absurd and wonderful, we go back to them to receive a welcome ration of disquietude. There are few rich enough to offer this gift. Of these Abner Dean is one.

G. K. C.

G. K. Chesterton was a rare man, and we shall not soon look upon his like again. Thousands who disagreed with much that he said would have vigorously defended his right to say it. Who would not have preferred to listen to him being dead wrong than to most others being dead right? Thus it was that he found it no less easy to make opponents than difficult to make enemies. With Shaw, for example, he conducted a practically lifelong argument, which never once turned into a quarrel. For his prejudices were often more appealing than the logic, his dogmas more human than the rational skepticism, of other men.

Chesterton was born at exactly the right time, by which, of course, one means exactly the wrong time. From his viewpoint the times were out of joint, but had they not been, he might have had no viewpoint at all. God, or the Life Force, provided him with George Bernard Shaw to act as his contemporary and his foil. The circumstance was of untold value to G. K. C., for he was never more himself than when debating with other people. He was happily fated (perhaps this was what made him an optimist) to spend his life surrounded by movements and ideas calculated to exasperate him into brilliant controversy. It is worth remarking that he did not always fight on the winning side, but his opponents, who often won, never seemed very happy about it, whereas G. K. C.'s gaiety was unflagging. Had he been born into his beloved

74

thirteenth century, he would have been at peace, but he would not have been Chesterton. It was his good fortune to be set down in the very center of all the "modernism" that for almost half a century was to furnish him inexhaustibly with pretexts for indignation.

It was "modernism" that converted him to Catholicism. The circle of the London intelligentsia of the 1890's and 1900's, full of weak and wandering souls, showed his irritable spirit the path to a creed that is neither weak nor wandering. It was through Bohemia and Eccentrica that he found his way at last to the country of the Cross. That is why he would never have thought blasphemous the notion that his love of God was stimulated by his lack of love for vegetarians. Cranks, fanatics, tuppenny freethinkers, puritans—all excited him to blasts of scorn that were basically religious. He had, after all, a monomania. It was monomaniacs.

Yet it is hard to think of him as a crusader, except as one of the Children's Crusade, for a certain childlike innocence clung to him all his life, as, indeed, he clung to it. What he fought may triumph or fail, but the joyousness with which he fought will continue to live a life of its own. This is no more than to say the obvious: that G. K. C. will endure as a humorist, in the classic English tradition. His most serious books—such as his great one on Charles Dickens—are full of jokes, and good jokes. It is when he is writing just for fun that he is most impressive, his weight lying largely in his levity. And this is what he would himself have wanted, for he would have said in all humility that his jokes and his religion partook of the same essence.

The Chestertonian laughter will, I think, wear better than its brother the Chestertonian romanticism. G. K. C. worked a little too hard at the business of being constantly surprised, not to say enchanted, by the ordinary. He was very careful to

be always taken unawares. He tried to live life and write
about it as if it were a cross between a Punch-and-Judy show
and a legend, and he himself a cross between a rapt small boy
and a mythical character. When, for example, he talks of
"Christendom," he transforms a great symbol almost into a
current reality. It is when he tries to transform every small
reality into a great symbol that he often fails. He could not
seem to see a thing clearly until he had thrown a halo around
it. And yet, just because he tried so joyously to live as if in a
legend, he may in time become a legendary figure.

She Did Not Know How To Be Famous

DESCARTES WAS unheroic, Leibnitz a fawning courtier, Willard Gibbs a recluse, Gauss cold and secretive. For all his nobility, Pasteur was tainted with chauvinism and race hatred. A dubious religiosity clouded to the end the magnificent minds of Newton and Pascal. Indeed, it is hard to think of many first-rate scientific careers in which some major flaw of character does not show itself, confounding our natural desire for wholehearted hero worship. But the lives of Marie and Pierre Curie, two of the most beautiful lives, I suppose, that have ever been lived, provide an exception. It was almost theatrically apt that this man and woman, with characters of shining purity, should have built their careers around a physical element recognizable by its indestructible and essential radiance.

The life of Marie Curie might have been conceived not by the accidents of nature but by the patterning brain of a tragic dramatist of genius.

One looks at a photograph of Marie taken in 1929, when she was sixty-two. The face is lined. From underneath the white and casually arranged hair arcs an abnormally spacious brow. She is dressed in a simple black dress that looks like a laboratory smock. The face is that of a truly beautiful

77

woman, the beauty lying in the bones and in the brain that
sends its clear signals through the deep, penetrating eyes.

The story of Marie Curie is not merely that of a poor Polish
governess who struggled against adversity and became a triumphant success. The story of Marie Curie lies precisely in
the fact that she was happiest during her struggles and least
happy when a vulgar world acclaimed her. Hers is a success
story with an ironic twist. Einstein has said, "Marie Curie is,
of all celebrated beings, the only one whom fame has not
corrupted." "She did not know how to be famous," says Eve
Curie in her classic biography of her mother. In one deliberate sentence she strikes to the heart of the secret: "I hope
that the reader may constantly feel, across the ephemeral
movement of one existence, what in Marie Curie was even
more rare than her work or her life: the immovable structure
of a character; the stubborn effort of an intelligence; the free
immolation of a human being that could give all and take
nothing, could even receive nothing; and above all the quality
of a soul in which neither fame nor adversity could change
the exceptional purity."

Recall that unbelievably dramatic life. She is born Marja
Sklodowska, youngest child of a Warsaw physicist and a sensitive, tubercular mother. The childhood is unhappy, torn
by the death of mother and eldest sister, rendered overseri-
ous by poverty, given a certain tenseness by the fact that
she is a member of a subject race, the Poles. She grows up, becomes the conventional intellectual rebel of her time, like
"all the little Polish girls who had gone mad for culture." She
is intelligent, but nothing yet reveals that "immovable structure" of which her daughter speaks. She becomes a governess,
a bit of a bluestocking touched with Tolstoyan sentimentality.
Now "the eternal student" begins to rise up in her. The little
child who at five stood in rapt awe before her father's case

containing the "phys-ics ap-pa-ra-tus" reawakens in the girl
of eighteen. Her duties as a governess do not prevent her
from studying. She has no money, not even for stamps so
that she may write to her brother. But "I am learning chemistry from a book." Back in Warsaw, she is allowed to perform elementary chemical experiments in a real laboratory,
and at last, after inconceivable setbacks and economies, after
years of weary waiting, she goes to Paris to study at the
Sorbonne.

On forty rubles a month Marja (now Marie) Sklodowska
lives, studies, learns. Solitude, near-starvation, an unheated
garret—none of these things matters, as long as at least a
part of her day is spent in the laboratory. Now even the miserable forty rubles cease. She is about to return in despair to
Warsaw when she is given a six-hundred-ruble scholarship.
A few years afterward, with the first money she earns as a
scientist, she returns the amount of the scholarship so that
some other poor student may be assisted by it.

In 1894 she meets Pierre Curie, already a physicist of note,
a mind "both powerful and noble." In an atmosphere of gar-
rets and laboratories, these two, very grave and serious, conduct their love affair. They marry. On her wedding day, to
the generous friend who wishes to give her a bridal dress, she
writes, "I have no dress except the one I wear every day. If
you are going to be kind enough to give me one, please let it
be practical and dark so that I can put it on afterwards to go
to the laboratory."

It is a perfect marriage, the marriage not merely of two
people who love each other but, what is incomparably more
interesting and important, of two great physicists who can
help each other. It is Marie, attracted by the uranium researches of Becquerel, who starts herself and her husband
on the long, tedious, glorious path at the end of which lies

radium. They know that radium and polonium (named by Marie to commemorate her beloved native land) exist, but they must prove it. From 1898 to 1902, in a dilapidated, leaking, freezing shed, with primitive apparatus, with little or no help, unaided by the scientific bureaucracy or by the State, these two gentle fanatics work in an absorption that is like a dream. The government is too busy spending money on armament to buy them the few tons of pitchblende they need. Somehow they get their pitchblende, paying for its transportation themselves out of their insufficient salaries. With "her terrible patience," Marie, doing the work of four strong men, pounds away at her chemical masses, boils, separates, refines, stirs, strains. Somewhere in this inert brown stuff lies radium. Marie loses fifteen pounds during these five years. At last they isolate the element.

All this time they have been bringing up a family. They have had sorrows, family illnesses. Pierre's mother has died of the very disease against which radium is soon to prove a weapon. All this time no provision is made for these selfless geniuses. The State, as always, cares nothing. Recognition comes first from other countries, from Switzerland, England. "With great merit and even greater modesty," says Montaigne, "one can remain unknown for a long time."

Now the full implications of their work begin to appear. The immovable atom moves; matter is touched with a mysterious life; physics revises its nineteenth-century conceptions of the indestructibility of matter and the conservation of energy. The Curies are triumphant; and their first major decision is to refrain from patenting their radium-extraction process. They give it freely to the world. This gesture alone is enough to lend their lives a depth that can never attach to a career like that of Edison. The difference between a Curie and an Edison is not merely one of scientific genius, it is a difference of order. The Curies are one kind of human being, Edison was another.

In 1903 the Curies, with Becquerel, receive the Nobel Prize for Physics. The world pursues them. Now they must flee the world. "In science we must be interested in things, not persons," says Marie, who was never to be interested in herself. One evening, at the height of their fame, as they are about to leave for a banquet, Pierre looks at his wife, with her ash-gray eyes, her ash-blond hair, her exquisite wrists and ankles, and he murmurs, "It's a pity. Evening dress becomes you." Then, with a sigh, he adds, "But there it is, we haven't got time."

They are offered the slimy vulgarity of decorations, ribbons, rosettes. But no laboratory. Pierre died without getting his laboratory.

Then on April 19, 1906, Aeschylean tragedy, cutting Marie's life in two, giving it at the same time a new emotional dimension. Pierre's head is crushed by a van in a street accident, and Marie becomes "a pitiful and incurably lonely woman." She refuses a pension (always the State makes its generous offers too late); she proceeds with the education of her daughters; she takes over Pierre's teaching post and, in a dry, monotonous voice, without making any reference to her predecessor, resumes the lectures at the exact point at which Pierre had left off.

The rest of her life is the story of her marriage with radium. For her laboratory, for science, she will do anything, even try to be "famous." In 1911 she receives the Nobel Prize for Chemistry. During the war she equips, with superhuman energy, a fleet of radiological cars so that the wounded may be helped by X-rays. She is no rotogravure ministering angel, no Queen Marie of Rumania. She actually works—works for the State which had done its best in those dark years to prevent her from working. Later, again for the sake of science, she comes to America to receive a gram of radium from the hand of an amiable poker player who could not possibly have understood even the most trivial of the thoughts in Marie Curie's mind. Then, applauded by all America, she goes back to France, and all America turns to the next celebrity, Carpentier, to lavish an identical adulation upon him. Almost blind, her hands and arms scarred, pitted, and burned by thirty years of radium emanations, she continues her work almost to the day of her death, caused in part by that very element which she had released for the use of mankind.

Puzzlements

Gertrude Stein

WHAT LADY would I most dread being cast upon a desert island with? A puzzling question, but not beyond all conjecture. For many years such now departed literary gentlewomen as Margot Asquith, Marie of Rumania, and Mabel Dodge Luhan ran neck-and-neck in the Stay-Away-From-My-Desert-Island Sweepstakes. But the late Gertrude Stein in a photo finish nosed them all out.

I have long been embarrassed by my anesthesia to Miss Stein, all the more because during her life she gained the affection of so many writers I admire, including Thornton Wilder, Glenway Wescott, and Ernest Hemingway. I can only assume that in person she exerted a charm she absent-mindedly forgot to insert into her books and her reported conversation; or, more probably, that I am in some way defective.

During her later years Miss Stein enjoyed a certain restricted mass-popularity. Even the *Saturday Evening Post,* whose editors hardly set themselves up to be connoisseurs of abnormality, published her. But these triumphs do not baffle me. They represent the capitulation we as a people sometimes make to successful eccentricity, the admiration we accord to anyone who can get away with it. During this period Miss Stein took her place, not among the literary *avant-garde,* but among other popular heroes spewed out by the internal necessities of the rotary press—goldfish eaters, flagpole sitters, and such gaudy gentry.

Her literary reputation is another matter. I have never understood it and I fear I never shall. I have made conscientious efforts not only to read her but to reread her. She remains for me a closed-circuit writer, using words, as far as I can make out, to establish contact with a receptive audience consisting of herself. Aware of the powerful barbiturate effect of her paragraphs' seashore mutter, I have even read her under the influence of benzedrine. Still no go. There she stands, a monitory barrier marking the parochial limits of my mind.

I can only account for the effect she appears to have had on many talented writers by citing, first, the feverishly experimental literary climate of the twenties when novelty was almost always given a warmer welcome than sanity, and, second, the youthfulness of her then devotees.

That she was on occasion intelligent I can believe. That she had intuitive insights I can believe. That her taste in art was courageous and well-founded one knows. That she was foolish, vain, arrogant, and a female Barnum is no less apparent, at least to me, from her work. She and G. B. S. were the two greatest literary egotists of their time. G. B. S. made good his claims and Miss Stein reiterated hers, reiteration being her specialty.

My public love affair with Miss Stein began on September 2, 1933, when I commented on her best-selling autobiography in the following intemperate manner:

> About a decade ago, Gertrude Stein and her sentences were fair game for the paragraphers. Then, after Mr. Hemingway had warned the comma and the semicolon away from American prose, Gertrude got to be taken seriously as an Influence.

She has now written her autobiography and goes to great pains to prove that the paragraphers were right in the first place.

Gertrude has always done justice to Gertrude, but this book sets a high-water mark in the delicate art of self-appreciation. Though written by the author of *Tender Buttons,* it represents itself to be the autobiography of Alice B. Toklas, her companion-secretary for twenty-five years. This reverses the usual process whereby secretaries ghost-write their employers' books and also allows Gertrude without immodesty to be fair to herself. Thus Alice, who is wired for sound, writes, "I may say that only three times in my life have I met a genius and each time a bell within me rang." Do you ask for whom the bell rang? It rang for Pablo Picasso; it rang for Alfred Whitehead; and it rang for Gertrude Stein. Lest the question of Gertrude's genius be considered in any way moot we are further informed: "She realises that in English literature in her time she is the only one. She has always known it and now she says it."

Gertrude bustles into Miss Toklas' autobiography on page 2 and doesn't leave till the very end, thus achieving a record in persistence eclipsing even her most typical sentences. There are also, to make the book's subject matter quite clear, a good many photographs of the great Stein face. Gertrude (and Miss Toklas) standing in front of Joffre's birthplace. Gertrude at work at her desk with Miss Toklas ectoplasmically materializing in the doorway. Gertrude (and Alice) in front of St. Mark's with Gertrude seated most oddly before a group of pigeons, representing the lost generation. Gertrude, hands folded, a Cumaean sibyl with a Ph.D. from Radcliffe. Gertrude, at four, in pantalettes.

The pictures are not all Stein. There is a photograph captioned "Room With Oil Lamp." This shows a room with an oil lamp.

In the early days Gertrude demonstrated courage and vision

in collecting the works of obscure modernist painters, many of whom have since achieved renown. On the basis of this, she gained a reputation as an *enfant terrible* of the arts. Whatever one may think of her style, this book hardly reveals Gertrude herself as *terrible*. The other half of the reputation is, however, confirmed. Wyndham Lewis, who is odd but ferociously intelligent, has frequently called attention to Gertrude's infantile traits. This book provides extensive proof of his thesis. With the exception of some interesting reflections on Hemingway, her judgments have little relation to life as it is understood by ordinary grownups. "I like a view but I like to sit with my back turned to it," says Gertrude. Also, says Gertrude, "I like being all alone with English and myself." Was ever a more candid confession of solipsism? She is the Radcliffe bluestocking, arty, snobbish, protected from practical life ("Anything can frighten her," says Miss Toklas), with a passion for the "advanced" reminiscent of the nineties. She is a tufthunter of no inconsiderable talents, possessing the arrogance of a wealthy, spoiled, bright child, together with the ability to impress impressionable people, particularly when they are at an impressionable age. There is no doubt that she is sufficiently eccentric to get away with the Mahatma pose, especially in the environment of Parisian artistic society. There is also no doubt that she has done things with the English language no one else has dared to do, which is much like praising the surgical ability of Procrustes. One should add that this Toklas book, though more conventionally written than her classic stammers and circularities, is still irritating enough to be an authentic Stein. At its best it sounds like Joyce's Mrs. Bloom, lacking her more colorful qualities but matching her garrulity. At its worst it is a pretty good burlesque of Stephen Leacock's *Nonsense Novels*.

It contains a few witty remarks. Like her pictures, these are mainly by Picasso.

The Autobiography of Alice B. Toklas enjoyed a great success in those dear old freewheeling days of the early thirties. It did not, however, as my notes remind me, meet with no opposition. Interestingly enough, the opposition came not from the comfortable middle-class world which a decade before had snickered at Miss Stein. The Philistines were now quite ready to welcome Gertrude, partly because she diverted them, partly because there was always an outside chance, they figured, that she might be an authentic even if incomprehensible messenger of culture.

No, the sour notes came from Miss Stein's own world of the Left Bank, from the artists and writers who, having met many examples of her type, understood it well and, like Queen Victoria, were not amused. A truculent pamphlet entitled *Testimony Against Gertrude Stein* emerged from the peace-hallowed Hague. Henri Matisse, after listing any number of misstatements and exaggerations, concluded that Miss Stein "contacted indiscriminately things about which, it seems to me, she understood nothing." Maria Jolas told of the career of *transition* in a manner at variance with Miss Stein's version. "She would eventually," wrote Mrs. Jolas, "tolerate no relationship that did not bring with it adulation." Tristan Tzara expressed his opinion of the book and its author even more forcibly, concluding: "Miss Stein, who understood nothing, contacted [this word was evidently part of a special *transition* vocabulary] in the final analysis only thanks to the weight of her pocketbook. If the exploitation of man by man has found its shameful expression in the conduct of business, we have, up to now, rarely seen the application of the principle to the domain of art in the unexpected form of the exploitation of ideas."

Georges Braque said flatly, "Miss Stein understood nothing of what went on around her. . . . For one who poses as an authority on the epoch, it is safe to say that she never went beyond the stage of the tourist." André Salmon came to the same conclusion: "It is evident that she understood nothing, except in a superficial way." Eugene Jolas summed up the evidence by remarking that the Toklas book, "in its hollow, tinsel bohemianism and egocentric deformations, may very well become one day the symbol of the decadence that hovers over contemporary literature."

On February 10, 1934, Miss Stein reappeared with a re-issue of her long and murmurous chronicle, *The Making of Americans.* I read far enough in this to grasp the fact that Miss Stein was a past master in the art of making nothing happen very slowly. But at page 133, line 30 ("Sometime then will be written a long book, a history of every kind of men and women and all the kind of being in them"), I dropped my tools.

Bernard Faÿ, I recall, wrote a foreword that should have cleared up everything. I retrieve from it two sentences. "Miss Stein's repetitions are really ideas, but living ideas still alive in living facts." This axiom is exceeded in lucidity only by this one: "She has lived, felt and understood so intensely and so clearly all the fact [*sic*] of her life that in truth her life is no more simply visited with a few ideas but is a living continuous essential idea." The style here, at once so Stein-esque and Toklasian, recalls James Branch Cabell's remark about a novel by Katherine Fullerton Gerould—it was so much like Henry James that it might have been written by Edith Wharton.

On November 17 of the same year I encountered the mama of dada again (something called *Portraits and Prayers*) and as usual withdrew worsted. Two cryptic sentences from that book still haunt me. The first is: "There is every reason why everybody loves me." The second is: "I am not amusing."

Well, let's see. Nothing much happened for a few years. Miss Stein consolidated her position and I withdrew to my second line of defenses. I was chivvied out and of course again routed by the appearance of *Everybody's Autobiography*. I need not add that *everybody's* was just Miss Stein's way of saying *my*. I found nothing really wrong with this autobiography except poor choice of subject. On December 4, 1937, I recommended it to my *New Yorker* patrons in the following forgettable lyric:

> According to Bennett Cerf, a valued friend
>   of mine
> Who, over an imprint aptly known as Random
>   House, publishes Gertrude Stein,
> This book records "five years of exciting
>   and soul-satisfying
> Experiences in France, England and America,"
>   making known
> What happened to Miss Stein when she decided
>   to stop trying
> To live Miss Toklas's life and instead to
>   live her own.
>
> Now, most of this book is about how it feels
>   to be
> Simultaneously Gertrude Stein and a celebrity.
> And to stay so.
> "It is very nice," she says, "being a celeb-
>   rity a real celebrity who can decide who
>   they want to meet and say so."
> But no nicer, perhaps, than being able to
>   assign your pronouns any particular case
>   you fancy.

Not many celebrities can do that;
That's flat.

Well anyway. (As Miss Stein so frequently
   says in her famous manière)
After a few stories left over from Miss
   Toklas's book, about Picasso and Apollinaire,
For after all, though she has been in the
   Saturday Evening Post, Miss Stein is still
   a grande salonnière,
And after telling us about her difficulties
   with publishers and lecture agents and
   about the amounts they *pay,*
And about her Mexican dog Pépé,
Well, after this, she tells us that William
   Seabrook came to visit her. (Sometimes
   she spells it Seabrooke; Shakespeare was
   a whimsical speller too.)
"He said he wanted to see if I was as
   interesting as my book was. I said I was.
   He said yes."
Now what do you suppose was meant by Mr.
   Seabrook?
Or perhaps by Mr. Seabrooke?

Well anyway. After these exciting and soul-
   satisfying experiences (one year of same)
The Champlain *wafted her to America, at*
   reduced rates, for the purser knew her name;
She became a great platform success.
Was it not an earlier showman who remarked
   that there was one bored every minute? Yes,
Everybody thought that to see a genius in the
   flesh would be fun.
Now, about genius Miss Stein has several def-
   inite ideas, and they are that she is one.

"It's funny this knowing being a genius," says
  Miss Stein. "It takes a lot of time to be
  a genius, you have to sit around so much
  doing nothing," says Miss Stein. "The earth
  is covered all over with people but geniuses
  are very few. Interesting if true and it is
  true," says Miss Stein.
But Miss Stein should remember that if the
  earth weren't so covered all over with people,
  there wouldn't be enough people to go to
  lectures at three dollars per to listen to
  the geniuses who are so very few.
Interesting if true and it is true.

Well anyway. Miss Stein revisits America after
  a thirty years' run as a transatlantic sibyl,
And she knows exactly what she likes, without
  hesitation or quibble.
"Windows in a building are the most interesting
  thing in America," says this fenestral
  connaisseuse who knows what's what.
Not that she didn't like other things, for
  "The ten-cent stores did disappoint me but
  the nut stores not."

Well anyway. Miss Stein liked college audiences,
  for "they are inevitably more flattering,"
And she liked Alexander Woollcott and Dashiell
  Hammett and Thornton Wilder and others who
  are currently mattering,
But she did not like Adler, Mortimer J.,
I regret to say.
On the other hand, she liked honeydew melon and
  the Burma-Shave highway signs, which must
  have brought her own prose home to her.

As for the Great Salt Lake, she does not say
  she liked it but it "satisfied" her, which
  is something.
Did I mention that she likes new shoes but
  does not care much for new clothes?
An interesting fact, almost as interesting as
  windows in a building or what she said about
  a rose.
There's also a lot in Everybody's Autobiography
  about Hollywood and its many beautiful faces,
But this part, to be frank, is not quite as
  good as the Abbe children's Of All Places!
Though perhaps naiver and more quaintly
  enfantine—
Qualities of which Miss Stein is not precisely
  what you might call unconscious, if you get
  what I mean.
Rouben Mamoulian and William Saroyan,
Jean Cocteau and Davidson, Jo,
And many others, including Mr. President Hut-
  chins and Mrs. President Roosevelt,
Must have been enthusiastic over Miss Stein,
  for "People always had been nice to me
  because I am pleasing," says Miss Stein.
Which is fine.

But do not run away with the impression that
  for Miss Stein everything is hunky-dory.
There are many saddening details in her story.
For instance, she worries about money being
  voted by Congress only in round numbers.
And another thing that disturbs her slumbers
Is the fact that the world is so covered all
  over with people that nobody can get lost
  any more.

And she broods over revolution and war.
"All the time that I am writing the Spanish
revolution obtrudes itself," she says; and
it's true.
Go away, you obtrusive Spanish revolution,
you!

"I have been the creative literary mind of
the century,"
"I am the most important writer writing today."
That is Gert's final word and, as it's clearer
than most of her prose,
To let her have it and let her keep it is
briefly what I propose.

It wasn't Gert's final word, of course. It never is. But it was
pretty nearly my own. This Left Bank Diotima in divided
skirts had worn me down till I was about ready to cry uncle.
I had left in me one small cry of pain, hardly more than a
peep. It was heard on February 15, 1941, when I seem to
have collided with a new Stein novel. I called my review
"Getting Gertie's Ida." The phrasing was overconfident.

A rumor circulating a couple of months ago hinted that
Gertrude Stein's new novel, *Ida,* was really about the Duchess
of Windsor. Now that I have tottered through *Ida,* I find I
cannot deny the rumor. It is certainly as much about the
Duchess of Windsor as it is about anything or anybody else.
If it is not about the Duchess of Windsor, what *is* it about?

Ida is Miss Stein's first novel in eleven years. "It is presented faithfully to you," says the amiable Mr. Bennett Cerf,
"by a publisher who rarely has the faintest idea of what Miss
Stein is talking about, but who admires her from the bottom
of his heart for her courage and for her abounding love of
humanity and freedom." This statement would seem to mark

an interesting departure in editorial policy. Doubtless we shall soon be reading the works of authors who cannot tell a lie, are kind to their younger brothers, or have contributed heavily to the Salvation Army.

Out of her abounding love of humanity, Miss Stein gives us an elusive creature named Ida. The story of Ida is divided, like a football game, into two halves, called, for purposes of ready reference, First Half and Second Half. The printer and binder have ingeniously arranged to make Second Half follow First Half, so that quite an effect of sequence and coherence is produced. It's never made quite clear whether Ida (who dominates both halves) is on her own or whether she is twins. On page 43 we have this: "Ida decided that she was just going to talk to herself. Anybody could stand around and listen but as for her she was just going to talk to herself. She no longer even needed a twin." This seems a forthright statement, but at other points the twin situation is not as lucid as one would wish. On page 52, however, Ida is definitely not a twin. Fifty-two is my favorite page.

Ida (or her twin) has certain quirks: she is very careful about Tuesday, she always hesitates before eating, and she rests a good deal during and between marriages. I should inform you that Ida is the marrying type. Among her husbands is a man named Frank Arthur, and why not? We do not learn much about her marital habits, but we are told that "she was always good friends with all her husbands."

This goodness of Ida's also extends to other matters. "She was kind to politics while she was in Washington very kind. She told politics that it was very nice of them to have her be kind to them." No record exists of politics' reply.

Furthermore, there is a man in the book named Philip. "Philip was the kind that said everything out loud." This sentence about Philip appears on page 40, and he is never mentioned again. Philip is my favorite character.

I have a theory about Miss Stein's novel which—give me

just a second—I should like to outline to you. My notion is that Miss Stein has set herself to solve, and has succeeded in solving, the most difficult problem in prose composition— to write something that will not arrest the attention in any way, manner, shape, or form. If you think this easy, try it. I know of no one except Miss Stein who can roll out this completely nonresistant prose, prose that puts you at once in a condition resembling the early stages of grippe—the eyes and legs heavy, the top of the skull wandering around in an uncertain and independent manner, the heart ponderously, tiredly beating. Take a sentence at random: "Ida instead of going on the way she was going went back the way she had come." Repeat it slowly once or twice and you will find that your head has fallen to one side and your eyelids are a little sandy. Try this: "Ida woke up. After a while she got up. Then she stood up. Then she ate something. After that she sat down. That was Ida."

See what I mean?

And there you have the brief history of a failure, mine of course. For Gertrude Stein, almost ten years after her death, has drawn about her the aura of what looks like a pretty enduring cult. Her letters and papers have been reverently deposited in the library of Yale University where subtle young scholars may accord them their due rites.

Perhaps as a people we are not old enough or confident enough cheerfully to accept our literary eccentrics merely *as* eccentrics. When we, like the English, have developed a really rich tradition of harmless lunacy we may be able to afford a little less intensity and a little more humor.

William Faulkner

In the London *Times Literary Supplement* of September 17, 1954, a critic, presumably British, discussing American fiction since the First World War, made the following statement: "It is pretty generally agreed that Faulkner—not the Faulkner of *Sanctuary* (1931), but the Faulkner of *The Sound and the Fury* (1929), *As I Lay Dying* (1930), *Light in August* (1932), and *Go Down Moses* (1942)—is the greatest American novelist of the century."

I imagine that this accolade marks high water in the flood tide of Mr. Faulkner's reputation. I quote it lest some readers misinterpret the subjoined commentary. I do not wish them to assume that I am ignorant of Mr. Faulkner's eminence, nor would I have them think me guilty of staging an exhibition of impertinence.

It should be remembered that twenty-five years ago there was no convenient bandwagon aboard which to climb. Twenty-five years ago many of the symbol-hungry young critics who have adopted Yoknapatawpha County as their second fatherland were still coiled in time's womb. At that time I appear to have written:

> No one can doubt that the author of *As I Lay Dying* has a really interesting mind, untouched by the platitudes of the day. His cosmos is awry; but it is his own, self-created. Genuine idiosyncrasy is rare among our younger novelists. For the most part they explain themselves too easily; they are con-

veniently ticketed. Mr. Faulkner cannot be so ticketed. That is one reason why he deserves attentive consideration.

This statement I still stand by. However, during the twenty-five years that have passed since these cautious words, Mr. Faulkner has become what he has become. Even as far back as 1944, André Gide, whose opinion one must respect, had singled him out as "the most important American writer."

I do not quarrel with the judgment or with that of the British critic already quoted. The comments that follow did not at any time in the past nor will they at any time in the future affect Mr. Faulkner's fame. Nor will they move to any shift of opinion the tens of thousands of critics and readers who find in him the accent of a master. I reprint them not in the spirit of controversy but for two reasons that can claim their own minor plausibility.

The first reason is that no master can talk to everyone. In the eighteenth century even Shakespeare fell on many deaf ears. It is a good thing for masters to be explained, analyzed, appreciated, and praised. But it is also a good, if lesser thing, to record the voice of the minority to whom these masters have little to say. That minority may be blind, crotchety, even stupid. None the less their rights are to be respected. Furthermore there is always the remote possibility that some small portion of the truth may be in them. My very insensibility to Mr. Faulkner's genius may serve to define it more sharply. Even the greatest of voices is characterized not only by what it has to say but by the distance it carries.

My second reason for recording my tiny nay is linked to the first. Over a period of a quarter of a century I have discussed Mr. Faulkner with many readers. Of these a great number admire him sincerely. A smaller number express admiration because they fear, unless they do so, to expose their own intellectual shortcomings. A still smaller but appreciable number recognize his talent but are unable to connect personally with its wave length.

The first group, though not always lucid, is extremely vocal. Mr. Faulkner may stand in need of interpretation but not of interpreters. He is the twentieth-century Robert Browning. He already occupies the semiposthumous position of having societies and even entire periodicals dedicated solely to the elucidation of his rebuses. He has been backtracked to his origins, broken down into groups of symbols, divided into periods, mythologized to a fare-thee-well, and in general given the complete A 1 Kafka treatment.

The second group, the fashionables, is not quite so audible. I am sure Mr. Faulkner, whose integrity is rocklike, has nothing but casual scorn for them.

The third group, of which I am a garden-variety member, has few spokesmen. Brendan Gill, reviewing *A Fable* in the *New Yorker,* was one of a small number who, rightly or wrongly, had the audacity to suggest that the emperor wore no clothes. (I can in these pages make no useful contribution to the controversy over Mr. Faulkner's masterpiece. It is simply not my book. Mr. Faulkner spent ten years writing it and I feel I spent a comparable period reading it.)

These non-Faulknerians, however, do exist. They are quiet through lack of self-confidence or as a consequence of intimidation by Mr. Faulkner's bully-boys. I have met many of them. They are, I think, passably intelligent, literate, and eager, as are all of us, to hail a new literary genius. But they don't *get* Mr. Faulkner.

To give a little aid and comfort to these baffled dissidents is the second purpose of what follows. These comments, drawn from reviews I have written of some of Mr. Faulkner's works, are not intended as analytical criticism. Let us put

it thus: They are the record of an insensibility, the diary of
a blindness, at best a case study of the non-Faulknerian mind.
Allons.

On January 15, 1930, writing in the *Nation,* I grappled
with *The Sound and the Fury*:

Frequently the intelligent reader can grasp the newer
literary anarchies only by an effort of attention so strained
that it fatigues his perception. He is so occupied in being a
detective that by the time he has to his own satisfaction clari-
fied the artist's intentions he is too worn out to feel anything
further. This is why the Joycean method of discontinuity has
been entirely successful only when applied to materials of
Joycean proportions. For it is obvious that if the theme is
sufficiently profound, the characters sufficiently extraordinary,
the plot sufficiently powerful, the reader is bound to absorb
some of all this despite the strain on his attention. But if, after
an interval of puzzle-solving, it dawns upon him that the
action and characters are minuscular, he is likely to throw
the book away in irritation. The analysis has taken too long
for the synthesis to be worth the trouble.

This seems to me to be the case with *The Sound and the
Fury,* a novel by an extremely talented young writer dealing
with the mental and physical disintegration of a Southern
family. Mr. Faulkner's work has been magnificently praised by
Evelyn Scott and other critics for whose opinions one must
have respect. It is in all humility, therefore, that I record the
feeling that the theme and the characters are trivial, unworthy
of the enormous and complex craftsmanship expended on them.
I do not see, for example, that Dilsey is more than a faithful
old Negress; she is not, for me at least, "stoic as some immemorial carving of heroism," nor does she "recover for us the
spirit of tragedy which the patter of cynicism has often made
seem lost." I admit that the idiocy of the thirty-three-year-old
Benjy is admirably grasped by Mr. Faulkner, but one hundred

pages of an imbecile's simplified sense perceptions and monosyllabic gibberings, no matter how accurately recorded, are
too much of a good thing. Similarly, Quentin and Jason are not
sufficiently interesting, not large enough, to make it worth
while to follow painfully the ramifications of their minds and
memories.

One has the feeling that Mr. Faulkner's experiments in the
breaking-up of consciousness, in the abolition of chronology
and psychological continuity, are both ingenious and sincere,
but not absolutely necessary to his story. The fact that his material includes imbecility, incest, paranoia, and sadism does not
mean that his tale is therefore complicated or obscure and in
need of oblique and bizarre treatment. The relationships between his characters are a trifle unhealthy, one must admit, but
must the prose in which they are described therefore be
feverish? After one has penetrated the mad, echoing labyrinth
of Mr. Faulkner's style one finds a rather banal Poe-esque plot,
a set of degenerate whites whose disintegration is irritating
rather than appalling, and two or three Negro characters who,
if they were reproduced in straight prose, would appear
as fairly conventional types. Sound and fury indeed.

That was over twenty-five years ago. Since then I have
read and reread Mr. Faulkner's novels as they appeared,
without being able (though I tried) ever completely to
emerge from my anesthesia. I seem, however, to have
struggled to a transient semiconsciousness on November 5,
1930, when I was permitted to review *As I Lay Dying*:

In his fourth novel Mr. Faulkner has to an extent departed
from the irritating obscurity which marked *The Sound and the
Fury*. It still seems that his is a far more involved technique
than his material actually requires; impudent analysis might
reduce this story to the dimensions of simple melodrama.

But, as people are always triumphantly reminding us, the same thing can be done with *Hamlet*.

Mr. Faulkner has a set of romantic obsessions which he treats in a highly intellectual manner. He is fascinated by characters who border on idiocy; by brother-and-sister incest; by lurid religious mania; by physical and mental decay; by peasants with weird streaks of poetry; by bodily suffering; by the more horrifying aspects of sex. Though his approach is always objective, he specializes in emotional extremes. He is a sort of prose Robinson Jeffers.

As I Lay Dying deals with the Bundren family who are transporting their coffined mother to her burial place in Jefferson, thirty miles away from the Bundren farm. During the course of this nightmare journey, which occupies nine days, we are taken inside the minds of the family and their neighbors. We learn that Dewey Dell is pregnant via her brother Jewel; that little Vardaman is a gibbering half-wit who believes his mother a fish; that Cash's mind is obsessed by his carpenter work on his mother's coffin. The strange tragedy of the dead Addie Bundren becomes clear as we listen to the weak-minded mutterings of old Anse, to the fanatic utterances of Cora Tull, a neighbor, and to the poetic, half-mad fantasies of Darl, another son. The whole affair is a psychological jigsaw puzzle, the pieces of which are represented by the distorted mentalities of half a dozen characters. The fascination of the story lies in the manner in which the phosphorescent rottenness of the family gradually reveals itself to the reader.

Despite the enthusiasm which has greeted Mr. Faulkner's work, it is difficult to believe him an important writer. His morbidity is interesting but tends to repeat itself. He seems acute in his portrayal of defective mentalities—but how, really, can one check up on this portrayal? The minds of idiots are more or less a closed book to us. We may be thrilled by the terrors of Vardaman and the mad vagaries of Darl, and nevertheless long for a few characters whose experience occasionally identifies itself, if only vaguely, with our own. If we are to judge from his first novel, *Soldiers' Pay*, Mr. Faulkner is quite capable of handling the more normal aspects of humanity; but out of an undoubtedly honest perversity he remains faithful to his old lechers, his brutal drugstore clerks, his sexual inverts, and his insane dreamers. Mentally disintegrated types (unless the disintegration is of a subtle and complicated character) are not a very rich mine for investigation, as, for example, T. F. Powys has discovered; and one hopes Mr. Faulkner before long will come to the same conclusion.

On April 15, 1931, *Sanctuary* almost drew me out of my coma. But I'm a little ashamed of my improvement. I didn't know it at the time, but it now develops that *Sanctuary* was a potboiler. Before writing it Mr. Faulkner figured out what would sell at least ten thousand copies and then "chose what I thought was the right answer and invented the most horrific tale I could imagine and wrote it in about three weeks." (It was, however, revised before publication.) As you will see, I fell for the potboiler, corncob and all, rather than for the masterpieces. I conclude that when Mr. Faulkner writes for the populace (me) he abandons about 50 per cent of the famous style. This relaxation of genius is just enough to give me a chance to find out what he's talking about. The material, however, potboiler or no potboiler, is not much different from what is to be found in his noncommercials. At any rate, here's how *Sanctuary* struck me:

Among the characters of Mr. Faulkner's latest novel are a murderer, an ex-harlot, a drunkard, two half-wits, a nymphomaniac, a degenerate child, three procuresses, and a *voyeur*. The action of the book includes two cold-blooded killings, an emasculation, a lynching by gasoline fire, a jazz party in honor of a gunman's corpse, and a particularly inhuman sexual assault. In his search for the perfect Inferno Mr. Faulkner makes no Dantesque journeys—his hell lies in the territory of northern Mississippi. There is no recent book better contrived to send Mr. Irving Babbitt into a non-inner-checked fit of delirium tremens.

But the book is real, there is no doubt of it. Mr. Faulkner has an almost Joycean power of exteriorizing his horror-obsession. His damned and distorted cosmos *is* a cosmos. It is not a private bellyache. And because it is a cosmos, obeying laws of its own, self-sufficient, shaped and dynamic, one cannot deny to Mr. Faulkner the title of creator. By virtue of this book alone he at once takes his place among the foremost of the younger generation of American novelists. He is an original.

And yet it is not hard to understand the point of view of the sweetness-and-lighters who are dismayed by his "sadism" and his morbidity. One cannot, of course, challenge an artist's choice of materials; one can only challenge his manipulation of them. Perhaps I am tender-minded, but it seems to me that *Sanctuary*, while startling and intensely interesting, is not overwhelming—and it might very well have been. It fails to overwhelm chiefly because it makes an exaggerated attack on the reader's nervous system. Here we have a book curiously akin to the eighteenth-century Gothic tale of horror. It makes use of similar mechanisms—dark hints, desolate backgrounds, unrelievedly black villains. But, instead of the flesh, it makes the mind and viscera creep. Each individual page is a calculated assault on one's sense of the normal, like the clever incantations and manual passes of the hypnotist. But while one succumbs to the hypnotist one does not quite succumb to Mr. Faulkner. His book induces a sort of stoic behavior-response; one wants to fight back against these repeated shocks, these impacts of horror. As a result, so much nervous energy is expended in this nervous resistance that the sensitive faculties which should lead you to abandon yourself to Mr. Faulkner's witchcraft are actually in part inhibited. The imagination gets charley horse.

Mr. Faulkner's descriptive style, too, for all its cleverness (I am speaking particularly of his cruelly evocative observation of unpleasant sensory impressions) is a little too taut, too strained. The hypnotist works too hard. Each sentence bears more than its due freight of tenseness, innuendo, horror, and fear. One's sense of the normal, at first paralyzed by the impact of this coiled and deadly prose, at last reawakens—and the spell is, for the moment, broken. There is a kind of artistic detachment so icy as to induce in the reader nervous terror rather than esthetic submission. Accordingly, the more thoughtless critic may find it easy to accuse Mr. Faulkner of mere maliciousness; he may urge that ugliness, while it can be pushed to the point of art, can never pass the threshold beyond which lies the genuinely tragic. But I do not think that there is anything gratuitous in Mr. Faulkner's morbidities. He has simply made a slight error in the calculation of his effects. He must learn when to pull his punches.

From almost every point of view *Sanctuary* is a better book than either *As I Lay Dying* or *The Sound and the Fury*. Its construction, however, is more open to criticism. It is really two novels, not one. The story of Horace Benbow, unsuccessful as lawyer, husband, and idealist, forms one novel. That of Popeye and Temple Drake forms another. They revolve about one another like the components of a binary star system, connected by lines of force but none the less separated. Also, there are certain bravura passages, gorgeous in themselves, but which as far as the necessities of the plot are concerned seem dragged in by the ears. Examples are the Hogarthian humors of Reba's gin party and the horrible grotesquerie of Red's funeral.

There are other weaknesses in the book but they all flow from the copiousness of the author's imagination. Possibly he has tried to do too much. His faults are the faults of excessive

eagerness. He remains, for me at least, with Ernest Hemingway and Conrad Aiken, among the most interesting young
novelists now writing in America.

After *Sanctuary* I relapsed. Mr. Faulkner passed from
strength to strength while my heart slowed down, my blood
stream languished and my eyes grew glassier. I was lost. I
had made my little effort but I felt a premonition that I was
not the man for Mr. Faulkner's Dixie dooms. I transferred my
apathy from the *Nation* to the *New Yorker*. On April 21,
1934, I wrote:

> The satisfaction felt upon turning the last page of one of
> Mr. Faulkner's Walpurgis Night narratives is akin to that of
> the neophyte who has successfully endured the college-
> fraternity initiation in the dark cellar. Even those who call Mr.
> Faulkner our greatest literary sadist do not fully appreciate him,
> for it is not merely his characters who have to run the gauntlet
> but also his readers. One does not so much finish *Sanctuary*
> as come through it in good shape. I have frequently felt that
> the publishers are missing a sure bet in not arranging to
> have every emergent Faulknerian met by a brandy-bearing St.
> Bernard. His best books give you the feeling that you have just
> spent (with those nice people, the Jukes and the Kallikaks) a
> weekend which would have been quite tolerable had it not
> been for the bleeding ghosts who kept filing through the bed-
> room all night long.
>
> *Dr. Martino*, a new collection of short stories, though much
> less scary than usual, is still not the perfect nightcap. There's
> a Svengalian doctor who sits quietly on a chair and manipulates
> a young lady's mind by remote control; a maniacal fox-hunter
> who tramples the fox dead with his heels; the corpse of a
> murdered man which is hidden in a tree and comes apart at the
> wrong moment; a story of the afterworld which I do not under-
> stand, but which, if I did, I am certain would terrify me; a sixty-
> year-old Mississippi peasant who in eighteen pages brings about

three murders and a suicide; some assorted assassinations in the grim defiles of the Tennessee hill country; and similar Faulknerian pleasantries.

Mr. Faulkner, of course, is interested in making your mind, rather than your flesh, creep. That is what renders his work so difficult to estimate. We all have the same flesh and it is set a-prickle by the same things, but we have different minds. A story like "Leg" will stimulate one reader to plucking madly at the chair arm. That reader is so constituted as to be able to fall through each and every psychological trap door laid down by Mr. Faulkner. Another reader may be so constituted that the trap doors don't exist for him. He will pass through the story with nothing but a feeling of bewilderment.

Mr. Faulkner is so subtle, so oblique in his effects that frequently I seem to miss the point altogether and escape without a single shudder. It is very much as if one were to go through *Dracula* by reading carefully every twenty-fifth page. One would have a general suspicion of dark doings, but the story as a whole would be a blank. The old-time thriller depended for its effect on our interest in and fear of what was going to happen. The thriller, new style, makes you wonder just what *is* happening, and as you're not quite sure, the assumption is it must be something pretty eerie. I am still trying, for instance, to figure out what the title story, "Dr. Martino," is about, and just what the trouble is with the doctor, and why the girl is so crazily linked with him, and how a fresh-cheeked Yale boy can possibly talk like Heraclitus. I don't think I'm any denser than the average reader, and I'm quite as willing to enjoy a good shriek. I just want to be sure I'm shrieking at the proper horror.

When Mr. Faulkner is least sibylline, he is for me most admirable. There are two stories in the book, for instance, whose every sentence I can understand, and so, as they are brilliantly written, they are for me very good jobs. One, a straight mystery-detection thriller called "Smoke," is as neat as anything by

Conan Doyle or Austin Freeman. The other is "Turnabout," a wartime melodrama involving bombers and torpedo boats, and full of old-fashioned, physical-danger thrills. There are also one or two stories, such as "Death Drag," which start out in a humorous vein. But the humor, instead of stopping at the grotesque, advances over the border straight into the horrible. I think Mr. Faulkner is the only living writer who can turn this particular trick, but whether it is intentional or not is a thing hard to be sure of.

From this point on I lost my way completely in Mr. Faulkner's hashish Southland. On March 30, 1945, I let out a plaintive but, I knew, hopeless cry for help:

I'm quite willing to turn Mr. Faulkner's new novel over to the Faulknerians. I've read it twice, once slowly and again in a burst of desperate speed, on the assumption that the first time I might not have seen the forest for the trees. It has me licked a dozen ways. Reaction analysis: one part repulsion, one part terror, one part admiration, three parts puzzlement, four parts boredom. I figure that disqualifies me as a reviewer of Mr. Faulkner's books, a conclusion I come to in all humiliation, because a few years ago I was cheering as lustily as the rest.

The scene of *Pylon* is a new airport just outside a Southern city that is clearly New Orleans. An air carnival, with pitifully small money prizes, is being held. Characters: an "air circus" consisting of Roger Shumann, pilot; Art, a parachute jumper (I *think* his name is Art, but Mr. Faulkner hates to tell you what people are called; it oversimplifies his narrative); Laverne, a woman who belongs to both of them; Jack, a child, fathered by either of them; Jiggs, a mechanic; a reporter who seems to have walked out of a waxworks show and who goes crazy over this strange quintet, follows them around, feeds and lodges them, and, finally, with the best will in the world, makes himself indirectly responsible for the horrible air death of Shumann.

There are some thrilling aviation scenes, a sickening but fascinating series of drunkenness vignettes in the author's most gelid and pitiless manner, and Mr. Faulkner's prose, more Joycean than ever.

It didn't register with me because (*a*) I understood what was happening only half the time, (*b*) the characters seem to be insane or nearly so, (*c*) the mainspring of the action—the fascination exerted by the traveling air circus on the reporter —is unconvincing to this primitive brain, (*d*) there seems a ludicrous disproportion between Mr. Faulkner's feverishly elaborate language and the sordid, rather simple plot, (*e*) I am bewildered by Mr. Faulkner's constant (and occasionally successful) attempts to scare the poor reader out of his wits, (*f*) I don't care about neurotic speed demons and can only with difficulty applaud heroism which is perilously close to lunacy.

But if your mind clicks with Mr. Faulkner's, pay no attention to all this and set me down as one so soft-boiled as to like his Caligari shudders without Dostoevski frills.

I am aware that *Absalom, Absalom!* was heralded by Mr. Faulkner's publishers as "his most important and ambitious contribution to American literature." For years I cringed in shame at my inability to share this opinion. I did not believe *Absalom, Absalom!* up to Mr. Faulkner's usual standard. For years I shivered in the chill wind of solitude. Only recently, coming upon some remarks by Mr. Gilbert Highet on the art of parody, I cheered up a bit. Mr. Highet owns a mind both subtle and muscular, well-equipped to grapple successfully with Mr. Faulkner. And yet here he is, saying "We could find some eminent authors who appear to be parodying themselves: dare I mention Mr. Faulkner's *Absalom, Absalom?*"

He dare; and on October 31, 1936, though with less authority, I did a little daring on my own hook:

At one point in *Absalom, Absalom!* William Faulkner makes Quentin Compson, who is telling the story, say to his auditor,

"You can't understand it. You would have to be born there."
This seems to me not merely one (or two) of the few comprehensible sentences in the entire novel, but also beyond a doubt
the truest. At any rate, it is my particular Out. Not hailing
from Mississippi (which Mr. Faulkner, in his best Greek-
tragedy mood, calls "a land primed for fatality"), I figure I'm
not required to understand Mr. Faulkner's novels. I should
like to state, therefore, in all humility, that I do not comprehend why *Absalom, Absalom!* was written, what the non-
Mississippian is supposed to get out of it, or, indeed, what it is
all about. Nor do I understand why Mr. Faulkner writes the
way he does. And, having gone so far, I may as well break
down and state my conviction that Mr. Faulkner's latest work
is the most consistently boring novel by a reputable writer
to come my way during the last decade.

One may sum up both substance and style by saying that
everybody in *Absalom, Absalom!* comes to no good end and
takes a hell of a time coming even that far. The story runs
from 1807 to 1910, with the major action concentrated between
1833, when Thomas Sutpen appears in Jefferson, Mississippi,
and 1869, when he is rather regretfully murdered by an old
family retainer. Thomas Sutpen is a monomaniac, known
familiarly to the other characters as The Demon. It is never
quite clear what makes him so villainous, except that he has
a habit of engaging in gouge-as-gouge-can fights with Negroes,
and has the odd power of scaring ladies first into marrying
him and then into conniption fits. However, he's the fellow
you're supposed to shudder at, and if you understand Mr.
Faulkner, you'll shudder. If you don't, I guess you just won't.
The Demon's second wife, Ellen Coldfield, gives birth to two
children, Henry and Judith, goes dotty, and dies after a while.
Her younger sister, Rosa, is insulted by The Demon and also
goes dotty, though it takes her much longer to die. The father
of Rosa and Ellen goes nuts when the Civil War arrives, nails
himself up in a garret, and perseveringly starves himself to

death. Now, young Henry, upon finding out that his best friend, Charles Bon, engaged to be married to his sister Judith, is (*a*) his half-brother and (*b*) part Negro, also goes dotty in a complicated way and finally shoots Charles dead. By the end of the story Henry has been reduced to straight, simple idiocy and is kept shut up in the attic. Judith, after some years passed in a vacant-eyed trance, passes out as a result of smallpox, a death so natural as to strike a jarring note. There is also Clytemnestra Sutpen, daughter of Thomas Sutpen (that's dat Ole Demon Sutpen) and a Negro slave. Clytie sets fire to herself and the idiot boy Henry, and so finishes her career in a fine blaze of pyromaniacal lunacy.

Then there are the Joneses. Wash Jones is a daft hanger-on of Ole Demon Sutpen. He has a granddaughter, Milly. Milly gives birth to a child (it's the Ole Demon's handiwork); Ole Demon insults her; Wash gets sore, shoots Milly, shoots the child, cuts Ole Demon in two with a scythe, and then commits suicide. The Joneses furnish the nearest thing to comic relief in the book. Now, if you'll think back a few lunatics or so, you will remember Charles Bon, preserved from incest and miscegenation by Henry Sutpen's fraternal bullet. Charles had an octoroon mistress, name and mental condition unrecorded, by whom he engendered the boy Charles Etienne. Charles Etienne, realizing that he is a few thirty-seconds Negro, promptly runs amuck. He dies prosaically of smallpox, but not before he has begotten, with the assistance of a full-blooded Negress, a son, Jim. Jim is the real McCoy, a legitimate idiot. (I mean one specifically so called by Mr. Faulkner.) At the end of the book, he is the only living descendant of the accursed Sutpens, which shows you what can happen to a family once it has committed itself to Mr. Faulkner's guardianship.

I think I've got them all in. There's a stray lunatic aunt here and there, but I'm no stickler for details. Come to think of it, there's the young man named Quentin Compson, whose grandfather had befriended Ole Demon Sutpen, and who tells the Sutpen saga to his college chum many years after all these murders, near-incests, fires, suicides, etc., had occurred down on the Sutpen farm in Old Mississipp'. Neither Quentin nor his roommate carries on what you would call normal conversations, but as there is no evidence of either of them having married his grandmother, or roasted his grandfather over a slow fire (under the impression that the latter was a mulatto first cousin with a trace of chimpanzee blood), I think they should be accepted as Mr. Faulkner's concession to the gray, tawdry, non-Mississippian universe in which the rest of us poor folks live, if Mr. Faulkner can bring himself to call it living.

This cheerful little fable is filtered through the medium of a style peculiar to Mr. Faulkner. It seems peculiar to me, too.

First, we have the Non-Stop or Life Sentence. The first two-and-a-half pages of *Absalom, Absalom!* consist of seven sentences, composed of 123, 155, 9 (something wrong here), 146, 66, 93, and 135 words respectively. Average: 104. To penetrate Mr. Faulkner's sentences is like hacking your way through a jungle. The path closes up at once behind you, and in no time at all you find yourself entangled in a luxuriant mass of modifiers, qualifications, relative clauses, parenthetical phrases, interjected matter, recapitulations, and other indications of style. All of Mr. Faulkner's shuddery inventions pale in horrendousness before the mere notion of parsing him.

After the Life Sentence comes the Far Fetch, or Hypertrope. Very few things in the book remain themselves. Each one reminds Mr. Faulkner of something else. "Her legs hung . . . clear of the floor with that air of impotent and static rage like children's feet." You don't see it? Join me at the foot of the class.

Then we have what may be called Anti-Narrative, a set of complex devices used to keep the story from being told. Mr. Faulkner is very clever at this. He gets quite an interesting effect, for example, by tearing the Sutpen chronicle into pieces, as if a mad child were to go to work on it with a pair of shears, and then having each of the jagged divisions narrated by a different personage: the author, Rosa, Quentin, Quentin's father, Quentin's grandfather. All these people do a neat job of mixing up the time sequences, delaying climaxes, confusing the reader, and otherwise enabling Mr. Faulkner to demonstrate that as a technician he has Joyce and Proust punch-drunk. I should add that everybody talks the same language, a kind of Dixie Gongorism, very formal, allusive, cryptic. Apparently the entire population of Jefferson, Mississippi, consists of rhetoricians who would blench at the sight of a simple declarative sentence. On the other hand, it is only fair to say that there are a score of pages (Rosa Coldfield's section of the narrative) full of remarkable prose poetry, beautiful in itself, if irrelevant.

Seriously, I do not know what to say of this book except that it seems to point to the final blowup of what was once a remarkable, if minor, talent. I imagine that many of my respected colleagues will see in it a tragic masterpiece, a great lament for the old dead South, a Sophoclean study of a doomed family. Perhaps they are right. For me, this is a penny dreadful tricked up in fancy language and given a specious depth by the expert manipulation of a series of eccentric technical tricks. The characters have no magnitude and no meaning because they have no more reality than a mince-pie nightmare. If we are to have tales of violence and sadism, let the violence and sadism be drawn from the behavior of grownups, let them be more than the melodramatic gestures of childish maniacs. A study of defeat can have great tragic weight, but only if the defeated are akin to us, which these mumbling, muttering, frozen-faced Sutpens surely are not. I fail to see why we must go into a spasm of ecstatic shivering just because Mr. Faulkner is a clever hand at fitting up a literary asylum for the feeble-minded. It takes more than these fake sepulchral voices, these synthetic incests, these Monk Lewis allusions, to scare ordinary sober citizens. Ole Demon Sutpen is a mechanical bogyman, and the rest of his gang are no better. The whole affair reminds one more of *The Tavern* than of Greek tragedy, and I have the horrid suspicion that if enough people were to say boo the entire structure of *Absalom, Absalom!* would disappear in smoke.

Well, I must have been wrong. No one cared to say boo. But doggedly I persisted. Mr. Faulkner, if he will forgive the image, was a hollow tooth which I could not help worrying though I knew it would do no good. On February 19, 1938, I did my best with *The Unvanquished:*

Any fool writer can be simple and dull at the same time; the real trick is to be subtle and dull. The only one who can turn this particular trick today with magisterial ability is Mr. William Faulkner. He has made an art out of the elaborate induction of tedium; he is tirelessly tiresome.

One opens his new collection of short stories, *The Unvanquished,* and finds a description of a horse's "steady gait which was not a walk and not a run, as if he had held it all the way from Tennessee because there was a need to encompass earth which abrogated sleep or rest and relegated to some insulated bourne of perennial and pointless holiday so trivial a thing as galloping." Now, what am I to do with this horse of Mr. Faulkner's, this abrogating, relegating, insulating horse? I am far too unsophisticated even to have thought of a horse like that, much less met him. And what is true of Mr. Faulkner's abrogating horse is true of the rest of his characters. I admit they're unusual, I admit only Mr. Faulkner can create them. But when I think of them I reflect on the thousands of extraordinary devices that have been patented in Washington and, for some reason or other, will never be of much use to the public.

The Unvanquished consists of seven short stories dealing with the fortunes of the Sartoris family during the last two years of the Civil War and the reconstruction-carpetbagging period immediately following. Five of these stories appeared in the *Saturday Evening Post*, whose readers are apparently attuned to Mr. Faulkner's ellipses, dark allusions, and generally recondite manner of narration. The style is not, I gladly acknowledge, as impenetrable as in *Absalom, Absalom!* but I would hardly care to be left out alone in it on a dark night without a lantern. Four of the tales revolve around the indomitable figure of Granny Rosa Millard, a heroic old Confederate who can outwit Union officers by the score and who is fazed by nothing. I rather like her; that is, whenever Mr. Faulkner doesn't get in my way. The tales are told from the viewpoint of Bayard Sartoris, who is twelve in the first episode and a young man in the last. Some of the stories are meant to be seriocomic, one is macabre, one or two are told in Mr. Faulkner's most somber and intimidating vein. All are intended to illustrate the notion contained in the title: that you can beat these Sartorises in battle, but in a spiritual sense they are unconquerable.

The Unvanquished is Mr. Faulkner's most Confederate book. I am forced to confess that I do not see why, in these days, it is necessary to be either a Yank or a Reb; there are so many more interesting things to be. But I fear that in order to enjoy *The Unvanquished* as more than a series of technical exercises in narration you'll have to adopt the unreconstructed point of view while you're reading it. If you can't do that you're out of luck. The effect of the stories depends on one's understanding of a special code of behavior, a code held by a few undoubtedly gallant, courageous, and masterful people on the plantations of the South up to perhaps the end of the nineteenth century. Their code, their special rituals of conduct, their stern lust for violence, their morbidity, their humorlessness, their unfailing personal courage have to be apprehended (unless you were brought up in the code yourself, as no doubt Mr. Faulkner was) by a terrific effort of the will. If

you can make that effort, Mr. Faulkner can give you something, perhaps a great deal. If you can't (and I can't), Mr.
Faulkner is not your meat. To me these stories, despite their
nervous brilliance of manner, are in a class with the hysterical
lost-cause fictions that pudgy, middle-aged English ladies used
to write about Bonnie Prince Charlie and the Jacobites. But
for many of us the King over the Water is water over the dam.

By this time I guess I have lost even those few readers
whose morbid curiosity has led them to follow this self-
exposure of a poor devil of a book-reviewer. It was around
this period, in the late thirties and early forties, that the
symbol-players and the mythanthropes discovered Mr. Faulkner. (Not, by the way, that he has ever paid any attention
to them.) The big and little drums began to beat, the parade
to form, and I was left far behind, occasionally tootling un-
heard on my penny whistle. Here's a sour note or two, dated
January 21, 1939:

William Faulkner, who provides monsters for all literate
American homes, is back again with another tale of terror,
The Wild Palms. The reader will detect no soft alteration in
Mr. Faulkner's Gorgon's-eye view of existence. In its very
first chapter, *The Wild Palms* offers for your consideration
a maddened woman bleeding to death as the result of an
abortion performed by her doctor-lover. Mr. Faulkner sustains
this mood throughout the book. Item: an engaging moron
who, armed only with an eight-inch knife, rips up alligators
in a Louisiana swamp. Item: a hill woman who, lying on an
islet of viscous mud, gives birth to a baby, her only help consisting of the aforesaid moron, who cuts the umbilical cord
with the jagged edge of an empty tomato can. Item—but no,
it's not fair to give Mr. Faulkner's horrors away in advance,
after he's worked so hard over them, too. I need merely say, to
reassure his many admirers, that *The Wild Palms* strengthens
his unchallenged position as the one living writer who could

retell "Snow White and the Seven Dwarfs" using for characters only Grumpy and the Witch.

Mr. Faulkner's interest in formal effects (friendly critics speak of this as a mastery of form) has led him, in *The Wild Palms,* to tell two stories instead of one. One is called "The Wild Palms," the other "The Old Man." They alternate like an endless sandwich: slice of "Wild Palms," slice of "Old Man," slice of "Wild Palms," etc. "Old Man" takes place in 1927, during the worst weeks of a Mississippi flood, whereas the action of "Wild Palms" runs through several months of 1938. The characters are quite distinct, as are the settings. Superficially, then, the two stories have nothing to do with each other. The publishers' blurb, however, invites us to believe that the book as a whole is a kind of exercise in counterpoint, with all kinds of subtle correspondences linking the alternating narratives. Those who like guessing games will be eager to trace these profound parallels and will doubtless succeed in doing so, which does not alter the fact that solving a puzzle and reading a novel are separate mental activities.

The theme of "Wild Palms" is flight: the flight of Charlotte and Harry, a sex-chained couple, from the conventions of a society which seeks to weaken and destroy their grim sexual absorption. On the other hand, the theme of "Old Man" is refuge (opposite of flight—neat pattern, eh?). A convict, sent out to labor on the levees during a flood, is swept away, forced to rescue a woman whom he does not want to be saddled with, compelled to undergo some of Mr. Faulkner's most ingenious special-patented tortures, when all the time what he desires most in the world is to get back to the safe, comfortable convict farm. Charlotte and Harry are punished for wanting freedom. The convict is punished for not wanting it. Heads I win, tails you lose; doomed either way, by arrangement with William Faulkner.

It would be silly to deny that there are extraordinary pages in this book—you'll discover them for yourself—but the net effect seems to me remarkably unmemorable. I am not convinced by the story of Charlotte and Harry that the modern world (I gather this is the moral) holds no place for love, nor am I convinced by the tribulations of Charlotte and Harry that love and suffering can be equated. Mr. Faulkner's Dostoevskian nymphomaniac and his naive young doctor, who has apparently never heard of ergot, are such a special pair of lunatics that their passion ceases to have any application to the world of general human nature. As for the love = suffering formula, it is simply an inversion of the traditional love = bliss equation, and no less absurd. If love = bliss is the wish dream of childish optimism, love = suffering is the wish dream of morbid pessimism. A ladies'-magazine serial is manic; Mr. Faulkner is depressive. Put them together and you get a complete psychosis.

The Charlotte-Harry story, however, is superior to the convict-flood-woman-in-labor narrative, because in the first you know what effect Faulkner is trying to create, whereas in the second you are never sure whether the mood is supposed to be one of grim hilarity or grim horror. The idea of a dim-witted convict forced into a freedom he doesn't want has its humorous side; the woman whom he is compelled to stick to and whose life he regretfully has to save may also seem funny to some. But whatever humor lies in this situation could and should be exhausted in twenty pages, not one hundred and fifty; and besides it is obscured by the atmosphere of brutal physical suffering in which the whole story is plunged. After a while this brutality becomes merely ludicrous; one begins to feel not only that Mr. Faulkner is trying his darnedest to see how much misery he can make his characters stand but also that he is trying to see how much misery he can make his readers stand. It's an interesting game, but nearer to old-fashioned melodrama than to literature.

The publishers may have had an inkling of this, for the blurb tells us that "*The Wild Palms* contains the most spec-

tacular situations yet created by William Faulkner." This is
true. But a novel that has to be praised for its "spectacular
situations" rather than for its power to mirror human nature
truly and movingly has, to my mind, two strikes on it. Not
meaning to be either paradoxical or frivolous, I think there is
something feeble about a creative imagination that, before
it can deal with human beings, must call to its aid a flood,
two abortions, various extremes of physical suffering, near-
madness, a woman in labor, quantities of blood (Mr. Faulkner's convict, for example, *has* to have hemophilia), and
human degeneracy ad libitum. Mr. Faulkner's mastery of
certain limited technical effects is indisputable, as is his
knowledge of certain subhuman types. But for his creative
power in general one reserves the same qualified enthusiasm
one has for the transient vitality that follows a shot of adren-
alin.

It's more than possible, of course, that my inability to see
in Mr. Faulkner what my respected colleagues see is simply
a demonstration of certain stupidities in myself. Sometimes
the best will in the world cannot produce sympathy or perhaps even understanding. I say this because I would not wish
my readers to believe that I am counseling them to avoid
The Wild Palms. On the contrary, please read it. If Mr. Faulkner can do more for you than set your teeth on edge or make
you snicker—my felicitations.

The Hamlet appeared. Down I went for the usual full
count, on April 6, 1940:

All in the line of duty, I have spent part of this week weaving through *The Hamlet*, by William Faulkner. From the intense murk of its sentences I emerge, somewhat shaken, to
report that the author apparently continues to enjoy as lively
a case of the 'orrors as you are apt to find outside a Keeley-cure
hostelry. While there is nothing in *The Hamlet* to rival the
bloody waxworks of *The Wild Palms*, still this chronicle has

its own special assortment of shudders. There's a troop of homicidal horses that ginger up things quite smartly. There's an idiot who falls in love with a beast of Borden—*chacun à son cow*—and comes to no good end. Odd bits of wife-beating, plain murder, near fratricide, and mania are also inserted here and there to provide a decorative effect. All in all, it's sound, Grade B Faulkner.

The Hamlet gives the reader the sense of being part of a family saga. The Snopeses are Mr. Faulkner's Mississippi Forsytes, and Flem Snopes is his Soames. Flem, who starts his career practically in the odor of sanctity as a mere barn-burner, comes to the hamlet and begins to show the stuff he's made of. With the aid of innumerable kinsfolk, who seep into the story like gas, he takes over by trickery and intimidation some of the holdings of the rich Varner family, gets control of the general store, quietly wins for himself the neighborhood Mae West, drives a man mad, mulcts the bold peasantry of their sweaty dollars, and departs to fresh woods and pastures new. (I forgot to mention that only bad luck prevents him from robbing a corpse.) Mr. Faulkner contrives the most extraordinary situations to drive home the fact that Flem Snopes is a mean, cruel, acquisitive villain, a proposition I for one would be willing to accept without all this argument.

I don't claim to understand everything that goes on in *The Hamlet,* or which parts are meant to make you laugh and which to chill your spine. Nor is its peculiar construction clear to me—it seems to be partly novel and partly a collection of short stories. Nor do I claim to understand just what Mr. Faulkner means to convey by his presentation of these niggling cruelties and this general-store gossip. In fact, I make no claims whatever to any ability to comprehend what Mr. Faulkner is about. I know when I'm licked.

I cannot leave him, however, without quoting, as is my wont, one of his representative sentences. It's really long enough to deserve a title all to itself: let's call it *The Curious*

Case of the Transmogrified Cattle. You'll find it by beating
your way to page 70: "Tull told him of a considerable herd
of scrub cattle which had passed the winter in pasture on the
farm which Snopes' father had rented from the Varners for
another year—a herd which, by the time Ratliff had been carried to a Memphis hospital and operated on and returned
home and once more took an interest in what went on about
him, had increased gradually and steadily and then overnight
vanished, its disappearance coincident with the appearance of
a herd of good Herefords in a pasture on another place which
Varner owned and kept himself as his home farm, as though
transmogrified, translated complete and intact save for their
altered appearance and obviously greater worth, it only later
becoming known that the cattle had reached the pasture via a
foreclosed lien nominally held by a Jefferson bank."

It was time for my swan song. I had established the fact,
ad nauseam, that Mr. Faulkner was too much for me. I
wished him well, I was proud that still another American
writer had won the Nobel Prize, I envied those who could
ride the cataract of his prose, I was about ready to paddle
my little canoe in quieter waters. But when *Requiem for a
Nun* came along I found myself responding to it, as a broken-
down retired fire-horse answers the sound of the alarm. One
last pitiful fling and I was through. This appeared in the
pages of *Holiday,* November, 1951:

Every anecdote I have heard about Mr. Faulkner leads me
to admire him. His character, as anyone acquainted with his
moving Nobel Prize address will agree, has extraordinary
purity and sweetness. As an artist he is as painstaking as
Flaubert. Furthermore, in the opinion of my myriad critical
betters, he is a genius.

It is also true—a fact of absorbing interest only to myself—
that when I read him I feel about as I would feel were I to
play chess with Alekhine. I just can't follow the moves.

Mr. Faulkner's latest Aeschylean whodunit has thrown me for my standard loss. For reasons apparent to any practicing clairvoyant, it is entitled *Requiem for a Nun*. It brings back Temple Drake, whom you may remember as the frangible heroine of *Sanctuary*, and who is beginning to shape up as the most fluent monologist since Mrs. Nickleby.

The plot is high voltage, even for Mr. Faulkner, involving incriminating letters (what the mellers of the last century termed "the documents"), blackmail, prostitution, infanticide, a last-minute appeal to the Governor, and a Negro murderess who acts out a levee version of Prince Myshkin. Part of the book seems to be a bardic account of the history of Jackson, Mississippi, but don't hold me to this statement. The remainder is cast in the form of a play whose relation to the narrative sections will be readily grasped only by the followers of the Oxford (Miss.) Movement.

For my befuddlement I have only myself to blame. As a mere pinafored child I was taught to diagram English sentences on the blackboard. Consequently, though I can honor Mr. Faulkner as the champion of lost clauses and though I concede the influence of his Doctrine of Original Syntax, for me his sentence structure passes the bounds of parsability. These relative clauses with mysterious antecedents; these parenthetical intruders who drop by for a minute and stay for a week; these qualifications that wear away the original statement till nothing remains but an impalpable verbal dust; these mazy paragraphs in whose dark corridors I wander, a blind, terrified Theseus minus Ariadne's thread; these non-commutable life sentences—the second one in *Requiem for a Nun* runs just under two pages: what can a simple country boy like myself, suckled on Fowler's *Modern English Usage*, do when set down in the middle of this grammatical Witches' Sabbath?

I am aware that Mr. Faulkner is a novelist, not a showman; that none of this is for effect; that he just can't write any other way, and shouldn't be asked to. Yet I cannot help feeling, particularly in this book, a gap between the actual weight of the content and the Alexandrian elaboration of the manner.

Maybe it's the latitude. In days gone by, well-born Southerners were noted for the flow and elegance of their conversation. (Even today, some Southern young ladies, believing a pause rude, keep moving their lips and larynxes almost continuously.) In general, however, the admirable Confederate tradition of sweet talk has tended to dilute into garrulousness. Chronic logorrhea is as common in Dixie as chronic laconism is in Vermont. I presume Mr. Faulkner's unremitting mutter, that rhetorical buzz which to my coarse ear is the ground-bass of his prose, comes naturally to him.

Mr. Faulkner and Jimmy Durante do not seem to have much in common. Yet in their approach to the language they shake hands. For Mr. Durante, as for Mr. Faulkner, English is not so much a refractory medium as an eager victim, hungry for plastic surgery. Like most men not dulled by too much schooling, both are fond of long words, and not words you can find in any old dictionary either. *Requiem for a Nun,* for example, offers, among other wonders, the following: *mammalinity, evictant, undeviable, incubant, impedeless, rejectant, toyment,* and *fissionating.* What the Schnoz (whose cognate genius transforms an oral translator into an *interrupter*) should do is hire Mr. Faulkner as his writer. Then things would really start fissionating.

By this time the reader (surely there can't be more than one) may have concluded that I have a prejudice against Mr. Faulkner. Not so. A prejudice is a pre-judgment. I came to every new Faulkner opus wearily determined to see in it what my betters saw. No more than the next man do I enjoy looking like a dunce. But, no matter how hard I tried, I was licked every time. Some major defect, some incurable myopia, prevented me from seeing in him more than a dazzling, though often unsuccessful technician, passionately and sincerely creating a private world whose inhabitants would be completely unrecognizable to the natives of Oxford, Mississippi, but are apparently immediately recognizable to a host of young academics and, let us be fair, to many non-specialized, average, intelligent readers.

For them there is no disproportion between Mr. Faulkner's Gothic-horrors material and the complex means used to embody it. No gap between the noble, free-floating utterances of the Nobel Prize speech and the moral chaos of most of the novels. No impatience with the violence, the humorlessness, the portentousness of his characters. No willful and, as I see it, unrewarding deformation of our English tongue. No feeling that at the heart of all his books there is, as an English critic has put it, "an abrogation of natural law, an act of violence." Nothing of the uneasy sense I get from time to time of Charles Addams trying to be Dostoevski.

If there exist, as I believe to be the case, a few other old-fashioned reactionaries who are like myself baffled by Mr. Faulkner and even more baffled by his commentators, the putting down of this record of bewilderment may not have been entirely wasted. I claim no more for it.

Lead-Ins

A Note on *Huckleberry Finn*

THIS IS the book with which we as a literary people begin. Two thousand years from now American professors of literature—if such still exist—will speak of *Huckleberry Finn* as English professors of literature now speak of Chaucer. For *Huckleberry Finn* is our Chaucer, our Homer, our Dante, our Virgil. It is the source of the stream, the seed-bed, the book which, read or unread, has influenced a thousand American writers, the first great mold within which the form and pattern of our speech were caught. It has spawned both Hemingway and Mickey Spillane.

First-rate writers existed on this continent before *Huckleberry Finn*. But *Huckleberry Finn* is the first important work written out of a simple, vast unconsciousness of the existence of any country except ours. It is not traditionless, but its traditions all have their roots in the Mississippi Valley. It is the nearest thing we have to a national epic.

And what an extraordinary national epic it is! It has its Achilles, but he is a fourteen-year-old boy. The hero has his Patroclus, but Patroclus is an illiterate Negro. It has its Kings and Dukes, but they are frauds and through them the whole principle of aristocracy (a principle upon which national epics rest) is ridiculed. It has its voyages and explorations, but they are undertaken on a raft. Its central episode is not some feat of high emprise, upon which rests the fate of a

129

people, but an elaborate hoax involving the unnecessary freeing of a Negro slave. And the tone of this epic! Not a heroic phrase, no elevation, no invocation to the Muses. On the contrary, a style casual, conversational, the first completely unliterary style to appear on the American continent. "I sing of arms and the man" begins the noble Virgilian strain. And how does our *Aeneid* begin? "You don't know about me without you have read a book by the name of *The Adventures of Tom Sawyer;* but that ain't no matter. That book was made by Mr. Mark Twain, and he told the truth, mainly. There was things which he stretched, but mainly he told the truth." These sentences announce the birth of a literature.

Yes, from one point of view, its language is the most important thing about *Huckleberry Finn,* more important than its humor, its characters, its story. For its language *is* in a way the humor, the characters, the story. Just as the Declaration of Independence (let us hope) contains in embryo our whole future history as a nation, so the language of *Huckleberry Finn* (another declaration of independence) expresses our popular character, our humor, our slant. This is the way we talk and think in those moods when we are most remote from our European or African beginnings. The smoking-car conversation, the Rotary Club address, the talk at a church social, the spiel of the traveling salesman, the lingo of Broadway—whatever is uniquely of this country has a smack, a tang, a flow, an accent, a rhythm, that go back to the language of *Huckleberry Finn.* For its language is not merely a comic device intended to convey the character of a rather unevenly educated boy of fourteen. It has in it the casual drawl of the frontier, the irreverent intonation of the democratic idea, and an innocent disregard of all the traditions of European writing. When Huck, complaining over the widow's preference for cooking each kind of food by itself says, "In a barrel of odds and ends it is different; things get mixed up, and the juice kind of swaps around, and the things go better," when he says this, we know we are listening to the idiom of a separate civilization.

Perhaps the word civilization is a bad one, for this book—and here lies its troubling appeal to us—is an epic of rebellion against civilization. We have become a people of cities and motorcars and vacuum cleaners and two-week vacations and commutation tickets. But that is not the way we began, and despite our childish delight in gadgetry, we have a deep hankering for the forest, the river, the rifle out of which this country came. *Huckleberry Finn* is our most typical novel precisely because it expresses this hankering. The typical novels of France or England or Russia are novels of civilization. They assume the permanence of certain sophisticated societal relations. *Huckleberry Finn,* on the contrary, is a book about primitive things: small boys and food and weather and murders and darkness. Though produced in the century of Balzac, Tolstoy, and Thackeray it is more akin to the *Odyssey* or the Norse myths than to any of the representative great novels of the European tradition.

Here, in this rambling tale about the unimportant adventures of a boy who will probably not amount to much when he grows older (except that he will never grow older) are the matters, the myths, the deep conflicts of the American people: the influence of the frontier, the unresolved problem of the Negro, the revolt against city-convention, the fascinated absorption in deeds of violence, the immense sense of a continent cut in two by a vast river, the type-figure of the self-sufficient frontiersman, the passion for exploration, the love of the hoax, the exaggeration, and the practical joke, the notion of basic social equality, the enskying of youth.

Dodsworth

Is *Dodsworth* still readable? Yes—and so it will be until our country's Sams and Frans are extinct. In the meantime, *Dodsworth* stands—no masterpiece, but nonetheless a novel so centrally conceived, so intimate with central American matters that it can still make its natural way into our mid-minds. What dates is negligible—the décor, the slang, the turn and curvature of the dialogue, a few minor, overcaricatured figures, a certain loose petulance of tone. What does not date is not at all negligible, being part of America's most important unfinished business—no more and no less than the discovery of her soul.

Ponder some of the themes and variations of this story of Innocence and Experience. Then look about you, not forgetting to cast a furtive glance at yourself. During the years since Dodsworth and his troubles first swam into our ken, how many of these themes have lost their point? I think only one: the Henry-Jamesian fairy-tale vision we have played with for fifty years, of a Europe possessing some magical secret, some snake-oil of Happiness-and-Culture, unpurchaseable within domestic boundaries. That Europe we no longer believe in. If it ever existed, the last war has bled it white; the next will tread its corpse into the ground; the survivors of the one after that will see to it that even its legend is forgotten and Christendom be no more alive in men's minds than is Atlantis. No, one particular pilgrimage the Dodsworth of the future will never again make; or, if he does, it will be to very different Londons, Parises, Romes, and Berlins.

In the meantime here are Sam and Fran, bound for the Europe we can still vaguely remember. Yet is it not true that their journey is only in a limited sense to a specific land area on the other side of the Atlantic? Does not their real journey lead into themselves, into their dissatisfaction with themselves and with what, be it motorcars or marriage, they, these restless builders, have built? In perspective this story appears less about the Dodsworths' hunger for Europe than about their hunger for some value, some stability, some coherence that they do not seem to have found in their spiritual city, here called Zenith.

Sam Dodsworth is but one of a long line of characters who express the deep and wondrous split in our most typical figure, the American businessman. What causes this split? It is caused by the fact that, generally speaking, the American businessman can neither give himself wholly over to the business of *being* a businessman nor give himself wholly over to the more difficult business of being a man. His vacillation between the part and the whole forms the basic theme of all of Sinclair Lewis's finest novels, including this one.

Sam Dodsworth has spent fifty years "in not letting himself do anything so destructive as abstract thinking." Instead, Sam Dodsworth, decent, truthful, attractive, energetic, intelligent, many cuts above Babbitt, has built good motorcars, married a pretty wife, and bred smooth-bodied, smooth-brained children. Of dollars he has made a million. Of researches into himself he has made not one. The casual observer would say of him that "he would never love passionately, lose tragically, nor sit in contented idleness upon tropic shores." Yet, before the story ends he is to do all these fatally human things, all these things that cannot contribute one smidgin of improvement to the Revelation motorcar. The fact that he does them, in pain, in indecision, not with all of him, yet with some of him, is the great and glorious thing.

Contemplate the struggles and victories of Sam Dodsworth, and say whether all about us these struggles and victories have ceased. Look at him discovering that leisure is not synonymous with "a vacation"; that leisure is something within which you rise, whereas a vacation is something into which you sink. Watch him concluding that mere command over one's environment does not mean maturity. See him finding out that "culture" is not buyable, that "freedom" is bigger than a mere release from the office. Look at him learning that play is more than being entertained, that conversation can be an *action,* not a time-waster. Look at him finally, aghast, desperate, exalted before the face of love. Watch him coming to the agonizing conclusion that marriage must be more than an adjustment to maladjustment, that a true woman must be neither a possession nor a possessor.

Look, too, at poor Fran, Fran the babied adult, the well-groomed female American monster, with no business on which to exercise her prehensility, a "success"—that is to say, a sulky-eyed, sulky-mouthed emotional virgin, immature in the home, the salon, the bed. You may see ten thousand Frans on Park Avenue in New York City any day of the year.

Look at these two (and they are ourselves) and then try to convince yourself that they "date." I do not think you will be able to. This Sinclair Lewis, for all his awkwardness, for all his bludgeon-strokes, his repetitiousness, his scorn of subtleties and shades, does one thing that few of his contemporaries can do. He takes hold of American life at its thickest point, where it is densest, where it is central. He has an instinct for what hurts most of us most, bewilders most of us most, threatens most of us most. And I think, too, that he has an instinct for what alone can save us at last, for that suppressed but still living spring of reflection and awareness that fountains up in Sam Dodsworth and Arrowsmith and Neil Kingsblood. He recognizes the eager whole man sleeping like a beautiful child within the part-men into which we have made ourselves, and from which, before it is too late, we must emerge. And will.

Moby Dick

SOME THIRTY-ODD YEARS ago, on May 18, 1921, Justice Oliver Wendell Holmes, then eighty, in a letter to his lifelong friend, Sir Frederick Pollock, wrote: "Did I mention 'Moby Dick,' by Herman Melville? I remember him in my youth. It seemed to me a great book—as ten years later may some of George Borrow's things, possibly influenced by him—but I should think a much greater man. It shook me up a good deal. It is wonderful already that a book published in 1851 doesn't seem thin now. Hawthorne did when last I read 'The Scarlet Letter.' Not so 'Moby Dick.'"

Holmes, a man given to wide and impartial decisions, made no judicial error here. By common consent—but, interestingly enough, a consent given only during the last three decades—*Moby Dick* is one of the great books of the world. It does not "seem thin now" any more than in the early twenties it seemed thin to the lucky Balboas and Columbuses who then rediscovered its Pacific rhythms and Atlantic rages.

A minor proof of its greatness lies in the circumstance (always true of masterpieces) that, while there seems nothing new to say about it, we are forever trying our hands at further commentary. In the case of a minor work, no matter how interesting, critics sooner or later, happily, have their say, the river of annotation dribbles off, and the position of the work is more or less firmly established. But men and women will always attempt the seemingly impossible task of
136

writing something new about Shakespeare and Dante—and Melville. That is, of course, because the meaning of a good minor work is clear and single, whereas the meaning of a great major work is multiplex.

The greatest books rise from a profound level of wonder and terror, a level common to all humanity in all times and climes, but a level so deep that we are only at moments aware of it, and none of us can ever glimpse it whole. From time to time a man—Cervantes or Dostoevski or Melville—lets down into this deep well the glorious, pitiful bucket of his genius, and he brings up a book, and then we read it, and dimly we sense its source, and know that source to be something profound and permanent in the human imagination. The mysterious liquid drawn from this well is never crystalline. Rather does each man, looking into it, see mirrored a different set of images, reflections, points of light, and layers of shadow. Most great books are overlaid like a palimpsest with the meanings that men at various times have assigned to them.

Moby Dick is, among other things, a book about Evil. Melville, with his characteristic irony, said of it, "I have written a wicked book and feel as spotless as the lamb." At no time in his life was Melville ever notably happy. At thirty-two, when he sat down to the composition of his masterpiece, he was notably miserable, a sick, worried, and not too happily married man. Some of the poison of his personal life was undoubtedly discharged, veiled in symbols, into the book. But if this were the only impulse behind *Moby Dick*, it would be but a subjective work of the second order, like *Childe Harold*. Melville's despair was metaphysical as well as personal; his awareness of evil goes beyond his own constricted circumstances. His book is not a lament but a vision.

Yet we must not lose ourselves in generalities, but remember always the kind of man Melville was—a magnificent Gloomy Gus, unquestionably ill at ease in his time and place, a romantic metaphysician whose affinities were with the Elizabethans rather than with his nineteenth-century contemporaries. He was by nature a solitary, not a half-and-half solitary like Thoreau, but a simon-pure one, akin to an Early Christian ascetic. It must have been hard living with Melville. Perhaps such men as he should be excused from the amenities of ordinary intercourse.

He was not a "literary man" in the sleek professional sense. His work was forced out of him; it is a kind of overflow of his vast interior silence. "Seldom have I known any profound being that had anything to say to this world, unless forced to stammer out something by way of getting a living." Again he says, "This whole book is but a draught—nay, but the draught of a draught."

A pessimism as profound as Melville's, if it is not pathological—and his is not—can exist only in a man who, whatever his gifts, does not possess that of humor. There is much pessimism in Shakespeare but with it goes a certain sweetness, a kind of radiance. His bad men—Macbeth, Iago—may be irretrievable, but the world itself is not irretrievable. This sense of balance comes from the fact that Shakespeare has humor, even in the plays of his later period. Melville had little. For proof, reread Chapter 100, a labored, shrill, and inept attempt at laughter. Perhaps I should qualify these strictures, for there is a kind of vast, grinning, unjolly, sardonic humor in him at times—Ishmael's first encounter with Queequeg is an example. But this humor is bilious, not sanguine, and has little power to uplift the heart.

We say that *Moby Dick* is a book about Evil; and so it is. It is the nearest thing we have to an unchristian (though not an antichristian) epic. But to believe in Evil's reality is not to espouse it. Ahab knows that Good exists in the world, he even has his own moments of softening of the heart, but at bottom he is mesmerized by the negative and disastrous. He cannot turn his mind away from Moby Dick.

The relationship between Ahab and the White Whale forms the central line of the story. Superficially this relationship is the same as that which animates any number of bloody Elizabethan tragedies of revenge. Ahab's leg has been torn off by Moby Dick; therefore he hates the whale; he pursues it to the death; and is dragged down, in the very middle of his vengeance, to his own destruction: a sufficiently familiar pattern. But any grown-up reader of *Moby Dick* senses at once that this pattern is a mere blind, a concession to the brute fact that at bottom we still have no better way of portraying the storms of the soul than by means of physical action.

The subsurface meaning of the Ahab-Moby Dick relationship is that the two are one. Moby Dick is a monster thrashing about in the Pacific of Ahab's brain. It is as much a part of him as his leg of ivory. The struggle that takes place on the vast marine or at the ends of a hundred harpoons is but Melville's method of exteriorizing the combat in the arena of Ahab's own chiaroscuro spirit.

> The White Whale swam before him as the monomaniac incarnation of all those malicious agencies which some deep men feel eating in them, till they are left living on with half a heart and half a lung. That intangible malignity which has been from the beginning: to whose dominion even the modern Christians ascribe one-half of the worlds; which the ancient Ophites of the east reverenced in their statue devil;—Ahab did not fall down and worship it like them; but deliriously transferring its idea to the abhorred white whale, he pitted himself, all mutilated, against it. All that most maddens and

torments; all that stirs up the lees of things; all truth with malice in it; all that cracks the sinews and cakes the brain; all the subtle demonisms of life and thought; all evil, to crazy Ahab, were visibly personified, and made practically assailable in Moby Dick. He piled upon the whale's white hump the sum of all the general rage and hate felt by his whole race from Adam down; and then, as if his chest had been a mortar, he burst his hot heart's shell upon it.

Like his cousins, Faust and Hamlet, Ahab is a divided man, at odds with his own mortality, at odds with all the grief in the world, at odds with his own incapacity to enjoy the world's fair show, and therewith be content. The whole complex narrative of *Moby Dick* with all its cetology and its digressions, is but the cunningly disguised soliloquy of a man in direst pain, pain which can cease only with suicide. And suicide is the true end of *Moby Dick*, the whale and the man, being one, turning upon each other simultaneously. There are certain men who are artists in suicide, who carve out for themselves over many years careers which have as their goal self-destruction. Ahab is such a man, and all his adventures, rages, conversations, soliloquies are but the joists and floorings of an immense structure of self-ruin.

If there is one grand type of character Melville knows to the last fiber and droplet of blood, it is the type dedicated to disaster. This dedication is a convoluted thing, never direct, never simple. Hamlet needs five acts and hundreds of lines of anguished poetry to achieve it. Ahab, in whom self-punishment is a complex art, cannot kill himself save in a roundabout manner, through the instrumentality of the White Whale. If there were no Moby Dick, it would be necessary for Ahab to invent one. In a sense, he *is* an invention, a white floating cancer in Ahab's own mind.

In the same way, to make sure that he will never deviate

from this road, however curving, to disaster, Ahab strips himself of all associations that might waylay him into joy. He throws away his pipe in fury because it might bring him pleasure. Gifted, as he bitterly reflects, "with the high perception," he lacks "the low, enjoying power; damned, most subtly and most malignantly; damned in the midst of Paradise." Just why he lacks "the low, enjoying power" Melville never tells us. He presents us with a fixed type; the causes of its fixity do not concern him. To give a certain surface rondure of motivation to Ahab's pessimism, he offers us the amputated leg. But we are not taken in by it; we know that this lightning-seared soul was deep in hell even in the days when he stood upon two feet of living bone. Moby Dick is a pretext, or, as Melville would say, a symbol.

Why do his men fear Ahab? Compare their emotion with that felt by the sailors toward Wolf Larsen in *The Sea Wolf.* In Jack London's novel the men are afraid of Larsen, another man, another creature; and therefore their fear is overcomeable. But no one on the *Pequod,* however brave he be, can overcome his fear of Ahab, because the fear is seated in himself. His Ahab-fear is a fear of *himself,* or rather of the pit of blackness, the central dark mother lode of despair which every man at times knows to be within him. But we are afraid to confess this primordial horror. When we come upon one who, like Ahab, *does* confess it, exulting in his confession, we shrink back, as if we had looked in the mirror and beheld there the horrid head of Gorgon. It is this self-fear that explains Ahab's unholy domination of his crew. It explains, too, the desperate joy with which the men pursue Moby Dick, as if they felt that, by killing the monster, they could exorcise the fear and dispel with their puny harpoons the gathered and oppressive malice of the world.

Moby Dick is a myth of Evil and Tragedy, as the Christian

epic is a myth of Good and Salvation. "Both the ancestry and posterity of Grief go further than the ancestry and posterity of Joy," ponders Ahab; and this central brooding conviction threads every page of the story, even when it seems most concerned with trypots, harpoons, and sperm oil.

The note is struck in the very opening sentence—surely the most magical first sentence in literature: "Call me Ishmael." Who is Ishmael? He is the narrator, but he is also Ahab (as all the characters of the book are partly Ahab) and he is also you and I, considered as eternal outcasts, which we are, the experience of birth being in a sense the casting-off of the moorings that attach us quite literally to mankind. The *Pequod* seems crowded with souls. Indeed it is a microcosm, with its philosophers, its men of action, its lunatics, its African savages and Polynesian cannibals. Yet, for all the shapes that man its boats or hoist its sails, the *Pequod* is a heaving hell of lonely and grief-touched souls, whose solitudes are gathered up and made manifest in the figure of Ahab. In a thousand ways Melville re-enforces this idea. He makes his devil-ship set sail on the day of the Nativity. "We gave three heavy-hearted cheers, and blindly plunged like fate into the lone Atlantic." Was ever voyage so morbidly begun, was ever theme so clearly announced?

The equivalences of the book are not allegorically plain, as in *The Pilgrim's Progress*, for Melville does not have Bunyan's simple Protestant certitude. They waver, shadow-like, at times emerging into the world of reality, at times descending into the underworld of myth. For instance, Fedallah and his Malays do not merely "represent" the evil spirits conjured up by Ahab's necromantic power. They are in truth these very spirits, akin to the fantastic figures with which Goethe peopled his Walpurgisnacht. Yet at the same time they fulfill a solid and specific function aboard the *Pequod*. They are at one and the same time part of a whaling cruise and of Hell. It is this extraordinary ambiguity that gives *Moby Dick* its special murky atmosphere, and which may have been responsible for the lack of understanding that was its portion for so many years.

Yet there should have been no misunderstanding, for Melville in a dozen passages reiterates that his story is not to be taken literally. The symbolism is not simple, no mere system of correspondences. It is rather the subtle atmosphere the whole story breathes. It is not imposed (except occasionally, and then the effect is creaky). "All visible objects," says Ahab, "are but as pasteboard masks. But in each event—in the living act, the undoubted deed—there, some unknown but still reasoning thing puts forth the moulding of its features from behind the unreasoning mask."

The poet is one, it has been said, who sees resemblances. Then Melville must be all poet, for he sees little else, the world being for him a shadow-show, a whale line but the halter round all men's necks, the very earth itself but the "insular Tahiti," in the soul of men, encompassed by the "appalling ocean" of "the horrors of the half-known life." "O Nature, and O Soul of man!" cries Ahab, "how far beyond all utterance are your linked analogies; not the smallest atom stirs or lives in matter, but has its cunning duplicate in mind."

This vivid sense of an extra, invisible dimension of all things can produce great poetry, as in Blake and Donne and Vaughan, and it can produce prose so charged with feeling that it is difficult to distinguish it from Shakespeare—as in *Moby Dick*. This sense, too, makes it possible for Melville's alembicating mind to mix such seeming incongruities as angels and spermaceti, and distill an essence of beauty.

Finally, *Moby Dick* is America's most unparochial great

book, less delivered over to a time and place than the work of even our freest minds, Emerson and Whitman. It is conceived on a vast scale, it shakes hands with prairie seas and great distances, it invades with its conquistador prose "the remotest secret drawers and lockers of the world." It has towering faults of taste, it is often willful and obscure, but it will remain America's unarguable contribution to world literature, so many-leveled is it, so wide-ranging in that nether world which is the defiant but secretly terror-stricken soul of man, alone, and appalled by his aloneness.

Portrait of a Misanthrope

As FOR Ambrose Bierce's life, we know something of its first seventy-one years only. In 1913 he vanished into the revolutionary wilderness of Mexico, and has not, for all the legends and rumors, been heard of since. If Bierce were still alive, he would be 113 years old. One doubts, however, that these added years could have mellowed his attitude toward the human race. Indeed, much of the conduct of civilized man since Bierce's presumed death in 1914 is happily calculated to confirm his misanthropy. Lidice, Belsen, Dachau, Hiroshima, Nagasaki, Bikini—all would have afforded him a satisfaction deeper and more bitter than that which he drew from the relatively paltry horrors of the nineteenth and early twentieth centuries. If he was killed, as some aver, during the Villa-Carranza fracas, it seems rather a pity. The current scene would have filled him with so pure a pleasure.

Whenever and wherever he may have died, Ambrose Gwinett Bierce began life on June 24, 1842, in Meigs County, Ohio. Born in a log cabin, he defied Alger's Law and did not become President. His father was a poor, eccentric farmer who begat nine children, Ambrose being the youngest. He was also the only one of whom the world has heard, thus supplying another bit of evidence to support the theory that exceptional persons are often the last, or among the later, of

145

a long series of progeny, and the issue, if not of exhausted, certainly of well-exercised loins.

The elder Bierce seems to have suffered an unhappy childhood. This formed the major part of his legacy to Ambrose, for his son hated the home and, except for one brother, Albert, the entire family. The unlovely circumstances of his early life may be in part the source of Bierce's later addiction to aristocratic heroes. Assuredly they played a part in the formation of his misanthropy. A by no means accidentally large number of his horrifying humorous tales turn on patricide and, less often, matricide, with an occasional avunculicide, if that be the word, thrown in for variety. (See, for example, *An Imperfect Conflagration,* with its masterly opening sentence: "Early one June morning in 1872 I murdered my father—an act which made a deep impression on me at the time.") To declare that Bierce's collected works are but a kind of inky revenge on his father is cheap, easy, and false; yet it does not require a Freud to trace in his fierce assault on all forms of authority some evidence of a clouded childhood.

The fact that Bierce wrote like an educated man is hardly explained by his education. When he was seventeen he spent a year at the Kentucky Military Institute. Not long afterward the Civil War broke out and he enlisted as a volunteer with the Union Army. (We have no evidence to indicate that he had any special sympathy with the ideal aims of the North and some slight evidence to show that he felt a mild tenderness for the ante-bellum aristocratic planter-culture of the South.) He began as a drummer-boy with the 9th Indiana Infantry, fought bravely, was wounded at Kenesaw Mountain, and emerged from the war a lieutenant, with the brevet title of major. It is evident that he possessed what military men call "qualities of leadership." It is no less evident that his Civil War interlude affected him in more important ways. It was directly responsible for some of his most finely felt, least posed stories. It very possibly helped to shift his perspective on mankind toward the dark end of the spectrum. And it may have been the spring of a certain military quality in him, for he writes like a conquistador, quick to take offense and to requite insult.

Shortly after the end of the war Bierce removed to San Francisco, the city which, though he lived there only intermittently, was to remain the focal point of his career. His first job was that of night-watchman at the Sub-treasury Building. However, his personality was ill-adapted to the least imaginative of all possible activities: guarding other people's money. He seems to have become vaguely involved in local politics and to have employed his talents as a controversial cartoonist, directing his ire with characteristic impartiality against both factions. But now journalism rose to mark him for her own, and in her dubious service he was to continue for many a year, writing well, writing badly, doubtless writing too much. From 1866 to 1872 he contributed various splinters of hackwork to the *Argonaut* and the *News Letter,* of which he finally became editor. In 1871, when he was twenty-nine and old enough to know his own temperament better, he married Mary Ellen Day, the daughter of a '49-er. The years from 1872 to 1876 were spent in London, where he engaged in the peculiar slashing journalism that had already won for him the sobriquet "Bitter Bierce." This London period appears to have left little impress on his work.

In 1876, his health having failed, he and the family (there were now two little sons, with a third child on the way) moved back to San Francisco. Bierce contributed again to the *Argonaut,* to the *Wasp,* and from 1887 to 1896 conducted a column in the San Francisco *Sunday Examiner,* a Hearst

paper. It is from these fitful contributions and weekly jottings that the contents of several of his books were drawn.
The *Examiner* period seems to have constituted his apogee.
During the late eighties and nineties he wielded extraordinary local influence as a kind of West Coast Samuel Johnson. It was, if any place could have been, the right place for
him. Then, as it does now, if to a lesser degree, San Francisco
tolerated and even encouraged salient personalities. Following the *Examiner* period Bierce worked as Washington correspondent for the *American,* and in later years was a con-
tributor to *Cosmopolitan.*

Dead ends, failures, and tragedies marked his personal life.
He was a man unfit by nature for socialized living, a non-
domestic animal. The family pattern of unhappiness repeated
itself on a tragic scale. In 1889 his older son was killed in a
vulgar shooting-brawl over a girl; two years afterward his
wife left him, finally divorcing him, thirty-three years too
late, in 1904; in 1901 his younger son died of alcoholism; and
at last in 1913 Ambrose Bierce, old, asthmatic, weary, his
creative power only an acrid memory, a bitter jester who had
outlived his time, made his queer escape from the civilization he had for forty years derided, and somewhere, presumably in Mexico, encountered his favorite character, the figure
who, so to speak, animates his finest stories: Death.

During Bierce's lifetime his vogue, except in and around
San Francisco, stayed within modest bounds, partly through
the efforts of his publishers, some of whom possessed a natural talent for bankruptcy. How to "handle" his talent so as
to make it yield the maximum public success Bierce never
learned nor did he care to learn. The emergence of his reputation was more or less coincidental with the disappearance
of himself. The tendency grew to concentrate on the Bierce

"legend" and to neglect his books. Nevertheless there has been a constant undercurrent of interest in him as a writer. Perhaps men love to hear themselves scorned and rejected if only the scorn and rejection are sufficiently eloquent. Jeremiah will never be out of a job. Calvinism is a success.

The dominating tendency of American literature and social thought, from Benjamin Franklin to Sinclair Lewis, has been optimistic. It has believed in man, it has believed in American man. It has at times been satirical and even bitter—but not negative. It gave the world the positive statements of the Declaration, the Constitution, the Gettysburg Address, Emerson, Whitman, William James, Henry George, John Dewey. This has been the stronger current. But along with it there has coursed a narrower current, the shadowed stream of pessimism. Perhaps its obscure source lies in the southern philosophers of slavery or in the bleak hell-fire morality of early puritan divines like Michael Wigglesworth and Jonathan Edwards. It flows hesitantly in Hawthorne, with fury in *Moby Dick* and *Pierre*, with many a subtle meander in the dark symbolisms of Poe. It may appear in part of a writer (the Mark Twain of "The Mysterious Stranger" and "The Man That Corrupted Hadleyburg") and not in the whole of him. It runs through Stephen Crane. You may trace it in an out-of-the-main-stream philosopher such as Thorstein Veblen. You will find it in the thought of H. L. Mencken and the stories of Ring Lardner. And you will see it plain, naked, naive, and powerful, in the strange fables of Ambrose Bierce.

Bierce's nihilism is as brutal and simple as a blow, and by the same token not decisive. It has no base in philosophy and, being quite bare of shading or qualification, becomes, if taken in overdoses, tedious. Except for the skeleton grin that creeps over his face when he has devised in his fiction some peculiarly grotesque death, Bierce never deviates into cheerfulness. His rage is unselective. The great skeptics view human nature without admiration but also without ire. Bierce's misanthropy is too systematic. He is a pessimism-machine. He is a Swift minus intellectual power, Rochefoucauld with a bludgeon, Voltaire with stomach-ulcers.

Nevertheless he may appeal to a generation which all over the world is being carefully conditioned to believe in nothing but Force. His cynicism, phrased with really extraordinary concentration, appalled his contemporaries; but it may attract rather than appall us. His *Fantastic Fables* may strike us as neither fantastic nor fabulous. He seems quite a man of our time.

I do not wish to overstate the point, for much of Bierce is old-fashioned. His prose at its worst is flawed with the bad taste of his period; his weakness for melodrama occasionally makes us squirm; he frequently overdoes his effects. Yet it is difficult to forget, for instance, the best of the stories in *In the Midst of Life:* "An Occurrence at Owl Creek Bridge," less interesting as a trick than as a heart-freezing symbolical presentation of the depth of the passion for survival; "Chickamauga," which, by a device of brilliant originality, rams home the pure insanity of war; "One of the Missing," which, like so many of his tales, shows a completely modern interest in and understanding of abnormal states of consciousness. Bierce, despite his almost Spanish admiration for "honor," was one of the earliest American writers to dismiss the flapdoodle of war and hold up to our gaze something like its true countenance. It is not so much that he hated war; indeed these stories are marked by a sort of agony of joy over war's horrors. Perhaps Bierce took a cold pleasure in war as the perfect justification of his view of mankind. He may even have liked war—no true lover of war has ever been so weak-

kneed or weak-stomached as to attempt to disguise its brutality. But, however complicated Bierce's attitude toward
war may have been, what he writes has the bitter-aloes taste
of truth. He helped blaze the trail for later and doubtless
better realists.

It is pertinent that Bierce, who disliked human beings and
scoffed at social relationships, should have written so much
and on the whole so well about ghosts, apparitions, revenants,
were-dogs, animated machines, extrasensory perception, and
action at a distance. It is as though the man's inability to
stomach the real world forced him to try to establish citizenship in the country of the occult. He was so obsessed by the
horror of real life that he had to call in the aid of another
dimension in order to express it. He seems to be saying to us:
"You do not have enough sense to shudder at yourselves; by
God, I will make you shudder then at spirits which are but
yourselves upon another plane! If I cannot make you shrink
from life, I will make you shrink from its goal and culmina-
tion—death!" Bierce's morbidity is too controlled to have
about it any touch of the insane; it merely expresses his fury
at our placid healthiness. *"N'importe où, hors du monde."* It
is this emotional drive behind his most calculated horrors
that makes him much more than an American Monk Lewis.
His Gothicism is no hothouse flower but a monstrous orchid.

Bierce's morbidity was exceptionally fertile—he made it
produce humor as well as chills. I should say that in this extremely narrow field of the sardonic, of the ludicrous ghost
story and the comical murder, he is unrivaled. He begins by
somehow making you accept his basic premise: death is a
joke. The rest is dead-pan elaboration, with the dead pan
occasionally relieved by the rictus of a ghoul trying to laugh.
Perhaps the two best examples are "My Favorite Murder"
and "Oil of Dog." "My Favorite Murder" really creates a new

shudder, a shudder in which laughter is grotesquely mingled. It is outrageous, it is frightening—it is funny. One finishes it in thorough agreement with the narrator that "in point of artistic atrocity" the murder of Uncle William has seldom been excelled. The humor of the unbelievable "Oil of Dog" depends on a careful, indeed beautiful use of ironical understatement, and the exhaustiveness of the technique whereby the macabre is pushed to such an extreme that it falls somehow into the gulf of laughter. One will not easily forget Mr. Boffer Bing's mother who had "a small studio in the shadow of the village church, where she disposed of unwelcome babes." The word "studio" is one of the happiest thoughts of the unhappy Bierce.

The nuclear Bierce is to be found in the *Fantastic Fables*. One should not read more than a dozen of them at a time, just as one should not read more than a dozen jokes at a time. Their quality lies in their ferocious concentration of extra-double-distilled essential oil of misanthropy. They are so condensed they take your breath away.

The theme is always the same: mankind is a scoundrel. But the changes rung upon the theme demonstrate an almost abnormal inventiveness. They have no humor—they do not resemble at all, for instance, the fables of George Ade. They have wit but little fancy, they are undecorated, and they sting painfully. The brutal Bierce allows no exceptions. He aims to make mincemeat of all civilized humanity—lawyers and weather forecasters, doctors and detectives, widows and photographers, editors and insurance agents, anarchists and female journalists, men and women.

Bierce is not, of course, a great writer. He has painful faults of vulgarity and cheapness of imagination. But at his best he is like no one else. He had, for example, a mastery of pared phrasing equaled in our time perhaps only by Wilde and

Shaw. When he defines marriage as "The state or condition of a community consisting of a master, a mistress and two slaves, making in all, two" he is saying something that many other unhappy men and women have said—but he is saying it in a way impossible to improve or forget.

His style, for one thing, will preserve him, though for how long no one would care to say; and the purity of his misanthropy, too, will help to keep him alive. It is good that literature should be so catholic and wide-wayed that it affords scope to every emotion and attitude, even the unloveliest. It is fitting that someone should be born and live and die, dedicated to the expression of bitterness. For bitterness is a mood that comes to all intelligent men, though, as they are intelligent, only intermittently. It is proper that there should be at least one man able to give penetrating expression to that mood. Bierce is such a man—limited, wrongheaded, unbalanced, but, in his own constricted way, an artist.

Three Notes on Henry James

IN A CERTAIN sense nothing happened to Henry James, or rather, the things that happened to him were negative things. The first large event in his life (after his birth in New York City on April 15, 1843) was an accident to his back that prevented him from becoming a soldier in the Civil War. He never married. He seems to have had no passionate relations with women or with men. He never had to earn his own living. He lived to be seventy-three, suffering only the normal illnesses that come to most mortals.

In his long life there is but a scattered handful of "dates." In 1875 he removed to Europe, and during the next year chose England for his lifelong residence. In 1897 he forsook London for a small house in Rye in Sussex. In 1904-1905 he spent ten months revisiting his native land. With the beginning of the First World War came a sudden outburst of emotion, formally symbolized by his becoming in 1915 a naturalized British subject. On February 28, 1916, he died.

Hardly an active life, one might think; yet, as you study its concretion—that is to say, his books—you begin to wonder whether it was not one of the most active lives of the entire century, though it went on almost entirely in his head. The word for James—it is his favorite—is awareness. He must have been aware of more impressions and reflected upon more ideas in the course of a single waking hour than is the lot of most of us in the course of a year or even a life-
154

time. Nothing happened to him except everything, everything that he could observe, relate, weigh, judge. These discriminations produced an incalculable amount of life, an entire population of human beings, a world of connections. And they were continually subjected to control, to a proper and harmonious ordering. Experience assumes meaning when the proper form for its expression is found. Thus the life of Henry James became identical with the search for and the discovery of the proper form. It became a work of art. This work of art was a growth, like the life of Goethe. James began as a mediocre imitator of Hawthorne, as a bright young reviewer, as a purveyor of genteel chit-chat. He ended as a great creative novelist and critic. The progression was not accidental. It was the result of constant self-examination, self-knowledge, self-control—and plain hard work. This is not to deny that the spring of it all—his genius—was in him from birth. It is merely to suggest that, more than any other writer of his time, he converted the potentialities of that genius into the fullest possible actuality.

James is a perfectly ordered, unified personality. He wrote nothing eccentric to himself. Like every human being, and particularly every writer, he occasionally lost confidence in himself; but he never really lost himself, Henry James, the man underlying the confidence or lack of confidence. The perfect recognition of the powers of his own personality is the mark of the master of any art.

From the point of view of the success-monger, James hardly lived at all. From another point of view, he lived a life so full, so passionate, so aware, that in comparison the careers of the success-men seem anemic and withered.

The "life" of Henry James need never be written by anyone, for he wrote it himself in fifty remarkable volumes and half a dozen supreme ones.

The case against James is firmly rooted and has a certain cogency. It rests on five main points.

1. *He, and hence his work, is rootless.* His alienation from America is exposed in his work and was formalized by his becoming, in 1915, a British subject. He ignored completely the great theme of the late nineteenth and early twentieth centuries—the rise of industrial America. His art is enfeebled by the malnutrition resulting from this split in his allegiance.

2. *His snobbery imposed on him a limited subject matter.* His mature life was spent among the rich, the well-born, the eminent—or among artists. He had little sympathy for the common man, viewed with apathy the democratic drift of his time, and (except for his literary friendships) attached himself to all that was decadent and artificial in European, British, and expatriate-American society. His characters, being drawn from this small and dwindling class, lack warmth, breadth, and social gravity. The *beau monde* he knew, but not the big world.

3. *Even within this world his emotional range is narrow.* His early injury may have been the reason for his never marrying. In any case his work shows little realistic expression of passion. It is bare of any representation of violence or of the larger, cruder, more elemental emotions. It is timid, even old-maidish. It lacks masculinity.

4. *He sacrificed content to form.* His elaborate esthetic theories stifled the free flow of his imagination. His interest in "effects," in the mere architecture of narrative, made him draw out his stories to excessive length. He disguised the poverty of his content with the artifice of formal tricks and mannerisms.

5. *His style is esoteric to the point of unreadability.* His dislike of banality swelled, in his later phase, into a mania,

the consequence of which was a prose so dense, involved, and allusive as to amount virtually to a dead language.

Thus, at its most vigorous, the arraignment of Henry James. Those who draw it up do not necessarily deny him genius, but they consider the genius so specialized and rarefied as to be insulated from the general reader. I have tried to be fair in my presentation of their case, all the more because, not many years ago, the shallowness of my own knowledge of Henry James would have placed me more or less in their camp.

I have tried to be fair, also, because the case is not without merit. It is based on what seem to be salient facts. James *was* a man without a country. His characters *are* drawn largely from the rich, the idle, the oversensitive, often the frivolous. Man as a sexual animal is *not* one of his specialties. He *has* a hypertrophied interest in the problem of literary form. His later style *is* difficult. All this is true. Yet, during the past twenty years or so, it has become apparent, at first to a small group of literary critics and scholars, then to an increasingly wider circle of perceptive readers, that it is not the whole truth. Somehow or other, after the charge has been drawn up and its points admitted, Henry James continues to impose himself. There is something in him, large, pervasive, and valuable, that eludes the indictment.

James's importance, its quality and extent, may take us some years to assess. We may not even be able to see it clearly, because our attitude toward him is in a sense impure. Perhaps we are getting solace from him, perhaps we are using him as a balm rather than a great writer.

For example, those who care passionately for our English speech find in the precision, the exquisiteness, the close workmanship of James's prose a relief from the careless, uncleanly,

and hyperthyroid jargon which currently passes muster for
sound writing. James's almost fussy concern for elevated,
even noble standards of craftsmanship operates in agreeable
contrast to our own fetish of relaxation, our cult of "informality" (a sweet name for mental laziness). Ours is a
period in which books are made easy for us to read; in which,
if this reading is too hard for us, we are given pictures ac-
companied by nursery-prose captions; in which, if pictures
are too difficult, we are furnished with comic-strips. Years
ago James saw all this coming. Indeed he described with
stunning accuracy the triumph of our most admired journalism when he spoke of "the bastard vernacular of communi-
ties disinherited of the felt difference between the speech of
the soil and the speech of the newspaper, and capable
thereby, accordingly, of taking slang for simplicity, the com-
posite for the quaint and the vulgar for the natural." Those
who find themselves unable to agree that the communication
of ideas and feelings must necessarily be on a pre-adolescent
level find in the careful complexities of Henry James a welcome challenge.

To those in reaction against the current passion for looseness of pattern and flatness of speech, James offers form and
subtlety in heaping measure. Furthermore, at a time when
no demands are made (except by scholar-specialists) for the
close, analytic appreciation of literature, James's uncompromising severity of approach, his perfect confidence that literature is a noble thing, worthy of the most unrelaxed attention,
has a certain tonic value. It is possibly true, as Spengler declared, that ours is an age of the conqueror and the technician, an age in which the artist will tend increasingly to be
contemned. Those unable to accept the conqueror and the
technician as paragons find in James's fervent—even feverish
—defense of the creative life a measure of consolation.

Finally, it may be that James's seeming unconcern with social and community problems, his unrelenting preoccupation with the individual (although always with the society-conditioned individual) comes as a welcome counterbalance to our own absorption in the Group-man.

Yet these are hardly sound reasons for praising James. Are we merely inclining to him because he offers something absent in our own environment, because he soothes some contemporary irritation?

Yes; but I would suggest that the return to Henry James is based also on something deeper, much harder to define. It is based on our sense that here is an author who is subtler than he seems, that there is hardly any end to his complexity, that underneath the surface vein are riches still to be mined. He is a writer with whom one does not easily finish. He exerts the fascination of those devious spirits whose message is neither slight nor immediate. He may be approached on more than a single level of perception. Reread and studied (for, I submit, he must be studied, he asks that we pay *attention* to him) he almost eerily reveals another James lying beneath the James of the familiar indictment.

All at once we perceive that his "rootlessness" furnishes him with an international viewpoint and, indeed, an international style, both far more relevant to our own time than they were to James's period. If Europe was once part of the American fate, America is now part of the European fate. Hence it has come about that those writers who can mediate between the two continents hold for us an enhanced value; and of these James is far and away the most meaningful.

As for his "snobbery," we note that while on occasion it can be irritating, it more often only half conceals the slyest satire on the leisure class. His unfinished novel, *The Ivory Tower*, is a work of social criticism as much as is *An American*

Tragedy; indeed, it shows the reverse side of that tragedy. To call him *tout court* a snob and Anglomaniac is to simplify an unsimplifiable temperament. Just as the typical Jamesian sentence is made up of qualifications rather than of statements, so is his "snobbery" composed of a hundred reservations and modifications. Part of James part of the time was a snob, but in the end this part always gave way to the central, the basic James. The basic James was not a snob, not an Anglomaniac, not a deracinated American, not a gentleman of the leisure class, though he was in part and at times all of these things. The basic James—I do not know how otherwise to put it—was an understander. His insight was so tireless that it was bound to comprehend finally even his own prejudices. In the end he saw through even himself. All things, including his own weaknesses, were soluble finally in the acid of analysis.

Seen in the light of what Freud has taught us, James suddenly demonstrates an extraordinary perception of the hidden and even sinister drives of men and women. I think it at least arguable that the distant manner in which he handles sex comes about not through ignorance or timidity but because, like the other Anglo-Saxon novelists of his time, he was forced by the taboos of his culture into reticence or ambiguity. That he does not, except rarely, represent passion directly, is true; but that he understood it and is compelled to express his understanding obliquely is, I believe, demonstrable. Certainly no one will deny ("The Turn of the Screw" is the most forcible instance here) that he had an almost intuitive perception of the unconscious and the part it plays in conditioning behavior.

His absorption in formal problems presents itself as a noble literary conscientiousness, pure, ascetic, but by no means frigid or remote; and the more we study him the more we become convinced that in him, as in any great writer, form and content are one. Even the famous style is seen to be a beautiful machine for the perfect projection of James's complex and curious perceptions. It is a weapon, not a toy.

One makes the general discoveries that James is wonderfully near to us; that he is a *modern* writer, to be ranked with Joyce, Proust, Mann, and not a nineteenth-century writer at all; that his studies of Americans in Europe in 1875 tell us a great deal about Americans in America in 1955; that from the embryonic prefigurings of his own time he foresaw many of the brutal dilemmas American society now faces—and is thus extraordinarily valuable, though dead for forty years, as a trenchant critic of the life around us; that (as *The Princess Casamassima* discloses) he knew or rather divined much about the conflict of classes; that his prefaces to his novels, his essays on Flaubert, Emerson, Stevenson, Turgenev, and others entitle him to rank as a master of literary criticism; that, in sum, while a moderate portion of his work *is* trivial tea-table chatter, the larger remainder is devoted to the most profound, ambiguous and touching of the moral experiences of man. I do not see how any unprejudiced reader can study "The Beast in the Jungle" (not to mention his larger masterpieces) without sensing that James, for all his fussiness, for all the cloistered quality of his experience, had somehow reached out and obtained a firm grasp of that stick whose two ends are labeled Good and Evil. He was, in other words, a philosophical novelist, his concern being generally, though not always, with what is persistent in the heart of man.

He did not, it is true, have the range of Tolstoy or Balzac, but, within his narrower compass, he worked to a great depth. Many of our current novelists exert their talents to "interest the reader." James exerts his genius to create a character. It is this attitude toward his job that makes James a writer. It is the lack of this attitude that makes most of our novelists merely men and women who write. James wants to *make* characters; the others want to *sell* characters. Both succeed, but in the difference lies the chasm between art and advertisement.

Not satisfied merely to present an understandable, easily graspable report on an individual consciousness, he would not stop, this patient, eager artist, until he had wrung that consciousness dry. When you have finished *What Maisie Knew,* for instance, you do not merely have a clear picture of Maisie. You *know* Maisie; you feel that there is nothing left in Maisie for James to tell you about; she is complete. You may not like James's characters, you may not think them "important," but it is hard to deny that they are exhaustively created. And it is from the exhaustiveness of the creation that one derives the sense that, while he at no time systematizes it, James has a wise and searching view of life. In his preface to *The Portrait of a Lady* he says that there is "no more nutritive or suggestive truth . . . than that of the perfect dependence of the 'moral' sense of a work of art on the amount of felt life concerned in producing it." Where there is enough knowledge, there is virtue.

To James, writing is not an opportunity for self-expression, or at least not merely for self-expression. It is first a problem, not first a solution. He thought about writing as Mozart must have thought about music, as the unsurpassable nameless architects must have thought about the cathedral of Chartres. That writing must express something goes without saying, but everything, for James, lies in the manner, the method of the expression. What is to be expressed must first be grasped in all possible relations (the opposite of impressionism); then a form must be discovered to enclose all these relations in the best conceivable way, which is, of course, the most economical way. James at his finest works on the principle of least action. He may seem elaborate, but that is only because he has seen all there is to express—and the all is multifarious, puzzling, "thick," to use his word. He speaks somewhere of "exquisite economy in composition"; and again of "that odd law which somehow always makes the minimum of valid suggestion serve the man of imagination better than the maximum"; and again—most revealing of phrases—of "the baseness of the arbitrary stroke." Accident James leaves to life, which specializes in it; but art cannot come out of the fortuitous. The artist by accident is a contradiction in terms; the true creator fights all his life against the temptation to take the easy road, to write the "readable," to gain effects by happy strokes. "The effort really to see and really to represent is no idle business," says James, "in face of the *constant* force that makes for muddlement." In James there is difficulty, there is complexity, but there is no muddlement. He is always clear, but only so after we have made a successful, if often an exhausting effort to perceive what it is he is being clear about.

Yeats, in his poem, "The Choice," tells us

> *The intellect of man is forced to choose*
> *Perfection of the life, or of the work.*

When we survey the life and work of Henry James we are filled with a sense that in a manner he resolved the dilemma Yeats poses. As we have seen, not a great deal "happened" to James; but he made everything that did happen pay. Indeed, out of his very sensation of nonexperience he constructed two masterpieces—"The Beast in the Jungle," which is about a man whose tragedy is that nothing ever happened to him; and *The Ambassadors*, which is about a man superbly equipped to react to the experiences which came to him too late. James put everything he saw, everything he felt, everything he thought, everything he was, into his books—but only after this everything had been subjected to the most rigorous scrutiny and organization. His work is not, in Yeats's phrase, "perfection"—no life work is—but it comes close to it. It is singularly rounded; it increases in importance as James ages. (He is one of the few writers of whom one might say that he would have written better at 170 than he did at 70.) It touches heights in several media—the long novel, the short novel, the short story, the literary essay, the familiar essay, the personal memoir. It is the harmonious record of a life that organized itself consciously, yet without pedantry, almost from its beginnings. And, because its creator rejected the shoddy, the easy, the second-best, because he was always hard on himself, because nothing but the essence, the economized, the beaten gold leaf was good enough for him, what he contrived speaks to us and will, in the years to come, be speaking still.

"THE BEAST IN THE JUNGLE"

FOR ME this is the best of James's shorter fictions, combining concentration of effect with inclusiveness of meaning. I know of few tales in any literature that I would rank above it. Its significance is absolute, being dependent on no wind of doctrine, no fashion of style. It gathers up in its sinuosities a part of the prime and universal experience of mankind. From it even the palest stain of the trivial is absent.

The concept of the Faustian man is one we accept as emblematic of our whole culture. Faust, we say, is ourselves, is Western man, the striver, the man to whom things happen, the man who makes things happen, the hero of experience.

He comes before us in a hundred guises, as Hamlet, as Ahab, as Don Quixote, as Leonardo da Vinci, as Huckleberry Finn.

Since the Renaissance the Western imagination has been so dominated by the idea of the Faustian man and has figured him forth in such powerful and magnificent embodiments that we have forgotten that where there is Faust there must also be un-Faust. We have forgotten that the Fausts are the exceptions, that they represent the aspirations, the hungers of men rather than their actual experience. The plain, bare, terrible fact of the matter is that most of us live pitifully un-Faustian lives and die pitifully un-Faustian deaths. The Preacher who said that all was vanity knew this; and many others after him. But, for the most part, poets and novelists have shrunk from presenting the un-Faustian life in imaginative terms. Their very business, they would say, is to show man amid experience. How, then, shall they show him as eternally waiting for the experience that somehow eludes him? The artistic problem seems to admit of no solution.

"The Beast in the Jungle" solves it relentlessly. Its subject is not the life we have had but the life we have missed. Whatever in us is nonsentient, nonperceptive, whatever in us makes us feel, as death approaches, that something has been slipping continually through our hands—this comes to expression in "The Beast in the Jungle." Who among us does not feel from time to time that somewhere ahead there is a magical, or it may be a dread, corner round which Life stands, her attitude full of promise? The saints, the artists, the thinkers, the lovers—these perhaps die in the certainty that they have lived. And (among the commonalty) the egotists, the success-men, the bank-balance men, the power-men—these too die in the same certainty. But most of the rest of us die in a kind of bewilderment, holding in our fail-

ing hands the thread that should have led us—but did not—
into the land of dense, exhaustive experience. This is the feeling, so intensely human, so nearly universal, and so seemingly
defiant of dramatic exploitation, that lies at the base of "The
Beast in the Jungle."

Marcher stands for un-Faust, for man the coward, not the
hero, of experience. "He had been the man of his time, *the*
man, to whom nothing on earth was to have happened." He
is the tragic, the terrible intensification of all those Jamesian
heroes who miss out because they lack the ability to make
the decisive gesture of gathering life into their hands. And,
before setting him down as an exaggerated, an unnatural
figure, let us ask ourselves in all honesty whether there is
more of Faust in us—or more of Marcher. "Has it ever happened?" is the key question May Bartram addresses to
Marcher when we first encounter them. It is life's key question too, the key question we are afraid to put to ourselves.
Many things happen to us, pleasant, unpleasant—but *it*, the
thing "rare and strange, possibly prodigious and terrible"—
this rarely happens. Most of us are only dimly aware that it
never happens; but it is Marcher's horrifying fate to know
it intensely. "It wouldn't have been failure," thinks Marcher,
"to be bankrupt, dishonoured, pilloried, hanged; it was failure not to be anything."

James's blinding insight into characters who are *manqués*
comes in part from the special pattern of his own life, one
lived largely—and with compensatory intensity—in the
mind. He must have felt that the circumstances of his parent-
age, the early accident that partially incapacitated him, the
removal to England—all had combined with many other factors to narrow for him the possibilities of direct and passionate experience. That he sensed in himself the troubling
pressure of his unlived life we can divine from the frequency

with which he exhibits characters who cry out for the experience which their temperaments deny them. Lambert Strether, in *The Ambassadors,* will be remembered as the perfect example of James's projection of his own inner conflict, his sense of the discrepancy between the plenitude of his imagination and the overrefinement of his experience.

But it is "The Beast in the Jungle" that develops this theme with the most concentrated power and greatest generality. Its meaning, as Philip Rahv has well said, is "so all-inclusive as to refer to every conceivable failure of human energy." It is not that we are all Marchers, but that Marcher is in all of us. He is in the medieval monk suffering from *acedia;* he is in the imperfectly sexed; he is in the ivory-tower dweller; he is in the scholar who establishes no connection with the pulsing outer world. Marcher looks out of the blank face of the subway strap-hanger and out of the equally blank face of the clubman of the whiskey ads. He is the epitome of the unlived life. He is in you and he is in me.

But he differs from most of us in the intensity of his consciousness. He is saved from blankness by the presence of May Bartram, personifying the life he might have had, holding always before him the possibility of real experience. It is May who, by merely existing, by talking, by an occasional question, and by her piercing insights into the horror of Marcher's predicament, keeps him perceptive. Without her he might have become one of James's nonsentient fools. But she cannot really save him, for his nature is his doom. "Of course one's fate is coming," says May at one point, "of course it *has* come, in its own form and its own way, all the while." One way of describing Marcher's fate is to say that he cannot love. He cannot love even after he realizes what the Beast is. When he perceives that nothing can happen to him, he throws himself on May's tomb, but it is in insane despair, not in passion, that he does so. The moment he understands his life (and that moment is the only real event in it) his life collapses about him. The sense of the collapse is conveyed in the relentless, terrifying last paragraph, an ending matchless in its condensation and finality of effect.

Marcher's special failure is part of mankind's general failure. It is the failure to communicate. The tragedy of men and women is not that we die, but that we die before we have had a chance to communicate to others even our pitifully small understanding of ourselves. Literature is but a protest against this inability, as are indeed all the arts. War, injustice, intolerance form the other side of the picture: they are the proofs of man's inability to talk to man.

The curious relationship between May and Marcher dramatizes this universal inability. For many years these two sensitive, articulate persons sit and talk to each other (only James could conceive of holding one's interest with so fantastic a situation) and yet do not really communicate. May cannot tell Marcher what she feels about him. He cannot tell her exactly what he feels about himself. Painfully they try to build bridges between them; but to no avail. In the end May, the more perceptive of the two, gives up. All she can do for Marcher is, as she says, "to help you to pass for a man like another." That, of course, is what most women are forced to do for their men—to cover up their weaknesses and inarticulacies and content themselves merely with helping them "to pass for a man like another."

It is customary to praise James for his subtle understanding of the smallest tricks and turns of the mind. This very praise carries with it the implication that he is deficient in large and powerful ideas. But in "The Beast in the Jungle" a large idea is developed with exhaustive subtlety. Masterful technique and overwhelming content have become one.

WASHINGTON SQUARE

ONE WONDERS how matters would have turned out if Henry James's stomach had been as delicate as his mind. Suppose he had been so subject to sea-sickness as to make his removal to the Old World an impossibility. Had *mal de mer* forced him to remain in his native land, he would have become the analyst of the American middle class. He would have written, we may conceive, no less copiously, but his work, instead of drawing its inspiration from English and Continental life, would have been purely American. Though we can only guess at the exact direction it would have taken, we may assume that much of it would have deepened and expanded the insights to be found in his American novels—*The Europeans, Washington Square, The Bostonians,* and the unfinished *The Ivory Tower.*

Some readers have felt that such novels as *Washington Square* and *The Bostonians* find no place among James's successes. They are not, of course, to be ranked with his greatest works—*The Ambassadors, The Wings of the Dove, The Princess Casamassima*—but to my mind they are, within their limited sphere, not only successful, but successful in large part by reason of the truthfulness with which they limn American manners. *Huckleberry Finn* is a great novel, and *Washington Square* is not. Yet neither yields to the other in the passionate exactness of its revelation of our national character, a character which flourished no less richly off the southern terminus of Fifth Avenue than on the banks of the Mississippi.

Throughout his life James, whatever his political and social loyalties, felt deeply the responsibility attaching to anyone ambitious to be an American novelist. As early as 1871 he commented, in a letter to Charles Eliot Norton, "To write well and worthily of American things one needs even more than elsewhere to be a *master*." (The italics, as is frequently the case, are James's.) It is harder to be the American Balzac than the French Balzac: perhaps that is why we are still waiting for his appearance. The very absence in our country of those traditional and firmly fixed institutions which helped to nourish James's genius makes the American scene a profound challenge to the novelist.

James felt this challenge. Whether he would have met it triumphantly, had he remained here, we cannot with certainty say. We do know, however, that whatever he wrote about his native land still possesses vitality.

This is notably true of the small, gracefully proportioned, low-toned masterpiece described by James himself, in a letter to William Dean Howells, as "a tale purely American." That its values are enduring is to some extent demonstrated by the success of the excellent dramatic version, *The Heiress*, and even, I am told, by a tolerable translation into images on celluloid. When we consider that the novel appeared in 1881, and that it chronicles the remote America of the 1840's and 1850's, we must acknowledge that *Washington Square* has in it somewhere the principle of permanence. It may not be the "work of great genius" Rebecca West once called it, but it has an extraordinary charm, deriving from an almost Mozartian combination of sweetness and depth.

Many of James's fictions sprang out of some chance remark or anecdote that a friend may have idly let drop, perhaps around the dinner-table. Writing about one of his finest stories, "The Pupil," he tells us that its source was just such a chance sentence or two. He goes on to speak of the "buried germ, implanted by experience and then forgotten," which "flashes to the surface as a fish, with a single 'squirm,' rises to the baited hook, and there meets instantly the vivifying ray."

The reader may be interested to make the acquaintance of the "buried germ" out of which came *Washington Square*. It was more than a germ; it was, as a matter of fact, the skeleton of the story. Here is James's notebook entry for February 21, 1879. (Mrs. Kemble was the famous actress and conversationalist, Frances Anne Kemble, whom James had met in London and greatly admired.)

February 21st. Mrs. Kemble told me last evening the history of her brother H.'s engagement to Miss T. H.K. was a young ensign in a marching regiment, very handsome ('beautiful') said Mrs. K., but very luxurious and selfish, and without a penny to his name. Miss T. was a dull, plain, commonplace girl, only daughter of the Master of King's Coll., Cambridge, who had a handsome private fortune (£4000 a year). She was very much in love with H.K., and was of that slow, sober, dutiful nature that an impression once made upon her, was made for ever. Her father disapproved strongly (and justly) of the engagement and informed her that if she married young K. he would not leave her a penny of his money. It was only in her money that H. was interested; he wanted a rich wife who would enable him to live at his ease and pursue his pleasures. Miss T. was in much tribulation and she asked Mrs. K. what she would advise her to do—Henry K. having taken the ground that if she would hold on and marry him the old Doctor would after a while relent and they should get the money. (It was in this belief that he was holding on to her.) Mrs. K. advised the young girl by *no means* to marry her brother. 'If your father does relent and you are well off, he will make you a kindly enough husband, so long as all goes well. But if he should not, and you were to be poor, your lot would be miserable. *Then* my brother would be a

very uncomfortable companion—*then* he would visit upon
you his disappointment and discontent.' Miss T. reflected a
while; and then, as she was much in love with him, she determined to disobey her father and take the consequences. Meanwhile H.K., however, had come to the conclusion that the
father's forgiveness was not to be counted upon—that his
attitude was very firm and that if they should marry, he
would never see the money. *Then* all his effort was to disen-
tangle himself. He went off, shook himself free of the engagement, let the girl go. She was deeply wounded—they separated.
Some few years elapsed—her father died and she came into
his fortune. She never received the addresses of another
man—she always cared in secret for Henry K.—but she was
determined to remain unmarried. K. lived about the world in
different military stations, and at last, at the end of 10 years
(or more), came back to England—still a handsome, selfish,
impecunious soldier. One of his other sisters (Mrs. S.) then
attempted to bring on the engagement again—knowing that
Miss T. still cared for him. She tried to make Mrs. K. join
her in this undertaking, but the latter refused, saying that
it was an ignoble speculation and that her brother had for-
feited every claim to being thought well of by Miss T. But
K. again, on his own responsibility, paid his addresses to
Miss T. She refused him—it was too late. And yet, said Mrs.
K., she cared for him—and she would have married no other
man. But H.K.'s selfishness had overreached itself and this
was the retribution of time.

The plot of *Washington Square* does not vary greatly from
this bald account. The important difference lies in the subtle
shift in values that took place when James decided to use a
quiet corner of pre-Civil War New York (familiar from his
own childhood) as his setting. As a consequence of this decision our literature was enriched by an acute study of a
small segment of American culture. It would be hard to find

many novels that draw so clear and delicate a picture of the
self-respecting, rather complacent, well-mannered upper middle class as it existed in New York City about a century ago.
The urge to accumulation that gathered force after Appo-
mattox was still in its infancy. Dr. Sloper and Mrs. Almond
had a confidence in themselves, their position, their prejudices, which could never be exactly duplicated after 1865.
Money was very important—indeed the story turns about
money as decidedly as does any novel of Balzac—but it was
still an adjunct to living, rather than a value in itself. New
York was a small town; what James calls "the long, shrill city"
was as yet not very long, not very shrill, not very citified.
The boom was still to come; ostentation was vulgar; society
was clearly stratified with no osmotic membranes between
the layers.

As a period piece, then, *Washington Square* presents obvious charms, of an order far superior, we may say, to the
somewhat derivative fictions of Edith Wharton. But James,
however fine his feeling for time and place, was not primarily
interested in historical reconstruction. His passion, as always,
was for the measurement of the invisible lines of force that
connect human beings with one another.

Of these lines of force the most interesting is that which
quivers between Dr. Sloper and his plain, dull, good daughter Catherine, and which is so disastrously disturbed by the
magnetic field of the venal Morris Townsend. The relationship between the doctor and his daughter is tenser and more
subtle than the transparent surface of the narrative would
seem to indicate. Dr. Sloper is a man of great intelligence
whose ability to love has been cut off by the death of his
wife. Instead of offering his daughter affection he offers her
irony. Had he been able truly to love poor Catherine, her
tragedy would never have taken place, for it is the emotional

starvation her father has imposed upon her that impels her to her unreasonable passion.

"Try and make a clever woman of her, Lavinia," says Dr. Sloper to Mrs. Penniman. He wishes Catherine to be a clever woman—but he is not willing that she should be something far greater, to wit, a woman. *Washington Square* is really about Catherine's desperate, pathetic attempt to become a woman despite the aridity her father has created within her.

In a way she succeeds with her life, though she is not very intelligent, just as Dr. Sloper, who is very intelligent indeed, fails with his. *Washington Square*, like all of James's novels, is a deeply moral book, and its moral is: to be right is not enough. Dr. Sloper is "right"; he is right about the character of Townsend, he is right about his own character, he is right about the character of Catherine. But because he can offer only the insufficient truth of irony where the sufficient truth of love is required, he partly ruins his daughter's life, and lives out his own in spiritual poverty. Catherine, however, merely because she is good, because the principle of love works in her, achieves in the end a certain stoic dignity and calm. She has, in James's beautiful phrase, an "undiverted heart." That is enough to sustain her even though she remains aware to the very end that "the great facts of her career were that Morris Townsend had trifled with her affection, and her father had broken its spring."

While the relationship between father and daughter is the major element in the story, the other characters, though properly subordinated, are presented with delicious humor and brilliant clarity. Mrs. Penniman is a small triumph—as obsessed by the stage, in a sense, as Henry James himself was, and just as unsuccessful in creating effective drama. The dialogue between Townsend and the doctor, when the former makes his bid for Catherine's hand, is as beautifully written as any comparable episode in all of James's work. Hardly less extraordinary is the conversation between Dr. Sloper and Mrs. Montgomery.

It is remarkable that so interesting a book could have been written about a heroine who is quite candidly described as dull, one to whom only one important thing happened in the course of a long life, and that one thing a seeming defeat. Had James centered his art on Catherine, had he made it pre-eminently her story, the novel would probably have remained, however skillful, rather banal. What he does is to direct our attention, not specifically to Catherine, but to the delicate lines of relationship which link her, in such subtly varying ways, with her father, with Townsend, with Mrs. Penniman.

Washington Square is a product of James's early period, of a time when he had not yet thought of the mandarin style of thinking and writing that has made his later books opaque to many readers. Here all is simple. The prose is pure and unmannered. The human secrets that are exposed are not uncommon ones. To the superficial glance even the characters seem overfamiliar: the rigid father, recalling Mr. Barrett of Wimpole Street; the naive, romantic daughter; the meddlesome duenna; the smooth-mannered fortune-hunter. Yet, out of these almost frayed materials, out of an old-fashioned plot revolving around The Will, James has woven a story which, though dealing with a way of life that has long since vanished, retains its soundness, its freshness, and its charm.

When a writer has utter respect for his characters, never imposes his own whimsy upon them, never uses them as instruments of self-exhibition, can reveal their weaknesses without malice, and can love them without sentimentality, he is apt to produce a book able to withstand the incisors of time. Many readers feel that *Washington Square* is such a book.

War and Peace

War and Peace hardly calls for comment. It is translucent. It seems to have been composed in the sunlight. Yet so fascinating is it that almost all critics who are interested in the novel have at one time or another had their say concerning it. I do not claim to add anything to their words. I hope merely to set Tolstoy's masterpiece before the reader in such a way that he will not be dismayed by its labyrinthine length or put off by its seeming remoteness from our own concerns.

War and Peace has been called the greatest novel ever written. These very words have been used, to my knowledge, by E. M. Forster, Hugh Walpole, John Galsworthy, and Compton Mackenzie; and a similar judgment has been made by many others. Note that it is particularly novelists themselves who hold this opinion. Is not this the book all novelists would like to have written? Is it not to the novelist what *Hamlet* is to the playwright?

That *War and Peace* is one of the greatest novels ever written is beyond question. But I do not know what is meant by calling it "*the* greatest." No calipers exist to measure the relative greatness of great novels. It is more useful, rather, to repeat the judgment of J. Donald Adams: "Reading it again and again is to realize the immeasurable gulf that is fixed between a merely good book and a great one." Let us not fret therefore over whether or not *War and Peace* is the greatest

176

novel ever written. Let us rather try to discover together why it is a great novel.

The first thing to do is to read it. A supreme book usually argues its own supremacy quite efficiently, and *War and Peace* is no exception. Still, we may be convinced of its magnitude and remain puzzled by certain of its aspects—for no first-rate book is completely explicit, either.

On finishing *War and Peace* what questions do we tend to ask ourselves? Here is a very simple one: What is it about? The title tells us it is about war and peace. But it deals also with other pairs of gigantic opposites—life and death, youth and age, good and evil, wealth and poverty, men and women, strength and weakness, love and hate, growth and decay. Smaller novels deal with one of these pairs of opposites or one aspect of one of these pairs. Here all are present.

"But," you reply, "these abstractions are too vague to be called the subject of this novel or any novel. They do not really tell us what the book is about." Very well. Shall we say, then, that *War and Peace* is concerned with the Napoleonic Era and its aftermath and with the varying fortunes of a large group of Russians, and of some French and Germans during the period? Or shall we say that *War and Peace* is a family novel tracing the careers of the Bolkónskis, the Rostóvs, the Kurágins, and the Bezúkhovs over a span of some fifteen years? Or shall we speak of it as a social novel painting a broad picture of Russian society from the Tsar down to the lowliest peasant? Or shall we alter our emphasis again and, with Tolstoy himself, say that in essence the book deals with the vast movement of men first from west to east and then from east to west—a movement that changes the lives of all those caught up in it? Or shall we see in *War and Peace* a philosophical novel whose purpose is to dramatize a particular view of history? Or, finally, shall we say, as does Percy Lubbock in *The Craft of Fiction,* that at least part of it is concerned simply with the spectacle of youth becoming age and of age giving way to youth: that is, with the procession of the generations?

But *War and Peace* is *all* these things. In fact, we are forced in the end to make the apparently vapid judgment that the subject of *War and Peace* is Life itself. Not life seen from a special angle, or given a special interpretation, but just Life. It is hard to name another novel of which the same statement can be made with equal justice.

We do not know what Tolstoy had in mind as the main subject of *War and Peace,* for he stated its theme differently at different periods of his career. Looking back on it, as a fairly old man, he said that his only aim had been to amuse his readers. There is a quirk in genius, a kind of last gasp of egotism in reverse, that makes it sometimes demean its own masterpieces. In the case of Tolstoy, of course, it is possible to explain this perverse judgment in terms of his religious conversion, after which he viewed such books as *War and Peace* and *Anna Karénina* as trivial and worldly. (No saint has ever been a good literary critic. Also vice versa.) More seriously, Tolstoy at times spoke of *War and Peace* as a picture of the wanderings of a people.

But whatever he thought its subject was, he transcended it. In one sense he put into this book everything that interested him, and everything interested him. That he managed to make it more than a collection of characters and incidents is equivalent to saying that in addition to being a man with a consuming interest in life he was also an artist who was not content until he had shaped that interest into harmonious forms.

Now, there are some who would demur, who feel that it is

precisely in this quality of form that *War and Peace* is defective. Percy Lubbock, for example, finds it unsatisfactory
because for him it is really two books. One book, he thinks,
deals with youth and age, with the procession of the generations, with the private lives of the Bolkónskis, the Rostóvs,
and all the others. The second book, inserted layerlike into
the first, is really the story of war and peace—of the movements of Napoleon's and Kutúzov's armies, of Austerlitz and
Borodinó, and of the laws of history which, in Tolstoy's view,
underlie these movements. Lubbock thinks that these two
themes never quite coalesce and that therefore, great as the
book is, it is deficient in the quality of form, deficient in unity
of subject matter.

Many readers would agree. Some would go even further,
arguing, on the ground that they are both extraneous and
indigestible, that Tolstoy would have done better to omit his
historical disquisitions and particularly the two epilogues.

Suppose we admit at once that there is no classic unity of
subject matter as there is, for instance, in the *Iliad*. Homer
tells the story of Hector and Achilles at the same time that
he tells the story of the Trojan War in general. But we feel
that he is telling one story, not two. This simple unity Tolstoy
does not have. But a profounder unity I think he does have.
When we have come to feel this unity, the philosophical and
historical disquisitions cease to seem long-winded and become both interesting in themselves and an integral part of
the Tolstoyan scheme. We are no longer disturbed as we
should be if such digressions appeared in a work of narrower
compass. We accept the fact that mountains are never pyra-
mids.

Let us see whether we can get this clear. In the course of
one of his digressions Tolstoy writes, "Only by taking an
infinitesimally small unit for observation (the differential of

history, i.e., the individual tendencies of men) and attaining
to the art of integrating them (i.e., finding the sum of these
infinitesimals) can we hope to arrive at the laws of history."
This rather obscure statement, if closely analyzed, gives us at
least a partial solution to the problem that worried Lubbock.
For in this sentence, perhaps, is concealed the theme of the
book: the movement of history which Tolstoy must examine
by observing "the individual tendencies of men," on the one
hand, and by attempting to "integrate them," on the other.
Putting it in another way, we may say that it is not enough
for Tolstoy to examine the individual lives of his characters
as if they were separate atoms. He must also sweep up all
these atoms into one larger experience. Now, this larger experience is the Napoleonic campaign. But the campaign
itself, which fuses or enlarges or focuses the lives of Andrew
and Natásha and Pierre and the rest, must itself be studied,
not merely as a background—that is how an ordinary historical novelist would study it—but as thoughtfully as Tolstoy studies each individual life. In order fully to understand
this focusing experience he is forced to elaborate a theory of
history to explain it. And so he is forced to understand the
major historical characters, such as Napoleon, Kutúzov, and
the others, who are the dramatic symbols of the experience.

The result of this integration may not please everyone, but
the integration is there. When one reflects upon the task, one
is driven to concede, I think, that Tolstoy, in his attempt to
understand history through human beings and human beings
through history, is undertaking the greatest task conceivable
to the creative novelist of the nineteenth century, just as
Milton, attempting to justify the ways of God to man, under-
took the greatest poetical theme possible to a man of his
century.

The titanic dimensions of the theme compel Tolstoy to ignore the usual canons of form. *War and Peace,* for instance, is a novel without a hero. Those who think of Pierre as the hero neglect the fact that Andrew, despite the circumstance that his death occurs long before the end of the book, is no less the hero—and no more. Indeed, we may say that if there is a hero in the antique sense it is Russia herself, rather than any single human being. Yet the herolessness of *War and Peace,* instead of decreasing the interest of the novel, merely gives it a more natural and lifelike quality. For in the eye of nature there are neither heroes nor villains, but merely striving human beings.

War and Peace is so vast that each reader may pick out for himself its literary qualities he most admires. Let us select three: its inclusiveness, its naturalness, its timelessness.

The first thing to strike the reader is the range of Tolstoy's interest and knowledge. His touch is equally sure and penetrating whether he is depicting the shelling of Smolénsk, or the progress of a hunt; a Freemasonry initiation, or a death-bed scene; Napoleon surveying Moscow from the Poklónny Hill, or a full-fig soirée; the bourgeois atmosphere of the household of Pierre and Natásha, or the sullen rebellion of a group of peasants; a party at Berg's, or a public hanging; Natásha in love with Andrew, or Natásha in love with Anatole Kurágin; a field hospital, or a dinner at a men's club; a woman's confinement or a drunken orgy.

He works, as J. B. Priestley says, like "a happy God, with a whole world to play with." There seems no limit to the characters at his disposal. The more life he touches with his pen, the easier it seems for him to create still more life. The more crowded his canvas, the more fluent his brush. Yet this

fecundity does not seem mere facility, as it does occasionally
with Jules Romains, and it is more than a natural overflow
of fancy as it often is with Dickens.

At first glance the inclusiveness seems so overpowering
that one inclines to agree with Hugh Walpole when he says
that *War and Peace* "contains everything," or with E. M.
Forster who is no less sure that "everything is in it." Naturally, these statements cannot be literally true. But it is true
to say that when we have finished *War and Peace* we do not
feel the lack of anything. It is only when one stops short and
makes a list of the things Tolstoy leaves out that one realizes
he is a novelist and not a god. We get very little awareness,
for example, of the Russian middle class which was just beginning to emerge at the opening of the nineteenth century.
Also, while Tolstoy does describe many peasants for us, the
emphasis is thrown disproportionately on the aristocratic
class with which he was most familiar. Another thing: obeying the literary conventions of his period, Tolstoy touches
upon the sex relations of his men and women with great
caution—and yet, so true and various is his presentation of
love that we hardly seem to notice his omissions. That, after
all, is the point: we do not notice the omissions, and we are
overwhelmed by the inclusiveness.

But inclusiveness in itself is no virtue unless informed by
understanding. *Anthony Adverse* and *Gone With the Wind*
also have an enormous range of scene and character. Still,
they are merely skillful fictions because the insight that the
author has put into these scenes and characters is of only
ordinary dimensions. It is Tolstoy's attitude toward his own
tremendous knowledge that makes him great rather than
merely encyclopedic.

What is this attitude? We say that Tolstoy had great understanding, but the secret of this understanding does not lie

only in his intellect, which is hardly among the first-order intellects of Europe. The secret lies elsewhere. Looking back on his work many years afterward, Tolstoy said, "To write a good work, one must love its basic, fundamental idea. In *War and Peace* I loved the people's emotions arising from the War of 1812. . . . I strove to write a history of the people."

The key word here is "love." One of the most penetrating comments ever made about *War and Peace* is Mark Van Doren's, "I think he can be said to have hated nothing that ever happened." This exaggeration contains a profound truth. Tolstoy's love for his characters in *War and Peace* is very different from the mystic and, some would say, morbid sentimentality of his later years. It is more like the enthusiasm of a young man for everything he sees about him during the period of his greatest vigor. It is not Christian tolerance or loftiness of soul. Indeed, it does not seem ethically based at all but is rather a product of that large animal serenity which at this epoch of his life formed the base of Tolstoy's character. He knows a great deal but it is his enormous capacity to love what he knows that makes his knowledge live for us.

At his best Tolstoy seems to write as if Nature herself were guiding his pen.

In *Opinions of Oliver Allston* Van Wyck Brooks (another of those who believe *War and Peace* the greatest of all novels) says, "It is true that to make the obvious not commonplace one has to be a Tolstoy." There is no formula to explain how Tolstoy does this. All we know is that he does it. Tolstoy is like Homer: he does not fear banalities because he is not aware that they are banalities. A small example: Captain Túshin, on the eve of battle, reflecting on immortality. Now, it is a fact that the simple soldier *does* think about life after death on the eve of battle, but most writers would never mention it for fear of being accused of senti-mentality or rhetoric. Fearing neither, Tolstoy avoids both.

The constant impression of naturalness one gets from read-ing Tolstoy comes partly from his lack of obsessions. He does not specialize in a particular emotion, as Balzac, say, special-izes in the emotions deriving from the desire for money. Per-haps we may say that if Tolstoy has an obsession, it is a pas-sion for showing people *merely living*. It is the quantity and quality of life in any particular scene or any particular person that interests him. In a sense all his characters are of equal value. He does not grade them in some fancied order of moral importance.

It is because his eye is always on the central current of life that his perceptions seem so inevitable. Indeed, they are in-evitable rather than searching, for there are writers—Dos-toevski, for example—who penetrate to levels closed to Tolstoy.

We could adduce a thousand examples of these Tolstoyan touches of nature. We think perhaps of the hospital scene toward the end of Book 5 in which the wounded men cast "envious, jealous" eyes at the healthy visitors. Sometimes it is a tiny touch of character: Prince Vasíli "who, like a wound-up clock, by force of habit, said things he did not even wish to be believed." Or it will be an insight, such as the one he gives us as he describes Pierre's taking leave of the young Borís after a pleasant conversation. "As often happens in early youth, especially to one who leads a lonely life, he felt an unaccountable tenderness for this young man and made up his mind that they would be friends." Nor is he afraid of giving us a man's character in a single, simple phrase: "Berg, with his joyful, pleasant smile, as if it were obvious to him that his success must always be the chief desire of every-one else."

Tolstoy's natural sympathy overleaps the boundary of sex; his women are as convincing as his men. Indeed, he has a special talent for the presentation of women at their most female. Who can forget his description of the pregnancy of Princess Lise?

For me, one of the supreme illustrations of Tolstoy's naturalness is the forty-odd words in which he describes the Countess Rostóva and her friend Anna weeping in each other's arms after the Countess has given Anna some money with which to outfit the latter's son Borís as he prepares to enter the army. "They wept because they were friends, and because they were kindhearted, and because they—friends from childhood—had to think about such a base thing as money, and because their youth was over. . . . But those tears were pleasant to them both." This is the touch of Shakespeare translated into prose.

We think of certain Tolstoyan scenes as other men would do them and then we realize the quality of his supremacy. Where coterie writers would use complex techniques, he uses the simplest. One can imagine what one of our smart young men would do with a scene like Andrew's delirium, cramming it full of Daliesque imagery and muddied streams of consciousness. Or take that great passage in which the daredevil Dólokhov balances himself on the window sill and drinks a bottle of rum on a bet. Imagine one of our more sophisticated novelists handling this scene. What subtle emotions that aren't really there he would put into it, what unnecessary underwriting, what overtones! But Tolstoy gives us only the scene itself, simply and vividly, yet with every desired effect obtained. Or take the death of Count Bezúkhov. Think of how Arnold Bennett would manipulate it, piling up the detail, smothering it with atmosphere. Tolstoy describes the death scene so that it becomes one of the most living scenes in the book. It is free of morbidity, false pathos, and extraneous sentimentality, but it is moving and passionate.

It is *normal*. Tolstoy is the epic poet of the conscious and the "normal," just as Dostoevski, complementing him, is the dramatic poet of the subconscious and the "abnormal." His instinct is always to identify the unnatural with the unpleasant. "But the smile did not enhance Véra's beauty as smiles generally do; on the contrary, it gave her an unnatural and therefore unpleasant expression." This genius for the normal operates with notable effect when Tolstoy is describing situations that, it might seem to another and lesser observer, should produce unusual reactions. Young Rostóv, for example, wounded, watching the enemy French approach him, cries, "Can they be coming at me? And why? To kill me? *Me* —of whom everyone is so fond?" At first this strikes us as absurd. But when we consider his youth, his sheltered childhood, his naïveté, his lovableness, and all the other characteristics that Tolstoy has shown in him previously, we perceive with a start of admiration that this is *precisely* the reaction Rostóv would have in the face of approaching death.

This almost abnormal normality in Tolstoy makes him able to do what would seem a very easy thing but is really very hard: describe people engaged in *nothing but being happy*. Some of the most moving scenes in *War and Peace* have little to do with profound emotions or great battles or lofty thoughts or critical conflicts. They are merely pictures of people doing things that seem pleasant to them. We think at once of the famous hunt scene in Book 7, the one that is followed by the Rostóvs' visit to "Uncle's" home. Here all is simple gaiety, charm, happiness. The ability to describe this sort of incident has died out in our time, perhaps because the simple glow of happiness itself seems at the moment so much less common than it did in the nineteenth century.

The inclusiveness of *War and Peace*. Its naturalness. Finally, its timelessness.

Here we have a story that deals largely, though not exclusively, with the members of a class long ago liquidated by war and revolution. The feudal nobility of which Tolstoy wrote is as dead as the feudal nobility of the tenth century. How is it, then, that these people still interest us so intensely? It is because Tolstoy does not describe them in terms of their class position only, but as whole men and women. And even when his characters seem almost pure representatives of their class, they still have a permanent value as symbols. For example, the dissipated exquisite, Dólokhov, exhibits that desperate courage his class has always had and always will have, though it may change its locale and its name.

Here is a book, too, that seems to deal with people caught in a particular cleft of history. As that limited epoch recedes, we might suppose the people should dim accordingly. Yet this is not the case. It is impossible to say just how Tolstoy manages to give the impression both of particularity and universality. Anna Schérer remains permanently the type of the fashionable hostess and yet she is herself and no other person. No one but Tolstoy could have created Pierre Bezúkhov, and yet, though he is not Hamlet, he calls out like a kinsman to the Hamlet hidden in all of us. Hélène is an individual and at the same time the personification of that radiant, completely self-assured imbecility which is the special quality of merely beautiful women. One could go on noting the same double character in all the other personages of the vast scene: Berg, the eternal *arriviste*; Borís, the fortune hunter; the wonderful Prince Andrew with his temperament at once so complex and so clear; the cynical Prince Vasíli Kurágin. As for the young Rostóvs, they are themselves and yet they are youth itself. There are other characters in other novels who

at the moment of reading are much more *vivid* than any of
these. But they have the vividness of glowing coals that fade
like ashes in the memory, whereas Tolstoy's characters live
with a steady light long after you have closed the book that
seems to contain them.

War and Peace may not have a classic form. But it does
have a classic content. It is full of scenes and situations which,
in slightly altered forms, have recurred again and again, and
will continue to recur, in the history of civilized man.

I once happened to observe a mother lifting her eight-year-
old boy in her arms. As she did so she laughed and said,
"You're getting so big you'll be lifting me soon." It was the
simplest of statements. Yet I felt something transiently touching about the scene merely because millions upon millions
of mothers reaching back into the dawn of history must have
said the same thing to their children at some time, and because other millions will say it in the remote future long after
this mother and child are dead.

You will find hundreds of these recurrent situations—
small and large—in the pages of *War and Peace*, and indeed
in the pages of any great novel or play. (See, in our own
literature, the finest of American dramas, Thornton Wilder's
Our Town.) It is as if the human race, despite its apparent
complexity, were capable of but a limited set of gestures. To
this set of gestures only great artists have the key. You may
recollect Aristotle's comment upon the dramatic value of the
"recognition scene" in Greek tragedy. One of the great
climaxes of *War and Peace* is just such a recognition scene,
after Natásha is told that the wounded officer who has been
traveling with her family is Andrew. The scene is not only
great in itself but it gathers up something of the greatness
of all the other supreme recognition scenes in literature.

A great many of the moments in the story most charged

with emotion have this quality of permanence: Andrew on the battlefield looking up at the sky and comparing its vastness with the littleness of Napoleon, Pierre listening to the peasant wisdom of Karatáev, Natásha at the ball, Mary receiving her mystical, fey peasants. These are timeless moments. They help to make a timeless book—as we May-fly mortals measure time.

Also the very looseness of the book's form, the fact that it has neither beginning nor end, helps to convey the sense of enduring life. As we read the first page we seem to encounter people who have been living for many years, and as we turn the last page, little Nicholas is merely carrying on the life that has been streaming through this vast story and these nineteen years of time.

We open the book at random and read a chance sentence. We are at the Rostóvs'. "In the drawing room the conversation was still going on." And it still is.

Has *War and Peace*, then, no defects? It has many. It is far from being a technically perfect novel, like *Madame Bovary*. It is filled with minor weaknesses of characterization. To take just one example: Pierre's complete unconsciousness of the fact that it is only his fortune that wins him both the regard of the world and the marmoreal breasts of Hélène. Despite his glasses, it is hard to think of Pierre as being quite so nearsighted as all that. There are also many places in the narrative where the pace lags. Certain characters in the crowded canvas tend to get lost in the shuffle and never become entirely clear. For example, I have a blind spot for Denísov—he never emerges quite plainly in my mind's eye. At times, so complex is the panorama that the reader has difficulty following the story, just as we have difficulty in following everything happening in a three-ring circus. Some of these defects seem to disappear on a second or third or fourth reading. Some are permanent. But none of them is so great nor are all of them taken together so great as to shake *War and Peace* from the pinnacle it occupies. Flaubert cannot afford to make mistakes. Tolstoy can.

This is not to say that *War and Peace* contains *all* the qualities of greatness. Tolstoy can project only what is in himself. And he is one man, limited, fallible, confined. We feel his limitations not when we are reading his novels, but when we read his novels and then, immediately thereafter, read the masterpieces of other writers dissimilar to him in temperament. If, for example, you follow *War and Peace* with *The Brothers Karamázov* you begin to perceive that Tolstoy's vision, far-ranging and humane as it is, is unaware of those murky depths to which the vision of Dostoevski could pierce. Tolstoy is vast. Dostoevski is vast too. But his vastness is vertical, Tolstoy's horizontal. Epic writing is generally of this horizontal character whereas dramatic writing—and Dostoevski is more akin to Shakespeare than he is to most novelists —is vertical. The insights in Tolstoy are at their best enormously moving and exactly true. But they rarely give us that uneasy sense of psychic discovery peculiar to Dostoevski. This is not to disparage Tolstoy or to exalt Dostoevski. It is merely a simple way of realizing the absurdity of the notion that Tolstoy "has everything."

So far in these comments I have emphasized those qualities—inclusiveness, naturalness, timelessness—that make *War and Peace* universal rather than Russian. But part of its appeal for us, I think, derives from the fact that though there is nothing in the book that is incomprehensible to the American or the Western European, everything in it, owing to its Russian character, seems to us just a trifle off-center. This gives the novel a piquancy, even a strangeness at times, that it may not possess for the Russians. No doubt the Russians get the same feeling from *Huckleberry Finn.*

There are certain central motives in *War and Peace* that are particularly (though not uniquely) Russian. The motive of moral conversion is a case in point. At some time in the story nearly all the major characters undergo this conversion experience—Pierre, Andrew particularly, Natásha, and even Mary, although perhaps we should say of her that, as the book progresses, her piety merely deepens. Note that the changes in the souls of Pierre and Andrew flow in both cases from suffering and pain. The sense of human freedom, it seems to Tolstoy, is given only to those who have suffered. In his later works we are to find this doctrine emphasized more dogmatically and more unconvincingly. In *War and Peace* it is presented with passion and power.

It is this longing for regeneration, present even in the rake Dólokhov, that makes Tolstoy's people at one or another point in their lives stop suddenly and ask themselves, as Pierre does, "What is life and what is death?"

Slavic characters do not ask themselves small questions. In Rebecca West's masterly book about Yugoslavia, *Black Lamb and Grey Falcon,* the narrator encounters an old woman somewhere in Montenegro, an old peasant woman, trudging the roads, absorbed in thought. Miss West and her husband greet her and ask her, as I remember, where she is bound. In three or four sentences she outlines for them, without any preliminaries, the curve of her life—a broken and tragic curve—and then says, quite simply, that she is now walking the roads and asking herself what her life means. Now, for Miss West this is a character one could meet only in a Slavic country, and I think she is right. Most of the characters in *War and Peace* are like this old woman. They ask themselves questions that would be impossible in, let us say, Steinbeck or Hemingway. Perhaps this is what marks our current American literature off from the greater tradition of such men as Dostoevski and Tolstoy. The characters in Steinbeck and Hemingway have no interest in themselves as wholes. They have no analytical curiosity about themselves. *They are studied by the author; they do not study themselves.*

In *War and Peace*, with varying degrees of success, the characters study themselves. All their critical experiences but lead them to further self-examination. Even the volatile and certainly not profound Natásha, after her sad experience with Anatole Kurágin, begins to explore whatever depths she possesses and emerges from these depths a woman ready for her reconciliation with Andrew and later on for her marriage to Pierre. She also emerges a much duller woman— evidence of Tolstoy's inability to sentimentalize.

This regeneration impulse, this desire for conversion, sometimes takes forms that may seem absurd to us and may even have seemed absurd to Tolstoy. But that does not deter him from describing these forms if they seem to him to embody the truth. Recall Pierre's Freemasonry. He is taken in, we say, by a combination of windy idealism and fraternity-house mumbo-jumbo. Yet, silly as the experience may seem to our eyes, it is a necessary one for Pierre. Without it he would perhaps be unable, at a later time, to absorb the far deeper spiritual message of the peasant Karatáev.

The purpose, if we may use so precise a word, of the regeneration experience is to enable the characters to attain to Pierre's state: "By loving people without cause, he discovered indubitable causes for loving them." In this sentence, a sort of moral equivalent of the James-Lange theory, lies the essence, the center, the inner flame, of the prerevolutionary

Russian novel. It is only after one has pondered its meaning that one can understand what lies back of the sudden changes in Tolstoy's and Dostoevski's characters.

It is interesting to speculate on why the Russians, and particularly the aristocratic class described in *War and Peace* and *Anna Karénina,* should have this thirst for salvation. One reason may be the circumstance that deep within the heart of the Russian aristocrat lay certain agonizing conflicts which could be resolved only by the grace of God, i.e., by regeneration.

One of these conflicts lay in the fact that culturally he was a mixture of barbarian, medieval Christian, Byzantine, and Western European. The attempt to reconcile these discordant elements produced those agonies of conscience that we find expressed in different forms in characters such as Andrew and Pierre. That there was a barbarian underlay in these apparently highly sophisticated people seems obvious to the Western European reader. Even such a minor survival as Natásya Ivánovna, the epicene buffoon of the Rostóv household, points backward to the Middle Ages and to even earlier times. The savage irritability of the old Prince Nicholas Bolkónski as well as the neurotic piety of Princess Mary are both examples of barbarian excess. They are the gestures of unstable souls. Only on the assumption that many of the habits of Tolstoy's aristocrats are derived from a more primitive culture can we understand certain actions. When, for example, Sónya, Natásha's best friend and a well-brought-up girl, does not for a moment hesitate to read a love letter addressed to Natásha, we find this somewhat startling. But even more startling is the fact that Natásha hardly seems at all indignant about it and indeed is even glad that it happened, as it gives her an opportunity to talk with Sónya about her love affair. Such behavior is not the behavior we should expect in aristocratic circles in the France or the England of the period.

These Russians must have been unconsciously aware of this barbarian underlay, for otherwise they would not have been so anxious to speak French rather than their native tongue. An impulse on the part of the upper class of any nation away from its own vernacular is generally an indication of lack of self-confidence.

There is a witty and not entirely cogent paragraph in Book 9 of *War and Peace* in which Tolstoy compares the self-assurance of various nations:

> Pfuel was one of those hopelessly and immutably self-confident men, self-confident to the point of martyrdom as only Germans are, because only Germans are self-confident on the basis of an abstract notion—science, that is, the supposed knowledge of absolute truth. A Frenchman is self-assured because he regards himself personally both in mind and body as irresistibly attractive to men and women. An Englishman is self-assured as being a citizen of the best-organized state in the world and therefore, as an Englishman, always knows what he should do and knows that all he does as an Englishman is undoubtedly correct. An Italian is self-assured because he is excitable and easily forgets himself and other people. A Russian is self-assured just because he knows nothing and does not want to know anything, since he does not believe that anything can be known.

There is a certain truth in all of these generalizations, even in the one about the Russian. But I think the reader will admit that the self-assurance based on the kind of negativism Tolstoy mentions is insecurely based.

The conflict in the soul of the Russian aristocrat derived not only from the conflict of cultures within him but from the moral falsity of his social position. Although Tolstoy—and this is one of his omissions—does not lay great stress on it, the Russian upper class in varying degrees suffered from a guilt-feeling arising from the institution of serfdom. While that serfdom was in many respects benevolent, it was nevertheless a basic moral evil. Why? Because there is beneath all our cruelty and lethargy something in us (most of us) which says that we must not enslave others or be enslaved by them, even when such a system seems to offer immediate advantages to both master and serf. Note that the form Prince Andrew's higher moral impulses takes is his successful endeavor to improve the lives of the serfs on his estate.

Much of the soul-searching in *War and Peace,* though it would seem to pivot only on each individual's personal problems, is in part a result of this vague pervasive guilt-feeling. Perhaps, indeed, a large part of the genius of the prerevolutionary Russian novel comes from the conflict born of this sense of guilt.

Finally, the Russian sought spiritual regeneration because he found no outlet for his idealistic energies in the state itself. On this point Tolstoy is clear and definite. He shows us an inefficient, slothful, uncertain Russian state, weakened by internal jealousies and rigid with hierarchy. The Russian upper class had at this time not developed the sense of national responsibility which the British ruling class has always had. Tolstoy's Russians are frustrated in their attempt to improve the character of their government—witness, toward the end of the book, Pierre's half-impressive, half-ludicrous political reformism. Because they cannot efficiently discharge, within the framework of politics, their impulses toward good, they are driven to discharge them in the form of personal spiritual crises and regeneration experiences.

I have made these perhaps hackneyed comments in order

to show that Tolstoy is a Russian novelist first and a universal novelist only by accident of genius. He did not know that he was writing for the world. He did not even know that he was writing for all of Russia because in his time the Russian reading class was limited pretty much to the (rather numerous) aristocracy. He wrote as a Russian about Russian people —indeed about his own family, for many of the characters in *War and Peace* are transcripts from reality. But he wrote about them not only as Russians but as people. And therein lies part of the secret of his greatness.

There remains for us at least one more aspect of *War and Peace* to consider—that is, Tolstoy's view of men, war, history, and their interrelationships. At the outset let me say that the truly conscientious reader should not be dismayed by the historical essays scattered throughout the book. He will find, if he reads them carefully, that he has been amply repaid for the effort. As I have tried to point out, they are not as extraneous as they seem. For those who prefer digests, however, I hesitantly submit herewith a brief account of Tolstoy's central thinking on history.

Tolstoy's theory of history is that there is no theory of history. Or, to put it more cautiously, if there are grand laws determining the movement and flow of historical events, we can, in the present state of our knowledge, only guess at them. Until our vision and our knowledge are so extended that they reveal these underlying laws, the most intelligent thing for us to do is at least to deny validity to all superficial explanations of historical experience.

Since *War and Peace* was first conceived, there have been numerous theories of history, such as the materialist theory, the cyclical theory of Spengler, Pareto's theory of the elite, Toynbee's vast interpretations. Tolstoy would doubtless have vigorously opposed each of these in turn on the ground that they were too simplified. In *War and Peace* he attacks those theories which were popular in his own time.

Of these, the most appealing was the notion that great events come about through the operation of chance and genius combined. It is part of the purpose of *War and Peace* to prove that there is no such thing as chance and no such thing as genius.

There is no such thing as chance, Tolstoy thinks, because each event, small or large, is linked by a thousand subtle chains to all other events. We, who cannot see the linkage, cry Chance. Thus to the fallible eye of man Luck rather than Destiny seems at moments to operate.

But the notion of mere chance as the only governing factor in human affairs is unsatisfactory to human egotism. To satisfy that egotism we project the idea of the hero, the *grand homme,* the military genius, through whom we vicariously secure the satisfaction which comes of feeling that in part at least the governance of human affairs is in human hands.

This great-man theory, of course, is most picturesquely developed by the vulgarian Carlyle. (It is the theory of history to which vulgar intellects are almost always drawn.) It is Tolstoy's particular bugaboo and abomination.

His method of exposing its falsity is threefold. First, he presents the typical *grand homme,* Napoleon. Second, he gives us a complementary presentation of Kutúzov. Third, he presents the battles themselves with intent to show their unmanageable waywardness and complexity.

Though Tolstoy has been dead now for almost half a century, one can almost hear the scorn vibrating in his voice as he speaks of "that genius, Napoleon." For him Napoleon was pre-eminently the fake *grand homme,* "that most insignificant tool of history who never anywhere, even in exile, showed human dignity." To understand this seemingly iconoclastic judgment it is necessary to remember that in Tolstoy's view evil and cruelty can never have dignity. Only the good man or he who strives for the good can have dignity. It follows then that no conqueror can have dignity. Someday the human race will learn this, and it will despise conquerors as it despises necrophiles.

Not only, however, is the fatuity of Napoleon depicted—his ill-temper, his peccadillos of conduct—but Tolstoy attacks him at his central point, his faith in himself. For Tolstoy, Napoleon, precisely because he is a "leader," is so limited in his freedom of action that only that capacity for self-deception which is the special characteristic of the conqueror type can give him the illusion that he is commanding events rather than surrendering to them. "Such is the inevitable fate of men of action, and the higher they stand in the social hierarchy, the less are they free."

To Napoleon, the pseudo-*grand homme*, Tolstoy opposes the Russian Kutúzov. Kutúzov is not, in the heroic sense, a great man. He is lethargic, old, slightly doddering, pietistic. He is incapable of "grand strategy," gives few orders, hardly listens to the reports of his subordinates. Yet just because Kutúzov is *not* a hero, he is able to understand or perhaps only to *sense* the historical undercurrents that will in the end defeat Napoleon and leave the Russians in possession of their own country. He is one of "those rare and always solitary individuals who, discerning the will of Providence, submit their personal will to it." This is not mere mystical verbiage. Kutúzov alone among all the Russian generals understands that Borodinó is not a French victory but a French defeat. He knows also that the abandonment of Moscow means the salvation of Russia. From Tolstoy's point of view, Kutúzov does not come to these conclusions through the exercise of the

rational faculty but by a kind of intuitive identity with the
ordinary Russian soldier. Kutúzov governs best because he
governs least.

Finally, with Tolstoy's conceptions of Napoleon and Kutúzov is associated his general contempt for the art of warfare.
For Tolstoy each battle is an affair of contingencies so numerous and so complexly related that no one mind or group of
minds can foresee them. Therefore, military experts are to
him a parcel of fools. The best expression of his contempt for
the military profession he puts into the mind of Prince Andrew as the Prince listens, in Book 9, Chapter 11, to the
council of war:

> Prince Andrew, listening to this polyglot talk and to these
> surmises, plans, refutations, and shouts, felt nothing but
> amazement at what they were saying. A thought that had long
> since and often occurred to him during his military activities
> —the idea that there is not, and cannot be, any science of war,
> and that therefore there can be no such thing as a military
> genius—now appeared to him an obvious truth. "What theory
> and science is possible about a matter the conditions and cir-
> cumstances of which are unknown and cannot be defined,
> especially when the strength of the acting forces cannot be
> ascertained? No one was or is able to foresee in what condi-
> tion our or the enemy's armies will be in a day's time, and no
> one can gauge the force of this or that detachment. Sometimes
> —when there is not a coward at the front to shout, 'We are
> cut off' and start running, but a brave and jolly lad who
> shouts 'Hurrah!'—a detachment of five thousand is worth thirty
> thousand, as at Schön Grabern, while at times fifty thousand
> run from eight thousand as at Austerlitz. What science can
> there be in a matter in which, as in all practical matters, noth-
> ing can be defined, and everything depends on innumerable
> conditions the significance of which is determined at a par-
> ticular moment which arrives no one knows when? Armfelt

says our army is cut in half, and Paulucci says we have got the French army between two fires. Michaud says that the worthlessness of the Drissa camp lies in having the river behind it, and Pfuel says that is what constitutes its strength. Toll proposes one plan. Armfelt another, and they are all good and all bad, and the advantages of any suggestion can only be seen at the moment of trial. And why do they all speak of a 'military genius'? Is a man a genius who can order bread to be brought up at the right time and say who is to go to the right and who to the left? It is only because military men are invested with pomp and power, and crowds of sycophants flatter power, attributing to it qualities of genius it does not possess. The best generals I have known were, on the contrary, stupid or absent-minded men. Bagratión was the best, Napoleon himself admitted that. And Bonaparte himself! I remember his limited, self-satisfied face on the field of Austerlitz. Not only does a good army commander not need any special qualities, on the contrary he needs the absence of the highest and best human attributes—love, poetry, tenderness, and philosophic inquiring doubt. He should be limited, firmly convinced that what he is doing is very important (otherwise he will not have sufficient patience), and only then will he be a brave leader. God forbid that he should be humane, should love, or pity, or think of what is just and unjust. It is understandable that a theory of their 'genius' was invented for them long ago because they have power! The success of a military action depends not on them, but on the man in the ranks who shouts 'We are lost!' or who shouts 'Hurrah!' And only in the ranks can one serve with assurance of being useful."

For Tolstoy the fate of battles therefore is decided less by prefabricated strategies than by the absence or presence of what he calls "moral hesitation," or what we would call morale.

This theory he carries to what may seem absurd lengths.

The military men he most admires are passive generals like Kutúzov, or subordinates like the officer Dokhtúrov who has no plans and no theories but is always on the spot when needed and who therefore succeeds while the strategists merely become "heroes." For Tolstoy, indeed, the victor in a historical crisis is usually he who does the opposite of what the textbooks lay down. A good example is his comment on the conduct of the citizens during their abandonment of Moscow: "Those who went about their business as Moscow was evacuated helped to save the city. Those who performed heroic labors hindered things."

It is essential to realize that Tolstoy's conception of war as something both too complicated to be foreseen and too complicated to be explained after the event is a conception based on his observation of the wars of his period. (He served for several years in the Russian army and was a soldier at the siege of Sevastópol.) In other words, his observations are of relatively unmechanized warfare—warfare in which the unit is still the individual soldier fighting on foot or on a horse, and able to communicate only with difficulty with his fellow soldiers and his superiors.

Were Tolstoy alive today would he moderate his views because the character of warfare has changed so radically in the interim? Have mechanization, three-dimensional battle and two-way radio communication abolished the individual soldier? Have they made possible a foresight and a planning impossible to Napoleon? Have they also changed the quality of the emotions within the hearts of those engaged in war? It is Tolstoy's great good fortune as a novelist that he is describing warfare in which, because the action is nonmechanized, the soldier himself is nonmechanized. Thus, he can show us the young Rostóv who, during his baptism of fire, feels "perfectly happy" and who, within a short time, is overtaken by an equally intense fear of death. Does the regimented totalitarian soldier have similar or different reactions?

Tolstoy, I think, would reply that any change is only apparent and only temporary. He would say that human nature is a constant, that it will rise to the surface despite all the deformation, the drill, the conditioning, the dehumanizing to which it may be subjected.

It is a constant, then, in war. It is a constant in peace. And it is a constant in *War and Peace*.

Pickwick and Dickens

SUCCESS STORY: A BRIEF HISTORY

AT twenty-three Charles Dickens had already made a reputation for himself as a transcriber of the words of others, being probably the fastest and most accurate shorthand reporter ever to take down the inanities of the House of Commons. Politicians have their uses: their dullness may have driven Dickens to original composition. At any rate, in his spare hours he began to jot down some humorous sketches of London life, and one evening dared to push one of them down the letter box of the *Monthly Magazine*. It was accepted and printed, anonymously; and the career of the greatest of English novelists began.

"A Dinner in Poplar Walk" preluded similar pieces. Soon Dickens, writing under the pseudonym of "Boz," was contributing regularly to the *Morning Chronicle* and later the *Evening Chronicle*. The sketches, most of them today just barely readable, attracted considerable attention. Dickens was fairly launched, and his inexhaustible energies at once began to deploy themselves in a dozen literary schemes.

By the greatest of good fortune, the perfect project, for which a publisher must be given a fair share of the credit, fell into his lap. Soon after Christmas, in 1835, to his door in Furnival's Inn came Mr. Hall, the managing partner of Chapman and Hall, a new publishing firm with which Dickens' fortunes, and a few misfortunes, were to be linked for some years to come. The proposal: that Dickens furnish some not

203

very important serial letterpress to accompany the humorous sporting plates of Robert Seymour, then fairly well known as a comic draftsman. The idea was to set up a "Nimrod Club" of amateur sportsmen who would become embroiled in a succession of difficulties, all laughable and all suited to the genius of Mr. Seymour.

Dickens, to whom publisher-fighting was to become as natural as breathing, bristled, and at once produced four reasons for handling the notion *his* way. His way involved dropping the Nimrod Club (Dickens knew nothing of sport) and subordinating the illustrations to the text. A fifth reason he did not voice, though he must have been aware of it: he was a genius, and Seymour wasn't. Chapman and Hall were among the first to feel the force of Dickens' fighting-cock, high-pressure personality. His views were "deferred to," as he remarked in the preface to the 1847 edition; he "thought of Mr. Pickwick, and wrote the first number."

In the quaint little bow-windowed office at 186, Strand, Dickens and the publishers worked out their arrangements. From a letter of February 10, 1836, to Catherine Hogarth, soon to become his wife, we learn that Chapman and Hall "have made me an offer of *£14 a month* to write and edit a new publication they contemplate, entirely by myself; to be edited monthly and each number to contain four woodcuts. I am to make my estimate and calculation, and to give them a decisive answer on Friday morning. The work will be no joke, but the emolument is too tempting to resist"—a questionable statement, for the "work" has turned out to be the merriest of jokes, and the "emolument" more tempting than the recipient was ever to know, for it is the love and laughter of untellable generations.

However, the mind of the businesslike Dickens was fixed less on fame than on the £14. By February 12 Chapman and

Hall had drawn up a letter of agreement for the monthly publication of *The Pickwick Papers*. Six days later their young author was able to write them, "Pickwick is at length begun in all his might and glory." On February 21 Dickens, who at no time found it any trouble to indite novels with one hand and reams of correspondence with the other, wrote his Catherine: ". . . I have at this moment, got Pickwick, and his friends, on the Rochester coach, and they are going on swimmingly, in company with a very different character from any I have yet described, who I flatter myself will make a decided hit." (The different character was Alfred Jingle, the "rather tall thin young man, in a green coat" who saved the Pickwickians from the onslaught of the pugnacious cabman.)

On March 26 there appeared in the London *Times* a literary announcement which we of a less restrained day can only call an unblurb:

> THE PICKWICK PAPERS—On the 31st of March will be published, to be continued monthly, price 1s, the 1st number of THE POSTHUMOUS PAPERS OF THE PICKWICK CLUB, containing a faithful record of the Perambulations, Perils, Travels, Adventures, and Sporting Transactions of the Corresponding Members. Edited by "Boz." Each monthly part embellished with four illustrations by Seymour. Chapman and Hall, 186, Strand; and all booksellers.

Of this first number, or installment, the cautious publishers printed only 1,000 copies. Of the 400 ordered bound up, perhaps fifty were sold. Apparently Mr. Pickwick set forth on his perambulations at a sluggish pace, for one month later the print order for the second number was reduced by fifty per cent, only 500 copies being issued.

The first notices were what publishers call "mixed"—that is, not very good. One reviewer found "some few instances of profanity which we could readily dispense with; and some jokes, incidents, and allusions, which could hardly be read by a modest woman without blushing." The book's reception was successful only in a Pickwickian sense.

Things hardly improved when on April 20, two days after he and Dickens had met for the first and only time, the artist Seymour committed suicide. He died, quite in character for a maker of sporting sketches, by pulling a string attached to a loaded fowling-piece. A pathetic claim was later made by his distracted widow that her husband had been the "originator" of Mr. Pickwick. In 1927 a letter of Dickens dealing with this claim sold for $2,800—a crass commentary on the relative importance of Dickens and his first illustrator. It is true, however, that in a book which Seymour had illustrated previous to *Pickwick*—it was called *Maxims and Hints for an Angler*—you will find a character who looks vaguely like Mr. Pickwick, one who slightly resembles Jingle, one even more remotely recalling Sam Weller.

As a direct result of Seymour's suicide there occurred one of the most unclimactic encounters in literary history. A tall, gangling young man, hearing that a job as Dickens' illustrator was open, made his way to Furnival's Inn, and offered his services. In the world of practical affairs Dickens always knew what he wanted. He did not care for the samples submitted. The tall young artist who moodily retired from Dickens' chambers was William Makepeace Thackeray, later to become friend, enemy, and then again friend to Dickens, and to share with him the affection of the British novel-reading public.

A new illustrator, R. W. Buss, did three plates for the third number of *Pickwick*, but he was a poor draftsman; and

Hablôt K. Browne ("Phiz") was subsequently engaged. It is the Phizical conceptions of the Pickwick characters, of course (as well as of many later Dickensian creations), that have become traditional.

Pickwick progressed rather slowly until the fifth number (August 1836). At this point Sam Weller sauntered in. From here on it was nothing but, as Dickens upper-cased it in a letter to a friend, PICKWICK TRIUMPHANT. Sales leaped from the hundreds to the tens of thousands (the printing order was 400 for Part One and 40,000 for Part Fifteen). Disregarding the reviewers, the British people as a body discovered a masterpiece. Dickens awoke to find himself Dickens. For the first time since 1066 England had been conquered— by a fat man in gaiters, attended by a cockney.

Carlyle wrote to John Forster, Dickens' biographer: "An Archdeacon, with his own venerable lips, repeated to me the other night, a strange profane story: of a solemn clergyman who had been administering ghostly consolation to a sick person; having finished, satisfactorily as he thought, and got out of the room, he heard the sick person ejaculate: 'Well, thank God, *Pickwick* will be out in ten days anyway!' " Sydney Smith, possibly the greatest wit of the time, admitted that he had "held out against Boz" as long as possible but had at last succumbed. Still another clergyman, Father Faber (*Pickwick* and ecclesiasts seem to have an affinity), was rumored to have asked for *Pickwick* on his deathbed. G. K. Chesterton has written: "In the days when Dickens's work was coming out in serial, people talked as if real life were itself the interlude between one issue of *Pickwick* and another."

Mary Russell Mitford, author of *Our Village*, wrote to a correspondent: "I did think there had not been a place where English is spoken, to which Boz had not penetrated." Rank-

ing with Wolfe's famous tribute to Gray's *Elegy* is Lord
Campbell's statement that he would rather have written *Pickwick* than be Chief Justice of England—a most judicious remark, in view of the fact that he is now chiefly remembered
for having made it. Walter Savage Landor, with characteristic energy, said *Pickwick* had drawn from him "more tears
and more smiles than were remaining to him for all the rest
of the world real or ideal."

The best judge of the book was its author. When, in a letter
of October 12, 1836, to John Macrone, he referred to Mr.
Pickwick as "that immortal gentleman," he was only half-
jocose. The most acute assessment came two weeks later, in
a letter to his publishers:

> If I were to live one hundred years, and write three novels
> in each I should never be so proud of any of them as I am of
> *Pickwick*, feeling as I do, that it has made its own way, and
> hoping, as I must own I do hope, that long after my hand
> is withered as the pens it held, *Pickwick* will be found on many
> a dusty shelf with many a better work.

Nor did its popularity diminish as the century wore on.
During his second American tour in 1867 Dickens met the
Secretary of War, Edwin Stanton, who told him that during
the Civil War, when he had served in Lincoln's administra-
tion, he had never gone to bed without reading a few pages
from *Pickwick*. The poet and furniture-designer William
Morris boasted that if every copy of *Pickwick* were destroyed
he could restore it to the world from memory without a word
missing—a statement no more exaggerated than many other
avowals of passion. Perhaps the simplest and best of tributes
is that of George Saintsbury: "There is no book like *Pickwick*
anywhere."

One might add that its fame has been somewhat meaninglessly enhanced by the circumstance that a complete set of the numbers in their original parts has become one of the great prizes of book-collectors. In 1837 one could have bought the twenty Parts for £5. At the moment a perfect Part One is worth about $1,000; a perfect Part Two about $2,000. (These Parts have their "points," of course, like pedigreed dogs; I assume the reader will be grateful to me for not explaining them.) In 1929, at the famous Jerome Kern sale, a complete *Pickwick* was knocked down for $28,000.

Final minor note: Dickens himself made perhaps £3,000 in all out of *Pickwick*. The publisher's profit came to about £14,000.

II

"I THOUGHT OF MR. PICKWICK"

The best way to read *Pickwick* is for fun. It is one of the few great books that do not call upon the reader for reflection. The laughing confounder of commentators, almost everything it has to offer lies on its sparkling surface.

It even defies classification. *"Pickwick,"* said George Gissing, "cannot be classed as a novel; it is merely a great book." If it has any structure at all, it is that of a dance, rather than that of a properly plotted narrative. It is not even a true picaresque; at best it is a pickwickaresque. Certain patterns recur: the appearances of Mr. Jingle, the visits to Dingley Dell. It may also be said to boast a comic climax in the Bardell-Pickwick trial and a serious one in Mr. Pickwick's incarceration in the Fleet. After his release, despite a few great scenes, such as the arrangement of the business affairs of the elder Weller, the story runs downhill rapidly. The whole Winkle-Allen marriage imbroglio is feeble stuff, and reflects a Dickens anxious to be off upon a fresh project.

No, *Pickwick* is not constructed at all—merely created. There never was a book in which such fun is poked at the mere notion of a plot. The only "plot" in *Pickwick* is a conspiracy on the part of the characters to take over the so-called story at every turn, bind it, gag it, toss it out the window. Progression in *Pickwick?* On the contrary, there is retardation. Everybody is hard at play, raising obstacles to the free flow of the narrative. When Sam Weller attends the "swarry," he does so not to advance the story but to detain it. He is there to afford Mr. John Smauker and Mr. "Blazes" Tuckle an opportunity to delay everything with their conversation, aimless and immortal.

It is apparent that *Pickwick* is not a "deep" book. But, disconcertingly, it is not a shallow one either. Still more oddly, it is not something in between. What it is is *simple*, like a fairy tale or a ballad. At bottom the charm of *Pickwick* resembles that of primitive works of folk-art, those evolved in a period before human life began to be analytically observed. It has far more in common with the story of Jason than with the modern novel. Written by one of the most complex of individuals, somehow it seems also to have emerged out of the popular imagination. Once Dickens met an old charwoman who, astonished to learn that he was the sole author of *Dombey and Son*, cried, "Lawks! I thought that three or four men must have put together *Dombey!*" This is even truer of *Pickwick*. It has a tang of anonymous composition, like a legend.

Dickens was an uncommon man not because he was ahead of his time, but because he was in touch with the simplicities that underlie all times. Here is André Maurois on *Pickwick*: "A whole picture of rural England rose up, a very eighteenth

century and rural England, alive with that sort of childlike
delight which the English take in simple pleasures, the enjoyment of roaring fires on the hearth, sliding in snowy
weather, a good dinner, and simple, rather absurd love-
affairs." Note that even our urbane Frenchman responds to
these "simple pleasures"—otherwise he could not write about
them so fresh and pleasant a sentence. As for these pleasures,
what are they if not what men for thousands of years have
been spontaneously responding to: fire, weather, food, and a
woman? Add to this brief list laughter, friendship, and movement—especially movement—and you hold in your hand the
true subject-matter of *Pickwick* and the secret of its appeal.

If for the moment we omit from consideration some of the
dismal (and dull) interpolated stories and virtually all of
the prison chapters, we may say that the tone of this vast
legend is set by a sentence directed by Mr. Wardle at the
Pickwickians on their first meeting: "And now you all know
each other, let's be comfortable and happy, and see what's
going forward; that's what I say." This is the tone of a merry
yarn of the commonplace—if we define the commonplace
as something that commonly takes place and also something
that takes place in common.

All human creation (and why not animals and plants?)
has an interest in the weather. The expression of that interest
may vary from "Nice out today, isn't it?" to Shakespeare's
Lear pitying the poor wretches who bide the pelting of the
pitiless storm; but the weather has moved us ever since, as
slimy cells, we slithered out of the ocean and began to set up
shop for ourselves as humans-to-be. Probably Dickens would
not have listened for thirty seconds to big talk about atavism
or racial memory. Nevertheless his novels, especially *Pickwick*, are charged with a deep sense of the intimate and
backward-ranging linkage of weather to man.

It is Christmas Eve at Manor Farm:

> "How it snows!" said one of the men, in a low tone.
>
> "Snows, does it?" said Wardle.
>
> "Rough, cold night, sir," replied the man; "and there's a wind got up, that drifts it across the fields, in a thick white cloud."
>
> "What does Jem say?" inquired the old lady. "There isn't anything the matter, is there?"
>
> "No, no, mother," replied Wardle; "he says there's a snow-drift, and a wind that's piercing cold."

It is apparent that the pleasure such a passage arouses comes partly from the images and rhythms Dickens employs, and partly from the implied happy contrast between the vigorously inclement *outside* and the warm, cozy *inside*. Dickens is rich in these interior scenes. They communicate a curious comfort, the comfort our ancestors, not many thousands of years ago, must have derived from the warm shelter of their caves.

The Cave may be one of the archetypal symbols, the symbol of the relishing of the private life, the nourisher of the sense of individuality. Its value is heightened when set beside another symbol: the Road. Just as the Cave makes man feel his transient personal victory over a whole universe, so the Road makes him feel the joy that comes of leaving the Cave and entering into association with his fellow-beings. The Cave offers the pleasure of the predictable: at home nothing bad can happen. The Road offers the pleasure of the unpredictable: away from home anything may happen.

When Dickens was first approached to do the sporting novel Seymour had in mind, he refused on the ground that he "was no great sportsman, except in regards of all kinds of locomotion." Many years later, in 1845, recalling the early newspaper training that preceded *Pickwick,* he wrote Forster:

There never was anybody connected with newspapers who, in the same space of time, had so much express and post-chaise experience as I. And what gentlemen they were to serve, in such things, at the old *Morning Chronicle!* Great or small, it did not matter. I have had to charge for half a dozen break-downs in half a dozen times as many miles. I have had to charge for the damage of a great-coat from the drippings of a blazing wax-candle, in writing through the smallest hours of the night in a swift-flying carriage and pair. I have had to charge for all sorts of breakages fifty times in a journey without question, such being the ordinary results of the pace which we went at. I have charged for broken hats, broken luggage, broken chaises, broken harness—everything but a broken head, which is the only thing they would have grumbled to pay for.

This, surely, is the spirit of *Pickwick,* quintessentialized in old Wardle's high exultant shout during the epic pursuit of Rachael and Jingle: "Ah! we *are* moving now!," expressed again in Mr. Pickwick's first statement after the trial: "And now the only question is, Where shall we go next?"

Two years of peregrination form the foundation of a narrative in which the author exploits an extraordinary variety of travel-aids, from shying horses to wheelbarrows. Of these the greatest is the post-chaise. Nowhere in Dickens (except perhaps in the wondrous description of Tom Pinch's journey to London) is the poetry of the post-chaise so rich. Gissing thought the best coach drive ever put into words was that of the Muggleton Coach. Another admirer has said: "You can't hold a copy of the 'Pickwick Papers' to your ear without hearing the coach-horns in it."

The Road and what happens on it have supplied a staple of narrative from the *Odyssey* almost up to our own day. With the advent of the railroad and particularly the airplane, however, this symbol began to lose some of its emotional charge. In his masterly *Technics and Civilization* Lewis Mumford describes what he terms the "paleotechnic" phase of our machine culture, the coal-and-iron age that reached its apex toward the end of the nineteenth century in England. He writes:

> . . . To quicken movement through space, whether the traveler journeyed for enjoyment or profit, was looked upon as a sufficient end in itself. . . . During the paleotechnic period, the increase in power and the acceleration of movement became ends in themselves: ends that justified themselves apart from their human consequences. . . . Technologically, the department in which paleotechnic industry rose to the greatest eminence was not the cotton mill but the railroad system.

What it amounts to is simply this: we have not "abolished space"—the phrase mirrors our paranoia—but we have, by the pointless, dehumanized acceleration of movement, abolished a part of ourselves. A man moving about on the surface of his home, the earth, *is* a man. A man in a jet plane is simply so much transportable material. Antaeus, detached from the soil under his feet, grew feeble and was easily overcome.

Dickens lived well into the Railway Age, but never took to it. (See Tony Weller's wry remarks on the "rail" in *Master Humphrey's Clock*.) He felt the immense chasm—no more and no less than the gap between the organic and the inorganic—that separates travel from transportation. But in 1832 his imagination was still happily anchored in the prepaleotechnic period. As Mr. Pickwick remarks in his speech to the Club, "Travelling was in a troubled state, and the minds of coachmen were unsettled," assuring us in this delightful sentence that travel was still far from its present state of dehumanization. The Road was all before the Pick-

wickians, where to choose their place of rest, and Providence
their guide.

The warm Cave and the open Road—to these primal symbols the simplest and deepest parts of us respond. And co-
primal with the Cave and the Road is Food-and-Drink. Take
the Cave and the Road out of *Pickwick* and you remove its
heart and arteries. Take out Food-and-Drink and you remove
its very guts.

> "Now, Sam," said Mr. Pickwick, "the first thing to be done
> is to—"
> "Order dinner, sir," interposed Mr. Weller.

Dickens, like Mr. Weller, knew what the First Things
were; *Pickwick* is made of them. He knew that on the whole
the lot of man is gaunt and uncomfortable; therefore he
smothers the reader with comfort, stuffs him with food, fills
him with drink. He mentions twenty-two separate and distinct inns and taverns. *Pickwick* is one long harvest-ritual of
abundance. It is filled with a primitive delight in the earth's
replenishing and consolatory generosity.

> The mottled-faced gentleman rose, as did the other gentle-
> men. The mottled-faced gentleman reviewed the company,
> and slowly raised his hand, upon which every man (including
> he of the mottled countenance) drew a long breath, and lifted
> his tumbler to his lips. In an instant the mottled-faced gentle-
> man depressed his hand again, and every glass was set down
> empty. It is impossible to describe the thrilling effect produced
> by this striking ceremony; at once dignified, solemn, and im-
> pressive, it combined every element of grandeur.

Dickens is half in earnest: it *is* a ceremony. Food and drink
for him are the serious, which is to say, the joyful, matters
that they would be for all of us were we able to approach

them freshly and innocently, instead of taking them for
granted.

Hot punch is a pleasant thing, gentleman—an extremely
pleasant thing under any circumstances—but in that snug old
parlour, before the roaring fire, with the wind blowing outside
till every timber in the old house creaked again, Tom Smart
found it perfectly delightful.

All the Pickwickians are heavy drinkers (indeed, the bland
Mr. Pickwick occasionally verges on the sot) but they drink
out of conviviality, which can be a profound emotion. Nothing more aptly measures the distance between *Pickwick's*
world and ours than the difference between that book and
Charles Jackson's remarkable and symptomatic *The Lost
Weekend.* All too often we eat and drink because we are
unhappy. In *Pickwick* they eat and drink because they are
happy.*

---

* Just for the fun of it, I once spent a happy and increasingly hungry and
thirsty hour tabulating the edibles and potables consumed in *Pickwick*.
I do not claim this to be a complete list but it may give the reader an idea
both of the daily habits of middle-class Englishmen in the early years of
the nineteenth century and of the importance that Dickens attached to food
and drink:

Chapter 1: meeting of the Pickwick Club; no specific refreshments mentioned, but the pleasing incoherence of the speeches indicates the presence,
as well as the disappearance, of considerable liquid nourishment.

2: brandy and water; soles, wine, broiled fowl and mushrooms; port;
negus; brandy.

3: brandy and water.

4: the Wardle hampers (fowls, tongue, pigeon-pie, veal, ham, lobsters,
salad, wine).

5: breakfast (broiled ham, eggs, tea, coffee, "and sundries").

6: a "substantial though homely supper"; punch.

7: mustard, beef, and beer at the cricket match; "plain dinner" at the
Blue Lion: cold fowls, meat pies, salmon, wine.

9: supper at Manor Farm: "a gigantic round of cold beef" in his
approach to which Mr. Pickwick was interrupted.

11: "a very excellent early dinner" partaken of by the Pickwickians as
they go in search of Mr. Tupman; as for the love-stricken swain, we find
him sharing his melancholy with a roast fowl, bacon, ale and "et ceteras";
later the happy reunion is celebrated with a convivial glass, and all start
back to London after a hearty breakfast.

Until we come to the Fleet the satire of Pickwick has a certain airiness, an amoral *commedia dell'arte* quality. The characters are like great clowns. The business of the clown is to make fun not of a specific local or temporal institution but of those absurdities which reside in the very circumstance of our being human, of having ridiculous appendages

---

13: the Eatanswill elections "at which exciseable articles were remarkably cheap at all the public houses."

14: drinking at the Peacock's commercial room, where the Bagman's story is told and at least five tumblers of hot punch are drunk to set Tom Smart off on his adventure. For breakfast: a very nice ham and a beautiful cold larded fowl.

15: lobster salad at Mrs. Leo Hunter's breakfast party; champagne.

16: Mr. Trotter and Mr. Weller partake of an "exhilarating compound, formed by mixing together, in a pewter vessel, certain quantities of British Hollands, and the fragrant essence of the clove."

19: shooting-party lunch: "weal pie," as Mr. Weller says, preliminary to the story of the pieman who kept cats; tongue; knuckle o' ham; cold beef in slices; beer; cold punch; chapter ends with a glass of brandy and water all round.

20: meeting of two Wellers: quart pot of ale; glasses of brandy. At the Magpie and Stump (Mr. Lowten's Club) the sign announces 500,000 bbl. of double stout in the cellars.

22: a poorish dinner at the Great White Horse at Ipswich: a bit of fish, a steak, "the worst possible port wine," brandy and water.

23: Mr. Weller, Senior, takes sustenance (breakfast): a pot of ale, a cold round of beef, and "a very respectable-looking loaf."

25: beer and cold meat in the kitchen.

26: Mr. Pickwick finishes his second pint of "particular port" at the George and Vulture Tavern and Hotel, George Yard, Lombard St. Mr. Weller, visiting Mrs. Bardell, encounters the widow, Mrs. Cluppins, and Mrs. Sanders, conversing over a quiet cup of tea "and a little warm supper of a couple of sets of pettitoes and some toasted cheese."

27: Stiggins and Mr. Weller: hot buttered toast, hot pineapple rum and water, with a slice of lemon in it.

28: Christmas at Manor Farm, with Mr. Pickwick contributing a huge codfish and a half-dozen barrels of oysters. First evening: hot elder wine, "well qualified with brandy and spice." Wedding breakfast: mince pies, wine, cake. Christmas Eve in the kitchen: wassail, with hot apples hissing and bubbling in the mighty bowl. The story of Gabriel Grub, in which a bumper of liquid fire is drunk by poor Gabriel.

29: Bob Sawyer and Benjamin eat a surgical breakfast; justice is done to a substantial lunch, "with the agreeable items of strong-beer and cherry brandy"; three bowls of hot punch are drunk to celebrate Mr. Pickwick's escape from the ice.

30: wine at the George and Vulture; affecting gastronomical tale of the ingenious gentleman who "rashly converted his-self into sassages."

like legs and arms, of acting oddly when we eat or drink too
much, of losing our dignity, our temper, our balance.

For the most part the Pickwickians are such clowns. This
is not to say that they are untrue to human nature, but only
that they are true to human nature seen in the very large and
often very crude. Mr. Tupman embodies the howling ridicu-
lousness involved in the mere spectacle of the male *vis-à-vis*

31: Bob Sawyer's Bachelor Party; punch, porter, and a quite bad supper
of unopenable oysters, underdone ham and beef, and very strong cheese;
cold brandy and water.

32: "a double glass o' the inwariable," for Mr. Weller, Senior.

34: buttered toast for the ferocious Mr. Dowler.

36: mainly concerned with the drinking of the waters at Bath, described
by Mr. Weller as having "a wery strong flavor o' warm flat-irons." The
swarry: baked leg of mutton, caper sauce, turnips, potatoes, "cold srub and
water," gin and water, punch plus oysters as the party develops.

37: meat-pie at Bob Sawyer's; beer; rum-punch; brandy.

38: Mr. Weller regales himself with moderation at the nearest tavern.

40: the Fleet: Mr. Smangle dispenses sherry.

41: still the Fleet: Jingle and the wretched loin of raw mutton.

42: shrimps and porter in the public house opposite the Insolvent Court;
Mr. Pell partakes of three penn'orth of rum.

43: a good lunch at the Fleet: roast leg of mutton, an enormous meat
pie, vegetables, porter, wine (*six* bottles); Mr. Weller's remarkable tale of
the man who consumed the crumpets on principle.

44: "a go o' wanity warm"; Mr. Job Trotter disposes of a pot of porter.

45: Mrs. Bardell and friends picnic.

47: Minced veal at Bob Sawyer's; also spirits-and-water; also the contents of a black bottle; the one-eyed Bagman ladles out a glass of negus.

48: a glorious supper at the baillie's: kippered salmon, Finnan haddocks,
a lamb's head, a haggis, and numerous tumblers of whiskey toddy.

49: on the roof of the chaise: Bob Sawyer eats a large sandwich and
imbibes the contents of a goodly sized case bottle (milk-punch); lunch at
the Bell at Berkeley Heath: "Everything they have cold," bottled ale,
Madeira; at the Hop Pole at Tewkesbury: more bottled ale, more Madeira,
some port.

50: Saracen's Head, Towcester: little dinner: "pair of fowls, Sir, and a
weal cutlet; French beans, 'taturs, tart, and tidiness," recommends Sam.

51: Mr. Stiggins' pineapple rum.

53: Mary and the Fat Boy: "There is such a jolly meat-pie"; "Oh, how
we should have enjoyed ourselves at meals."

54: arranging Mr. Weller's affairs: a drop o' beer, a little bit o' cold beef,
a oyster, brandy and water.

56: decanters are passed around, bumpers are drunk, and the Club
dissolves.

the female. Mr. Winkle is the clown as predatory hunter, Mr. Snodgrass the clown as poet and visionary. His "wash-up," the majestic Mr. Nupkins, does not arouse resentment of bureaucracy; he merely stimulates delight in Nupkinsism. We say to ourselves, wouldn't it be fun *if* military maneuvers were as absurd as those at the Rochester field-day; *if* visiting celebrities were as great geese as Count Smorltork. Those weird animals, Dodson and Fogg and Perker and Buzfuz, constitute about as cogent a criticism of the law as the Fat Boy constitutes a criticism of greediness. Are Jack Hopkins and Bob Sawyer intended as satire of the medical students of the period? One supposes so: as knowing an authority as Logan Clendening calls these grotesque portraits the best of their kind in literature, and goes on to say that their dialogues have "the spirit of practice . . . only Dickens divined that patients are bores." True; but they are also buoyant with a helium-life of their own, soaring at once to those upper airs where live their greater clown-brothers, Falstaff and Uncle Toby.

Opening it almost at random, one sinks back into *Pickwick* as into a dream; indeed the book has a dreamlike quality, as though it were partially exempt from the restrictions of space, time, and (particularly) gravity. In this dream, as in most dreams, nothing really comes to a head. Forever shall the villainous Captain Fitz-Marshall be unmasked and forever shall the Pickwickians be taken in by him, for neither the deceptions nor the unmaskings are meant seriously, being but feints and lunges in a harmless comic duel. Mr. Pickwick says to the temporarily crestfallen Jingle, "I might have taken a greater revenge, but I content myself with exposing you, which I consider a duty I owe to society." It is Mr. Pickwick's duty to "expose" Mr. Jingle—that is, to exhibit him in the clearest possible comic light.

Even a not particularly sympathetic reader of *Pickwick*, such as George Orwell, cannot help sensing this dreamlike atmosphere. Orwell believes the characters of Dickens are *static*, not *functional*, which is true of *Pickwick* but only partly true of the other novels. He comments: "Consequently his greatest success is *The Pickwick Papers*, which is not a story at all, merely a series of sketches; there is very little attempt at development—the characters simply go on and on, behaving like idiots, in a kind of eternity."

Take Buzfuz. He is an unfair, hypocritical, prevaricating shyster. Logic tells us he should be disbarred. But Buzfuz laughs at logic. He reminds us that his disbarment would be an irreparable loss to the human race. It were almost better that the legal profession should remain a mass of futility than that we should not possess Buzfuz. He may behave like an idiot, in a kind of eternity, but, if so, he is an indispensable idiot, and his eternity gives greater savor to our mortality.

The relation of these people to the real world, though far from non-existent, is joyfully tenuous,* like the antics of the Marx Brothers or, to descend to a lower level, perhaps the lowest, like the moron-absurdities of our national reading, the comics. They should be judged not as satire, but as jokes.

---

* But it is easy to exaggerate this notion. The flower of *Pickwick* is a bloom never seen on earth, but its root is in actuality. At first glance nothing would seem more cheerfully fantastic than Tony Weller's story of the time he upset the voters in the canal—were it not for the fact that something very much like this actually happened at an election in the borough of Great Yarmouth. Indeed the whole Eatanswill election is uncomfortably close to the facts and owes much to Dickens' observations as an itinerant political reporter. One might mention also that the Rochester maneuvers are probably in part a memory of the "Lines" review of the 43rd and 52nd Light Infantry which Dickens witnessed as a boy, plus a recent memory of a book—*Field Exercises and Evolutions of the Army*—read in a Chelmsford inn one dreary evening. Dingley Dell, Eatanswill, and Muggleton are the only invented place-names in the entire narrative. The remarkable bony shying horse Dickens got from his recollection of a day's journey in a gig when he was covering a provincial election: "Every time the horse heard a drum he

Of these jokes the best is the relation between the two Sams, Pickwick and Weller, who transform into gleeful absurdity the notion that a human being is a dignified animal. Mr. Pickwick is the Eternal Innocent disguised as the Eternal Respectable; Mr. Weller is the folk-philosopher who protects the innocence, and sees through the respectability. They form an alliance—Don Quixote-Sancho Panza is the classic example—over which men have always smiled with pleasure.

It is exquisitely right and humorous that the benevolent Mr. Pickwick should call himself "an observer of human nature"—and that Mr. Weller should do all the observing. It is quite proper that Mr. Pickwick should suppose he is attaching Mr. Weller to his person, when in truth Mr. Weller proceeds at once to attach Mr. Pickwick and everyone else to *his* person. It is true that when Mr. Pickwick enters the Fleet he becomes a different man; but the Fleet Pickwick is not the one we remember. The Pickwick we remember is the one who falls asleep drunk in the wheelbarrow; or slides on the ice; or dashes his spectacles insanely on the floor; or listens with blessed gullibility to the extraordinary medical narratives of Jack Hopkins. The real Pickwick is just what the strong-minded Mrs. Pott calls him: "a delightful old dear."

And what shall we say of his good fairy, Sam Weller? He

---

bounced into the hedge, or the left side of the road; and every time I got him out of that, he bounded into the hedge on the right side." The Eatanswill rival editors, Pott and Slurk, may have been suggested by Edward Sterling, editor of the *Times*, and John Black, editor of Dickens' own paper, the *Chronicle*. The Blotton-Pickwick set-to may be a parody of a somewhat more dignified interchange between Canning and Brougham in the House of Commons. The originals of Dr. Slammer, Sam and Tony Weller, Mrs. Leo Hunter, Sergeant Buzfuz, Mr. Justice Stareleigh, the Fat Boy, Jingle, Tracy Tupman, Pickwick himself—all these have been conjecturally supplied. But it matters little: the originals are shades, the copies are now the originals.

represents that best-beloved of human types: the clown, the hind, the peasant, the cockney, who turns out wiser and wittier than his betters. It is he who sees in Mr. Pickwick the lovable man beneath the ridiculous gentleman. His mind is keener than that of anyone else in the story (except perhaps his begetter, Mr. Tony Weller). His wit is more searching, his energy more tireless, his worldly wisdom more applicable. It is he who infuses the warm, popular life of the street into almost every page. He democratizes the book but in a spacious, imaginative manner that confounds the critic who would make of him a hero of the proletariat. He tells tales of the street, but they are mythical tales. He issues moral quips, but they are odds and ends from a gigantic underground system of folk wisdom. He has that most uncommon of talents, the common touch.

Incomparably the greatest character in *Pickwick,* Sam Weller is one of the greatest of Dickens' creations, and among the greatest in literature. Perhaps the secret of his hold on us lies in the simple fact that he is a poet, a lord of language, one for whom the word is quite literally life. Mr. Weller stands with Falstaff, Panurge, Pantagruel, Huck Finn, Hotspur—all vast and poetical *talkers.* His trade, of course, is not that of a Boots, or a gentleman's gentleman, or anything so minor and transitory. What he is is a professional conversationalist, like Socrates. He lives in anecdote and dialogue. Take his story of the crumpet-eater "as killed his-self on principle." It is pure dramatic legend, perfect in form, alive in every word, loaded with nuance. For him humorous, detached observation is a way of life, as for Hamlet tragic, subjective observation is a way of life: complementing each other, they represent the two poles of the English imagination working at high speed.

Never again was Dickens to write anything so purely

comic as *Pickwick*, so free of bitterness and indignation. Yet even *Pickwick* foreshadows the future novels, with their increasing somberness and ferocity. *Pickwick* contains the farce which later on is to darken into satire. Mr. Nupkins faintly indicates the bureaucrats to come, as does Lord Mutanhead Dickens' view of the upper classes. Stiggins is a freehand sketch preliminary to the full-dress portraits of Chadband and Pecksniff. The Fat Boy (a perfect observation, by the way, of a hyperpituitary case) is the first and one of the greatest of a long series of Dickensian half-wits and flutter-minds. Dickens' contempt for politics and Parliament was to explode in novel after novel; we note it first at Eatanswill. As for his great enemy, the law—perhaps it is the great enemy of all imaginative men—he sounds his preliminary battle cry with the Bardell-Pickwick trial. In Alfred Jingle's rather callous view of the female sex we catch more than a hint of Dickens' own mature attitude toward women —or, rather, a component of that attitude.

There is, moreover, a large and important section of *Pickwick* which we cannot properly call comic or farcical. Many readers have felt this section, describing Mr. Pickwick's incarceration in the Fleet Prison, to be badly out of key with the rest of the book. It seems odd that a young man of twenty-four, cocky as the very devil, with a best-seller on his hands, apparently bursting with energy and optimism, could have conceived it. The Fleet scenes might have been drawn by Hogarth: they are at once ferocious and sorrowful.

In them the character of Mr. Pickwick undergoes a change many have found unconvincing. The corpulent innocent in tights and gaiters is transformed into a thoughtful spectator of man's inhumanity to man, and finally into an indignant reformer. With Sam Weller as his Virgil, Mr. Pickwick enters the hellish gates of the nineteenth century.

A similar transformation is undergone by some of the lesser characters, in particular the extraordinary Mr. Jingle, the glandular polar opposite of the Fat Boy. Mr. Jingle, who up to now has been merely a great grotesque, a grimacing Punchinello, suddenly reveals unsuspected capacities for suffering. There is real imaginative power in his broken ejaculations as he contemplates what he conceives to be his inevitable death in the darkness and dankness of the Fleet:

> "Lie in bed—starve—die—Inquest—little bone-house—poor prisoner—common necessaries—hush it up—gentlemen of the jury—warden's tradesmen—keep it snug—natural death—coroner's order—workhouse funeral—serve him right—all over —drop the curtain."

These chapters seem almost to comprise another book. It is as if during the rollicking high jinks of the pre-Fleet *Pickwick* Dickens had unconsciously been repressing a part of him that now suddenly rises and clamors for attention. There is a tone, difficult to define, in these chapters that makes one feel they are the involuntary translation of some actual episode of Dickens' life.

We can point to one such episode. It took place in Dickens' boyhood during the short period when his father was confined in the Marshalsea Prison for nonpayment of debt. In the Fleet Mr. Pickwick hears the pathetic cry: "Pray, remember the poor debtors." Dickens remembered them.

But the harsh, wild tone of this section springs from something in Dickens that lay deeper than the effect of any single incident of his biography. The Fleet is in part a re-creation of the Marshalsea. But it is more than that. The Prison is one of the central symbols that recurs in Dickens' novels almost to the very end. It is his Moby Dick: it has a terrible special agonizing meaning for him.

This has been pointed out with superlative brilliance by Edmund Wilson in *Dickens: The Two Scrooges,* a profound study from which all future serious interpretations of England's second greatest creative imagination must take their lead. Wilson demonstrates, within the compass of a relatively brief exposition, that Dickens, probably from childhood, was a sorely divided human being, and that as he grew older the chasm in his soul grew wider. Part of him was a Victorian gentleman, part a guilty outcast. His sense of guilt expressed itself, among other ways, in an obsession with crime and criminals. All his life this good Victorian, the prose-laureate of the family, the celebrant of Christmas, the lover of little children, writhed in painful and only half-conscious rebellion against the institutions that had blighted his boyhood and whose hollowness he had systematically observed during his novitiate as parliamentary shorthand reporter and traveling newspaper correspondent.

For Wilson, therefore, even the great comedy of the Bardell trial represents, "like the laughter of Aristophanes, a real escape from institutions." For Wilson, "*Pickwick,* from the moment it gets really under way, heads by instinct and, as it were, unconsciously, straight for the Fleet Prison."

I cannot feel as Wilson does about the Bardell trial but with respect to the Fleet he seems to me essentially right. Dickens did not know that his epic of laughter was to rise to its climax there; but something in him forced that climax upon him. The underground Dickens rose to the surface, to remain there for the rest of his life. The Fleet episode *is* at variance with the rest of the book; but it is not at variance with the complex temper of the man who, to our twentieth-century eyes, is the real Charles Dickens.

III

WHAT DICKENS DID FOR THE VICTORIANS

For the men and women of the nineteenth century Dickens was a robust humorous optimist, his kindly heart crying out against every instance of injustice or cruelty. Though his material may often have been "sordid," to the Victorians he seemed essentially a lover of children, Christmas, "characters," sentiment, home, morality, and innocent laughter. His "radicalism," while deplored in gentlemanly quarters, was generally considered no more than a benevolent person's natural indignation at the abuses of the period. His happy endings were thought to contain his final thoughts as well as his concluding words. Even so acute a critic as George Gissing (the vicissitudes of whose own life should perhaps have given him a deeper insight) wrote: "Forced into contemplation of the gloomiest aspects of human existence, his buoyant spirit would not be held in darkness; as his art progressed, it dealt more gently with oppressive things."

It is this latter notion that has, in the last few decades, been seriously challenged. Any good contemporary biography, such as the excellent one by Hesketh Pearson or the now classic recent full-dress affair by Edgar Johnson, does not even bother to assault this Victorian view. It assumes that Dickens, whatever he was, was far more than an indignant optimist with a gift for creating odd characters.

The Victorian culture during which Dickens flowered was one directed, as Lewis Mumford puts it, "toward the quantification of life." "In this paleotechnic world," continues Mumford (perhaps overstating his case, but not by much), "the realities were money, prices, capital, shares: the environment itself, like most of human existence, was treated as an abstraction.... The values of the paleotechnic economy were topsy-turvy. Its 'abstractions' were reverenced as 'hard facts' and ultimate realities; whereas the realities of existence were treated by the Gradgrinds and Bounderbys as abstractions, as sentimental fancies, even as aberrations." "The state of paleotechnic society may be described ideally, as one of wardom. Its typical organs, from mine to factory, from blasting furnace to slum, from slum to battlefield, were at the service of death. Competition: struggle for existence: domination and submission: extinction."

Now such a culture was bound to produce, in both its creators and its victims (really one and the same), tensions, fears, and guilt-feelings that cried out for release and relief. Certain elements in Dickens provided that relief and release. These were the elements the Victorians seized upon and most readily appreciated.

Take the Dickensian pathos. Oscar Wilde, speaking for the post-Victorian world, said, "He must indeed be a hard-hearted man who can read the death of Little Nell without laughing." Yet it sent Lord Jeffrey into a convulsion of tears. The audience that witnessed *The Frozen Deep* (a play Dickens wrote in collaboration with Wilkie Collins) sobbed *en masse* so violently that the drama had to be followed by a farce, to supply the necessary relief. Even the actors would cry during rehearsals.

In a letter of December 2, 1844, Dickens, writing to his wife, describes a reading-aloud of *The Chimes:* "If you had seen Macready last night, undisguisedly sobbing and crying on the sofa as I read, you would have felt, as I did, what a thing it is to have power." When Dickens completed *The Chimes,* he felt, he said, "as haggard as a murderer" and let himself go in "what the women call 'a real good cry.'" Both parts of this sentence are worthy of note: in a sense the entire guilty culture of his time felt "as haggard as a murderer" and similarly found relief in "a real good cry."

The Victorians reveled in Dickens' most mawkish scenes because these scenes provided a convenient lightning rod along which their feelings of guilt could be harmlessly discharged. To sob over the death of Little Nell is one way, however indirect, of keeping out of one's mind the realities of child labor. These poor guilty folk were thus provided with an opportunity to feel kindhearted without incurring any financial loss.

His contemporaries made use also of Dickens' satirical humor. This was something they could live with and enjoy—it did not make them too uneasy, it did not humiliate them too much. Why? Because Dickens' comedy plays on two levels. In part, but only in part, it is the expression of rebellion against institutions that Dickens disliked. Here it is akin to the direct satire of Molière or Swift. But it exists, by some mystery, on another level at the same time. On this level it can be enjoyed without regard to the institutions or conventions it is attacking. It was both necessary and possible for the Victorians to enjoy Mrs. Gamp almost without giving a thought to the atrocities of nineteenth-century midwifery which she embodied.

The part that Dickens played in the abolition or mitigation of the abuses of his time has been considerably exaggerated by those critics who see in him the social revolutionary *manqué*. A certain amount of educational reform can doubtless be traced to *Nickleby*; but for the most part whatever basic changes came about in the Victorian era were the consequence of deep-lying social and economic evolutionary forces. Only in a minor degree were they the effect of the novels of Charles Dickens.

The secret of his comedy (the ability to enlarge without losing definition) is also the secret of the Victorians' enjoyment of that comedy. Satire hits home and incites to action when it is adjusted to the proportions of the reality from which it springs. In his comedy Dickens exceeded these proportions, exactly as Shakespeare did in his. Micawber and Falstaff are both so large (about of a size, I should say) that there is nothing one can do but admire them. They are both, in a way, reprehensible men; but their reprehensibleness is so small when set beside their poetry, their aliveness, the quantity of swift-flowing blood in them, that they freeze the moral-critical faculties at once. To the guilt-ridden Victorians this freezing was a kind of salvation. Hence Dickens was not merely admired but genuinely and heartily loved, as are all saviors who do not demand from their disciples concrete changes in conduct.

Even Dickens' bitterest and least funny satirical portraits, such as Gradgrind and M'Choakumchild, fed the fires of the audience's virtuous indignation without increasing their sense of guilt. Gradgrind did not recognize himself, as Babbitt did not recognize Babbitt. How could he? For the Gradgrind of Dickens was far more interesting, far clearer in outline, far more effective in speech, than the real Gradgrind. Great satiric art is an arrow that, from the viewpoint of the practical reformer, always overshoots its mark.

Thus the Victorians appropriated to themselves Dickens' pathos, Dickens' humor. Both ministered to their inner sickness.

That sickness was relieved by still another medicine: Dickens' seeming benevolent optimism. The essential truth about Dickens' optimism has been stated, with his usual bald clarity, by Bernard Shaw: "He gave us no vitally happy heroes and heroines after Pickwick (begun, like Don Quixote, as a contemptible butt). Their happy endings are manufactured to make the books pleasant." I do not agree that Mr. Pickwick is either contemptible or a butt (Shaw is misled here by his excessive admiration for rational heroes and heroines) but the balance of the statement is true enough— or at least seems true to our mid-twentieth-century sensibility.

Shaw adduces as the prime case in point the happy ending of *Great Expectations*. This would have been among the greatest of Dickens' novels had not its author acceded to the persuasion of Bulwer-Lytton, the Victorian novelist at his most canting and dishonest. Bulwer-Lytton urged Dickens to contrive a close whereby Pip and Estella in the last chapter would be drawn together in happy union. Actually both Pip and Estella are fascinating characters largely because of their *un*happy, their doomed quality. Originally the author planned to leave them lonely and sad. But Dickens the tragic artist surrendered to that part of him which feared and therefore yielded to the convention of Victorian optimism; and the conclusion we now read, and which seems to us so false, was tacked on.

The fact is that the Victorians—and who shall blame them? —could not face squarely the consequences of their doctrine of the quantification of life, with its corollary, the worship of power. But they were still human enough to feel dimly that something was grievously wrong in their idolatry. The happy ending served as one of the mechanisms enabling them to evade that most dreadful of all human experiences—a look in the mirror. (Today we have advanced so far in the direction of dehumanization that we no longer need the happy ending. The characters in our most representative novels are miserable throughout. We accept their misery as proper to human life, just as in general we accept war as the natural behavior of man.)

It is not entirely fair to Dickens to say that he catered to an external social demand for optimism. It is more accurate to say that he surrendered to an internal demand for absolution. In himself there lay a profound guilt, an omnipresent and dominating restlessness, a sick awareness of the evil both in his own soul and in his environment. His benevolent characters, beginning with Mr. Pickwick, are instruments of exorcism. Through them he temporarily persuades himself that the world is good, that Christ works, however occultly, in the hearts of men. His rationalization was the Cheeryble Brothers and Tiny Tim and the reformed Scrooge, as Browning's rationalization was Rabbi Ben Ezra, as Tennyson's was Galahad. It is not hard to find in many of the greatest Victorians this same agonizing split. It is not until Hardy that we find tragedy faced without evasion; and it is with Hardy that the contemporary English novel, finding its bitter flowering in Graham Greene, Evelyn Waugh, and George Orwell, really begins.

The superimposed, *willed* character of Dickens' benevolence has been noted by many modern critics, particularly Orwell, Rex Warner, and the Marxist T. A. Jackson. Things are "fixed up" by the charitable uncle, the checkbook, the legacy, a convenient death, an appropriate marriage, a last-minute reformation. The optimism is not internal, as with Fielding. The difference is plain: Fielding is at bottom a healthy and happy man, Dickens is not. He has vitality, but not health. He is exuberant, but not happy.

Pathos, humor, mechanical benevolence: in addition to these Dickens supplied the Victorians with something more: the sensation of life itself.

Those who dwelt in the paleotechnic world tended to misprize character, originality, spontaneity, in favor of "facts," physical expansion, economic accumulation, imperial power. They were drunk with the first large-scale evidence that the environment could be made to yield "returns." This intoxication led them to avert their attention from the merely human, from the wayward and nonprofitable character of the organic. But this excessive torsion of their attention inevitably set up strains which had somehow to be relieved. The more they denied life, the more a deeply hidden part of them craved it in some form that nevertheless would not interfere practically with the drive toward quantification.

The simple fact is that the more than two thousand vividly realized characters of Dickens helped to allay this craving. These Victorians who mechanized themselves, who attached the deepest of meanings to the word convention, went mad over the eccentricities of Dick Swiveller, the orchidaceous verbiage of Chadband, the delightful lunacies of Mr. Dick. Dickens became a wholesale supplier of life. Every artist, of course, is such a supplier; but he supplied a greater quantity of higher quality to a larger group of customers who stood in greater need of this particular commodity than had their predecessors. One notes that in a period whose conversational tone was set by the formal dullness of the court of Victoria and Albert, the most popular of Dickens' characters were precisely the greatest, the maddest, the most unrestrained of talkers—Weller, Mrs. Nickleby, Mantalini, Dick Swiveller, Sairey Gamp, Micawber, Chadband, Skimpole, Flora Finching, Pumblechook.

Finally, Dickens celebrated one of the nineteenth century's vastest and most fascinating creations: London, the Giant City. We are learning in our time to hate and fear large cities as a symbol of petrifaction; but to the Englishman of the period, as was only natural, London was a miracle. If he was not proud of it (and often he was not) he could not fail to be awed by it. And it was Dickens, alone among the novelists of his time, even more surely than Balzac, who understood Megalopolis in all its horror and grandeur, its pullulating, animal-like vitality, its inexhaustible variety, its terror and color and beauty. He was London's first, perhaps its last, poet. He gave back to England, in symbols of overwhelming force, its most admired production: the Great Wen, the Hive, the Man-swarm—London. At the very moment when a laureate of Megalopolis was most urgently required, providence supplied him in the person of Charles Dickens.

IV

DICKENS THROUGH TWENTIETH-CENTURY GLASSES

Perhaps all that our time has contributed to a deeper than the Victorian understanding of Dickens is the simple insight that he was an unhappy man, along with some crude notion of the reasons for that unhappiness.

The Dickens revealed to us by the most searching of our modern critics, such as Edmund Wilson, is two men. One is the respectable Victorian who grew increasingly rich and famous, spoke out nobly on the side of the angels, was famous for his energy, optimism, and humor, fathered eleven children, wrote books of seemingly matchless moral purity, was beloved by millions, and lies buried in Westminster Abbey. This Dickens existed, and only a jaundiced eye would disregard him. But, along with him, lived and struggled another Dickens: one whose fame and wealth never gave him true satisfaction, who was morbidly attracted to the spectacle of evil and crime, who was frequently a very devil to his household, who was inordinately and increasingly restless, who wrote books of deepening bitterness, and died a self-questioning, perhaps even a despairing, soul.

Unless we assume the coexistence of these two Dickenses, it is hard to explain the fact that the progression from *Pickwick* to *Edwin Drood* is one of almost steadily deepening darkness. The Rochester in which the Pickwickians' travels begin, all jollity and jokes, is a far cry from the Rochester (Cloisterham) of his last book, all corruption and choking tradition. It is a long journey from the open-air bustle of *Pickwick* to the foul opium-dens of *Edwin Drood*. Yet the same man conceived them both, and the second man must have been alive in the first.

Even his biographer, John Forster, who did so much to conceal for so long the seamy side of Dickens' life, is forced to speak of "the underlying tone of bitterness that runs through the books that followed *Copperfield*." Many commentators have pointed out that few, if any, of *Pickwick's* riotous company (I would except Mr. Jingle) could have fitted into the somber pages of *Our Mutual Friend*.

Was the later Dickens "realer" than the earlier one? Was the hearty Dickens nothing but an act? Shaw, himself one of the greatest self-dramatizers of all time, thinks so, believing that Dickens' "exuberance was imagination and acting . . . and his outward life a feat of acting from beginning to end." He goes on to say: "When he was not infectiously laughing he was a melancholy fellow."

I do not think it necessary to assume Dickens' exuberance to be mere play-acting, unless we believe the high spirits of the manic-depressive less "genuine" than his fits of melancholy. The key to Dickens' character (and to the distress of his whole life) lies in the rapid and almost desperate *alternation* of these moods, an alternation so dizzying that it left

Dickens himself bewildered and frightened. We have the sense, reading his correspondence, of a man unable to *control* his life—and, perhaps by the same token, all the more masterful in the creation and control of the surrogate life of his characters.

There is a daguerreotype of Dickens taken when he was thirty-five, in the full flush of his triumphant career. It is hard to look at this face, and particularly at the piercing, almost mad, eyes, without feeling this man's intensity to be most precariously balanced, without feeling that the laughter of such a man, however vast and uproarious, must have somewhere hidden in it a gleaming knife-edge of hysteria.

Doubtless we shall never penetrate to the heart of Dickens' mystery, never understand what he himself never understood —the deep, deep reason for the sense of grief and oppression that pervaded his life, growing stronger as he grew older and more successful. Certain things we know, for Dickens himself has told us about them; others have come to light since his death; others we can make a shrewd guess at.

We know that his grandfather was a footman, and his father, immortalized in Mr. Micawber, a ne'er-do-well, constantly in debt. (There may be some connection between the fact that the elder Dickens was an extremely bad businessman and his son an extremely good one—perhaps, with Trollope, Shaw, and Arnold Bennett one of the four best businessmen English literature has produced.) We know that Charles, a victim of his age, hungered and thirsted after respectability. His father and grandfather remained as immovable clouds, forever casting a shadow over Charles' persistent and never quite successful pretensions to the estate of gentleman.

As "a very queer small boy," to use his own revealing

words, he looked at the elegant property at Gad's Hill, and determined he would one day own it and live in it. So ferocious was his drive that own it he did, live in it he did, and die in it he did. There is nothing excessive or uncharacteristic of the time in such an ambition; but there is something feverish about the urge that enabled Dickens to achieve it.

It is generally recognized (since Dickens himself recognized it in a letter written in middle age to John Forster) that the boy Dickens' brief career as a label-paster in Warren's Blacking Factory marked his life decisively. Recollecting the episode (which certainly lasted no more than four months and may have lasted only six weeks) he wrote to Forster: "My whole nature was so penetrated with the grief and humiliation of such considerations that even now, famous and caressed and happy, I often forget in my dreams that I have a dear wife and children; even that I am a man; and wander desolately back to that time of my life."

It is difficult for us to understand why Dickens felt this as a desperate humiliation, but feel it he did, and for many years concealed even from his family this early episode in his life. It seems to have re-enforced his vague sense that somehow he was an outsider. Artistically it helped to provide the impetus which enabled him to depict with such burning vividness a succession of street urchins, from Oliver Twist to the extraordinary "Deputy" of *Edwin Drood*.

It is interesting to note that what most revolted Dickens in his later memory of the blacking-factory job was that, as he worked, all the world could stare at him through his little window. Apparently what ate into his soul was less that his occupation was menial than that it was *public*. And this was the small boy who grew up to be the most public of the Victorians, to exhibit himself on every occasion, to wear waistcoats that rivaled Disraeli's in splendor, to impress a Kentuckian on his first American visit as "flash, like one of our river gamblers," to announce loudly in the public prints the fact of his separation from his wife, to achieve, finally, as great a reputation as actor as he had won as novelist. It is almost as if he were drowning the recollection of his early public humiliation by a later parade of himself under circumstances externally quite different from the sordid factory window.

The other great shock of his boyhood—contemporaneous with the blacking-factory job—is associated with the imprisonment of his father for debt when Charles was twelve. For three months John Dickens lived, probably quite cheerfully, in the Marshalsea Prison. Here almost daily the little Charles visited him. These visits worked intensely on the child's imagination. They aroused in him a constellation of powerful emotions—humiliation, rebellion, the fear that must have gripped him as he identified himself with his father, and the strange, passionate sense that this scene was connected with some vague capacity in him, his then unsuspected creative imagination.

Years later he gives in a letter an extraordinary description of one of the debtor-prisoners, a Captain Porter, reading a petition aloud to the other debtors. He writes:

> Whatever was comical in this scene, and whatever was pathetic, I sincerely believe I perceived in my corner, whether I demonstrated or not, quite as well as I should perceive it now. I made out my own little character and story for every man who put his name to the sheet of paper. I might be able to do that now, more truly; not more earnestly, or with a closer interest. Their different peculiarities of dress, of face, of gait, of manner, were written indelibly upon my memory. I would rather have seen it than the best play ever played; and I thought about it afterwards, over the pots of paste-blacking,

often and often. When I looked, with my mind's eye, into the Fleet Prison during Mr. Pickwick's incarceration, I wonder whether half a dozen men were wanting from the Marshalsea crowd that came filing in again, to the sound of Captain Porter's voice.

There is no other recollection of his boyhood or youth that Dickens describes with such particularity. It is difficult not to conclude that this was a key experience, one helping to explain why, as Wilson has pointed out, the Prison—and the Criminal—are recurrent symbols throughout his books.

They appear first in his earliest and gayest novel, *Pickwick*. Criminality is the very stuff of *Oliver Twist*, the workhouse itself being a kind of prison. So indeed is Dotheboys Hall in the succeeding *Nicholas Nickleby*. One can trace the motif, expressed more or less directly, through the entire Dickensian corpus. Murdstone is but a jailer, Bleak House but a jail. A convict, revenging himself on society, forms the hinge on which turns the whole plot of *Great Expectations*. In *Little Dorrit* the prison dominates almost every page.

Someone more learned in these matters than the writer will one day cast a clear light on the peculiar mechanism that not only attracted Dickens to scenes of crime, but in some distorted manner made him identify himself with the criminal.

This identification became most luridly apparent when, against the advice of all his sensible friends, Dickens persisted in portraying, as the climax of his public readings, the brutal murder of Nancy by Bill Sikes, from *Oliver Twist*. After the first of these readings, he wrote to a friend: "The crime being completely off my mind, and the blood spilled, I am (like many of my fellow-criminals) in a highly edifying state today." The sentence, though jocular, is by no means wholly so. (It reminds one of a similar ironic sentence by a man similarly tortured—Herman Melville, who, upon finishing *Moby Dick*, said, "I have written a wicked book and feel as spotless as the lamb.") One feels that Dickens' identification with Bill Sikes was so neurotically complete that he *had* to portray the murder on the stage in order to relieve his own mind of a vague, oppressive weight of guilt. The portrayal was more than a piece of acting: it was so powerful that women in the audience would faint and Dickens himself emerge from it nervous almost to the point of hysteria. But he would not cease the reading; he would not cease trying to exorcise the Bill Sikes in himself; and in the end, by a piece of entirely Dickensian melodramatic irony, it was Bill Sikes, as much as any other specific factor, who may be said to have so weakened Dickens as to kill him at fifty-eight.

All his life Dickens seems to have felt hemmed in, imprisoned, like a criminal. Indeed his travels should hardly be considered in the light of pleasure-trips, but rather as a kind of escape. During these restless pilgrimages in America and on the Continent he rarely missed an opportunity to visit jails, not to mention morgues. During his second visit to this country, he was fascinated almost to obsession by a dossier of thieves' portraits in the New York police station.

"Like Dostoievsky," writes Rex Warner in a discerning study, "Dickens was both fascinated and horrified by the criminal type, and in his later work he seems to suggest that criminality, or the impulse towards it, is much more widely spread and much more closely connected with the morals of respectability than the majority of his readers would be willing to admit." In his middle and later period, Mr. Warner suggests, "Dickens seems to be using an allegorical method in his analysis of society and to be indicating, as Dostoievsky did, the massive forces of violence and lawlessness which are the counterparts of that legitimate selfishness and personal accumulation on which society rests."

I am not suggesting that the Marshalsea visits were the *cause* of Dickens' feverish interest in crime; but they may well have comprised one of the trigger-episodes that re-enforced in the little Charles a sense, already highly developed in his unconscious, that he was somehow an alien, with odd parents, a confused background, an imperfect education. To be an alien is next to being a criminal.

Had the boy, however, been of a stoic, a lethargic, or what is called a "normal" temperament, all this might have made little impression. Fortunately for his art, however, and for us, he was precariously balanced. As a small child he suffered from what was called "spasms," painful onsets of dizziness, a lucky handicap which turned him into an indoor boy, fond of reading, daydreams, and "showing off" before visitors. Dickens was never well; he suffered all his life from a variety of physical troubles, including insomnia, colds, a weak kidney, hardening of the arteries, hemorrhoids, or fistula, and other illnesses. This was not necessarily a bad thing; a combination of continuous high energy and intermittent illness often provides a favorable condition for the artist.

The boy Dickens' stature was slight, and remained so. (What long shadows have been thrown on history by short men!) Between his fourth and eighth years he and his brother and sister, more or less neglected by their bohemian parents, came under the care of a favorite nurse (her interesting name was Mary Weller) who loved to tell bloodcurdling stories. Possibly she helped start the young Charles on a career in which the delights and terrors of melodrama were to play a decisive role.

In short, Dickens passed a childhood calculated to draw out the kind of genius that probably lay in him at birth— or so it seems to us who enjoy hindsight. He experienced the changes and upsets that arise out of shifts in the economic level; he passed through a few traumatic experiences that were serious without being emotionally paralyzing; he was never constricted by the strait jacket of a formal education; the persons nearest him, his mother and father, were great characters, full of vast and interesting weaknesses; and he very early developed that sense of rejection by society which is one of the generators, liberators, and developers of artistic capacity.

Dickens himself recognized his childhood as the seminary of his genius. Even as he recalls with horror how, after he had been withdrawn from the factory, his mother tried to have the little Charles taken back to his humiliating job, he writes: "I know how all these things have worked together to make me what I am."

His young manhood was equally fortunate. He spent five years in and around law courts and four years in the House of Commons as shorthand reporter and later as correspondent for the *Chronicle.* He spoke of these latter years as "the usefullest of my life." They were. They afforded him an opportunity, during a plastic period, to observe casually the common run of men, as later, when he became a public figure, he could no longer observe them.

His first passion proved no less stimulating. Maria Beadnell was the kind of coy semimoron with whom men of genius frequently fall in love. Geniuses do not seem to *need* superior women. Some strange economy of the imagination attracts them to their inferiors, as if the mismating were a necessary stimulus to the creation of more memorable ladies of the imagination. Balzac persisted doggedly in his tedious romance with the unappetizing Mme. Hanska; Dickens was no less stubborn in his pursuit of the mediocre. Perhaps they were both well guided by some mysterious law of their natures, for in both cases sexual infelicity lent to their work a dimension it might otherwise have lacked.

Dickens, ambitious to win Maria, was moved to make up, by hard reading in the British Museum, some of what he had missed by reason of his helter-skelter education. But more important was the fact that for years he could not quite get over Maria's rejection of him. It tortured him to write and read about her (Dora) in *David Copperfield*. Dickens was a poor loser, touchy, irritable, quick to sense criticism or insult. The petty loss of a stupid girl worked deep within him at a time when he was just beginning to exult over his superiority to most men. He began his sexual life with a defeat. That defeat was to influence the conception of women in his novels. It was also to render him highly vulnerable, at a later period of his life, to second- and third-rate women.

Now Dickens made what to many would appear the greatest mistake of his career. He married Catherine Hogarth, a plump, dull girl, with whom he was to lead a life of gradually increasing boredom, punctuated only by the arrival of baby after baby. Catherine and Charles were profoundly at odds. Charles was one of the most imaginative of men; Catherine, poor soul, appears to have possessed no imagination at all. The worst of it was that apparently they could not talk to each other. Had Charles been able to cleanse his bosom of some of the perilous stuff already weighing upon it in his early manhood, he might have turned out a happier man—and a very different sort of novelist. What was poor, stupid Catherine to make of a husband who could write her in phrases such as these: "The more you see of me, the better perhaps you may understand that the intense pursuit of any idea that takes complete possession of me is one of the qualities that makes me different, sometimes for good; sometimes, I dare say, for evil, from other men"?

It is probable that upon the hapless Catherine Dickens projected, quite unfairly, a large part of his spleen and general self-dissatisfaction. At twenty he could already refer to his "gloomy ideas, of which I always have a very plentiful stock." Doubtless Catherine did little to relieve this gloom; and it was only human for Charles, later on, to imagine her its chief cause, which was not the case.

A large part of his trouble was simply a consequence of what in a letter to Mrs. Winter (who had been the Maria Beadnell of his youth) he called "a habit of suppression." This habit was both an agony and a boon. It was an agony because it sharpened in him his pervading sense of guilt. It was a boon in that it exerted pressure on him to release his fears and shames through imaginative creation.

If we assume that in the young Dickens there worked a poison of shame and humiliation, the heritage of his childhood experiences, it takes no great acumen to suspect that such a nature would seek eagerly for some incarnation of purity that might act as a kind of antidote or neutralizer. Dickens thought he had found such an incarnation in the silly Maria Beadnell; he thought for a time he had found it in his wife; in 1844 he discovered another (temporary) angel in a Miss Christiana Weller; and there is no doubt that he deceived himself similarly with the apparently quite colorless Ellen Ternan, with whom he went to live in 1858. There was a dreadful need in him to create out of quite ordinary women Beatrice-like images of innocence. His books, of course, are full of lily-girls, quite impossibly pure and sweet. But it is an error to suppose that these heroines, this repulsive succession of Little Nells, sprang, as the Victorians thought, from an imagination dedicated to the worship of virtue. They sprang instead from a mind frenziedly endeavoring to compensate by these creations for its own grievous impurity, or, rather, imagined impurity.

This search for the innocence-symbol might not, perhaps,

have been so intense had it not been that, early in Dickens'
married life, in 1837, Mary Hogarth, his seventeen-year-old
sister-in-law, died suddenly in Dickens' arms. There can be
little doubt that Mary was the one Dickens really loved; or
perhaps we should say that in her sweetness and purity of
heart she came nearest to embodying in reality Dickens' crazy
ideal.

Her death was probably the greatest single emotional experience of his life. At her deathbed he slipped a ring from
her hand and put it on his little finger. It was found there,
thirty-three years later, at his own passing.

Dickens' grief passed all reasonable bounds. We can only
assume that he had built Mary up in his imagination until
she possessed for him a symbolic value of vast proportions.
It is not too much to say that with her death something broke
in Dickens. The spirit of melancholy that was to live with
him to the end stole into his heart.

Dickens, thus maimed so early in life, was never to know
(as far as his correspondence would indicate) a mature and
satisfactory sexual experience. Nor did his home life make
any sense; it was obvious he felt little affection for his brood.
Somerset Maugham says, shrewdly enough: "There is something of Pecksniff in the way he assured himself that he had
been a good father and had done everything possible for his
children." In his later Gad's Hill years Dickens would say
with bitter humor that he ought to be signalized "for having
brought up the largest family ever known with the smallest
disposition to do anything for themselves." Somehow Dickens
ruined his children, perhaps by treating them as an audience
rather than as human beings, crushing them by the display
of his own superior vitality, using them as a kind of play-
ground on which to exercise his exuberance. Or perhaps the
central truth lies in a pathetic comment by one of his boys,

the young Charley: "I am certain that the children of my father's brain were much more real to him at times than we were." At any rate, the contrast between Dickens' real attitude toward the hearth and the attitude expressed in his novels is as glaring as is the similar case of Rousseau.

Dickens' social life was lived almost entirely among males, a circumstance that may help to account for the obsessive, adolescent character of his few contacts with women. The frustrated woman (Rosa Dartle is the great example here) he understood by instinct, or perhaps by a kind of introspection; and elderly females he could draw by the hundreds. But he found it difficult to create a normal, healthy heroine; almost all of them are namby-pamby or otherwise unconvincing. Dickens was never really interested in love. A woman for him was either a symbol of the purity he felt his own life lacked, or a miracle-helper who, he hoped, would resolve the painful chaos within him.

Santayana has pointed to this defect: "In Dickens love is sentimental or benevolent or merry or sneaking or canine; . . . but love for him was never chivalrous, never poetical. What he paints most tragically is a quasi-paternal devotion in the old to the young, the love of Mr. Peggotty for little Emily, or of Solomon Gills for Walter Gay." One might add here— or the love of Charles Dickens for the long-dead Mary Hogarth.

On the whole we must agree with George Gissing that, if we are to judge by his characters, Dickens did not like women very much—unless they bore the stamp of infantilism, that is, unless they were equatable with his pink-edged memories of little Mary. His acidulous portraiture must to some extent have arisen out of the circumstances of his own life, for the woman he knew best, his wife, he disliked.

In fifteen years the uncomplaining Catherine bore him ten

children and had four miscarriages; and Dickens greeted each new arrival with an irony in which the modern reader cannot help sensing both vulgarity and brutality.

Finally the situation became too much for him. In a letter to Forster Dickens confessed at last: "You are not so tolerant as perhaps you might be of the wayward and unsettled feeling which is part (I suppose) of the tenure on which one holds an imaginative life, and which I have . . . often kept down by riding over it like a dragoon. . . . The gist is that it is a mistake to marry too young and that the years are not making things easier. . . ."

But Dickens was blaming an early marriage for a tragic restlessness which had its roots in his childhood, in his essential nature, even though it had been re-enforced by a grievous misalliance. Dickens would have been unhappy had he married late in life; and the proof lies in the fact that when he left Catherine and took the pretty young actress Ellen Ternan as his mistress, he found no real solace. All he succeeded in doing was to make his large family unhappy. His daughter Kate, recalling the Ternan affair many years after, wrote: "More tragic and far-reaching in its effect was the association of Charles Dickens and Ellen Ternan and their resultant son than that of Nelson and Lady Hamilton and their daughter. My father was like a madman. He did not seem to care a damn what happened to any of us. Nothing could surpass the misery and unhappiness of our life."

This misery and unhappiness Charles Dickens fully shared. His genius may have showed no signs of diminution, though it altered its direction somewhat: *A Tale of Two Cities, Great Expectations, Our Mutual Friend,* and even *Edwin Drood* are not the products of a failing talent. But the man himself began to fail. His restlessness increased. "He walked about the black streets of London," says Dickens, describing himself, "fifteen and twenty miles many a night when all the sober folks had gone to bed." In an endeavor to avoid recognizing the inadequacy of his private life, he multiplied to absurdity the number of his public appearances, at dinners, at meetings, on the lecture platform.

Some inner devil was driving him, a devil that lent him a spurious strength. During his second American tour in 1866-1867, evening after evening this tortured invalid, almost incapable of movement, his foot dragging, his heart pounding, would, when the time came, mount the platform and go through an exhausting series of readings with incredible energy and art.

But nothing would serve: energy and genius and public triumphs were not enough to fill the deep void in his temperament. In his middle years he had written to Forster: "Why is it that, as with poor David [Copperfield] a sense comes always crushing on me now, when I fall into low spirits, as of one happiness I have missed in life, and one friend and companion I have never made?" This basic loneliness could not be assuaged by the dutiful caresses of Ellen Ternan. It was linked to an unhappiness so deep-rooted that we are forced to say that it was almost identical with Dickens himself.

In his last year of life his gloom deepened to a kind of wholesale self-revulsion, the self-revulsion that had always underlain his apparent self-complacence. One day, engaged in destroying packets of old letters, all mementos of happier times, he exclaimed bitterly: "Would to God every letter I had ever written was on that pile!"

The shift in our view of Dickens, as we have seen, is largely the consequence of our simple conviction that he was a grievously unhappy and divided man. This division, however, was a double one: he was dissatisfied with society as well as with

himself. The Victorians preferred to interpret this dissatisfaction as a generous heart's resentment of the period's abuses,
but to our eye Dickens' attack on society seems more than a
natural overflow of kindly feelings. For all his surface con-
ventionality, his joinerish civic-mindedness and public speech-
making, his kowtowing to the Victorian idols of Activity,
Accumulation, and Display, Dickens, like most of his more
sensitive contemporaries—even Tennyson—was profoundly
at odds with the very culture that sustained him. In Edmund
Wilson's opinion, "Of all the great Victorian writers, he was
probably the most antagonistic to the Victorian age itself."

This antagonism is interpreted by Marxists such as Bernard
Shaw and T. A. Jackson as the rage of a revolutionary *manqué*.
Shaw: "The difference between Marx and Dickens was
that Marx knew that he was a revolutionist whilst Dickens
had not the faintest suspicion of his calling." Jackson: "He
had completely lost faith in bourgeois society; but, unfortu-
nately for himself—although he went as near to its attainment
as a man can go without actually achieving it—he never quite
acquired a faith in the proletariat and its historical future. . . .
It is this fact which constitutes the real tragedy of Charles
Dickens. . . . He was, ever and always, the petit-bourgeois
in revolt."

It is not hard to make out some sort of case for the Shaw-
Jackson theory. Obviously the entire Dickensian corpus can
be viewed as an attack on the institutions of his day. From
the rough-and-tumble burlesque of the parliamentary election system in *Pickwick* to the stinging satire on the newly
rich Veneerings in *Our Mutual Friend*, Dickens strikes with
increasing fury at the pillars of Victorian society.

Nor is it difficult to find in his correspondence savage out-
bursts of what to one kind of dogmatist will seem the most
out-and-out radicalism. Has anything ever been written in

purer acid about the Mother of Parliaments than this: "My hope [is] to have made every man in England feel something of the same contempt for the House of Commons that I have. We shall never do anything until the sentiment is universal"? Could anything be more downright jacobinical than this passage from a letter of March 1844 to Forster: "I declare I never go into what is called 'society' that I am not aweary of it, despise it, hate it, and reject it. The more I see of its extraordinary conceit, and its stupendous ignorance of what is passing out of doors, the more certain I am that it is approaching the period when being incapable of reforming itself it will have to submit to being reformed by others off the face of the earth."

Yet there is something that bids us pause before accepting the easy view of Dickens as the revolutionary whose socioeconomic libido was insufficient to make him fall in love with the proletariat. To be even an unconscious revolutionary one's temper must be dominantly political—and the feeling comes over one that Dickens was not only nonpolitical, but antipolitical. *Hard Times* is full of sympathy for the oppressed factory-worker, though hardly for the union. Yet its central theme is not political but, in a sense, poetical: at bottom *Hard Times* is a plea, not for the claims of the worker but for the claims of the imagination. Its anger is directed against Gradgrindism. Gradgrindism is a state of mind that may prevail in any society, capitalist or communist, and indeed tends to flourish much more tropically under communism.

As all readers of *Barnaby Rudge* know, Dickens had little sympathy for the masses as the instrument of insurrection; and the extraordinary figure of Simon Tappertit in that book must stand as the embodiment of at least one of Dickens' attitudes toward social rebellion. As for *A Tale of Two Cities*, it is a case of a plague on both your houses.

The true revolutionary, like the true reactionary, has as his prime passion a thirst for order; and this Dickens lacked. He could hate, as he did, the hollowness and cruelty of the dominant institutions of his time, and to this extent he was a radical; but he would have hated even more fiercely the institutions his contemporary Marx wanted to substitute for them. His position is Rousseauist, even anarchistic.

I would suggest that his unhappiness stemmed in part from an unconscious feeling that the Victorian age, in its dominating aspects, threatened his very life, his quick, leaping, creative heart. Dickens was mad, not for order, which is the concern of the state, but for personality, which is the state's deadly enemy. His attack on institutions was an inverted defense of his deadly enemy. In his day the impulse to power and the itch to modify the environment were beginning to assume those forms which in our own time have congealed into the Russian police state. Dickens shivered before the first chill exhalations of that congelation, of the process which could reduce to cold slag the vast, roaring furnace of his imagination.

The killing of the human being and his replacement by a set of conditioned reflexes appear to some as the chief duty and necessity of the next hundred years. Dickens scented this, as any great creative temperament scents the future; and his novels, which seem to deal with specifics such as the Circumlocution Office and the schools of Yorkshire, are, beneath their local and temporal satire, anguished pleas for the preservation of personality against the encroachments of the Moloch state.

Thus Dickens' unhappiness was nourished not alone by the concrete miseries of his personal life but by an abstract threat pervasive in the social atmosphere around him, a threat that cried then, and cries now, Death to all creators.

Conversation

Conversation

I HAVE JUST noticed an advertisement for a small object known as the Conversation Ball. "In it," say its enthusiastic sponsors, "are thirty conversational subjects. Throw it to anyone nearby. He or she extracts one slip which introduces the subject to be discussed. Each one present is supposed to contribute his views, then the ball is thrown to the next person. . . . You'll never have a dull party with everyone sitting around wondering what to talk about or do."

This Conversation Ball lends support to my conviction that if, as everybody says, there is a dearth of good talk nowadays, one reason may be that conversation is given too much aid and comfort.

What do we do when we converse? Surely, as Doctor Johnson said, conversation is more than asking questions and receiving answers. Surely it is more than the mutual exchange of monologues. It seems to me a kind of popular art, open to all, like whittling, or doodling, or singing in the bathroom, only more social. It is the translation of one's personality into evanescent words intended to reach a few persons at most. It is a retail catch-as-catch-can method of finding out what the human race, including oneself, is like: easy-chair anthropology.

Now, if this notion be accepted, who is the better conversationalist: the man, fresh from a reading of the latest expert on China, who says, "Here's what *I* think of the mess over there"; or the man who, consulting no one, but genuinely convinced that it's a fine day, remarks, "Fine day, isn't it?" I'd rather listen to the second fellow; he sounds more like himself.

The overavailability of authority, much of it well intentioned, much of it doubtless sound, nevertheless makes it hard for us not to transform our conversation into a kind of game of quotations. Newspapers, magazines, radio and TV forums, lecturers, commentators, all thrust conversational crutches at us, encumber us with aid, and lessen our chances to use talk as the translation of our own personalities.

> *What does Mr. Alsop say*
> *In the* Trib *at break of day?*
> *Let me make it clear, says Alsop,*
> *Reader, let me talk away.*
> *Alsop, talk a little longer*
> *Till my little mind grows stronger.*
> *If you talk a little longer,*
> *I'll know what to say.*

If the overavailability of authority forms one conversational crutch, the overavailability of timely information comprises another. Our news services are undoubtedly the most efficient and reliable in the world. The question is, are they not a little too efficient for our own good—that is, our good as conversationalists? Chatting with a friend for a few minutes, I find myself giving him a crisp, knowledgeable summary, drawn from my newspaper, of the day's events. I may touch this up with shrewd comment derived from the morning editorial. My friend now performs the same service for me, his source being a different newspaper. After this exchange of newspapers, we part, congratulating ourselves on being so well informed. Perhaps we are; but we have not really been talking with each other.

If conversation is an informal try at the expression of one's personality, too copious an infusion of the timely may enfeeble rather than strengthen it. Perhaps a certain detachment from the "reality" of the day's news is a help, not a hindrance. It is surprising, indeed, how nicely the delicate craft of conversation will float on the shallowest of waters of fact, how much fresh and pungent talk can come from that almost extinct animal, the ill-informed man.

Our third conversational crutch we may call the multiplicity of models. Breakfast programs, forums, interviews, "panel" shows (as a small-time sinner myself, I'm particularly sensitive on this point), teams of radio comedians, ad-lib quiz shows—all pour out an endless stream of what passes as conversation. Of this much is pleasant, much amusing, much instructive; but, considered as imitable talk, it is perilous stuff. Yet, how much of it *does* sink in, to reappear in our own words—bits and pieces of slang, "smart" phrases, wisecracks, whole structures of opinion and attitude.

Air-wave talk is not really conversation at all, but a kind of informal discourse presumably taking place spontaneously among people in the studio, but actually directed at millions of outsiders—you and me. Mass communication is exactly what its name implies. The average mass communicator cannot afford to be too uncompromisingly himself lest he startle or offend or puzzle or bore large sections of his public. And, because he is, unavoidably, a departure from himself, talking wholesale to millions, he is not in a position to produce the personal, retail stuff called conversation.

Yet our broadcasting system is flexible and tolerant enough to permit naturalness and spontaneity to break through, despite all restrictions. Sometimes a program is so conceived, as in the case of *Invitation to Learning,* or, if I may say so, *Conversation,* that sincere, easy, unself-conscious talk is frequently generated. You will hear the same kind of thing, on an entirely different but equally legitimate level, from Arthur Godfrey or Dave Garroway, whose "showmanship" consists in being themselves.

In general, however, to take our conversational cue from the multiplicity of air-wave models is to drain from our own talk some of its blood and salt. Broadcasting is broadcasting. Conversation is narrow-casting.

I can recall two novels, both of them about the Irish—Irish-Irish in one case, Chicago-Irish in the other. The first is *Children of the Rainbow* by Bryan MacMahon. It consists of a loosely strung-together collection of sketches about the natives of a small village in southern Ireland called, by the author, Cloone. The book's quality flows from its dialogue, by turns earthy, absurd, poetical, windy, vehement, tragical, musical, witty, or some combination of these adjectives. Now I do not believe this dialogue a pure invention of Mr. Mac-Mahon, for too many Irish novels continue to appear, all touched with the same genius for fresh speech. The reason is not far to seek. The people of Cloone are isolated in space and in time. In some respects they are marooned in the eighteenth century; in others they have not progressed beyond the age of Homer. Their backwardness helps to make them poor, dirty, uncomfortable, shiftless, and violent. It also helps to make them great talkers. Without mass communication on hand to offer its crutch, they are forced to invent conversation in order not to bore each other to death. Talk is their comic magazine, their television set, their playhouse, their newspaper. The village of Cloone is nothing but a swarm of engaging lunatics, lovers, and poets, seething in a frenzy of fine talk.

Turn the pages of one of James Farrell's recent novels, *This Man and This Woman,* and you are living in another world. Here the chief characters—a pathetic, aging Irish-American and his equally pathetic wife—have been so worn down by their environment that they can feel the spring of life only by mutual nagging. One finally kills the other; but the reader has been talked to death long before this. The fact is that Mr. Farrell's distressing couple speak so dully, so flatly, that one can hardly tell whether his novel is good or not: before one can make a judgment unconsciousness supervenes. The irony of it is that, in a way, this is Mr. Farrell's intention —to portray the absolute, sordid depersonalization into which a certain kind of big-city American may degenerate.

And yet Mr. Farrell's dead-eyed, dead-voiced Irish-Americans and Mr. MacMahon's parti-colored eccentrics come of the same wonderful, imaginative racial stock. Can the folk of Cloone have gained something by their parochial isolation? Can Mr. Farrell's Chicagoans have lost something by living in the heart of megalopolis, the tension of their imagination at last loosened by the mighty pull of a million broadcasts, headlines, billboards, comic papers?

Some years ago, it was my happy fortune to be involved in a book publishing venture under the genial leadership of George Macy, the man who makes salable books beautiful and beautiful books salable. We (my colleagues were Sinclair Lewis, Alexander Woollcott, and Carl Van Doren) met monthly to enjoy Mr. Macy's Roman hospitality, transact a little business—and talk.

That is, Messrs. Lewis, Woollcott, and Van Doren talked. Mr. Macy and I, having sense enough to know a good thing when we heard it, listened.

What was good about the conversation?

Well, for a starter, it was unspecialized. We were all what is called literary men, but the talk was not particularly literary. It ranged freely, if not always soundly—why should conversation always be sound?—over a dozen fields, including that of gossip, with letters occupying a proportionate place, and politics coming in a bad last. Though often ribald, it was never rude. No man tried to stop another. No man tried to top another. They were all aware that part of the art of conversation is the art, learned with difficulty, of not interrupting. Very little of the talk, as I recollect, dealt with the day's happenings. Much of it dealt with the century's or millennium's happenings.

Each man was himself. Each gave with delight something the others lacked. Each received with the same delight what the others had to give.

Carl Van Doren was the most learned. Often, in these tricky days, when scholarship has to apologize for itself, learned men are ashamed of or self-conscious about their erudition. Not Carl. He was quite cheerful about what he knew and used it to lively advantage. Like his hero, Ben Franklin, he had endless curiosity, edged always with a serene humor. Almost dogmatically tolerant, if he had a weakness it was for weakness itself—the weakness of our ridiculous human nature. If a man can make conversation out of a liking for people, that was how Carl made conversation.

Alec, accused of tolerance, would have exploded like a trick cigar. His talk was a constant busy erection of prickly palisades. Much of the prickle was an act designed to amuse, for Woollcott could be as kind as he could be cutting. The trouble lay in the limitations of his talent for expression. When exposing pretense or stupidity, his phrases rounded to an easy perfection. When he was genuinely moved by goodness or courage, they fattened into sentimentality. If Carl was a vest-pocket Franklin, Alec was a vest-pocket Doctor Johnson. He had the great Doctor's flair for the perfect phrase, and of the three talked most naturally in balanced sentences that cried for a Boswell.

But the best of them was Sinclair Lewis. He possessed more energy than the two others combined, a famous power of mimicry, a capacity to spurn the solid earth of rational discourse and leap with a ballet dancer's ease into an upper realm of the fantastic and absurd. Remembering Lewis, one always felt, after we parted, that there had been a dozen men in the room. Behind everything he uttered, whether a mad pun or a long monologue that could have been inserted into one of his better novels, there worked a pressure of personality to which neither Alec nor Carl could lay claim. He was Mercutio.

They are gone, all three, and—for they were very human—I presume they are in Purgatory. If so, and if Purgatory contains three chairs, and Carl and Alec and Red are in them, and talking, then Purgatory can boast some of the pleasures of a Paradise.

If one could only move this Paradise into one's living room . . .

One hundred and twenty-nine years ago William Hazlitt made up a pleasant fancy that he called *Of Persons One Would Wish to Have Seen*. I am no Hazlitt, but this is a game anyone may play at any time; the imagination recognizes no closed season. Let us put the matter thus: an obliging god from the Time Machine undertakes to introduce into your living room any fourteen historical characters with whom you hanker to spend an evening of general conversation. They will be supplied in good talking condition, one an evening for two weeks. Fourteen only; and no second helpings.

Which would you choose? Whatever your selection, of course, you are giving yourself away, for we are known by the company we keep, even a company of spirits.

For those who do not care to play there are Canasta tables in the next room. The cosy little group now remaining must keep clearly in view our only purpose—fourteen evenings of the best general conversation possible. Therefore it avails little for our guest to be wise or witty, good or great, if he be not talkative or so reputed. Make sure, too, that he is congenial rather than merely notable. The elder Rockefeller and Daniel Webster are outstanding chaps, but I am content to leave them in limbo. It is difficult to spend one's time making as many pennies as Rockefeller or as many platitudes as Webster without turning into a bit of a bore. I warn you also against opting for mere greatness. Archimedes, Newton, Darwin—each would waste for us a precious evening. To such master minds (Hazlitt tells us) Charles Lamb objected: "They were not persons—not persons . . . not characters, you know." What would be the point? Most of the best of what they had to say is already part of our mental world. Though we rarely think of it, which of us does not live every day of his life in closest intimacy with the laws of the lever, gravitation, and evolution?

Nor is my latchstring out to any man, however admirable, of too intense a temperament. I do not care to exchange an evening of grumps and glooms with Dante. I must have outgoers, men whose minds continually walk abroad. Thus saints and mystics are not to my purpose, unless they be such antic and irregular ones as the poet William Blake, who might well arrive companioned by his daily familiars, the angels. Nor is the virtuous man my meat. Let me read Emerson, not talk with him, for though I am willing to be improved during the leisure of a lifetime, I object to sudden moral elevation in a single evening.

Perhaps you are already thinking of such great talkers as Samuel Johnson or Lincoln or Shaw. But reflect: you have but fourteen evenings. Can you afford such men, who spent their lives making sure that posterity would know all about them? With little difficulty I can hold in my hands between two covers the kernel of their minds. An evening with Doctor Johnson would be interesting enough—but how often shall you be forced to interrupt with "But, sir, I have heard all that from Mr. Boswell!"

On the other hand it would be no less risky to entertain characters as to whom we are quite in the dark. How tempting to chat with Shakespeare or Homer—but how rash! We know nothing of either. Shakespeare may have put the last ounce of his loquacity into Hamlet and Falstaff; Homer, reputed blind, might turn out deaf to boot. Why talk with a pig in a poke?

I warn you also against the mere satisfaction of curiosity. Had I more than fourteen evenings at my disposal, I would gladly welcome the composer Rossini and even feed him his own *tournedos,* could I but ask him why, after completing *William Tell* at thirty-seven, he wrote no more operas during his remaining forty years. I should be glad, too, to interview the playwright Sir William D'Avenant and ask for the real dirt behind the rumor that he was the son of William Shakespeare. But the satisfaction of curiosity on such single points does not create good talk.

To reverse the situation, it would be equally tempting— and equally prodigal of our limited time—to *tell* rather than ask. To watch the face of the Greek scientist Heron of Alexandria as we explain the later career of a little toy he put together around 100 A.D., a toy now called the steam engine; or alternately to gratify and horrify the thirteenth-century Franciscan monk Roger Bacon with the story of what has happened to a few of his many anticipations—flying, explosives, mechanical propulsion; to—but no, we must sidestep such seductions.

With no less regret we shall bar our door to that vast army of out-of-step eccentrics: to interesting fanatics like the Populist politician Ignatius Donnelly who knew that Shakespeare was Bacon, located the whereabouts of Atlantis, and is remembered today only because he compared the Democratic party to a mule "without pride of ancestry or hope of posterity"; to quaint freaks like "that fantastic old great man" Robert Burton, who devoted his cloistral life and stupefying talents to the compilation of a half-wise, half-crazy Stonehenge of a volume on melancholy; to prodigies of nature like John Lewis William Thudicum, who founded the science of brain chemistry, wrote *The Spirit of Cookery* and *A Treatise on Wines*, and might have become, had he wished, a great concert singer; to the Marquis de Sade who—but the school of odd fish is not for us. Once we have fathomed their oddity, there may be too little left. To talk with a rhinoceros would be interesting; but not interesting enough.

There is a large class of men who have always fascinated all of us but whom nevertheless I would hesitate to include among my fourteen. They are the power men—those who pass their lives widening the gap between themselves and their fellow humans, whether by force, or politics, or the amassing of wealth. There have been interesting conquerors —perhaps Alexander the Great was one. There have been interesting politicos—one thinks of Disraeli and Burke. There have been interesting money men, though at the moment their names do not occur to me. And there have been men both great and even good among these three groups.

But on the whole, power men are too successful to be really interesting conversationalists. A man who passes his life dominating the world rarely has the temperament to reflect upon it. Napoleon may resemble a vast force of nature but by the same token be diminished in his humanity. He must settle for power, not wisdom, and assume as the normal human relation that between superior and inferior. How can one really *talk* with a Stalin, a Hitler, a J. P. Morgan? There is bound to be too much ego in his cosmos. "The love of liberty," says Hazlitt, "is the love of others. The love of power is the love of ourselves." There are few charming tyrants. If I may revise Lord Acton's well-worn dictum, all the powerful bore; the absolutely powerful bore absolutely.

So—let my fourteen be given to talk. Let them not be fixed aggressively on one idea, whether the idea be a great one, as with St. Paul, or a dangerous one, as with Karl Marx. Let them, or some of them, have that added charm that comes of a division in the mind, or even a flaw in the character; monuments are for veneration, not conversation. Let them not agree too patly with their time (a Joseph Addison, a Calvin Coolidge), for while rebels may be, conformists always are, tedious. Let them be of high general intelligence, lively in manner, rich in experience and, if possible, touched with humor.

There's the doorbell.

Ancient Greece produced more interesting human beings per square foot per year than did any other time or place in history. So, for my first two evenings, I choose two Greeks, a good Greek and a naughty one.

The good Greek is Europe's first great diner-out, SOCRATES.

I will have him in part to discover how much of him was made up by Plato (for, like Jesus, Socrates wrote not a word that has come down to us). But mainly I will have him because of all mortal men we know, he seems least tethered to his time. An evening is too short to spend with a provincial.

My naughty Greek is the pupil of Socrates, ALCIBIADES, who learned everything from his master except how to lead a Socratic life. Alcibiades is the cynical young adventurer *par excellence*, the eternal gilded youth, the aristocratic mind flawed by the desire ever to impress, to make an effect. All the world's Byrons are but carbon copies of him. He exerts the fascinating charm of the able dilettante and will bring to my table, if not virtue, the perfection of worldly elegance and that hard radiance of manner possessed only by those free of a sense of sin.

I am almost stumped when I come to Rome, a city that abounded in men both able and dull. I think I will ask one who was far from the noblest Roman of them all, the lyric poet CATULLUS, lustful, obscene, tender, burning like a flame and as short-lived, a specialist in excess. And when he comes I shall take pains to hustle the children from the dining room.

From the Middle Ages I will have my Time Machine transport CHAUCER, as healthy-tempered as Catullus was not, the road-walker, the man of daylight, the eternal good companion.

From the Renaissance give me the one who spoke of himself as "the unlettered man" and who was probably the maniest-sided human being that has ever lived, possessing also the great attraction of the divided soul, for his powerful reason seems always to be measuring itself against what is vast and indefinable in nature: LEONARDO DA VINCI.

The great century of talk is the eighteenth. I shall invite that century's greatest talker. You may object that I have already disqualified him, for has he not in a hundred volumes unpacked his restless mind? Perhaps—but this single risk I shall venture, persuaded that to bore me VOLTAIRE would have to make extensive preparations. Here is the one man who cannot be dull *ad lib.*

Somewhere in a publisher's strong-room in Leipzig lie moldering in unguessable obscenity the complete memoirs of one who knew Voltaire. Yes, I would like to entertain CASANOVA, assured that he would return the compliment. Learned in a learned century, witty in a witty one, unscrupulous in an unscrupulous one, a magnificent taker of chances, this charlatan-abbé knew more, let us confess it, about the mysterious country of women than most men have even fancied, for he had not merely the explorer's energy but the philosopher's mind with which to mull the meaning of his conquests.

Let us start a fresh week with BENJAMIN FRANKLIN. Franklin is interesting because he had the liveliest mind that it is possible for an utterly *sensible* man to possess. For flights of fancy I must send out to others, but if there are such things as flights of sense, Franklin is their master. Like Chaucer he will make me feel, as he made all with whom he spoke, joyfully at home in a not always friendly world.

We often elect able men to the presidency, rarely interesting ones, particularly since the death of Lincoln. Not many of our Presidents have combined vast personal charm with a first-class brain. Perhaps this is as it should be: we do not believe in the philosopher-king theory and generally distrust leaders who are too lively of mind. We came nearest, I think, to running counter to our deepest feelings when we elected my next guest, THOMAS JEFFERSON. Exalted in character but without pomposity, a master of the English tongue, one of our few well-educated Presidents (I suggest that we have had seven such in all), curious about everything, he will step to my fireside on his own vigorous two legs, scornful of the politician's almost invariable crutches—cant and the platitude.

In Mr. Jefferson there was little darkness of soul; we are in part the children of his faith in men and women. Yet the world has its evil face and only the fool refuses to front it. So, to hear the other side, I shall follow Jefferson with JONATHAN SWIFT and listen to the creator of Gulliver unburden the bitter indignation of his lacerated heart. I will gladly forgo most men's benevolence if I may enjoy Swift's misanthropy.

And then for a change of pace let me have CHARLES LAMB. I will take Lamb solely on the say-so of his judicious friend Hazlitt, who calls him "the most delightful, the most provoking, the most witty and sensible of men" and states flatly that Lamb "always made the best pun, and the best remark in the course of the evening."

From Hazlitt's circle of super-talkers I shall select one more guest, the man who spoke "well on every subject," the torrential COLERIDGE, whose mere digressions mesmerized his audience. This I know will be an evening of monologue; perhaps the rapt metaphysician, caught in the ever-thickening web of his airy speculations, will not even be conscious of his host's existence.

There are but two evenings left. Shall it be Mark Twain—but, please Heaven, without his wife? Or Disraeli, who could touch with his incomparable style utterances of the most dubious taste? Or Samuel Butler, who combined so oddly acute intelligence and ridiculous cantankerousness? Or G. K. Chesterton, shedding sparks of paradox like a Catherine wheel? I will sacrifice them, reluctantly, in favor of the nineteenth-century Anglican parson, SYDNEY SMITH. If Smith could send Sarah Siddons, the Tragic Muse, into convulsions, he is bound at least to make me laugh; and it is time for a pure entertainer. This man who remarked of a bishop that he deserved to be preached to death by wild curates; that he had no relish for the country, because it was a sort of healthy grave; that gout was the only enemy he did not wish to have at his feet; who observed that his wife was as pregnant as the Trojan Horse; who dismissed an oratorio with "How absurd, to see 500 people fiddling like madmen about the Israelites in the Red Sea"; who said that he never read a book before reviewing it, because it prejudiced a man so; that Macaulay had flashes of silence that made his conversation perfectly delightful; that his idea of heaven was eating pâtés de foie gras to the sound of trumpets; that Webster impressed him much like a steam engine in trousers—this man I shall ask to the largest dinner I can manage, so that I may overhear my guests whisper in pleased anticipation, as they did in his day: *"Mr. Sydney Smith coming upstairs."*

My fortnight is almost up. I have only a single evening left. Better to take not even the slightest chance; better to call in someone I have myself known at first-hand. I shall ask for WILLIAM BOLITHO, the British journalist who streamed like a meteor over New York in the late twenties and died too soon in 1930. "To hear Bolitho talk," said Alexander Woollcott, "was to listen to one who himself dwelt outside of time." It is true. They called him the man from Mars, and he was. I knew him only slightly, yet well enough to get the impression of a supercharged being, filled with gunpowder, ready to explode at a touch. He was so original as on occasion to be almost unintelligible; but the unexpected in conversation is so rare in our day as to be welcome in any form. His books, such as *Murder for Profit* and *Twelve Against the Gods*, are written in a strange prose that one can only call Bolithian, and are packed with the quirky, furiously independent judgments that catapulted out of him in talk. Compared with my other guests he is of course a mere bush leaguer; but at least I shall be sure of what I am getting. Bolitho was one of the best talkers, as he was surely the most bewildering one, I have ever known. Twenty-five years after his tragic and probably needless death I—and how many others!—miss him sorely.

Onstage

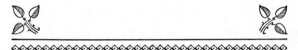

Clowns, Humorists, Comics

IN THE course of my immersion in the wild waves of radio and television, I've worked with perhaps a hundred and fifty professional funny men. They split up into three main classes: clowns, humorists, comics.

There are very few great clowns. One is Jimmy Durante, whose art is that of making quietly despairing men suddenly catch a vision of the surprisingness of life, the breakability of rules, the spirit-cleansing power of the irrelevant.

The Marx Brothers and W. C. Fields in their finest period about two decades ago were unsurpassed clowns. Fields dealt in understatement, the Brothers in overstatement. Fields' face expressed resignation, varying from the quiet to the desperate. Groucho's expressed exaggeration. Harpo's was exaggeration itself, a kind of *ne plus ultra* in faces. Even in his juggling act Fields seemed to move slowly, whereas the Marx gestures were all rapid. There was something *reasonable* about Fields, but the Marxes were so confidently unreasonable as to awaken in the spectator bitter doubts as to the worthwhileness of not being a fool. Fields was a Stoic, the Marxes Anarchists.

Fields, Harpo, and Groucho were "smart" clowns. Bert Lahr is the supreme type of the yokel clown. He is organized mental innocence, his face one question mark.

If great clowns are rare, humorists are almost as rare. The great remainder are comics.

271

They're all comedians—that is, they make us laugh. But we laugh in different ways at the clown, the humorist, the comic.

The clown is a creator, like a poet or a great tragic actor. He cocks a snook at the quotidian, and makes up his own world. Often he does this by his power of transforming himself into a whole cast of characters. This protean capacity for impersonation is part of the genius of Danny Kaye and Groucho Marx. The clown's power over us is vast and deep; he moves us out of ourselves into a bright new universe of happy accident.

While the clown works with fantasy, the humorist is realistic. He reports on some aspect of his own experience and makes us realize, with a start of delight, that it is our experience too. His humor is a direct reflection of his own unchanging character. The less he departs from himself, the more effective he is. This is Sam Levenson's secret, though no one can predict what may happen to a humorist once he has fallen among jokesmiths.

The comic is simply a pro. He has no character, in the sense that the humorist has one. Instead he has "personality," which is an odd power of projection. This depends pretty much on the possession of great stores of energy. The "personality" is sometimes sharpened by the exploitation of a notable personal trait (Cantor's eyes, Benny's "stinginess," Bob Hope's nose).

The finest comics are far better at making up gags than are their paid writers; but all depend more or less on gagmen. The comic is an efficient machine for distributing a certain standard manufactured product.

The product, the delivery—these are the two important factors. The product—the joke—must fall into one of a smallish number of patterns. These patterns are familiar to us; we have been taught to react, like Pavlov's dog, with the rictus known as a smile, or the nervous explosion known as a laugh, to a certain kind of statement about the ugliness of the comic's wife, the high cost of living in Florida, and similar "tested" material. These jokes have long ceased to be very funny in themselves; we would not laugh at them were it not for the "delivery."

The comic makes us laugh by overpowering us; his relation to us is that between aggressor and aggressee. Before we have time to reflect upon the possibility that the gag is not really side-splitting, the comic has hit us over the ribs again with another gag. Thus he builds up a kind of hysteria which must release itself in laughter. In a way he tires us into laughing. Some comics I have worked with will cock their heads fiercely after a joke, make a threatening grimace—anything to induce the nervous reaction of cachinnation.

The art of the comic, however synthetic, is a real and admirable one. He is a hard worker—actually he expends more foot-pounds of energy than does the clown or the humorist. He must always "deliver"—that is, beat down his audience whose normal initial attitude is one of I-dare-you-to-make-me-laugh. The radio and television comic does not distill true humor any more than the newspaper comics do. But he gets what he goes out for: the laughs.

We love the clown. We feel affection for the humorist. The comic is—popular.

Emlyn Williams, Charles Laughton, and the Art of Reading Aloud

On April 29, 1858, at St. Martin's Hall, London, Charles Dickens gave his first paid public reading from his own works. When on March 15, 1870, he finished his Farewell Reading, his brain children, working through his vocal cords, had earned for their father a total of £45,000. He had convulsed and terrified audiences on two continents. And he had signed his own death warrant.

Seventeen years later one who had heard him set down these words: "And I *see*—yes, I declare I *see*, as I saw when Dickens was reading, such was the illusion of voice and gesture—that dying flame of Scrooge's fire, which leaped up when Marley's ghost came in, and then fell again."

Thomas Carlyle, who enjoyed himself under protest, spoke of Dickens as "a whole tragic, comic, heroic *theatre* visible, performing under one hat, and keeping us laughing—in a sorry way, some of us thought—the whole night."

G. K. Chesterton, recalling a tradition that had come down in his family, wrote that Dickens "could make his face fall suddenly into the blank inanity of Mrs. Raddle's servant, or swell, as if to twice its size, into the apoplectic energy of Mr. Sergeant Buzfuz."

274

As a reader there had never been anyone like Dickens. He owned and operated a hundred gaits, faces, accents. As Mrs. Gamp he sounded as though his voice were coming through a tissue-paper-covered comb. In the trial scene from *Pickwick* he contrived by a series of sudden snorts and starts to keep continuously present to the audience the somnolent Justice Stareleigh. In the scene between Fanny Squeers and Nicholas Nickleby he seemed to split his face in two, one side representing Fanny, the other Nicholas.

Dickens' power of creeping whole into the skins of his characters was almost frightful in its intensity. His most celebrated performance (Sikes' murder of Nancy, in *Oliver Twist*) involved real hazards for both audience and actor. One friend, echoing the general feeling, wrote him: "I am bound to tell you that I had an almost irresistible impulse upon me to *scream* and that if anyone had cried out I should have followed." During this reading Dickens' pulse rate would leap from its normal 80–100 to about 120; and there is little doubt that his frenzy hastened his death, at the age of 58.

On February 4, 1952, I attended the American première of Emlyn Williams's performance as Charles Dickens, which had been a London sensation. I am now reconciled to having missed the original. Indeed I am convinced not only that Dickens *could* not have been better, but that he could not have been very different.

The mere mechanism of impersonation was, as far as the rather full tradition can instruct us, perfect. The stage bare, except for the red-velvet-covered reading desk, an exact replica of the one Dickens used, with its ledge to the right on which to deposit the white gloves, its small elongated cubical rest to support the left hand. The entrance of the master, the gait a trifle stiff, the right shoulder a bit forward, the manner precisely that of the self-confident public idol. The red geranium in the buttonhole—"In Ireland, ladies sitting with their chins against the platform, would gather up the petals falling from [Dickens'] red geranium and even beg the denuded stalk as souvenir." The flowing hair (home-grown by Mr. Williams), the mustache, the parted chin whiskers with their slight suggestion of Napoleon III, the whole somewhat dandiacal getup.

But, beyond this machinery of mimicry, something eerier. The very expression of the actor Dickens—"a corpse galvanized by a god," as Chesterton put it. The piercing eye that mesmerized Dickens' audiences and had enabled him at one time in his life to cure by hypnosis a female hysteric. The sensation of reality rather than impersonation. Broadway died about us and an effluence of the Victorian epoch seemed to waft from the stage and drift impalpably about the aisles.

And then the "readings," done of course with no reference to the books themselves except for an occasional casual flick of a page. Done with an easy perfection of intonation and gesture: the pomposity of Podsnap, the pathos of little Paul Dombey, the whine of Mrs. Raddle, the sporting cigar-gestures of the medical student Jack Hopkins, the delicious unconscious cockney humor of the narrator of "Mr. Chops," the impressive drama of the episode from *A Tale of Two Cities*. Inanimate objects corporealized with a movement of the arms or hands or shoulders: a guillotine, a rocking horse, an epergne. All exquisitely shaded and timed, down to a flicker of the eyeball, a muted dying fall of the voice. Dickens once said that before risking the public stage he had rehearsed one of his readings ("Dr. Marigold") two hundred times. Mr. Williams must have worked almost as hard.

And the effect on the audience? A small but sizable portion, displaying the rudeness so marked in a certain type of ultra-smart first-night New Yorker, left as soon as Mr. Williams had finished casting his pearls before them. They crowded down the aisles even as he, with an aplomb just faintly pointed, I fancied, with irony, was delivering his, or rather Dickens', curtain speech. This group, it was clear, had all along been stoically resisting Mr. Williams. Perhaps they had been nursing a dull indignation at the mere idea of one man doing well what a score of fancy actors, hip-deep in lights, scenery, props and "production," would do grossly. For them this was a "stunt."

The rest of us were interested, some to the point of enthrallment. I think we were unaware that we were being tested. We were being tried, to determine whether there still lived in a mid-twentieth-century audience the vestigial faculty of attention, the ability simply to listen to sound English prose delivered without benefit of paraphernalia. An old-fashioned art—call it reading, recitation, declamation—was being revived before an assemblage that had for years or decades been fed on the simplicities and topicalities of radio and television, or on the artful bounce and tempo, the "stars" and "personalities" of stage and screen.

I think most of us sensed a mysterious stir of joy, as if we had discovered a use for a muscle long since semi-atrophied. Though on a higher level, it was the satisfaction children two generations ago felt by the chimney corner as the members of the family read aloud in turn, creating entertainment out of themselves.

I had had the same sensation a few days before, listening to Charles Laughton at New York's Town Hall in a series of readings that, to the astonishment of the theater-wise, have been so successful throughout the country. Mr. Laughton is of course an excellent actor, as his memorable performance with the First Drama Quartette attested. For all his abilities, however, Mr. Laughton's performance was hardly in a class with that of Mr. Williams.

Using a severely formal art, Mr. Williams re-created a personality, Dickens, and an epoch, the Victorian. With obvious relish Mr. Laughton played himself, treating the audience pretty much as though it consisted of a covey of Helen Hokinson's amiable ladies. Jovial and arch, not above an occasional giggle, he spoke of "Larry" Olivier and "Charlie" Boyer, commenting on his material with chatty informality, quite unconscious of the fact that it takes two to make an intimacy.

He waded joyfully through a purple patch out of Thomas Wolfe. He read a sincere but rather callow confession of religious faith by an eminent sculptor friend. He exuded corny bits from movies (Bligh, *Rembrandt*) and hammed up the rehearsal scene from *A Midsummer Night's Dream*.

On the other hand, in a long selection from *Pickwick* ("Christmas at Manor Farm"), he was superb. With the Old Testament story of Shadrach, Meshach, and Abednego, he did remarkable things. An unfamiliar Lincoln speech was vastly effective, and his Gettysburg Address had great quiet and dignity.

It does not really matter that Mr. Laughton's platform style (he is hardly built for the kittenish) may not charm all comers. What is important is that he and Mr. Williams are making a noble and successful effort to revive the almost-lost art of reading or reciting aloud.

Some years ago a similar attempt was made in England. I learned about it from John Masefield's autobiographical memoir *So Long to Learn*. This is mainly a record of the early impressions that created the temperament of a romantic poet. A large part of it, however, deals with the inception and growth from 1923 to 1930 of the Oxford Recitations. In these contests artists in oral speech from all over the British Isles competed in the reading of great verse before juries of experts, including poets such as Mr. Masefield himself. From these public recitations flowed a general sharpening of interest in good poetry; the training of a corps of professional reciters, capable of giving delight to large audiences anywhere in the English-speaking world; a fresh enthusiasm for English beautifully spoken; and a general spread of the notion of reading aloud.

Suppose, not impossibly, that something of the same sort were done here, perhaps under the aegis of a great university. Perhaps a minor renaissance might result, a renaissance of reading that would spread to radio and TV (remember Alexander Woollcott) and do something to compensate for the absence of a nationwide theater. Would it not also work subtly against that degradation of our fair English speech of which so many of us are conscious? Would it not supply some slight counterweight to the emphasis on the trivial and the topical so manifest in our mechanized entertainment? Best of all, might it not encourage us to become our own readers-aloud, helping to make our centrifugal homes what they once were, a kind of informal playhouse?

Reflections on Musical Comedy

EARLY in January, 1952, Broadway witnessed a revival of *Pal Joey*. It seems hardly possible that only eleven years had passed since *Pal Joey*, opening at the Ethel Barrymore Theatre, made musical comedy not only turn over in its grave but throw off the graveclothes and walk friskily out of the cemetery. In the history of the arts that night of Christmas, 1940, may come to be as notable a date as February 25, 1830, when the première of Hugo's *Hernani* marked the victory of the embattled French Romantic school; or the night of May 29, 1913, when Stravinsky's *Le Sacre du Printemps* declared in percussive tones that modern music was here to stay; or, in that same *annus mirabilis*, the opening of the Armory Show, when Marcel Duchamp's *Nude* first descended her staircase and an enchanted or enraged public met abstract art face to cube.

In his notes to a fresh recording of the songs from *Pal Joey*, Richard Rodgers, composer of the permanently delightful music, recalls its première. "The effect on the public was startling, to say the least. Approximately one-half of the first-night audience applauded wildly while the other half sat there in stony, stunned silence. The press the next day reacted in somewhat the same ratio, with those in favor slightly in the lead." Such a ferocious division of opinion often marks

280

a turning point in the career of any art (see *Hernani*, etc.),
and its occurrence is an all-round good thing.

There were giants before Agamemnon, and there had been
unconventional musicals before *Pal Joey*—notably *Of Thee
I Sing*. But John O'Hara's book and Lorenz Hart's lyrics,
brass dissolved in vitriol, really ticked off the end of the gag-
and-girlie show.

The attack was all-out. As backgrounds *Pal Joey* offered
appallingly convincing honky-tonks, night clubs, and over-
employed bedrooms. The cast was outcast: an assortment of
heels, rats, and frail ladies. The only unspotted character was
also a female dolt of the first order. The heroine stacked up
as a nymph of fairly mature charms, her world view neatly
bounded by four posts and a mattress. By the exercise of his
natural endowments the go-get-her hero extracted large sums
of cash from this lady, the plot revolving around this touching interchange of gifts.

The lyrics matched the book. One celebrated Joey's favorite sport, quail hunting. Another sang the praises of a "little
den of iniquity." Still another dwelt on the envy with which
the heroine regarded the contiguous relationship between
Joey and Joey's trousers. If, as someone has said, vulgarity
conceals something whereas coarseness reveals something,
then these lyrics were coarse but not vulgar, being supreme
examples of what can only be termed single *entendre*.

In those days the word for *Pal Joey* was "mature"—a word
characteristic of any period forced to grow up beyond its
intelligence. The judgment needs qualification. Maturity is
not necessarily identical with the discovery, however firmly
announced, that as a general thing the human race is in
favor of sex. Still, compared to its mentally innocent predecessors, *Pal Joey* was grown up. Its cynicism may have been un-
wholesome ("Can you draw sweet water from a foul well?"

worried Brooks Atkinson). Nevertheless, that cynicism lay closer to certain of the facts of life than the sentimentality of the routine musical lay to any of them.

The difference between the O'Hara-Hart-Rodgers combination and the ordinary team of cheerful hacks was that while both had a legitimate desire to make money, the first was also interested in compelling words, songs, and dances to say something. In so doing they declared implicitly that the butter-and-egg audience was becoming a thing of the past.

The revolution was on. It was taken over and organized on a systematic basis by Rodgers and Hammerstein. Their work, in addition to enchanting millions, has permanently changed the meaning of the term "musical comedy." The musical comedy turns into the musical play. The form is not profoundly different; the content is. That content, for all the high jinks and pretty tunes, is astonishingly serious, even weighty. The underestimated *Allegro* says much the same thing as *Death of a Salesman*. The underlying theme of *South Pacific* is not romantic love but, strange to say, race and color prejudice. As for *The King and I*, one may indeed fairly ask whether the delicate structure of the musical play was sturdy enough to bear the burden of reflection with which it was laden—for what *The King and I* was about was nothing more or less than the conflicting claims of freedom and authority. We're a long, long way from the Shuberts.

What marks the work of Rodgers and Hammerstein (and Joshua Logan) is that while they took over the realism of *Pal Joey*, they quietly veered away from its cynicism. The simple-minded carnality of "There is Nothing Like a Dame" has little in common with the sensual obsession of "Bewitched, Bothered and Bewildered." (I refer to the original lyrics of the latter, not the vacuum-cleaned versions of the air waves.)

It is not only that Mr. Hammerstein's temperament is naturally sunnier than was Larry Hart's. The difference has to do with a change in our temper as a people. With the coming of the forties (and the war) the whole ideal of "sophistication" had the air let out of it. We were now compelled to grow up for real. The "knowingness" of *Pal Joey* began to seem very unlike true knowledge. The slick wisdom of the opportunist began to seem inopportune. The lessons any nubile human being can learn in a boudoir began to seem trivial compared with the lessons the whole world was being forced to learn on a battlefield.

And so, listening to this recording of *Pal Joey*, or rereading in the handsome *Rodgers and Hart Song Book* some of the diabolically clever lyrics of Larry Hart, one is filled with an odd mixture of emotions. Shock, embarrassment, and wistfulness mingle easily.

Some shock there is bound to be, for the Rodgers-Hammerstein purified musical comedy, with its stress on the wholesome, has weaned us away from the indiscretions, with their mild suggestion of the street corner, of the Larry Hart school. One feels some embarrassment, too, the embarrassment that comes of listening to the small boy saying something shocking in the drawing room.

And, along with this shock and embarrassment, goes a kind of wistfulness. In retrospect the twenties and thirties seem to assume a certain coloration of innocence. In those far-off days people, some of them, seem to have had a pure-hearted, shining faith that somehow the good life and the "good time" were connected, that in the release of inhibitions (another favorite word of the time) lay the passport to freedom. Now we know that freedom is a thing much harder won, much more dearly bought. And so we feel ourselves wiser than the Noel Cowards and the Larry Harts of that

day, with their reliance on gaiety and cleverness, their confidence in trick rhymes and trickier immoralities. Wiser?
Perhaps we are—but also a little sadder. They may have
been silly and excessive, those odd, faraway People of Be-
tween-the-Wars, but they enjoyed their silliness and their
excess. Never again in our lifetime will we be able to feel
the innocent joy of sheer impudence. Only once can the first
glass of champagne be drunk. They who lived in the era
that found a sort of climax in *Pal Joey* thought of themselves
as part of a world of unfettered and perhaps slightly wicked
freedom. To us, looking back a little ruefully, they seem to
be singing and dancing in a vernal wood stirred by the airs
of Arcadia.

Judy and Juan

A. E. HOUSMAN once said he felt confident a line of poetry was good if reading it made the skin of his face prickle. A similar phenomenon has often been noted in the theater. When something great is happening onstage you can almost feel a kind of electrical discharge from the audience. This is generated only when the attention is so condensed, so absolute, and so uniform that it creates a force peculiar to itself.

In the past I have felt this several times. I felt it during almost the entire performance of Laurence Olivier in *Oedipus Rex*. I felt it again in *Henry IV, Part II*, when Olivier pierced you with his Justice Shallow. I felt it once more during many moments of Thornton Wilder's *Our Town*, which I am persuaded will some day be ranked as the finest American play yet written.

Twice in two weeks during 1952 I sensed this powerful vibration. I felt it rise from an audience that had come to hear and see Judy Garland. I felt it rise from a quite different audience that had gathered to listen to the First Drama Quartette perform, for the first time on this continent, Bernard Shaw's extra and presumably unactable dream sequence from *Man and Superman* entitled "Don Juan in Hell."

Judy Garland is a pop singer and her songs are frankly pop songs. The Quartette, on the other hand, is a group of burnished actors, manipulating material about as intellectually complicated as the modern stage can handle. Yet it would be an error to declare the first inferior as a dramatic performance to the second. Both worked the miracle of the playhouse. Both enforced the attention of the audience, an attention condensed, absolute, and uniform. Both transformed that audience into something beyond and above the separate selves of which it was made.

I saw Judy at the Palace Theatre, where she was being held over for an unprecedented, indefinite run. Her act climaxed a program of sound, old-fashioned vaudeville. Eight amiable young male assistants once or twice trotted quite nicely around the stage to give her a chance to change costume, but for most of the forty-five minutes—in vaudeville that's eternity—it was Judy Garland, and nothing but.

She led off with a song about the great performers who have played the Palace in the past. Many vaudeville stars have sung similar nostalgic ditties—it's part of the tradition, and a very good one. She sang half a dozen of the melodies, gay or sad, that she had introduced in various Metro-Goldwyn-Mayer musicals and which make it barely possible to remember those high-budget monstrosities without excessive pain. Assisted by an agile male partner, Jack McClendon, she did the "We're a Couple of Swells" tramp dance—the one she used to do with Fred Astaire. She finished—how else?—with "Over the Rainbow." By that time you were pretty well convinced that Judy Garland could sing anything except suggestive songs and the phonier kind of operatic aria.

From time to time she talked with, not to, the audience. She kidded herself about her advancing age and increased poundage. (Yes, she's put a little on, but her legs are still as beautifully and smoothly turned as a couplet by Alexander Pope.) With a comic sigh she removed her shoes and moved into the heart of every woman in the theater. She mopped

her face candidly with a red silk handkerchief. And she
drank a glass of water, first offering it to her audience with
a tiny comic gesture so sweet that no trace of contrivance
clung to it.

Well, that was all. Where lay the magic? Why did we
grow silent, self-forgetting, our faces lit as with so many
candles, our eyes glittering with unregarded tears? Why did
we call her back again and again and again, not as if she
had been giving a good performance, but as if she had been
offering salvation?

Some of the effect may be traceable to the extraneous
drama of Judy's personal life. After a period of too highly
publicized grief and failure and misfortune, this was her
comeback. Of *course* we wanted her to be wonderful, as if
her triumphs could somehow help to wipe out our own sorrows and weaknesses. But there was more to it than that.

Much more. As we listened to her voice, with its unbelievable marriage of volume and control, as we watched her, in
her tattered tramp costume, telling the most delicious jokes
with arms, legs, head, and eyes, we forgot—and this is the
acid test—who she was, and indeed who we were ourselves.
As with all true clowns (for Judy Garland is as fine a clown
as she is a singer) she seemed to be neither male nor female,
young nor old, pretty nor plain. She had no "glamour," only
magic. She was gaiety itself, yearning itself, fun itself. She
expressed a few simple, common feelings so purely that they
floated about in the dark theater, bodiless, as if detached
from any specific personality. She wasn't being judged or
enjoyed, not even watched or heard. She was only being felt,
as one feels the quiet run of one's own blood, the shiver of
the spine, Housman's prickle of the skin. And when, looking
about eighteen inches high, sitting hunched over the stage
apron with only a tiny spotlight pinpointing her elf face, she

breathed the last phrases of "Over the Rainbow" and cried
out its universal, unanswerable query, "Why can't I?" it
was as though the bewildered hearts of all the people in the
world had moved quietly together and become one, shaking
in Judy's throat, and there breaking.

A week or so later I listened to Charles Laughton, Charles
Boyer, Cedric Hardwicke, and Agnes Moorehead, compris-
ing the First Drama Quartette, as they half read, half talked
Shaw's two-hour dialogue, published as a sort of interlude
within *Man and Superman* and known as "Don Juan in Hell."
My mind went back to Judy Garland. She had been pure
feeling. Here was something quite other—pure, relentless
mental brilliance. Nothing Judy had done or said or sung
could not have been felt by any child of nine, if only in anticipation, or by any man or woman of ninety, if only in
memory or regret. And here was Shaw at his most unconcessive, writing, if ever man wrote, for a highly intelligent
posterity.

Yet the same lightning struck both audiences. Our emotions, all tender and alive, had lain cupped in Judy's hands,
cradled in her voice. And here our minds, all tense and eager,
followed so closely upon Shaw's argument that they, too,
seemed to leave their local habitations and become one with
the fountain play of the dramatist's brain. In both cases
attention was so condensed, so absolute, so uniform as to
become raptness, the feeling of being unexpectedly greater
than oneself.

This is the fresh, immemorial miracle of art, the art of the
theater no less than other arts. How was it accomplished?
In both cases the material was familiar—for no one can main-
tain that any great novelty still attaches to Shaw's views on
the shortcomings of human nature, or his notion of woman

as hunter and man as quarry (with both the prey of the biology of the Life Force), or his conception of the inferior rank of beauty and pleasure, or his vision of mankind as hungering to surpass itself in ever deeper and broader mental self-consciousness.

Here the secret of the miracle lay in the presentation. This was radical in the sense that it went to the root of the matter. The root only. No foliage.

The scene was Hell, but Hell was a bare stage, furnished with four high stools, four chairs, four microphones, four lecterns on which reposed, quite brazenly, four typed playscripts. The characters were not characters but minds—four separated sections of Shaw's brain. There was Donna Ana (Agnes Moorehead), clothed in an evening gown; there were her former lover Don Juan (Charles Boyer), the Devil (Charles Laughton), and the Statue of Donna Ana's father (Cedric Hardwicke)—all dressed in moderately impeccable dinner coats. There was no change of scene, no movement, no opening and closing of doors, no exits or entrances, no lighting effects, no orchestra, no "realism," no "production." Though the parts had been fairly well memorized, the actors followed their scripts, unconcernedly turning the pages as the play progressed. On occasion Mr. Hardwicke made vast comic play with his tortoise-shell spectacles. That comprised the "action." Four beautiful voices, whose every intonation and minuscule rise or fall breathed understanding. Two hours of dazzling epigrams and closely knit sinuosities of abstract thought. One dead man's mind galvanizing the whole. Beyond this, nothing—that is, nothing to distract your attention from the play.

The result: great theater—and the audience knew it. Nobody sighed for a plot. Nobody wanted anything to happen. Nobody longed for beautiful costumes or carefully designed stage sets. The "theater" was not missed because we were being given something far more dramatic than the "theater" —the play of life itself, in this case one of the most fascinating kinds of play, the play of the life of the mind. It mattered little whether we agreed or disagreed with Shaw's ideas. The point was that those ideas were being projected with such clarity of profile and such simplicity that the leaping joy of following them, becoming a pro tem part of them, dominated the earth-tethered faculty of mere criticism.

This was especially marked during Boyer's reading—in both senses—of Don Juan's great rhetorical outburst, in which he excoriates mankind. I had always thought of Boyer as a movie actor—that is, not really an actor at all. I could not have been stupider. He is a versatile and intelligent artist, and a law should be passed exiling him forever from the country of the camera. For about eight minutes, without a break, Boyer-Shaw insulted the audience, railed at our folly, stripped us of our pretenses, unmasked our lies, withered us with wit, until we were left crawling like insects on the floor of the very cellar of the universe. At the end of the speech our applause erupted like a volcano. Instead of feeling resentful or depressed, we were updrawn into delight, the delight that comes of the recognition of truth. And upon this was imposed the superdelight that came of our ability to follow, almost as if we were so many Shaws ourselves, the convoluted art of the demonstration of that truth.

Judy Garland at the Palace, Don Juan in Hell: polar opposites in many ways, yet both supplying evidence that great theater is founded, not on "production," but merely on words, arranged in the best possible order and spoken or sung in the best possible way; on human beings who, like Judy Garland, are passionate in themselves, or, like these four actors, sincere, alert conduits for the passion of another greater than themselves.

The theater dead? I have rarely seen it more alive than when Judy Garland, crouched on the edge of the stage in a darkened vaudeville house that had seen a thousand animal acts and brassy comedians, voiced a lost child's pitiful lament; than when three men and a woman, assisted by nothing but their brains and throat boxes, thought aloud for two solid hours while we animal creatures joyed in the revelation that we were also rational souls.

"Ladies and Gentlemen, Your Host—"

THE LYRIC-WRITER Gene Buck used to be fond of starting a festive evening's proceedings with his Steeplechase grin and the words "I am merely the toastmaster—the punk that sets off the fireworks." Inelegant but apt. The Moderator (airwave English: Your Host) is a creature at once lowly and useful. I invite a moment's consideration of this harmless, necessary drudge.

I speak as an M.C. of twenty years' standing and sitting. At benefits and banquets, on radio and television shows I have practiced to excess the art of moderation. I have introduced five thousand people who need no introduction to this audience. I have passed untold man-hours being genial. And so today I am master of a profession which in my more melancholy moments I range about midway between that of the bubblegum chewer and that of the bathroom baritone.

There *are* M.C.'s of a hue more vivid than my own. There is the Stentor of the giveaway (*He's* GOT *it, folks!!*), honorable descendant of the medicine-show barker, capable of generating every sixty seconds as much excitement as would normally greet an announcement that the first interplanetary flight had been completed. There is the folksy M.C. who gets down on all fours with his guests. There is the hearty M.C. whose voice is a brisk rubdown. There is the rapid-fire, pre-
292

pared-gag M.C. who is a hard-working vaudevillian doing his best to adapt himself to a new medium.

My plumage cannot hope to rival theirs. I am but a good gray moderator of the standard variety, suitable for the family trade, mild-mannered, ordinary-voiced. I am supposed to represent the audience. But as no one knows who or what the audience is, an M.C. like myself is best off without distinguishing marks. His talent lies in showing none. Like a point he has position, indeed a central one, but no dimension. Careful never to overstep the thin line separating smoothness from nullity, he is generally acceptable and, with more brains, would make a middling-good president of a very small freshwater college.

In my present trade—I preside, when hired, over TV and radio shows—the most important requirement is the ability to tell time. Any man who can simultaneously move his lower jaw and furtively eye a stopwatch may well awake some morning to find himself an M.C. Once he has learned how to get the show off the air at 28.30, all he needs is a network, a sponsor, and a half-hour not opposite *Dragnet*.

Biting the mike that feeds me? Not in the least. Sometimes, eavesdropping on my own copious banalities, I reflect that few men lead lives of less quiet desperation. But for the most part I enjoy my work, do it as well as I can, and respect it for what it is. That doesn't mean, however, that I must respect it for what it is not.

My kind of M.C. (your genial host) makes no pretense of being a real entertainer. He does not even do what is often claimed for him—hold the show together. That is done by a group of invisible, almost supernatural beings: producer, director, cameramen.

If he *seems* to hold the show together he is probably not a real M.C. Groucho Marx, for instance, does not hold the show together. He *is* the show. His guests are but the occasions of his wit; he passes his entire public life among straight-men. Bowing to the current fashion that frowns on the non-gim-micked stand-up comic, he has merely supplied his mono-logue with built-in interruptions. Groucho is no M.C. Groucho is an artist, and I don't mean a television artist but a real one, which means that on the whole he is himself.

The M.C. is not quite himself. (In the days when I worked with Oscar, whose mike suffered from permanent Levant-fright, I was often beside myself, but that's not the same thing.) The M.C. is not precisely dishonest but he is con-tinually undergoing the beveling, leveling process of per-sonality-attrition that is the occupational hazard of those who must be all things to all men. He's not a fake but he is a bit artificial—in a nice way, of course. If seeing is believing, M.C.'ing is often make-believing.

Essentially the M.C. is a convention born of the special needs of mass entertainment. The average TV or radio variety show is part human, part machine. Its mechanical elements are assembled like a motorcar. The human element has to shine through the mechanism. The ideal M.C. is one who, without losing touch with this human element, keeps a fore-man's eye on the moving parts of his vehicle, oils them, ad-justs their speed, reduces excess vibration, and arrests them in the required split second. Within this pattern of entertain-ment-plus-engineering he performs his proper, necessary, and on the whole harmless function.

For example: one small cog in the machinery of most variety and panel shows is the presumption that no one has a last name. This convention has a psychological basis con-nected with the nature of a mass audience. The audience in a hall or theater is a true audience. It is a group separated by observable space and tangible matter from the people onstage. But on the air this formal separation does not exist. In reality there *is* no audience. There are only some millions of groups in millions of living rooms who through the courtesy of Marconi feel themselves in immediate contact with the performers. This immediacy—literally an absence of medium—is symbolized by the use of first names among the entertainers. The informality corresponds roughly to the informality of the spatial relationship between entertainer and viewer or listener.

Some years ago, M.C.'ing *Information Please,* I decided that this informality was ill-advised. It seemed discourteous for Mr. Adams, Mr. Kieran, Mr. Levant, and myself to call each other Frank, John, Oscar, and Kip before millions of utter strangers, however amiable. For ten years, therefore, with occasional lapses, we called each other Mister. On *Information Please* this worked. People (in those days they were known as people, not folks) liked it. They *wanted* to feel a certain distance between themselves and the panel. The experts really *were* experts, demonstrably superior men. The audience liked to have the experts' dignity marked by the emblematic use, often humorous of course, of the formal mode of address.

On the TV program *This Is Show Business* I tried the same thing. No dice. I floundered back and forth between Mr. Levenson and Sam, Mr. Kaufman and George. Finally I tried to think the thing out. *This Is Show Business* was by ordinary TV standards a fairly original show. Still it was a far more standardized product than *Information Please*. It was so machined as to be unable to tolerate too much deviation from the norm. The one-big-happy-family pattern demanded—what I should have realized earlier—the first-name convention.

On any future variety or quiz show to which I may be

attached I intend to obey this convention. Not because I
think it a gracious one, for I don't, but because it is part and
parcel of standard mass entertainment. The machine has its
own laws. If you don't want to obey them, don't monkey with
the machinery.

M.C.'s on dramatic shows must fall in with another requirement of the machine. They must speak "narration" English. This, like Announcer's English, is a highly specialized
language. It is built up tenderly, cliché by cliché. It is so
terse that naturalness of expression must be sacrificed. Finally
it is infected with a toniness that the ad-agency brain identifies with distinction of style. Consequently a truly interesting
personality such as Robert Montgomery is made to sound,
as he walks through his M.C. chores, like a vocal robot.

Nothing can be done about this. Perhaps nothing should,
for we are now quite comfortably conditioned against genuine English on the air, and any wholesale use of it might
prove decidedly annoying. For example, the speech Dr.
Lyman Bryson, M.C. of *Invitation to Learning*, uses is personal, informal, with not a punch in a paragraph. But no
advertising agency in its right mind, a somewhat restricted
environment, would or should stand for it. It does not have
the mechanical efficiency of Agency or Announcer's English.
It is too organic. Announcements are safe. Real talk is
dangerous.

What makes my trade interesting to me is first that it
offers a living, second that it offers a challenge. The challenge is this: to satisfy, by producing a smooth show, the
legitimate demands of the machine and at the same time to
outwit it by giving the audience the suggestion of real life,
real laughter, and real character. To do only the first is
profitable but a little monotonous. To do only the second is

quixotic. Mass entertainment cannot afford to confine itself exclusively to creating sensations of actuality. But a mixture of the two is often feasible and gives the M.C. whatever esthetic pleasure the poor soul gets.

Now the sponsor is paying generously for a satisfactory mechanical performance certified to sell his product. He's entitled to get what he's paying for. Any M.C. who does not admit that his first obligation is to his sponsor is a trouble-maker and should go in for social work. But mass entertainment is a funny business. Everyone knows who the sponsor is, but no one is sure who the boss is. The sponsor meets the payroll but that doesn't make him the boss. The boss is the one who lays down the rules of entertainment. But who does this? Sponsor, agency, network, producer, director, and even audience—all do certain kinds of bossing at different times and in different ways. Amid this fine chaos the wily old M.C. can slip in and occasionally do a little bossing himself. But he must be as unobtrusive as a chameleon on a branch.

Let me illustrate. W. C. Fields once remarked of sex that there may be some things better and some things worse, but there's nothing exactly like it. There have been better radio shows than *Information Please* and I'm positive there have been worse, but there's never been anything exactly like it. It was unlike most quiz shows in two respects. First, the questions, chosen by producer Dan Golenpaul with skill and edited with humor, were generally interesting to the literate audience, of whom there were and are many millions. Second, the experts were not smart showmen but complex, quick-witted human beings. Wisely Mr. Golenpaul gave them their heads, which happened to be good ones.

In theory my job was to pose the questions and rate the answers. In practice I found that this was not my job at all. My real task was to get four lively minds, all with a low boredom threshold, *interested* in the questions. Merely answering them correctly (or incorrectly, a point of quite minor importance) engaged their memories but not their minds. But it was their minds as much as their memories that amused the audience. I had to prevent them from degenerating into dull answering machines.

To do this I was forced to goad them, tease them, set them arguing, poke them into free association, stimulate them to bits of autobiography, even in some cases to take their minds *off* the questions. The result was that a quiz show turned into something better. It turned into a four-man conversation, sometimes good, sometimes ragged, always real. I was well aware that my own talents were as nothing compared with those of Frank Adams, Oscar Levant, or John Kieran. But I was also well aware that I was so placed as to be able to do one thing better than they could do it themselves. That one thing was to prod them into being Adams, Levant, and Kieran.

At the same time I had to remain comparatively characterless, a task which, considering their colorful temperaments, presented few difficulties for me. Finally I was being paid to assure the show's mechanical efficiency. A minimum number of questions must be asked, each of the quartet must have his fair chance to shine or flop, fluffs must be covered, incomplete statements completed, a certain number of audience laughs secured, and so on. Mere chauffeuring, but necessary.

Once in a while I felt that I had contributed my small mite to a successful performance. That is, with the aid of a bag of professional tricks, I had persuaded three intelligent men and quite frequently an intelligent guest to talk almost as well as if they were not on the air.

My next chore, *This Is Show Business*, posed a different

problem. The variety component was standard: dancer, comic, singer. They added up to about half of the show's appeal. The other half was supplied by three show-business "experts": the witty playwright George S. Kaufman, the anecdotal family humorist Sam Levenson, and a visiting fire-woman. This trio ad-libbed comment teeing-off from some question asked by each of the three entertainers.

For this ad-libbing the average time available was 8 minutes, 40 seconds for each half-hour program. This had to be split fairly among the three panelists. That meant little or no conversation. As for the questions, they were usually interesting enough but hardly of a nature to draw profundities from the panel. The M.C. had little to do. I kept the machinery going, but I.B.M. could have devised a little plastic man to do it as well. The panel did most of the talking. Indeed on those occasions when we had a lovely Gabor sister as a guest, I could hardly get a word in edgewise. For the most part I remained, if I may modify Sir James Mackintosh's well-known words about the House of Commons, in a wise and toastmasterly inactivity.

All I could do was what any adequate M.C. would have done in my seat. I sharpened for the audience the personalities of Mr. Kaufman and Mr. Levenson. I ignited a mock feud. From week to week I used as running gags their peculiarities, of which each had a complete set. Standard procedure, of course—still, it allowed me a little play. Not that Mr. K. and Mr. L. were unable to express their temperaments without me. But I was Mother's Little Helper.

During the summer of 1954 I was hired for eight weeks to M.C. a panel show. It was one of those game-shows built around a comic who is both inanimate and unpaid. The comic is the "answer" to certain clues, an answer to which the audience but not the panel is privy. The theory back of this kind of show is sound: most laughs for least dollars. The laughs come from the unconscious and ludicrous errors made by the panelists in their efforts to get the answer. You know.

Here the game was the thing. Not the panelists, though they were all amusing and agreeable people. Certainly not the M.C. The latter's job is clear. He must see that the game is played well, fast, comprehensibly. Acting as audience-surrogate, he must point up the panel's blunders. At the same time he must encourage them and keep them happy. That's the setup.

The show was neither bad nor good. It failed for a number of reasons, one of them being that, as it progressed, it inclined more and more to the mechanical as against the spontaneous. This is natural enough: the machine is "dependable," the human being an unknown and therefore suspicious quantity.

If my trade requires so little talent, it may well be asked why there are so few of us. Comics come by the hundreds, singers by the thousands, M.C.'s by the dozens. Why?

Good M.C.'s of the order of Steve Allen, Alistair Cooke, and John Daly are rare, not because they are geniuses but because they must combine in proper balance a fairly large number of necessary abilities. An ambitious tyro is apt to have one or more of these abilities, often in high degree. But the chances of his having all of them are small. What are they?

1. Time-sense.

2. Natural warmth of manner, under which lies

3. Coolness of mind capable of coping with the minor accidents that pop up on any show.

4. Ability to make most of the audience tolerate or even mildly like him over a long time-period. But he should not be *too* much liked because he must have the

5. Ability to subordinate himself to other performers without losing his

6. Ability to dominate them when the interests of the show demand it. This connects with his

7. Possession of a constant feeling for the structure of the program as a whole, so that each segment may be given its proper weight.

8. A nonprofessional sense of humor which works for smiles, not laughs.

9. Ability to fill a hole in the air—5 seconds, 20 seconds, 60 seconds—with immediate chatter, any kind as long as it is noise cut up into words. This ability is common: mid-twentieth-century mass entertainment produces the ad-libber in wholesale lots.

10. Good manners. Of the whole lot this is the hardest quality to find in the profession. Entertainment genius links psychologically with exhibitionism, not restraint.

11. Class. This is a show-business word. Nobody knows what it means but to a greater or less degree the competent M.C. has it. I think class (in an M.C.; it's a very different thing in a true entertainer) is what the audience feels when the M.C. possesses these ten abilities in equilibrium. But, beyond this, class is an X-quality that seems to be tied up with at least a moderate amount of mental cultivation. That does not mean that the M.C. is learned or even well educated. It merely means that his manner, choice of words, intonation appear to suggest some connection with a world that, oddly enough, is supposed to have nothing to do with mass entertainment. The presumably non-intellectual pop audience seems to like an occasional suggestion of intellectual good manners. Many network and agency executives find this infuriating.

Remember, these eleven abilities do not make up a great

showman or even necessarily a good one. All the M.C.'s now laboring in the TV vineyards do not in combination possess the talent Ethel Merman contains in her little finger. They're minor gifts, highly specialized, unexciting, and, quite properly, never rewarded with top money.

But, such as they are, they make up, ladies and gentlemen, your host.

The Reading Lamp

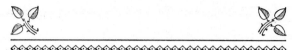

The Book-Reviewing Business

FOR MORE than fifteen years I made a living as a reviewer of new books, and still, from time to time, like an old firehorse, respond automatically to the clang of the publishers' announcements.

I propose to talk for a few pages about this odd business. Note the word "business." I employ it as a wedge with which to separate book reviewing from literary criticism. Literary criticism is an art, like the writing of tragedies or the making of love, and, similarly, does not pay. Book reviewing is a device for earning a living, one of the many weird results of Gutenberg's invention. Movable type made books too easy to publish. Some sort of sieve had to be interposed between printer and public. The reviewer is that sieve, a generally honest, usually uninspired, and mildly useful sieve. My colleagues and myself are often called critics, a consequence of the amiable national trait that turns Kentuckians into colonels and the corner druggist into Doc. But true literary criticism is a subtle and venerable art, going back to the ancient Hindoos, who doubtless wrote sanskriticism. Aristotle was the first great literary Pooh-Bah. He had no more charm than an old knothole, but the things he said about narrative and drama are so sensible that they're still useful today. Aristotle had a first-rate mind, which is what most really good literary critics have, or something pretty near it. You can number the top-notchers on your fingers and toes—that's the way I taught my small son to count: Aristotle, Horace, Coleridge, Lessing, Sainte-Beuve, Taine, Goethe, Arnold, Shaw (one of the greatest), and a few others. In our own time and nation, literary criticism is almost a lost art, partly because no one except a few other literary critics cares to read it. A real literary critic is a whole man exercising his wholeness through the accidental medium of books and authors. A reviewer is not a whole man. He is that partial man, an expert. All experts are monsters.

Let's examine the monster.

We must first of all remember that reading maketh not a full man, despite Bacon. I suppose I have read five or ten thousand books—it doesn't matter which—in the last few decades. Every so often I catch myself wondering whether I wouldn't be a sight wiser if I had read only fifteen, and they the right ones. You see, a reviewer does not read to instruct himself. If he remembered even a moderate quantum of what he read, he would soon be unfit for his job. Forced to comment on book Z, he would at once recollect everything that books A to Y, previously reviewed, contained that might throw light on Z. This is not the mental attitude that makes for useful book reviewing. As a matter of fact, what the reviewer should have above all things is a kind of mental virginity, a continual capacity to react freshly. I said that he was an expert. He is. He is an expert in surprisability. The poor fool is always looking forward to the next book.

This does not mean the reviewer has the memory of a moron. He doubtless remembers something of what he has read, but not enough to handicap him. His mind is not so much well stocked as well indexed. If challenged, I think I could tell you the authors and titles of the three or four best books of the last ten years dealing with the ancient Maya civilization. I can even make a fair fist at grading the books in the order of their completeness, authority, and readability. But what I don't know about the Mayans in the way of real information would fill several volumes and has done so.

The reviewer, then, granting him any mind at all, has a fresh one. The critic Frank Moore Colby held a different point of view. In 1921 he wrote a little piece from which I quote:

Beans Again

If a man had for one day a purée of beans, and the next day *haricots verts,* and then in daily succession bean soup, bean salad, butter beans, lima, black, navy, Boston baked, and kidney beans, and then back to purée and all over again, he would not be in the relation of the general eater to food. Nor would he be in the relation of a general reader to books. But he would be in the relation of a reviewer toward novels. He would soon perceive that the relation was neither normal nor desirable, and he would take measures, violent if need be, to change it. He would not say on his navy-bean day that they were as brisk and stirring little beans of the sea as he could recall in his recent eating. He would say grimly, "Beans again," and he would take prompt steps to intermit this abominable procession of bean dishes.

If change for any reason were impossible he would either conceive a personal hatred toward all beans that would make him unjust to any bean however meritorious, or he would acquire a mad indiscriminateness of acquiescence and any bean might please. And his judgment would be in either case an unsafe guide for general eaters.

This, I believe, is what happens to almost all reviewers of fiction after a certain time, and it accounts satisfactorily for various phenomena that are often attributed to a baser cause. It is the custom at certain intervals to denounce reviewers for their motives. They are called venal and they are called cowardly by turns. They are blamed for having low standards or no standards at all. I think their defects are due chiefly to the nature of their calling; that they suffer from an occupational disease.

Now, I can understand why Colby felt this way. He could afford to be superior. He was an encyclopedia editor, which is several cuts above a reviewer. But his beans-again notion, though plausible, is not cogent. The truth is, that a competent reviewer's stomach does not summon up remembrance of beans past. Though there are exceptions he does not hail or damn novels out of a kind of hysteria of surfeit. If he makes a stupid judgment it is simply because his judgment is stupid. It may be stupid for a variety of reasons, no one of which will have anything to do with the fact that he reads half a dozen novels a week. In other words, a jaded reviewer sooner or later realizes that he is not a good reviewer, and tries to get another job. A good reviewer is a perennially fresh hack.

But this doesn't work out 100 per cent of the time. For example, I confess that I no longer look forward to next week's American historical novel with any bridegroom eagerness. I have read too many such. I am positive that they (not I, you see) have slipped into a groove, are standardized products, and therefore there is nothing helpful I can say about them.

Never to be bored is merely an active form of imbecility. Do not trust the man who is "interested in everything." He is covering up some fearful abyss of spiritual vacancy. Ennui, felt on the proper occasions, is a sign of intelligence. All this is by way of saying that, of course, no reviewer is interested in every book he reads. He should have the ability to be bored, even if this ability is much feebler than his ability not to be bored. A competent reviewer knows his blind spots, tries to counteract them, and, if he can't, never drives himself into phony enthusiasm. Indiscriminate love of books is a disease, like satyriasis, and stern measures should be applied to it.

I, for example, do not react eagerly to books on the delights of gardening; to novels about very young men lengthily and discursively in love; to books by bright children Who Don't Know How Funny They're Being; to diplomatic reminiscences by splendid gaffers with long memories and brief understandings; to autobiographies by writers who feel that to have reached the age of thirty-five is an achievement; to thorough jobs on Chester A. Arthur; to all tomes that aim to make me a better or a more successful man than I would be comfortable being; to young, virile novelists who would rather be found dead than grammatical; to most anthologies of humor; to books about Buchmanism, astrology, Yoga, and internal baths, all of which seem to me to deal with the same subject matter as does the last of the four subjects named.

It is books like these that make a successful appeal to my apathy. Every reviewer has his own list. He does his best to keep it a small one, for he knows that his responsibility is to his public, not himself. He knows that he cannot afford to any great extent the luxury of indulging his own prejudices. A reviewer is not in the self-expression business. If he were he would run the risk of becoming an artist. He is, by the nature of his trade, uncreative, or, if his creative impulses are too strong, he sooner or later finds himself a dud at his job, and turns into a writer. But if he is a good reviewer and keeps in the groove fifteen or twenty years, he has no more chance of becoming a writer than a pig has of flying. There is nothing tragic about this and no reviewer who has any respect for his trade wastes any sentimentality over it. One decent hack, to my mind, is worth a stable of would-be Pegasuses.

Reviewers interest the public. I cannot fathom the reason, for we are among the mildest and most conventional of citizens, pure Gluyas Williams types. A life spent among ephemeral best sellers and publishers' announcements is not apt to produce characters of unusual contour. But the fact remains that people are curious about us and are likely to ask more questions of a reviewer than they would of a successful truss manufacturer, though probably the trussman leads the more abundant life.

To satisfy this curiosity I list herewith a few of the queries most commonly directed at my tribe, together with one man's answers:

Do you really read all those books? This question is generally put with an odd inflection, combining cynical disbelief with man-of-the-world willingness to overlook any slight dishonesty. There is no need for this hard-boiled attitude. A reviewer reads the books he reviews, exactly as an accountant examines his cost sheets, with the same routine conscientiousness. It's his job, that's all.

Back of this question, however, lies a peculiar condition, which baffles me and I think many others who are forced to read a great deal. The reason people think we bluff is that they themselves read so slowly they cannot believe we read as "fast" as we actually do. Now, I do not believe dogmatically either in fast or slow reading. I believe tripe should be read practically with the speed of light and, let us say, Toynbee's *A Study of History* with tortoise deliberation. And most books are nearer to tripe than to Toynbee. But the trouble with practically all of us is that we suffer from chronic reverence. We make the unwarranted assumption that because a man is in print he has something to say, and, acting on this assumption, we read his every word with scrupulous care. This may be good manners, but it's a confounded waste of time.

If I am at all partial, it is to the man who reads rapidly. One of the silliest couplets ever composed is to be found in *The Art of Reading*, by one William Walker, a seventeenth-century hollow-head who wrote:

> *Learn to read slow; all other graces*
> *Will follow in their proper places.*

This is unmitigated balderdash and if taken seriously can easily result in the wasting of 10 or 15 per cent of the few waking hours God has put at our disposal.

For example, I am simply unable to understand those—and there must be millions of them—who spend hours over the daily paper. Why, if you add up those hours, you will find that some people pass more time with the *Herald Tribune* than they do with their wives or husbands. I do not draw from this any conclusions about the state of either American journalism or American matrimony. I merely infer that such paper-maniacs simply do not know how to skip, to take in a paragraph at a time, to use the headlines, one of mankind's most blessed inventions.

No, reviewers do their job, but they know how to read quickly, in large units, to seize a point and be off to the next one while the author is still worrying the first one to death. Anybody can learn to do this; the reviewer simply is forced to learn it. I happen to be an exceptionally rapid reader, which is no more to my credit than would be the possession of exceptionally bushy eyebrows. Of the average novel (a description that covers virtually all novels) I can read one hundred pages an hour. Of the average historical novel I can read two hundred pages an hour, but that is because I am so familiar with the plot and characters. It took me two weeks, about five hours a day, to read Thomas Mann's *Joseph in Egypt*. I submit that in all three cases I did my reading with the proper speed and with conscientious attention to the value of what was being said.

How do you select books for review? Well, each reviewer has his own system. I used to try to juggle five factors, whose relative importance varies with each book.

First, I asked myself whether the book was apt to interest me. This is only fair. I will write better, more usefully, about something that naturally engages my attention. I don't have to like the book, necessarily. It may interest me because its author happens to represent a great many things I dislike, as is the case with Gertrude Stein, Mabel Dodge Luhan, Charles Morgan, and William Faulkner.

Second, does the book have news value? A book reviewer is partly a purveyor of news. Any book by Ernest Hemingway would have to be reviewed whether it were a good one, like *The Old Man and the Sea*, or a poor one, like *Across the River and Into the Trees*, for Hemingway is news. This does not make him a better or a worse writer, of course. It has nothing to do with his literary value, but it has a great deal to do with whether or not the public expects information about his new book.

Let me give you another example. Many years ago everybody was all worked up over the Edward-Simpson affair (remember?). I said then and I say now (nobody listened then and nobody's listening now) that the whole mess was of very little political importance and that the persons involved were not sufficiently interesting even for the thing to have much scandal value. I was in a chilly minority of one. One week, with public interest at fever heat, three or four books bearing on the case appeared. Not one of them would have been worth a line of comment had it not possessed at the moment an inflated news value. To my mind they weren't worth a line of comment anyway, but I would have been an incompetent reviewer had I not given them considerable space. A reviewer is a journalist.

The third factor is allied to the second: Is the book apt to be of interest to the reviewer's particular audience? I used to have a job with *The New Yorker*, a humorous and satirical family magazine. There is no such animal as a typical *New Yorker* reader, but most of the magazine's readers did not enjoy, let us say, Frances Parkinson Keyes. Mrs. Keyes had and has many virtues but they were not the virtues that happened to interest the people who read my small screeds. Hence Mrs. Keyes did not get a look-in in my column. Her sales did not suffer in consequence.

The fourth factor is the only one that might not occur to a non-professional. A reviewer, in selecting books, takes into careful account the opinion of the *publisher* with respect to his own publications. If a publisher writes me that Hyacinthe Doakes's novel is terrific, that it is his fall leader, that he is going to lay ten thousand dollars' worth of advertising money on the line—why, I make a note to read Hyacinthe's book with care. I may not like it, and in that case will say so. (I did not once, in more than fifteen years in the trade, receive a letter of protest from any publisher whose offering I had panned, except in a few cases when I had made misstatements of fact.) But the truth is that I am more apt to like it than I am to like some little yarn that this same publisher is so ashamed of he hides it away in the back of his catalogue. Publishers have their faults (a profound remark that I have often heard them apply to reviewers), but they know a good deal about books and their judgment of the relative values of their productions is hearkened to by any sensible reviewer.

Finally, a book may not be of great personal interest, it may possess no news value, my audience may not care deeply about it, and the publisher will not be in a position to give it any special publicizing. Nevertheless, I will review it in some detail. Why? Because I feel it to be important. That is to say, it is a book of literary or instructive value by a criterion (a cloudy one, I admit) that has nothing to do with the four factors already mentioned. Some years ago there appeared a long, scholarly, rather solemn work of literary criticism, *American Renaissance*, by F. O. Matthiessen. Factor 1 applied moderately; factors 2, 3, 4 hardly applied at all. But I gave it a column and a half. I did so because the book was clearly an important work of creative scholarship and in years to come was bound to take a considerable place in its restricted field. It was my duty (to whom I don't know; I suppose to Literature itself) to comment on such a book to the best of my ability. Every reviewer feels the same way and does the same thing.

How reliable are reviewers' estimates? There's no exact answer to that one. If his estimates weren't appreciably more reliable than those of your dinner-table companion, he wouldn't hold his job long. But he is several light-years distant from infallibility. He works under pressure, he's human, he's been out too late the night before, his eyes bother him —for one reason or another, the result may be a stupid verdict. I've rendered many. At the end of each year I used to give myself something life itself, less generous than I am, doesn't allow us: a second chance. I went over the books I had reviewed and corrected my first estimates.

As to this question of reliability, I would say that on the whole we reviewers err in the direction of overamiability, though not so noticeably as was the case twenty-five years ago, when the Great American Novel was being hailed about as regularly as a Fifth Avenue bus. What has happened, roughly, is that the old type of book reviewer, to whom the job was a game, has gradually been replaced by a new type, to whom the job is a job. In the days of Laurence Stallings and Heywood Broun you would on occasion get superb pieces of enthusiastic journalism, but more frequently sickening examples of hullabalunacy. Today book reviewing is staider, duller, but unquestionably juster and more serious. It has a professional touch. It is growing up.

Nevertheless, I should hazard a guess that its standards of judgment are still too relaxed. Just what my tribe has to be mellow about I can't figure out, but we are mellow, and the result is a certain lack of acerbity. There's too much good-nature-faking among us, a continuous observance of Be-Kind-To-Dumb-Novelists Week. Literature does not grow only on praise. It needs the savage and tartarly note, even the astringence of insult.

In order to keep his sword sharp, the reviewer should see to it that he does not make too many close friends among writers. Two decades or so ago, during the heyday of the literary tea and the publisher's cocktail party, this was a difficult assignment. Today, now that book publishers have finally put on long pants, the problem is easier. A reviewer may go from one end of the year to the other without flushing a single novelist, and I have known some reviewers, now quite grown men, who have never met a literary agent in the flesh. This alienation from what used to be known laughingly as the Literary Life is a good thing for us. It makes possible a cool inhumanity toward authors, which in turn results in more detached comment. The road to a reviewer's disintegration is marked by many milestones, each one a statue erected to commemorate a beautiful friendship. I am sure of this even though I would not go so far as to agree with the man who thought the proper relationship between reviewer and author should be that between a knife and a throat.

What, then, is a reviewer to do when unavoidably confronted with a book written by a close friend? I have had to face this situation perhaps a dozen times in the course of my daily work, and it is not an easy one to handle if one wishes to be scrupulously honest. In my case the difficulty was never disastrous, for it is my policy, when choosing friends who write, to choose of course only those who write well, thus making it a matter of duty for me to praise their work.

The fact is that no reviewer is really objective when dealing with a friend's book, for if the book has anything to it at all, he is really dealing with the friend himself. He does the best he can, trying not to crack his spine in an attempt to lean over backward. But I doubt the final accuracy of his judgment. For example, I have praised rather heatedly two books by close friends of mine: Mortimer Adler's *How to Read a Book* and Oscar Levant's *A Smattering of Ignorance*. I still do not know whether these books are as good as I made them out to be. On rereading my admittedly amiable pieces, I detect no conscious dishonesty. Of course, as one of my most sympathetic readers, I may be giving myself the benefit of the doubt. There are some Alexanders among us who cut the Gordian knot, such as the famous literary commentator (as a matter of fact, his first name *was* Alexander) who is reported to have said with dulcet candor, "Any reviewer who won't praise a friend's book is a louse."

How influential are reviewers? This is a hard one to answer. All the publishers' questionnaires, scientifically designed to discover just why a given book is bought, throw but a dim light on the subject, though they provide any desired quantity of statistics. Reader A buys a book because his friend B has mentioned it; that is apparently the strongest single definable factor. But this means nothing unless you know why B happened to mention it. You ask B. B replies, let us suppose, that he himself bought, read, and recommended the book as the result of reading an advertisement. Now you have to find out what in that particular advertisement caused the positive reaction to the book. Was it the publisher's statement of the book's merits? Was it a quotation from a reviewer? If the latter, B bought the book because the reviewer liked it— and therefore A indirectly did the same. The whole matter is very complex.

With a great best seller, a large number of factors operate simultaneously or follow rapidly on each other, causing an irresistible, constantly mounting wave of popularity. If we take the case of Hemingway's *For Whom the Bell Tolls*, we might list these factors somewhat as follows, in the order of their conceivable importance:

(1) Author's reputation (but that didn't make a best seller of his previous book).

(2) Timeliness and importance of the subject matter.

(3) Literary excellence.

(4) It was a Book-of-the-Month Club selection, which automatically set in motion a wave of bookish conversation, for the club members form a mighty army of talkers.

(5) Almost unanimously favorable reviews.

(6) Erotic and "shocking" passages.

(7) Book-store recommendation. (A factor very difficult to judge—perhaps it should be placed much higher in the list.)

(8) Publisher's advertising and general promotion—in this case, I should say, a minor factor.

( ) Talkability. I don't give this a number because any of the factors (1) to (8) might have contributed to the book's talkability, and no one can determine the relative importance of any of them.

Now, this casual analysis (whose arrangement would probably be sharply questioned by my colleagues, the publisher, and Mr. Hemingway) would not apply identically to any other great best seller. In some cases (8) might be very near the head of the list. *Anthony Adverse,* for example, benefited by one of the most skillful advertising campaigns in publishing history; *Jurgen* was made mainly by (6), or rather by a Vice Society's alert appreciation of (6); and so it goes.

The reviewer alone cannot make a book popular. A superb novel such as Elizabeth Bowen's *Death of the Heart* may be praised by every reviewer who knows his job and still sell but a few thousand copies. Only factors (3) and (5) applied to this book; other factors would have been necessary to push it over into solid popularity.

Columnists, radio commentators, editorial writers, lecturers, even big businessmen will on occasion influence the sale of books more sharply than reviewers can. On the other hand, preachers, whose literary influence a generation or so ago was marked, have now sunk to a minor role as book recommenders.

One of the paradoxes of bookselling, observable only during the last few years, is that a book may be helped by one or more of the so-called competitive media. A book's sale will be increased by its translation into a moving picture. Alice Duer Miller's *The White Cliffs* became a best seller largely because it was so successfully broadcast. And, to take a more striking example, the condensations of popular books to be found in the *Reader's Digest* frequently tend to accelerate the sale of these publications in their original form. There is no such thing as bad publicity for books.

I am inclined to think that one thing that does *not* sell them is the publisher's jacket blurb. This is generally written after much brow furrowing and is almost completely ineffective. Sometimes blurbs help the reviewer, but not much; more often they aid the harried book seller. Yet I have never seen a potential book buyer influenced by them. My own practice was to be wary of them. Their extravagance is often so absurd that the reviewer loses his detachment and is unduly severe with the innocent book. "One of the outstanding biographers of our time," said the blurbist about a journalist who has devoted himself to the extremely dull task of composing official slop about the English royal family. A tedious Scandinavian named Trygve Gulbranssen was once tagged by his publishers as "One of the great writers of the day," the day being unspecified. This jacket racket alienates reviewers.

To THE READER: Pay no attention to the blurb on the jacket of the book you are now reading.

An Experiment in Teaching

MORE THAN a quarter of a century ago, when all the trees were green, I was one of twelve poor but earnest young men who had recently taught or taken the John Erskine-inspired Columbia College course in General Honors. Here for two years we had read, talked, and floundered our way through the greatest books of the Western tradition from Homer to William James. Then, as I remember, the Carnegie Foundation announced itself willing to take a long chance on Plato, Shakespeare, Tolstoy, & Co. If we would lead free classes for adults the Foundation would shell out fifteen dollars weekly to each of us twelve disciples.

Masking our glee at the hard bargain we had driven, we began to seek among New York's faceless millions for those sufficiently tetched in the head to believe that one can learn more from dead poets and philosophers than from live editorial writers. We cast our nets, we caught our odd fish. We led our classes in Y.M.C.A.'s, churches, public libraries, our own homes. Recalling that Socrates had taught in the market place, we saw nothing wrong in continuing our discussions over cafeteria tables. Our students were wildly random. Merchant mariners marooned until the next voyage. Burly truck drivers who had read Bob Ingersoll and nothing else. Brash dogmatists who had read Marx and didn't want to understand anything else. Pale-faced Emersonian clergymen. Young stenographers, their eyes reflecting the solitude of the dismal hall bedroom. Comfortable matrons pouncing on a bargain in culture. Professional arguers trailing their soap boxes. Recent immigrants seeking a key to a bewildering America. Those too poor to go to college. Those thirsty for something college had been too poor to give them.

We were not good teachers. We did not have to be, for the discussions were led by unpaid spirits named Rousseau, Montaigne, or Melville. With the impalpable forceps of symbol and idea they began to deliver the rational minds that lay coiled within us. The Marxist launched fewer manifestoes. The arguer stepped down from his soap box. The truck driver grew less arrogant, the immigrant less humble. Introduced to each other by the most radiant hosts the world has ever known, our reasons cautiously shook hands. We were becoming members, however modest, of the only aristocracy that has lasted for three thousand years, the aristocracy of those who refuse to lead the unexamined life.

Since those first Great Books classes more than twenty-five years have passed. Today there are about two thousand of them. One in Highland Park, a suburb of Chicago, was started in 1930. It is still meeting weekly, though sons and daughters have replaced some of the original students.

Speaking of Chicago, a New York journalist recently published a book about that city. Of its Great Books classes, he says, "Two chapters of the *Decline and Fall* become mysteriously equivalent to the whole work when exhaustively discussed in a group led by one's chiropodist." I admire the efficiency of this sentence: in a few words it manages to define the limitations of its author's understanding, sympathy, and manners. For I still think it better to talk about a few chapters of Gibbon than not to know him at all. Nor have I any more objection to learning from my chiropodist than from a lens grinder named Spinoza, a bankrupt veteran named

Cervantes, or a slave named Epictetus. The only kind of teacher I might draw the line at is a really smart twentieth-century New York journalist.

Obviously I wear my bias on my sleeve. I suspect I cannot outgrow the pride I feel in those two years from 1927 to 1929 during which, with all the fervor of youthful ignorance, I helped lead Great Books discussions.

What can the Great Books do for you? I can only tell you what they have done for me. I do not know them well. Many I do not know at all, and will never know. But ever since my college days almost thirty years ago, I have not allowed myself entirely to lose sight of them. I remain poorly educated. But if it is education I seek, at least I know toward what compass point to turn.

Two things, among others, these books have done for me and will continue to do.

First, they have lifted from my imagination the curse of the contemporary. No matter how rude may be my understanding of them, the Great Books have enlarged my mental living space. As the shell lifted to the ear seems to carry in its curves the rumor of the seas of the whole world, so this brief shelf of books, placed against the mind, makes audible to me the living voices of three thousand years of my civilization. He who has once heard these voices is forever freed from the thralldom of the current. He begins to see that all great minds are contemporary—not that they have receded into their common past, but that we have not yet advanced into their common future. They do not so much compel us to look back as to look up and, where once our eyes met a ceiling, to glimpse the vast sky of possible ideas.

Second, they have given me ground to stand on. Today we see those like the Communists, who would jettison the entire Western and Christian tradition because it makes nonsense of their vision of a closed history and a static state. And we see those like the French writer Jean Paul Sartre, who believes that "man's long dialogue is coming to an end." I think we will not vanquish either the iron faith of the Communists or the leaden faith of the defeatists unless we deploy in the struggle the armament of a deeply felt and superior creed of our own. And I cannot see on what that creed can ultimately found itself if it be not the whole scripture, sacred and profane, of our Western world, that long dialogue, which, I trust, will never come to an end. We who make that dialogue part of ourselves are helping to preserve against the onslaught of the barbarian the ideas, the visions, the laughter, the deep cries of anguish, the great Eurekas of revelation that make up our patent to the title of civilized man.

The Wild Child

A NOVA, BLAZING out of deep space, is remarkable, but, except by astronomers, unremarked. Alike remarkable, alike usually unremarked is that rarer nova from out the mind's deeper space: a really new literary form. Edgar Allan Poe could not have known that his *Murders in the Rue Morgue* would breed ten thousand smaller Dupins and Sherlock Holmeses. Nor could Jules Verne, hoisting his dullish characters into a balloon or plummeting them under the sea, have foretold that in less than a century the form he so casually devised would mushroom into a new kind of literature.

For that is what science fiction is: something new on earth —I mean Terra. So fast has it shot up that it already threatens the popularity of the detective story. Books of science fiction, whether grown up or "comic," stream from the press. On the newsstands several good magazines (examples: *Astounding Science Fiction, Fantasy and Science Fiction, Galaxy*) bravely hold up their heads amid a Sargasso Sea of pulp. Television, a natural outlet for ingenuity and fancy, is becoming more and more hospitable to science fiction. In fact a radio-and-television critic of my acquaintance (Timothy Crouse, aged seven, the son of Russel Crouse, a playwright regrettably mired in mere realism) informs me that Hopalong Cassidy now ranks with the dodo. In young Crouse's set you're either a Space Cadet, able to astrogate your nuclear-fission-driven rocket on a routine run from Antares to Aldebaran—or you just don't rate.

324

The beanstalk growth of science fiction is no accident, any more than was the growth of the detective story. The detective story mirrored the development of organized police forces in London, Paris, and New York. Suddenly society felt itself to be not a haphazard, unregarded affair, but something precious and worth systematic protection. Felt danger from the criminal, felt safety from the cop—of these two thrills was the atmosphere compounded that distilled the detective story. Peril and coziness—and they found their emblems in the Sherlock Holmes tales: the eerie London fog, the snug Baker Street sitting room.

If the nineteenth century birthed the detective story, the twentieth has fathered science fiction.

A dynamic social invention is apt to produce its epic: the Roman Empire called upon Virgil, and the *Aeneid* was born. In our time that social invention, the victorious, ever expanding Machine, was sure to evoke some expression of its dangers, its triumphs, and its possibilities. Begotten by Imagination on the body of Technology, there springs forth the wild child, Science Fiction.

It would seem that poetry, painting, music, drama, and the ordinary novel have failed to create, for people in general, exciting images that will convey our sense of what the Machine is doing to us, and will do. These traditional disciplines lie rooted in the past, and for the past the Machine cares little. It marches well with the needs of a generation which finds it quite easy to live with little consciousness of its forebears. As the sunflower to the sun, so the Machine's iron face turns forever toward the shape of things to come. Its brain is packed with cells, not of memory, but of pre-vision. Its eyes are fixed on possibility, including that most recent of possibilities, the impossible. Science fiction is a kind of archeology of the future.

To express the Machine's future-mindedness, its powers of generation (for the master-machines are those that breed other machines), its capacity to alter humans by replacing them, its magnificence and its direness, its generosities and its cruelties—to express all this a new form was needed. That this would turn out to be science fiction no one could have foreseen.

Science fiction began, with Jules Verne, as a mutation of the adventure-yarn. It reached its first peak with H. G. Wells, who used it largely as a means of popularizing applied science. In the hands of Stapledon, Huxley, and Orwell it became philosophy, satire, and admonition against the Communo-Fascist state. In our own day it has mushroomed into a new form of mass-entertainment.

The philosopher Olaf Stapledon writes *Last and First Men,* a dazzling, speculative "history" of the next 5,000,000,000,000 years (quite right, 12 zeros). A space-opera hack manipulates his androids, intergalactic ships, telepathic monsters. Between the two minds stretches an abyss. Yet both are responding to the same challenge, to a fantastic but real machine age, an age of vacuum tubes, electronic calculators, and proximity fuses, an age only tenuously connected with the gross, clanking, dirty, iron-and-steamy nineteenth century.

However weird the form it takes, science fiction is solidly here, ready to satisfy certain needs and fulfill certain functions.

Were it unable to satisfy these needs, it would have remained on the Edgar Rice Burroughs level, displaying its primitive attractions before a relatively unexacting audience. But such has not been the case. During the last ten years (particularly since Hiroshima, which acted as a kind of trigger to the popular imagination) science fiction has gained not merely a large and growing audience, but an increasingly discriminating one. Literary men of parts have turned their pens to it, as have scientists of talent and learning. Well-edited popular magazines, such as *Collier's* and *The Saturday Evening Post*, have published it. *The New Yorker*, whose standards are rigorous, has done so also. *Astounding Science Fiction*, edited by the brilliant John W. Campbell, Jr., consistently presents, along with much tosh, substantial articles and witty, imaginative stories. A glance at J. O. Bailey's compendium of science fiction (*Pilgrims Through Space and Time*, Argus Books, Inc., New York, 1947) or E. F. Bleiler's useful compilation (*The Checklist of Fantastic Literature*, Chicago, 1948) demonstrates the existence of an entire new literature, already obeying or modifying its own laws and traditions.

In his hand the wild child grasps—the gadget. The gadget may be around the corner. It may be heat-conditioned furniture, collision-proof automobiles, celestial television, electronic noise killers, electrostatic dust absorbers—all forecast for the near future by the science-fiction veteran, Hugo Gernsback. Or the gadget may be something quite fanciful, a rocket ship to Mars. In either case it is already more or less part of our mental world. The imagination of Western man has moved a certain distance away from its traditional center, the human heart, toward a new focus, technology. Science fiction is the attempt, however crude, to cope in popular terms with this displacement.

Now it is apparent that science fiction does not give a "true" picture of the possibilities of technology. President Conant's recent warning against a naïve acceptance of science fiction as such a picture was justified. Some writers impose self-restrictions: their wonders (for example, the televiewer, the telephone's visual mate) are reasonable extrapolations from current technical knowledge. But many others go hog-wild, their offerings bearing about the same relation to the future of science as soap opera bears to American home life.

As an intelligible statement of the probable, science fiction cannot be defended. It is poetry rather than truth, stimulating at best, childish at worst—but poetry nonetheless. It is a vision dissolving at times into a nightmare or mere fantastic japery. And, like all visions, it does not explain or instruct. It is a form incorporating the fears, the hopes, or the bewilderments of the unconscious.

Though we may act casually toward the Machine, below the surface there works a welter of inchoate emotions. The Machine has come too quickly, there is too much of it, there are too few of us intimate with its brief history and complex structure. Its priesthood, the scientists and engineers, is not given to talk: we find it hard to connect with them.

As a consequence our deepest feelings about the Machine comprise a muzzy mixture. Will it kill us? Will it save us? Do we control it? Is it beginning to control us? Will it bring us infinite leisure, infinite ennui, or infinite slavery? Do its masters know what they are doing? Because the Machine is omnipresent and intrusive, such questions never cease to trouble us. But as yet the answers are not, even to our sages, apparent.

In this uncertainty some of us, without being quite aware of what we are doing, may begin to attach to the Machine pseudo- or quasi-religious emotions. A child will form a more than casual relation to his television receiver. The juke-box and the slot-machine become objects of absorbed devotion. Nevil Shute's interesting novel, *Round the Bend*, shows how a reverent attendance on the Machine may become the channel of some of our purest aspirations.

Henry Adams' Dynamo has not yet replaced the Virgin, nor is it likely to; yet it is already something more than a dynamo. Does it seem too fantastic, then, to suggest that space-ships and flying men and roads that move at inhuman speeds can be for some the outlets through which flows an odd impulse of tentative worship, somewhat as ritual drama channeled for the early Greeks their uprush of awe in the face of nature's generative powers?

This feeling has its baser version: superstition. It is no accident that today at every subway-stand manuals of astrology are vended along with nickel candy. Nor is it an accident that the able writer Gerald Heard should present us with a book (*Is Another World Watching?*) suggesting that flying saucers are not only real but manned by super-intelligent Martian bees about two inches long; or that Kenneth Heuer in *Men of Other Planets* should discuss the airy possibility that "there is an immense army of intelligent beings in the universe." Even if these are dismissed as deadpan hoaxes the question still stands—Why is just this kind of hoax being perpetrated as against other possible kinds? What kind of credulity is it exploiting?

It is a credulity generated by the Machine's ineffable triumphs. The imagination, grasping the fact that radar, television, nuclear fission, the proximity fuse, and mathematical thinking-machines are merely the forerunners of what (and *what* indeed?) is to come, begins to tremble. If A is possible, why not B? And if B, why not X? And if X, why not X^n?

How shall the imagination come to terms with such conceptions? Perhaps it could make some reasonable adjustment were our environment favorable to reason and adjustment. But with the entire planet in a state of social disorder, menaced, not in the vague future, but now, today, by the Communist threat of a world termitarium, it is harder to do so.

Then, upon this disordered world, crowded with dismayed humans, are suddenly loosed the giant gadgets of technology.

What shall we do? Reject them? But Gandhi's crusade is already lost. If we cannot reject the gadgets, and do not quite know how to accept them, the affrighted, boggling imagination still has a seeming way out. It is the way of the dream.

The Machine can be transferred to the plane of fantasy. Contemplating it through the eyes of the science-fictioneer, we can ease ourselves of the burden of interpreting it. The reason, faced with work too hard for its muscles, can for the moment harmlessly abdicate. Thus science fiction appears to be, not a way of *understanding* the Machine, but a way of escaping from the fear of our *inability* to understand it. We temporarily suspend our disbelief in monsters on Mars so that we may cancel in our minds our incapacity to come to terms with the monsters on Earth. By fleeing to the impossible Then and There we may evade the incomprehensible Here and Now. Hence the reading of science fiction offers us the illusion of power without its responsibility. It acts as an outlet for our daydreams. Some years ago the novel, the travel book, even poetry performed this function for us. We could "lose ourselves" in a book. Today anyone who wants to lose himself in a book must do some pretty careful picking and choosing. (In fact, I know a literary critic who uses ordinary living as a method of escaping from the harsher realities of the novels he has to read.)

I am a member of the selecting committee of a well-known book club. Each month I examine a hundred-or-so reports based on an advance reading of forthcoming books. From the last batch I herewith select, practically at random, a few brief descriptions.

1. "In the end he (the hero) is a broken man, the family ruined." (A novel.)

2. "Just one horror after another." (A travel book.)

3. "Will make the sensitive reader's blood run cold." (A

book about the Germans' extermination of the Polish Jews.)

4. "The horror of it, like something out of Kafka." (A true story of the persecution of an American by Communists.)

5. "Full of mad futile characters and diseased brains." (A novel.)

6. "Mainly a record of a succession of degradations: one long wail about how hard life is for the girl born with black skin." (An autobiography.)

7. "A good, realistic novel . . . spoiled by a lot of medical details and a morbid obsession with epilepsy."

Is it any wonder that, with this sort of fare being grimly offered up by the publishers, readers should turn for relief to dreamworlds of the future, in which at least *some* kind of order is to be found? The imagination must exercise itself *somehow*. If conventional literature refuses to give the imagination a chance, then an unconventional literature will come into being to redress the balance. That literature is science fiction.

The poet W. H. Auden has termed ours the Age of Anxiety. It is as fair to call it the Age of Expectation. Koestler's phrase, the Age of Longing, bears both suggestions: we long for some absolute order because we fear the visitation of some absolute disorder.

This will to believe in the future, coupled with violent doubts about it, is reflected in science fiction with a vividness denied to conventional narrative.

Science fiction is utopian. Upon its screen it throws a picture of a world of unlimited power and comfort, unified by science. War and poverty have been abolished, man is an improved animal. His intellectual enterprise has colonized the farthest stars.

Science fiction is anti-utopian. It tells sad stories of the death of man. Science, uncontrolled, has laid waste the earth or even blown it up. Man is reduced to the level of the lower animals, or subjected to the iron mastery of a ruthless élite, or even assimilated to the condition of the Machine itself. Sometimes he has given way entirely to another species.

Often the two moods mingle or alternate in the same story. Men develop the ability to think telepathically—but their thoughts hardly seem worth transmitting. Their society is ordered with an efficiency beyond the dreams of the classical utopists, but in this society men are conceived as means rather than ends. Man can do more; he feels less. The theme of the Superman seems to identify itself with that of the robot-ruler.

The infinite expansion of science is often linked with an unquestioning surrender to it. If force and violence are no more, it is not because man's heart has become good, but because he is now subject to control by mental suggestion or the techniques of pharmacology (a not completely fantastic notion, if we are to believe some reports that have filtered out from the laboratory of terror behind the Iron Curtain).

A sense of man's illimitable powers is shadowed by an equally present sense of his vulnerability. The favorite *leit-motifs* of science fiction come readily to mind: fourth-dimensional flight from the present (Baudelaire's *"N'importe où, hors du monde!"*); the Last Man; the coming Dark Ages; the Absolute Weapon; the conquest of earth by space-visitors, animals, plants, or even a filterable virus. I am aware that much of this is mere mechanical bugaboo-making; everybody likes to be scared a little. But I cannot help feeling, after ten years of immersion in science fiction, that it is not all a matter of crying "Boo!" A whole literature of dismay cannot arise unless the conditions are there to produce it and the audience is there to digest it.

But to take only the apocalyptic view is a form of self-indulgence. A great deal of science fiction is more level-headed and, in its way, even sensible. Many writers emphasize the possibilities for good that lie in the applied sciences, particularly the biological and sociological ones. Technology is exploited humanly; the Machine is defied or tamed. It should also be remembered that virtually all writers of science fiction assume as a precondition of our future world the existence of a single government and the permanent leveling of all barriers of race, color, religion, and nationality. In their minor way the less frenzied and more thoughtful writers of science fiction are charging with a new and daring meaning that antique notion of never ending progress to which we now so wistfully look back. That such stories should be rather fewer in number than stories of doom or social immobilization is natural enough, our time being what it is: one in which man has gained the power to remold himself nearer to the image of God, without commanding, as these lines are written, the will to do so.

Pillow Books

READING in bed, like other gentle customs of the pre-Tension Age, may be on the way out. Yet it is a minor art we should not willingly let die.

There are three schools. At one extreme are those who say, with Sir J. C. Squire, "The bedside book for me is the book that will longest keep me awake." I suspect such literary night owls of being less avid of reading than fearful of sleeping, like the student Lia Hsun who, according to Giles's *Chinese Biographical Dictionary*, had "a lighted twist of hemp arranged in such a way as to burn his hair if he began to nod from drowsiness." They would do as well to stuff the pillow with a pair of spurs.

At a far remove from those who misuse books to keep themselves awake are those who misuse books to put themselves to sleep. When laudanum failed, the poet Coleridge was forced to administer something stronger—the blank-verse odes of his friend Southey. We have no Southeys today, but a dose of current historical romance might do as well, or a bitter ounce of novel by any of our young men who have reached the land of despair without bothering to pass through the intervening country of reflection.

I hold with neither the benzedrine nor seconal school. As for the first, to read the whole night through is to trespass upon nature. The dark hours belong to the unconscious, which has its own rights and privileges. To use the literary lockout against the unconscious is unfair to the dreamers' union. Hence the wise bed-reader, rendering unto Morpheus the things that are Morpheus', will shun any book that appears too interesting.

Nor, in my view, should a book be used merely as an opiate. Indeed, I do not understand how it *can* be. Dull books soothe only dull brains—a moderately healthy mind will be irritated rather than rested by a dull book. (This irritation is of a special kind; it is known as boredom and no one need blush for it. He who boasts that he is never bored confesses himself half-dead, irritability being one of the marks of all living tissue.) But is this capacity to irritate through ennui really what we seek in a pillow book? I doubt it. Books that bore you into a kind of dull paralysis are committing mayhem on your mind. I avoid them as I do the man with total recall of his morning paper, the woman with total recall of her shopping day.

As a middle-of-the-roader I have found (nothing surprising about it) that the ideal book to read before sleep should neither bore nor excite.

Take newspapers, which tend to do both. Charles Lamb said, "Newspapers always excite curiosity. No one ever lays one down without a feeling of disappointment." I do not urge upon anyone my own reactionary notion, which is that the proper time to read a newspaper is when passing the newsstand. For me much daily journalism might as well be condensed to skywriting.

But even if this extreme position be disallowed there is something to be urged against the habit of reading newspapers before sleep—apart from the legacy of smudge they leave upon sheets, pillows, and fingers. Pre-slumber reading should be a kind of small private devotion during which we beat a quiet retreat from the practical. Now the newspaper is but the daily reiteration of the practical. It is the enemy of the settled mind, which is the province of those truly important concerns that are not practical at all, but speculative. The newspaper, with its unkillable obsession with the actual, is the systematic generator of worry. All newspaper readers furrow their brows. This may be a good thing during the active day, but to read the paper in bed is to open Pandora's box at the very moment when we are least able to deal with its contents. It is to fall asleep with a gadfly inside your skull.

There is a famous essay, *Mr. Bennett and Mrs. Brown.* In this essay Virginia Woolf attacked novelists like Wells, Bennett, and Galsworthy on the ground that reading their books left one feeling incomplete, even frustrated. Such novels, she said, seemed to call for action on your part: reform the economic system, improve education, divorce your wife. I think Virginia Woolf thought up this pretty theory to camouflage the fact that she just didn't like novels so different from her own. However, applied more narrowly to bedside books it makes fair sense.

The man of Wall Street should not take to bed the stock-market quotations; the quiet counterpane is no proper field for raging bulls and bears. Problem novels (usually produced by problem children) should never companion your pillow; midnight is no hour to worry about the time being out of joint. Avoid political arguments that step upon your toes, whether the toes be Republican or Democratic. Await a more fitting hour than bedtime to scare yourself stiff with the latest volume on the atom bomb. Above all, put from you all reading matter that aims (like this essay) to persuade you of something, or change you into a finer and more alert citizen. The state of a man comfortably tucked in bed is already kingly; it will not brook improvement. All books too close to

our worn and fretted daily lives make dubious bedtime reading. Avoid the call to action.

In my own case I can think of two seeming exceptions to
this rule. The first is travel books. The normal human being
is made restless by such reading, and quite properly so. But I
am of such rooted and stationary nature that I can enjoy
the most seductive tales of gypsying without feeling any
impulse to kick away the blanket and phone for reservations
on the next plane to Rio. However, if I owned an itching foot
I would confine such unsettling reading to the non-horizontal
hours.

The second exception concerns my favorite bedtime pabulum, books about food and drink. For me there are few
nobler experiences than to read myself almost to sleep over
a classic like P. Morton Shand's *A Book of Food* or André
Simon's *Concise Encyclopaedia of Gastronomy* or M. F. K.
Fisher's *Here Let Us Feast.* I say *almost* to sleep, for of course
such reading can have but one outcome—a 2 A.M. invasion of
refrigerator and cellar. This would appear a flat contradiction
of my rule: no calls to action. Yet the contradiction is apparent, not real. Such reading, it is true, maketh a full man,
but a full man is a better sleeper, and so books on food and
wine lead roundabout to sweet slumber.

In sum, for me the best bed books are those that deny the
existence of tomorrow. To read in bed is to draw around us
invisible, noiseless curtains. Then at last we are in a room
of our own and are ready to burrow back, back, back to that
private life of the imagination we all led as children and to
whose secret satisfactions so many of us have mislaid the
key. Not that the book need be "good." Indeed, like another
bedtime favorite of mine, science fiction (some of it), it can
be pleasant trash. But, "good" or "bad," it should act as a
bridge, a middle term between the sharp fact of daily ex-

istence and the cloudy fact of the dream life. It must commit me to nothing, least of all to assent or contradiction. All the better if it be removed in some degree from my current time, my current place—life is too short for us to spend more than a few hours a day being up-to-date. Finally, it should not be in any way excessive, whether in humor or depth or even originality.

Nevertheless if for you the *World Almanac* satisfies these conditions, then by all means bed yourself with the *World Almanac*. The books that do the job for me may quite well bore you to a catalepsy or infuriate you to a raging insomnia. The following paragraphs may therefore be of no use to you. On the other hand, they may.

Most intelligent bed-readers will get a not too stimulating pleasure from any well-conceived general anthology, such as Huntington Cairns's *The Limits of Art* or Somerset Maugham's more conventional *Traveller's Library*. Maugham's own tales, published complete in two stout volumes, *The World Over* and *East and West*, are perfect for the alcove. I like detective stories, if good, but must confess that most of the current crop read as if they had been punched out on an IBM machine. Sound collections, like those by Dorothy Sayers, of short whodunits, are most satisfactory. E. C. Bentley's two detective novels and his handful of short stories have recently been put into a single volume, *Trent's Case Book*: a superior affair; and there is also available a Josephine Tey omnibus. Other-worldly tales (but they must stop just short of the gruesome) do nicely. The contrast between their shudders and one's own snug safety supplies a childish pleasure whose roots lie too deep for us to scorn them. Of anthologies of the weird there are dozens—Alexander Laing's *The Haunted Omnibus* and the Modern Library's *Great Tales of Terror and the Supernatural* are among the better ones.

I like also to roam around in the General Catalogue of the Oxford University Press, a publication that costs you nothing and is rich with peculiar treasures. There is nothing quite like these endless book titles and brief descriptions to produce in the reader a gentle, serene amazement at the quantity of extraordinary matters, from *Acrocephaly and Acrocephalosyndactyly* to the *Zla-ba-Bsam-'grub*, that have engaged the minds of our fellow human beings. Here we find Galen's *On Medical Experience*, with this bit of useful information: "Since the original Greek text of this work was lost, except for two small fragments, this ninth-century Arabic translation is the earliest known complete version." Who follows Galen? Why, no others than Gall, Alice and Crew, Fleming, whose *Flat Tail* is described as "The story of a beaver during the second and most interesting year of his life, told with imagination and accuracy." What a brave and perennially new world this is that can contain cheek to cheek such creatures as Galen and Flat Tail!

Books about people who lived lives fantastically different from my own I have found excellent for the bedside. I like to read about the Middle Ages; you may prefer Polynesia or even more alien climes, such as William Faulkner's Southland. Books of popular science please me, but there are few writers today who have the liveliness and wit of Eddington, Jeans, and H. G. Wells. (Rachel Carson's *The Sea Around Us* and Guy Murchie's *Song of the Sky* are delightful exceptions.) Non-academic books about words and language are first-rate for me, but this may be a narrow professional interest.

As for novels, give me no profound Russians, no overlucid Frenchmen, no opaque Germans. Give me solid Englishmen of the nineteenth century or early twentieth—William De Morgan, Wilkie Collins, George Borrow, Charles Reade. (I omit Dickens and Thackeray as too obvious.) Above all give me Trollope, from whom I have received so much pleasure that I would willingly call him another St. Anthony, Trollope who breaks through the time barrier and teleports the horizontal reader instantly to a divinely settled, comfortable, income-taxless vanished world. His half-a-hundred novels are good for five years of bedside reading. Of those who minister to the tired, night-welcoming mind, Trollope is king. He never fails to interest, but not too much; to soothe, but not too much. Trollope is the perfect novelist for the bedside.

The Voice of the Dodo

THIS MONTH's inspirational thought: Dale Carnegie has now been winning friends and influencing people for nineteen years, or over half a generation. By this time the persuasive powers of the Mahatma of How-to have leaped all frontiers. Along with the citizens of 24 other countries even the Indo-Chinese are Carnegie converts. As for the home grounds, over four million of us—about one out of every twenty-five adults—have bought the good book. Now while of course no Carnegie man would ever try to influence another equally irresistible Carnegie man, each one must by now have won as friends at least a couple of dozen non-Carnegie men. The impressive result is visible at every turn—a happy band of All-American brothers, cemented in love and friendship by Simon and Schuster.

Seriously, as we old broadcasting hands put it, I had all this while supposed that the last grim decade had blown the How-to boys to bits. I would not have predicted that they could survive both history's rude onslaught and satire's sharp barbs—for the double-domes have not been kindly. To write any more about them would have seemed to me like flogging a dead horse.

But a dead horse that can run up a total of four million copies and keep right on traveling has Native Dancer left at the post. The fact is that the evangel of How-to has now become a standard product and an everyday necessity. The advertising shamans are still telling me how to keep up my social prestige with the right kind of abdominal belt. The digests are more helpful than ever, vending success at every newsstand. And, to clinch the matter, a sample issue of *Publishers' Weekly* not so long ago included in its listing of summer releases about a hundred titles that are clearly the handiwork of the How-to boys. Of these, thirty-seven actually begin with the sacred words, ranging from *How to Make Doll Clothes*, setting you back $2.25, to *How to Solve Your Problems*, which comes a little cheaper.

To say that such books are begot by the publishers' ingenuity upon the public's gullibility is easy enough. Easy— but too pat. The gullibility, at any rate, doesn't in the least resemble the pure traditional innocence of the rustic, but is rather a queer mixture of self-confidence, fear, bewilderment, and quasi-religious faith: mixed-up stuff indeed.

First let me say that I don't intend to lump all How-to books together. There's not a thing wrong with useful manuals that tell you (now and hereafter I'm taking my examples from the *Publishers' Weekly* list) *How to Build or Remodel Your House, How to Build Your Own Garage and Save Up to 60%* or even—though the *terra* here is a little less *firma*—*How to Buy a House*. The worst you can say about such How-to's is that they are more eagerly bought than frequently consulted. There's something in our human nature that makes us fall less violently in love with the How-to book that makes good on a small promise than with the one that doesn't make good on a big one. Remodeling my house, even if I succeed, still remains something pretty plain and practical. But remodeling my personality is such a wingy and inspiring vision that it seems vulgar to question its mere feasibility.

Years ago, when I was a student-librarian at Columbia College, one of the freshman courses required the reading of John Dewey's *How We Think*. About half the freshmen kept right on asking for *How to Think*. I'm convinced many students finished the book satisfied that Dewey had slipped them the secret of infallible thinking when all the poor fellow had in view was an explanation of how the mind works.

This little experience taught me the simple lesson that we are always anxious to improve ourselves as long as it requires doing something impossible. Let's go back to my list and take *How to Run a Gift Shop*. Now there's an honest title. It promises nothing that the contents, if equally honest, cannot deliver. But suppose we change the title by inserting the miracle-adjective: *How to Run a Successful Gift Shop*. There you have the real How-to touch, the Carnegie touch, the divine touch of the impossible—for *success* in running a gift shop, like success in painting the Sistine Chapel, depends of course on factors that escape book covers. Take *How to Make Beautiful Gifts at Home*. Gifts, yes; beautiful gifts, doubtful. Beauty dwells in the eye of the maker, beauty dwells in the eye of the beholder, beauty dwells not in the typewriter of the How-to miracle worker.

How about *How to Play Par Golf?* Doubtful again. My own limited experience plus the leaden hours I've spent listening to golfers' post-mortems lead me to the opinion that the relations connecting a small ball, a stick, eighteen oddly placed holes, and a man calling upon the Lord are too complicated for any book. The book can give the cozy *feeling* that you're learning how to play par golf. But the actual learning is a weird business involving millions of almost instantaneous messages darting around the wires of your nervous system and generally getting all jammed somewhere in the vicinity of your wrists. Just try to write *that* up.

As I look at my list I notice a large number of titles intended for what I would guess to be a small number of people. Here we have *How to be a Chalk Artist, How to Make Mobiles, How to Make Aprons.* Fair enough if I happen to burn with an unquenchable passion for chalk drawings or mobiles or am an inveterate apron-buff. But there's something uneasy-making about manuals that minister to such splinter-interests. Long ago Mencken taught us to laugh at centers of higher learning that offered courses in hog-calling. Not that there's anything wrong in calling hogs. It's as legitimate a calling as any. But most of us are troubled by the conviction that a student who has elected hog-calling has done so because he has rejected more difficult and more general disciplines. Harmless enough in itself, *How to Make Aprons* appeals in the same way to a tendency in us that's really a mild form of lunacy, the tendency to excessive specialization. It's like trying to start a fire with kindling split too small.

This free elective or How-tutorial system rests on a brace of dubious notions. The first is that books can teach you everything. The second, more dangerous, is that books *should* teach you everything. Example: the publishers will for a trifling $2.95 sell you *How to Live With a Cat.* My feeling is that anyone who has to study a book on how to live with a cat ought to give up cats and live with books. The whole point in keeping pets lies in the gradual, unending, almost instinctive mutual adaptation of animal and master. Dependence on a book suggests a loss of this capacity for adaptation. Does my cat read *How to Live With People?* Not on his nine lives. He has too much self-confidence. I have too little.

Such books, it is quite true, are short cuts. They save me time and trouble so that I have more time for other trouble. But also they cut me off from a certain quantity of warm, relaxed life-experience, from those necessary mild pleasures arising out of meeting difficulties. They are like airplane travel which, by obviating the need of looking it over slowly and reflectively, will end by snatching the whole world away from us. Short cuts? Yes. But short circuits too. It seems to me there's a limit to the benefits accruing from the economy of energy. The logic of the How-to School, Short-circuit Department, really leads to an escape from experience altogether. When you come right down to it, the only completely efficient labor-saving technique is to stick your head in a gas oven.*

Perhaps I can make my point clearer by reference to another class of How-to's. These tell us how to be the one thing we've been ever since our amoeba-ancestors got bored with simple fission. I'm talking about being fathers and mothers.

The How-to boys have given us, among other similar earnest guides, *How to be a Successful Parent, How to Live With Your Teen-Ager,* and, no kidding, *How to Plan a Party for Teen-Agers.* In suggesting that such books tend to form a less perfect union, establish dullness, and insure domestic stupidity, I mean no disrespect to those contemporary scientists who have made many brilliant discoveries in the field of child psychology. But I would point out that the better the psychologist the more closely he sticks to his last, the description of the child's mind. By the same token, not wishing to be caught with his panaceas down, he is wary of distributing universal formulas for "handling" or "living with" the child.

He knows what deep down in us we all know—that the parent who is "successful" (Lord, what a word!) is simply a wise and good person who also happens to be a father or mother. The nub of the matter lies in getting to be wise and good, which takes a bit of doing. It does not lie in reading

---

* *How to Stick Your Head in a Gas Oven,* by Empedocles Schnitzelfresser, Ph.D., Utopia House, Inc., New York, $2.95.

How to Plan a Party for Teen-Agers, which takes six bits of currency. I would far rather have my son plan his own party whose entire program should consist in having the young guests throw large lumps of coal at each other than organize one for him out of a book by some well-intentioned but total stranger.

Of course I'm overstating the case. Many manuals for parents are well researched and well written. But there are other brasher ones that assume a standard, factory-made child on whom you are expected to practice "techniques." Many of these books seem to believe that the normal American household is in a continuous state of civil war, a kind of miniature reflection of twentieth-century humanity. To outwit the child seems to be the main object, or to "get along" with him, or, in the more relaxed tomes, to "enjoy" him.

But whether the volume tells you *How to Live With Your Teen-Ager*, *How to Carry On a Conversation*, *How to Sell Your Way to Success*, *How to Read the Bible*, *How to Believe*, or *How I Can Make Prayers More Effective*, it seems to me, for all the honorable intentions of the authors of some of these books, to boil down to faith in magic. The faith may be a modish one, the magic may be gimmicked-up, but it's faith in magic nonetheless. The savage uses incantations. We listen to formulas, "facts," techniques. For a people which prides itself on its no-nonsense practicality we have the most sublime confidence in mere words.

Now in magic the thing is to secure very big results by dint of very little effort and to secure them without enlisting the aid of any verifiable law of cause and effect. The medicine man claims to produce rain with a bull-roarer and a series of charms. If certain things are done according to ritual, he says, certain wished-for results will follow. Similarly the How-to boys assure me that if I learn certain words, follow certain rules, wear certain objects, swallow certain pills, I will become a good conversationalist, or sell more goods, or increase my powers of sexual attraction, or decrease my body odor, or even actually learn how to live with my own children. There's a key for every door and a door for every key and he must be subversive who whispers that these are wax keys to unopenable doors.

In certain respects our faith in magic differs from that of the primitive. For one thing, primitive magic flows out of the savage's relative ignorance of reality. He quite literally does not understand the world, but his ritual practices at least substitute forms and traditions for what would otherwise be chaos. We, however, are not so much ignorant of reality as in the process of moving away from it, losing touch with it, forgetting it. Friendship is a reality of whose existence we are sure. But when four million of us have to buy a book on how to make friends it must be because that reality is slipping from our grasp. About 20 per cent of the How-to books promise to remove the sense of alienation and loneliness that apparently afflicts so many of us. The rituals suggested are equivalent to the communal chanting and dancing through which the tribe periodically re-establishes its sense of solidarity.

Primitive magic is aristocratic. The innermost secrets are known only to a superior class of professionals. Our magic is democratic. The last thing Mr. Carnegie wants is to keep his special knowledge to himself. Primitive wonder-working we would expect to be pessimistic, as aristocratic societies often are: propitiation of the gods is a tricky business and only the tribal big shots have the know-how. But our democratic magic is optimistic, constructive: share the voodoo.

The primitive's faith derives from his helplessness before the mysteries of Nature. Ours, oddly enough, springs from our control over these same mysteries. Drunk on technological happy dust, elated with know-how, manic with our superb victory over things, we have almost unconsciously attempted to apply our knowledge in fields where it works poorly. It is as though Yankee ingenuity had mated with Los Angeles cultism—a union guaranteed to prove sterile.

There *is* a formula for the internal-combustion engine. There is none, I fear, for making prayer "effective." We suspect somehow that because there is a learnable trick to making things behave, there must be a similar learnable trick to making ideas and feelings behave. When I confidently apply a trick to materials that cannot respond to trickery, I am practicing magic. If I know that this is what I am doing, I am a faker. If I don't know, I am a savage.

The heart of magic is the notion of the infallibility of the absolutely right formula. The charm of our own special magic springs from the fact that mass communication makes the right formula immediately available to everybody. The logic is inescapable. Everybody reads *How to be a Consistent Winner in the Most Popular Card Games* (note how long the titles are—powerful incantations are rarely terse) and the money starts to flow in only one direction—toward everybody. Everybody reads *How to Add Years to Your Life* and the population gradually jells into one solid mass of oldest inhabitants. Everybody reads *How to Master Your Fears* and all the world's big bad wolves drop dead. To quote from another well-known book of magic: "At last the Dodo said, '*Everybody* has won, and *all* must have prizes!' "

For, lo! the winter is past, the rain is over and gone, the flowers appear on the earth: the time of the slinging of words is come, and the voice of the Dodo is heard in the land.

A Gentle Dirge for the
Familiar Essay

SAY WHAT you will of our manners, surely our essays grow
less familiar. With such masters as E. B. White, Christopher
Morley, Bernard DeVoto, and John Mason Brown exerting
their delaying action the eclipse of the familiar essay will be
slow. Nonetheless it is setting to the horizon, along with its
whole constellation: formal manners, apt quotation, Greek
and Latin, clear speech, conversation, the gentleman's library, the gentleman's income, the gentleman.

Some months ago over in London Sir Harold Nicolson held
a pocket mirror to the mouth of that fabulous invalid, the
novel, and pronounced it moribund. It can flourish, he thinks,
only in an age of settled social relations governed by at least
a minimum of agreed-upon conventions. A society ruled, like
ours, by a kind of universal uncertainty principle cannot, he
believes, nourish great fiction.

Busy as I am holding the hand of one of my own patients,
I would not for the world deprive Sir Harold of his. Yet I
should have thought that the novel, sly as Proteus and as
quick to alter, might make itself at home even in our house
of chaos. To my mind Fielding's *Tom Jones* and Faulkner's
A Fable have in common only the fact that both tell some
sort of story about imaginary persons. (This is no less true of
a good solid nightmare.) Yet *A Fable* is as much entitled to

349

call itself a novel as is *Tom Jones*. Furthermore, Mr. Faulkner's reputation stands higher than Fielding's ever did. He is currently pleasing tens of thousands of Champollions eager to decipher his latest Rosetta stone.

No, the novel may be suffering from fits, jaundice, and Cheyne-Stokes respiration, but I believe it will live. The patient Sir Harold should look for on tomorrow's obituary page is not the novel but the familiar essay. It is the familiar essay that is being starved by our time. On what does it live? The vitamin essential to it is the reader's willingness to hold casual ideas in suspension. In an age of order that vitamin abounds. But not in our age of anxiety.

Explaining the decline of the familiar essay is one of the few pleasures now available to the familiar essayist. One will blame the creeping politicalization of man, and it is true that different bloods course through the veins of the political animal and the polite essayist. Another will heave his half-brick at the big, black giant, Science, seeing in him the foe of the personal and the informal. The critic David Daiches points out that "there are too few people who know enough about enough matters to afford an audience for the attractive discussion which is expert without being specialized." Here the guilt is placed not so much on the shortcomings of our education as on the wildfire spread of our knowledge. There is something to the notion that the intimate discourse, bright with its thousand flowers of allusion, grows more richly in the climate of *omne scibile*, or at least in one in which a large number of people all know the same things. In the country of the specialist the merely educated man is lost.

The world of the personal essay is small. It has its own limits. They resemble neither the hard bounds of that vaster world in which all the answers are given, nor the blurred ones of that equally vast world in which no questions are asked. The familiar essay is not argument and it is more than entertainment. It was invented to seduce the reader into mental play during those intervals in which his mind prefers to hover like Mohammed's coffin between the purposive and the passive.

With the death of that kind of mind the familiar essay will die too. As the areas of both the purposive and the passive enlarge, the familiar essay's plot of ground narrows. It offers little to us when, hot for certainties, we read to improve ourselves, or compete with our neighbors, or bring ourselves up-to-date. And it offers even less when, swinging toward passivity, we cast about for the soft ottomans of print, finding them in the comics, the columns, and the picture magazines. Being neither quite useful nor quite trivial the familiar essay ends by being, like all outmoded reminders of a vaguely recalled lost paradise, somehow exasperating.

Almost 400 years ago in 1580 Montaigne laid down its pair of lenient laws. "What do I know?" he asked his own skeptic mind, and for an answer came up only with "It is my self I portray." The question marked out the method of the familiar essay, digressive and noncommitting. The answer marked out its subject matter, the ego of the essayist.

Its method, to those who think of words as either mental weapons or mental lullabies, seems quaint. So too does its subject matter.

The familiar essayist invites me to rest in the shade of the perpendicular pronoun. His connection with me is a personal one, chancy and fragile, a friendship sustained only by a few dozen paragraphs. He does not raise, much less settle, the kind of issue known as crucial. He is full of opinions and void of conclusions. He has the impertinence to solicit my interest in such useless topics as old china or getting respected at inns or the feats of Indian jugglers. By a cunning display of his personality he seduces me into a co-consideration of these small matters. He exerts charm, not that he may persuade me to anything, but solely for the pleasure of it. He demands only that I do my best to march with the humor or eccentricity of his mind. If I cannot follow him, the devil take me. He wants to involve me but not if it means truckling to my prejudices, streamlining his style for my greater ease, or pretending that in the veined shell of his paragraphs lies hidden the pearl of the Truth. The familiar essayist is his own man. At no price will he be mine.

His kind of ego is out of fashion. Others are in. We can and do admire the grand strut of the politician and the general. From the fact that they deal with important matters, such as war and politics, we conclude that their egos are of corresponding weight. The peacocking confessionals of film stars and odd-larynxed crooners attract us too, though differently. Since they live in a world so fabulous that no road leads from it to our own workaday one, the play of their egos becomes pure exciting spectacle, committing us to no response beyond gap-mouthed wonder and the pleasure of vicariously sharing in fairyland.

Our indifference to Montaigne as opposed to our lively interest in Marilyn Monroe is not explainable solely on the ground that one is dead, the other rather aggressively alive. The point is that one kind of ego is dead to us, the other alive to us. Montaigne is a private sort of fellow, with a queerly shaped mind. He takes a deal of knowing and, though he is willing to make me a temporary and partial gift of himself, it is only at the cost of effort on my part. But Miss Monroe's ego is a public one, adapted to general consumption and enjoyment by nature collaborating with the press agent. Montaigne is an individual able to converse at any time with only one other individual. Miss Monroe is an idol, ready at any moment to receive the worship of millions of communicants.

The ego of a twentieth-century "personality" is a kind of public utility, developed and expanded systematically by the techniques of publicity. In a way all of us feel that we own a small piece of Senator McCarthy or Debbie Reynolds. But the ego of a Charles Lamb or a Robert Louis Stevenson is a private non-utility. No matter how frankly it exposes itself, it never in either sense quite gives itself away.

The transformation of the private ego of the typical Renaissance hero into the public ego of the typical modern "leader" is reflected in our conversation. On all sides we hear talk about "the individual" and "individualism," talk inconceivable at the Mermaid Tavern or the court of Lorenzo de' Medici. Individuals don't champion individualism. They live it.

Of all the forms of writing it is the familiar essay, I think, that has suffered most from this transformation. The novelist can mount a soapbox and so compete with other public egos. The playwright, by the very nature of his trade, has always been half-public, half-private. The poet can retire into the fastness of himself, or content himself with talking to other poets. The essayist of another stripe—the travel essayist, the historical essayist, the propaganda essayist, the formal literary critic—can find his proper audience and remain, however perilously, in business. But to whom shall a man talk if he has some notions to advance on the decline of the walking stick? Who listens to the man who, varying the outburst of the old lady in the nursery rhyme, cries

> *Lawk a mercy on me,*
> *This is some of I!*

The Decline of Attention

ALMOST fifty years ago Henry James, a novelist desperately in search of an audience, isolated, in the course of a letter of December 11, 1902, to William Dean Howells, one reason for his commercial failure. He wrote:

> The *faculty of attention* has utterly vanished from the general anglo-saxon mind, extinguished at its source by the big, blatant Bayadère of Journalism, of the newspaper and the *picture* (above all) magazine; who keeps screaming, "Look at *me*, I am the thing, and I only, the thing that will keep you in relation with me *all the time* without your having to attend *one minute* of the time." . . . Illustrations, loud simplifications and *grossissements*, . . . the prose that is careful to be in the tone of, and with the distinction of a newspaper or bill-poster advertisement—these, and these only, meseems, "stand a chance."

The first thing that strikes one about this pronouncement is its accuracy if considered as prophecy. All the evils of which poor James complained would seem to have intensified since his day. Yet James did not think of himself as prophetic; apparently the decline of attention in the reading public was already, in 1902, a salient phenomenon.

Let us move back another hundred years. We find Wordsworth writing, in the preface to the 1802 edition of the *Lyrical Ballads*:

> For a multitude of causes unknown to former times are now acting with a combined force to blunt the discriminating

354

powers of the mind, and, unfitting it for all voluntary exertion, to reduce it to a state of almost savage torpor. The most effective of these causes are the great national events which are daily taking place, and the increasing accumulation of men in cities, where the uniformity of their occupations produces a craving for extraordinary incident which the rapid communication of intelligence hourly gratifies.

It is interesting to note, first, that the decline of attention had been clearly spotted as far back as 1802; and, second, that some of its causes—nationalism and industrialism—were more philosophically identified in that early era than in James's time. What James took to be the sources of the decline of attention—the blatancies of journalism and particularly of pictorial journalism—are really secondary effects or symptoms. At most they lend a helping hand; they are aids to inattention.

Let us be clear as to what we mean by attention. The faculty of attention itself cannot disappear. But it may be paralyzed by various pressures: the pressure of the German torture chamber, of the Kremlin propaganda mill, of the sensational journalism of James's complaint. It may also be displaced as to its objects; that is, attention may be unwilling or unable to fasten on the matters James cared for—the world of art and thought—and quite willing and able to fasten on a quite different set of objects: the mechanisms of industrial production, of a baseball game, of war.

It seems fairly clear that in our time the attrition of one kind of attention—the ability to read prose and poetry of meaning and substance—is becoming more and more widespread; and that the faculty of attention in general is undergoing a wholesale displacement away from ideas and abstractions toward things and techniques. The movement toward displacement is the result of calculated policy in such police states as the Soviet Union. It is a natural phenomenon, by no means universal, in free countries such as our own. The displacement may be glimpsed in the pages of those Utopias which begin with *Erewhon,* continue with *Brave New World,* and culminate in George Orwell's *Nineteen Eighty-four.*

When reflecting on these Utopias, it is important to remember that they were conceived by literary men, that is, by men belonging to the class most gravely menaced by the attrition or displacement of attention. Such men—Wordsworth, James—are naturally the first to notice the phenomenon from which they have most to fear. But there is a larger class—technicians, generals, Mr. James Burnham's "managers," certain kinds of journalists, certain kinds of government and labor bureaucrats—which has much to gain from the same phenomenon; and there is a very large class indeed which simply feels more comfortable in a society that does not demand from it any considerable systematic effort of the mind.

Here is Cyril Connolly:

The great artists of the past, despite the love lavished on them by scholars and esthetes, are becoming more and more remote and unfamiliar. They are not replaced by others because we are moving into a world of non-art. One has only to compare the world of the long sea voyage: sunsets—leisure—complete works of so-and-so—with the still mildly esthetic world of the train and then with the completely incurious existence of the air-passenger with his few reassuring leaflets issued by the company, his meals wrapped up in cellophane in a cardboard box, his copy of *Time* in case the sleeping pill doesn't work. This unseeing, unreading traveler is a symbol of the new public. Poetry for this civilization may well cease to exist, for no one except a few professors will possess the necessary ear to follow its subtleties. Reading aloud is almost extinct and the poet who wrestles with his subtle tone-effects secures his victories for himself alone. The hopeless are the irresponsible, the irresponsible are the lazy: we must accustom ourselves to a reading public which is both too slothful and too restless to read until a sense of values is restored to it.

But what meaning would this tirade hold for a publisher of comic books or a seller of big-magazine advertising space: men who are quite as good citizens as is Mr. Connolly and possess souls quite as immortal as his? To them all the things of which Mr. Connolly complains seem good, not bad; inability to read poetry is for them a sign of decency and inner happiness. No cheap irony is here intended. I wish merely to suggest that the decline in the ability to read is distressing only from a certain traditional—indeed, one might say reactionary—point of view. In larger perspective it may seem merely an inevitable change in man's mental outlook as he moves into a new phase of culture—or anti-culture. The poet will view this change differently from the anthropologist, who will view it differently from the grand masters of pictorial journalism, who will view it differently from the straphanging reader of a tabloid newspaper.

Let us try to consider the decline of attention as objectively as possible.

The first thing to make clear is that excellent books are being consistently produced and eagerly read. The question to ask, however, is this: do such books, read by a minority, make a connection with the *center* of our culture in the same sense that the latest issue of a picture magazine or the latest product from Hollywood *does* make such a connection? Our anthropologist would be forced to answer in the negative. I think he would have to admit that the success of such a book as Toynbee's *A Study of History* is an eccentric rather than a normal phenomenon.

I believe, furthermore, examination would reveal that such books are the consolation of the few (still fairly numerous—possibly a million in all) whose faculty of attention has been neither paralyzed nor displaced, but who fearfully sense such paralysis and displacement all about them. The cults of Faulkner, James, Eliot, Kafka; the excitement over the often admirable "new criticism"; the multiplication of little magazines with littler and littler circulations; the flowering of "difficult" poetry; the modest successes of such an uncompromising publishing house as New Directions, or such a vanguard magazine as *Partisan Review*; the limited but definite triumphs of the Great Books movement; the attention given to such educational "experiments" as St. John's College and such traditional pronouncements as those by educators like Hutchins and Conant—all these apparently disparate phenomena are really symptoms, not of the *numerical* growth of those who cultivate the faculty of attention, but rather of the growth of *the intensity of their need* for some mental pabulum other than that supplied by the central culture-purveyors of our time.

We may put it another way. From the time of the Greeks and early Hebrews up to the triumph of the nationalist spirit and the industrial revolution, the "highbrow"—Moses, Socrates, Thomas Aquinas, Voltaire—was instinctively regarded, however vaguely, as a leader of the human race. He fought, even if unsuccessfully, a vanguard action. Today the "highbrow"—Schweitzer, Hutchins, Einstein, Freud, Toynbee, Sir Richard Livingstone—is instinctively regarded, even when accorded a certain mechanical respect, as contrary to the trend of the times. He fights a rear-guard action.

If we limit our attention to literature alone, the fact that this action is rear-guard shows itself in dozens of ways. For instance, in a nation of 140,000,000, we have only two serious monthly magazines of general appeal—*Harper's* and *The Atlantic Monthly*. As we should expect (for they satisfy the intense thirst of a cultural out-group) their circulation is faithful, but it is also limited, and does not keep pace either with the growth of the general population, or with that of the specifically "literate." These and a few other serious magazines make valiant efforts to print material that demands a real effort of the attention.

But it is needless to point out that the magazines that really talk to the heart of our country are not these, but the others—the digests, the pulps, the picture magazines, the weekly news catalogues, the smooth-paper monthly mammoths. These vary widely in literary finish and "sophistication" (*Life*, for example, has published brilliant examples of scientific popularization). But they have in common this: in general they make no rigorous demand on the faculty of attention.

Some of the characteristics of this journalism are: brevity, simplification, the emphasis on timeliness (with its corollary, the conscious neglect or unconscious ignorance of the past), planned non-literary English, the avoidance of abstract ideas, the compartmentalization of life (this compartmentalization, as in the news magazine, is the verbal analogue of mass production's division of labor), the emphasis on "personalities" as well as the avoidance of *personality*, the exploitation of the "column" as against the discursive essay, the preference of the wisecrack to wit, the featuring of headlines (here, as elsewhere, modern journalism reveals its kinship, quite proper and natural, with advertising), the often remarkable ingenuity displayed in "packaging," an almost religious veneration for the "fact" (to be "well informed" is our substitute for the capacity to reflect), the rapid alternation of appeals (known as "balance," or something for everybody), and the careful exploitation of certain not highly cerebral interests, mainly in the areas of vicarious sex, criminality, violence, "inspiration," gadget-worship, and the idolization of contemporary gods, such as cinema stars, sports heroes, and clean-faced high-school girl graduates.

In general, a successful, technically admirable attempt is made to *attract* the attention without actually *engaging* it; to entertain rather than challenge; or, to use the editors' quite legitimate phrase, to be "readable"—that is, to present material which can be read easily and forgotten quickly.

The reader is reminded that the above description is not intended to be scornful. No reflection is here cast on the editors or publishers of these magazines. The appeal to inattention is as natural a development of our culture as is the mass-produced washing machine. There is nothing Machiavellian —with a few exceptions—about those who manipulate this appeal.

Pater thought the goal of all the arts was to approach the condition of music. It would seem that today the goal of the word is to approach the condition of the picture. The great triumphs of modern journalism have been accomplished not with the typewriter but with the camera; the lens is mightier than the sword. This is natural enough: the photograph (I am not referring here, of course, to the occasional production of a great camera-artist, such as a Steichen or a Gjon Mili) makes less demand on the attention than even the simplest sentence. It attracts at once; it induces an immediate stimulus, and it is forgotten directly. It is the ideal medium of communication without real connection, so ideal as to make it inevitable that the two great communications inventions of our time—the radio and the movie—should somehow copulate and engender television.

It was advertising that did most of the pioneering for modern journalism, that discovered the value of the pictorial and the visible. Advertising led the assault on the solid page of prose, led it so successfully that nowadays even the editors of serious magazines worry about "breaking up" the page, introducing "white space," and similar problems. Visibility is the thing: the comic strip represents its outstanding triumph, and sky-writing its enthronement in heaven.

The victory of the visible is closely associated with another victory—that of the clock. The long piece, the discursive essay, the attempt at a complete view of anything—these find publication only with difficulty. When *The New Yorker* devoted an entire issue to John Hersey's *Hiroshima*, admiration for the narrative's qualities was far less intense than astonishment (shock is really the word) at the mere fact that so long a piece of prose should be presented to the magazine reader for a single reading. The shortened paragraph, the carefully measured column, the "punchy" sentence are, of course, minor by-products of our clock-worship which began, as Mumford has brilliantly demonstrated, in the late Middle Ages with the advent of the commercial spirit, and underwent a vast development with the triumph of industry and technique. We modern readers want to "understand" a piece of prose as quickly as, let us say, we can understand the dashboard of our new cars. In both cases we wish to increase the sense of our own "efficiency" by subordinating ourselves to the errorless perfection of a machine.

We must beware of assuming that the prime *causes* of the decline of attention are to be found in such symptoms as the digest, advertising, the radio, television, the gossip column, the picture magazine, the soap opera, the mass-newspaper, the comic book, the pulps, the mammary-glandular "historical" work of fiction, the inspirational best seller, the cinema, the juke-box, the monosyllabic novel. They aid in the relaxation of attention, but they do not cause it. They are merely carriers of the germ.

Similarly, it is both ungenerous and superficial to blame our educational system. That, too, is a carrier, not a cause. It is true, as educators such as Bernard Iddings Bell have pointed out, that on the whole our primary schools no longer really teach the child certain basic skills (how to read, write, speak, listen, and figure) the non-possession of which works against the development of attention. It is true, as Bell says, that many of our primary schools, through the system of mass-promotion place a premium on mental laziness. It is true also that many of our high schools proceed on the make-the-work-interesting-to-the-student theory—which hardly conduces to the development of the intellect. Finally, it is true that the college, therefore, is forced to neglect its true function—which is to produce mentally mature leaders—in favor of performing, belatedly and therefore inefficiently, the elementary education duties that are properly the province of the primary and secondary schools.

The school is an instrument of our society; it cannot be that and at the same time be an agent of intellectual ferment. It cannot teach the virtues of attentiveness if the society of which it is a part indoctrinates the child hourly with the virtues of inattentiveness, or, rather, with the virtues of attentiveness to things, techniques, machines, spectator sports, and mass amusement, as against the virtues of attentiveness to knowledge, wisdom, and the works of the creative imagination.

The school—there are, of course, notable exceptions—has in general become a kind of asylum or refuge rather than an educational institution. In his noble jeremiad *Crisis in Education*, Dr. Bell quotes a high-school principal as saying:

"My real business is to keep adolescent boys and girls, regardless of educational aptitude and desire or the lack of them, from running the streets, getting into trouble, and becoming an intolerable nuisance in the community. The easiest way to keep them willing to submit to the school's control and so, incidentally, to hold my job, is to provide for them a vast amount of amusement and a minimum of work to do."

This seems a fair statement. All it means is that if our culture desires to produce, not rational men, but producers and consumers, the school becomes a useful place in which to quarter and divert the youthful citizen until he is old enough to produce and consume. The point is well put, entirely without irony, by Professors Russell and Judd, of the University of Chicago, in *The American Educational System*: "Most young people today are not able to enter industry or other types of gainful employment before age eighteen; in many cases not before age twenty. The best method of occupying the time of such young people is an important problem, and the solution of this problem by requiring an extended educational period, regardless of the immediate value of the education as such, may be socially wise." Dr. Bell further quotes them as saying that American education may have to depart from the usual academic and vocational disciplines if it is to be "made of sufficient interest to appeal to most young people in this country."

It is clear that this conception of the school is not at all eccentric or cynical. It is realistic. It simply tunes in on the wave-band of our society in general. However, it is also clear that it will hardly be apt to produce men and women capable of paying attention to a reasonably complex story or exposition, much less capable of reacting to the highest types of literature, such as poetry, tragic drama, philosophy, or religious reflection.

The phrase quoted above, "of sufficient interest to appeal," is the crux of the matter. The future citizen is made the criterion; you must "appeal" to him, or be lost. Thus the reading public becomes a "consuming public" that must be *sold* words and thoughts. In consequence the writer tends more and more to obey the doctrine of cultural Jacobinism—to wit, that he is equal to his audience, but not superior to it. He must "please," and the quickest way of pleasing involves simplification, overemphasis, and all the other ingenious techniques of modern communication.

Naturally, a great many writers, members of the outgroup, reject this theory. They believe that if they do not know and feel more than their audience, there is no particular point in being a writer. They write, therefore, in accordance with outmoded standards—and to date have succeeded, as a general thing, in finding an audience of people more or less like themselves, relics, holdovers. This audience, particularly in free countries like our own, is still quite numerous. It supports many excellent publishers, several book clubs, a multitude of good bookstores. It welcomes eagerly such novelists as Graham Greene, Miss Compton-Burnett, Elizabeth Bowen—writers who are not ashamed, nay, are proud, to make stiff demands on the attention of the reader. But, whatever it may contribute to our culture, it does not appear to be solidly in the mainstream.

That mainstream is composed largely of men and women whose faculty of attention is in process either of decay or displacement. In decay it is incapable of grasping reasonably complex works of literature or speculation. In displacement it is highly capable of grasping the often formidable intricacies of business, machinery, technology, sports, and war.

For the fundamental causes of the decline of attention, we

shall have to go back to our quotation from Wordsworth. They lie deep in the history of the last three hundred years and are almost surely connected with the rise of aggressive nationalism and the victory of the industrial revolution. At some point in the not very remote past a profound shift in our thinking took place. An interest in altering and vanquishing the environment by means of mechanical techniques plus an interest in material accumulation began to oust our traditional interest in discovering the nature of man and expounding his relation to God. Nationalism set itself up against universal thought, substituting for it local and temporal dogma. Industrialism erected definite, easily understandable standards of values, quite at variance with the ethical, religious, and esthetic standards that had, at least in theory, prevailed before its time. These standards "paid off"—that is, the man who lived by them found himself becoming "successful" or "adjusted."

It seemed more useful to fix the attention on a new system of double-entry bookkeeping or the mechanism of the internal-combustion engine than on *Hamlet*. It *was* more useful: it was also more enjoyable.

If the man who likes *Hamlet* finds himself a member of an outgroup, even a tolerated outgroup, sooner or later he may wonder whether it's worthwhile to like *Hamlet*. If there are no, or few, social rewards accruing from the exercise of the faculty of attention, he may tend increasingly to permit its attrition. If the rational man is made more and more to look like a fool he may cease to prize his rationality. Very few like to be reactionary, setting themselves against the current of their time. Most of us want to be part of contemporary history, and if contemporary history does not demand of us any rigorous ordering of the faculty of attention, we will either allow it to decline or we will fix it upon those objects or processes in which the majority of our fellow-citizens seem to be genuinely interested.

The humanist will cry out against all this; but he forgets that humanism itself is no more than three thousand years old, a short parenthesis in history. At one time the mental habits of the caveman prevailed over the earth. There seems no absolute reason why the mental habits of George Orwell's robot man of 1984 should not come to prevail during the next few hundred years. Those reactionaries who believe that man is unchangeably a rational soul will have faith that Orwell's world, too, will pass; and that man is bound to return to the pursuit of those goods Socrates and Jesus pointed out to him. But it is doubtful that this return will on a large scale come to pass in our own time. For the moment the humanist would seem constrained to bide his time and conserve the faculty of attention as the church conserved the riches of the classical tradition during what is unfairly called the Dark Ages.

Children's Reading

Portrait of the Author as a Young Reader

THOSE to whom reading is fated to become important generally shake hands with books early. But this is not always true. Many distinguished writers were blockheads at their letters until a comparatively advanced age. I think, however, of an undistinguished one who was a busy reader at four: me. My first book was entitled *The Overall Boys. The Overall Boys* was and doubtless still is a rousing tale of two devoted brothers, aged five and seven, and their monosyllabic adventures on a farm. The style was of transparent lucidity. I found *The Overall Boys* a perfect job then, and, looking back, I haven't been able to detect any flaws in it. I remember it in greater detail and certainly with greater pleasure than I do the 576-page novel I finished yesterday. At four I was convinced that *The Overall Boys* represented the peak of the art of narrative and sternly rejected all attempts to make me continue my reading adventures. This resistance endured for a lengthy period—about a week, I should say. Then I broke down, tried another book, and have been doing the same sort of thing ever since. But all devout readers will agree that my first literary judgment was correct. Everything after *The Overall Boys* has been anticlimax. One's first book, kiss, home run, is always the best.

Between the ages of four and ten I read but moderately

and with absolute catholicity. We had in our household the usual meaningless miscellany that accumulates if the parents are not specifically literary. Thus I read whatever lay behind the glassed-in shelves of two dreary-looking black-walnut bookcases. I devoured the standard "boys' books" scornfully discarded by my elder brother. I bored my way through at least ten volumes of an unreadable set of historical novels by some worthy named Mühlbach, I think, and got absolutely nothing from them; the same result would be achieved were I to read them now. I read an adventure story about the Belgian Congo that made an anti-imperialist out of me when I was eight; I have seen no reason to change my views since then. Something called *Buck Jones at Annapolis* similarly made me permanently skeptical of the warrior virtues.

I read an odd collection of "daring" books that many families of the period kept around the house, often hidden under lock and key: Reginald Wright Kaufman's *The House of Bondage*; something called *The Yoke*, which was on the same order; Maupassant complete, though this may not have been until I had reached the mature estate of twelve or thirteen; and similar luridnesses. These had no effect of any sort on me, as far I can recollect, though I suppose a psychoanalyst could, at a price, make me tell a different story.

The child reader is an automatic selecting mechanism. What he is not emotionally ready to absorb, his mental system quietly rejects. When in later years I became a teacher of literature I could never see the point in censoring my young charges' extracurricular reading. Very often the mothers (never the fathers) of my high-school students would ask me to explain my refusal to forbid Mary or John to read James Joyce's *Ulysses*. I never offered any satisfactory explanation except to say that if John or Mary were ready to understand *Ulysses* then they were ready to understand *Ulysses*, which was a Good Thing. If they were not ready to understand it, which was apt to be the case, then *Ulysses* would at most waste their time, on which I was not prepared to set any exaggerated value. Often an anxious mother would inquire whether I didn't agree that the last chapter (Mrs. Leopold Bloom's uncorseted memories of an exuberant life) was shocking. My reply may have been frivolous, but it seems to me it contained the germ of the truth: that she found it shocking mainly because she had not had the chance to read *Ulysses* when she was seventeen, wherein Mary or John had an advantage over her. This generally closed, without settling, the controversy.

As you can see, part of my four-to-ten reading was orthodox for a small child (I forgot to tell you that I also toddled through a volume of Ibsen, and found him impenetrable) but the unorthodoxies had no effect whatsoever. What I really liked was what any small boy or girl would like— what I was ready for. This included, of course, a moderate amount of what is called trash—the Rover Boys, Horatio Alger, Wild West yarns, Jack Harkaway, the whole conventional canon of those days.

I say trash. Actually such books are "trash" only by standards which should not be applied to children's reading. They have the incalculable value that listening to perfectly inane adult conversation holds for children: they increase the child's general awareness. They provide crude paradigms of character, motivation, life experiences. That is why it seems to me that the trash of my generation was superior to the trash of today. I submit that *The Rover Boys in the Everglades* and *Frank on a Gunboat* are preferable to Superman and his kind on two counts: they were cleanly and clearly written, and their characters were credible and not entirely unrelated to the child's experience. When I was nine I could learn something interesting about life from even such highly colored affairs as the Frank Merriwell series, but I know that my son can learn nothing whatsoever of genuine interest (that is, which he can check against the expanding universe within himself) from the comics. I believe firmly that the current juvenile literature of the impossible is meretricious compared with the honest hackwork my own generation enjoyed.

Between ten and seventeen I did the major bulk of my reading. I have never read as many books per year since, nor do I expect to in the future. Those were the splendid years, and it is my notion that they are the splendid years of most devoted readers. After seventeen (in some cases a year or two later) the books choose you, not you the books. You read within limits. Reading becomes a program. You read as part of your college curriculum, or to gain knowledge in a specific field, or to be able to bore your neighbor at dinner-table conversation.

Even the reading done during one's college years lacks the spontaneity, the high waywardness of one's pre-adolescent and adolescent reading. It circles around the classroom. It consists of authors recommended by authority or who you feel should be "covered." Or it has to do with books you know a good deal about in advance, one of the most effective ways to spoil one's reading pleasure. Such reading may be mentally stimulating or socially useful. It may benefit you in a dozen ways. But it is not an adventure in quite the same sense that reading in your second decade so often is.

I am not, in this random biblio-autobiography, proposing to list the books I have read. Nothing could be duller or less useful, except when he who does the listing owns a mind whose operations are really of interest to mankind, as was the case, for example, with John Stuart Mill. All I am here endeavoring to do is to outline some of the processes whereby an average person became an above-the-average reader, which is what I immodestly claim to be. To understand these processes a mere catalogue of titles is of no avail.

Yet I would like to list a few names, mainly to indicate the kind of writer that, as I recall, influenced the more bookish boys and girls of my generation. Shaw, Galsworthy, Bennett, Conrad, Merrick, Barrie, Moore, Dunsany, Yeats, Synge, Swinnerton, Chesterton, Meredith, Wilde, Hewlett, Gissing, Zangwill, and above all H. G. Wells—these, to confine the list to Englishmen only, are a few of the authors I remember devouring from my tenth to my seventeenth year, miscomprehending many, overprizing some, but getting from all an exultant sense of discovery, a peak-in-Darien thrill rarely enjoyed since.

The secret of second-decade reading, of course, is that you are not really finding out what Shaw thinks or Conrad feels, but what *you* think and *you* feel. Shaw and Conrad and the rest are but handy compasses to guide you through the fascinating jungle of your young self. When I read Wells' *Tono-Bungay* at fourteen or fifteen, I found myself saying in delight, "But that's just the way *I* feel!" When I now read Thomas Mann's *Joseph* story I find myself thinking how true it is to the experience of men in general. There is a difference in the quality of the emotion. The grown-up emotion may be larger and wiser (and probably more pompous), but the boyish one is unique just because it is so utterly, innocently self-centered.

During this adolescent period of my reading life I had a lucky break. My brother, five years my senior and a student at Columbia College, was at the time taking a conventional survey course that used a sound standard anthology known, I think, as *Century Readings in English Literature,* edited by

Cunliffe, Pyre, and Young. For some reason, possibly a mild
fraternal sadism, he made me take the course along with him
—he at college, I at home. The whole thing was over my
head—I was fourteen—but when I had finished my *Century
Readings*, which took a year, I had at least a hazy notion of
the course and development, from *Beowulf* to Stevenson, of
the most magnificent, after the Greek, of all literatures. I remember writing essays, perhaps no more interminable than
my subjects, on Hakluyt and Spenser. I am still unable to dis-
lodge from my memory—which is not a good one—odd lines
of verse from minor poets like Drayton. That is all of no account. The important thing is that I got through my head at
an early age a few simple truths: that the proper reading of
a good writer requires energy and application; that reading
is not mere "diversion"; that it is impossible to admire writing
you do not understand; that understanding it does not destroy but rather enhances its beauty; that unless a writer's
mind is superior to, more complicated than, your own, it is a
bore to read him. (That is why I never recommend a book
to a person if it is on his own mental level.)

I learned also that daydreaming and intelligent reading do
not go together. There is a story told by Dr. Sandor Ferenczi,
the psychoanalyst, about a Hungarian aristocrat who, while
devouring a quick lunch between trains, was recognized
by a boorish acquaintance.

"My dear Count! How are you?"

"Umph."

"And how is the Countess?"

"Dead."

"How shocking! It must be terrible for your daughter."

"She's dead."

"But your son—"

"Dead! Everybody's dead when I'm eating!"

During my all-out period everybody was dead when I was reading. Most children and adolescents know this magical secret of concentration, though it is not till they are older and duller that they realize it was magical.

I remember that, when I was fourteen, we lived about two miles from the nearest library. I had a choice. I could cycle there, borrow my books, and cycle back in a very few minutes —but those few minutes were lost to reading. Or, if I wished, I could walk to the library, reading the last fifty or seventy-five pages of my calculatedly unfinished book en route, make my borrowings, and walk back, reading a new volume on the way. I usually preferred the latter procedure. It is no trick at all to read while walking, to step off and onto curbs with unconscious skill, to avoid other pedestrains while your eyes are riveted to the page. There was a special pleasure in it: I had outwitted Father Time. I think Providence meant me to be an ambulant reader, for I never once even stumbled. But one afternoon when I was cycling home from the library with my wire basket full of books, I was hit from behind by a car and sent sprawling.

This absorption, this "losing yourself" in a book, though clearly quite remote from "practical life" (for children "practical life" is simply what grownups want them to do), is not daydreaming. The child does not interpose a continuous, fuzzy, wavering screen of personal desires and wishful visions between himself and the page. On the contrary, he and the page are one. The Victorian female, with whom novel reading was a disease, was the real daydreamer. For her, reading became a drug, a kind of literary marijuana, an instrumentality for the production of needed visions. The child's hearty relation to his book is devoid of this sick quality.

Well, the course my brother gave me, via that blessed trinity Cunliffe, Pyre, and Young, was calculated to make me understand that literature, beyond helping one to discover oneself, has a higher, more impersonal function. It is a challenge issued by a higher mind, the author's, to a lower mind, the reader's. Even if the challenge is not met, much pleasure may still result. But if it is met, or if a sincere attempt to meet it is made, a finer, rarer pleasure is experienced. If you read for pure diversion, well and good, but if you read for any other purpose, always read above yourself. One of the reasons for the general mental fuzziness of most "cultivated" people we know is that publishers have become too shrewd. They have learned, the cunning little fellows, just how to temper their books to the lamblike mental innocence of their readers. The result is that every week we are deluged with books which, the publishers assure us, we can understand. It is quite true. We *can* understand them, all too easily. It would be much better for us if now and then we read a book just a few rungs beyond our mental capacities in their most relaxed state.

My second-decade reading—and I think this is sadly true of most of us—was in this sense educationally more valuable than any I have done since. During adolescence our feeling of bewilderment and insecurity tends to be greater than at any other time. Hence the need to know, to learn, is greater. Therefore whatever reading is done is intense. It is utterly assimilated. We pay absorbed attention to it, as we would to the instructions of an expert before venturing into a trackless forest.

It seems to me that in my late teens I did more "heavy" reading and digested it more thoroughly than at any succeeding period. In this connection I recall two antithetical experiments I made extending over an interval of six months. The first was an experiment in difficult reading. The other was an experiment in non-reading.

One summer I decided to spend my evenings reading only "hard" books. I went at it with the humorless obstinacy of a sixteen-year-old—and I was more humorless and more obstinate than most. I staggered wildly through stuff like Ueberweg's *History of Philosophy*, Winwood Reade's *Martyrdom of Man*, Saintsbury's *History of English Prosody*, Taine's *History of English Literature*, Gibbon's *Decline and Fall of the Roman Empire*. It was enough for a book to seem important and forbidding—I read it at once. No novels, no light literature of any sort, no magazines for three solid months—hot months, too. Now, as I look back on this extravagant experiment, it seems like the disagreeable behavior of a young prig. Yet I was not really priggish; I didn't read for show-off purposes. I read my Ueberweg as a challenge to myself, as a test, as a deliberate gesture, if you will, of self-punishment. The boy of sixteen by overexercise will punish his body deliberately just to see how much it can take. That same boy may punish his mind in the same way. It is a kind of initiation ceremony that he performs upon himself, a queer, grotesque test of approaching manhood. Sometimes he will decide to go right through the Encyclopaedia Britannica.

Well, that was Experiment Number One. The second was its opposite. I decided to spend three whole months reading nothing at all, not even a daily newspaper. (The three months coincided with a long absence from school, so the conditions for the experiment were at their optimum.) Now, why did I want to do this? It was again a matter of self-testing. I felt I had grown too dependent upon other people's ideas. The only way I could perceive to cure myself of this dependence was to abjure other people's ideas completely. The mental life of the adolescent is frequently characterized by this oscillatory quality. He can find out what his real nature is only by leaping from one extreme to the other.

And so for three months I read, as nearly as I can recall, virtually nothing. It was by no means a fruitless experiment, and to those held too tightly in the grip of the reading habit I heartily recommend it. The effect is purgative. The mind disgorges a good deal of waste and clutter, it slows down, for a time it seems vacant. Then gradually it fills again, this time not with the myriad, second-hand impressions induced by non-stop reading, but with the few clear ideas and desires that reflect more accurately your true self. The experience, in addition to being cleansing, is humbling; you realize how sparse is the net content of your mind.

I have known men and women who read so voraciously and continuously that they never have the time or opportunity to discover who they really are. Indeed, I suspect it is precisely because they prefer not to make that discovery that they cling so limpetlike to books. I suppose this is better for them than alcohol or hasheesh, but it is not very different. All of us, I am sure, have noticed people who suffer from reader's fidgets. If there is a book, a magazine, any piece of print within easy reach, they will at once take it up, idly, without real intent to peruse it, but out of a kind of mechanical compulsion. They will do this while they are talking to you, while you are talking to them, while engaged in some other activity. They are victims of print. Perhaps some dim premonition that unless I watched out I too would become afflicted with reader's fidgets made me carry through with entire success my three months' literary fast.

Some years ago I helped to manage a bookstore featuring a circulating library. The main body of customers consisted of commuters. Every evening, a few minutes after five, the commuters would dash in.

"Give me a novel!"

"Any special title?"

"No, any novel will do: it's for my wife"—as if that somehow made everything clear.

These commuters' wives—there are tens of thousands of them—were not really in any active sense doing any reading at all. They were taking their daily novel in a numbed or somnambulistic state. They were using books not for purposes of entertainment, but as an anodyne, a time-killer, a life-killer. Many "great readers" are of this class. Truth to tell, they have never read a book in their lives.

Akin to these novel-addicts are the newspaper fiends who read three, four, or five papers a day and supplement them with radio and TV news reports. There is only one Keeley cure I can recommend for this weakness, and that is for these people to save their papers for a week, and go back and read the news of seven days before. They will then see, even in the short perspective thus provided, how unimportant most "spot news" is. They will perceive that, if taken in overfrequent doses, its main effect is to bewilder or even to frighten, rather than to inform. A ration of one newspaper a day ought to be enough for anyone who still prefers to retain a little mental balance.

Serious reading is an art. An art is something you have to learn. To learn an art requires a teacher. There are too few such teachers of reading in the United States, and that is one of the reasons why we are still only a semi-educated people. I, like my fellow Americans, was never taught, in elementary and high school, how to read properly. Thus, when I reached college, I was but ill-equipped to understand any really original book that was handed to me, though I found no particular difficulty in getting through the required textbooks, manuals, and other predigested matter. I do not think I would ever have learned how to read had it not been for one man and one college course.

The man was John Erskine and the course was, rather absurdly, called Honors. Erskine himself was largely responsible for the conception underlying Honors, which in turn was the only begetter of Robert Hutchins' Chicago Plan, of the St. John's College classics curriculum, and in fact of the whole return in modern education to the great tradition of Western thought. John Erskine was a man of such varied talents that his original contribution to American education is often forgotten.

It is very hard to explain why Erskine was a great teacher. He was not a character as Copeland of Harvard was. Although always genial and fair, he never attempted to make the students like him. He did not act as if he were a perennial contestant in a popularity contest. (I am convinced, by the way, that those teachers who year after year are voted Most Popular by the undergraduates are rarely educators of great value.) In his literature courses Erskine never swooned over beauty or tried to make you "feel" the lines or the paragraph.

There were two things about Erskine that may help to explain the influence he wielded over his students, even over those who didn't care greatly about literature. One was his enormous respect (not merely liking) for his subject matter. This may seem a commonplace, but it is not. Many teachers —no more surprisingly than other frustrated human beings— have a silent, gnawing contempt for what they teach. Unaware of this contempt, they often find it subtly translated into a resentment of their students. The result is vitiated teaching, teaching of a purely formal sort.

Erskine not only loved his subject but reverenced it and respected himself for teaching it. There was thus a good moral relationship between himself and his work. It may seem high-flown to say that this moral relationship was a vital aid in the production of good teaching. Yet I'm sure this was the case.

He could teach his students to read because he had a large and lofty attitude toward what we were reading.

At the same time, if Erskine had been able to communicate only this attitude, he would not have been the great teacher he was. He went beyond this. To put it simply, he challenged us to *understand* what we were reading. He called upon us for a kind of mental exercise that is ordinarily devoted to mastering such "hard" subjects as philosophy and the sciences. (Actually, there are no "hard" or "easy" subjects. Donne is as difficult and as rewarding as Euclid.) Erskine made us work and the odd thing about it was that the more we understood, the more we liked the particular book we were reading.

The Honors Course was but a systematic extension of the Erskine educational program. For two years, under the guidance of a group of selected instructors, we read and talked about one great book a week, beginning with Homer and concluding, as I recollect, with William James. That was all there was to the course, and it was by far the most valuable one I took at college. You will find a good account of it and its influence in *How to Read a Book*. (Mortimer Adler was also one of my teachers, and a first-rate one, too.)

Well, Erskine and a few other teachers (particularly the poet Mark Van Doren) plus the two years I spent in the excellent company of fifty or sixty of the great writers of all time taught me, I hope and believe, how to read. I was lucky.

Books for Children

DURING MY younger years, mainly between the ages of eight and ten, I, like my contemporaries, read a few "good" books, though they were not recommended to me as good. Such recommendations are hardly necessary. The child, if reasonably intelligent, has almost infallible good taste. Probably his good taste reaches its peak at that time. We all felt, when we encountered *Tom Sawyer* or, to hit a lower level, Thomas Bailey Aldrich's *Story of a Bad Boy* or, on a still lower level, that fine New England classic *Lem* (is it still read?) that these books had something not possessed by *The Pony Rider Boys in the Ozarks.* It wasn't that they were more exciting, for sometimes they weren't, but that they were more "real." The other books were read eagerly and with joy, and then forgotten—indeed, they were read *to* be forgotten, to be "finished." But *Tom Sawyer* was something you caught yourself remembering a week later, and a year later. I know now, of course, the reason the child feels these books is that the authors felt them. It is as simple as that. That is why the so-called "better" juveniles that flood the bookdealers' shelves every year—the skillfully constructed, highly educational, carefully suited-to-age, morally sanitary, psychologically impeccable children's books—don't really make much of a dent on the child's consciousness. They are constructed for "the market." I don't mean the commercial market, but the market that is supposed to be the child's brain, as if that brain were

382

a kind of transaction center in which each transaction was expressible in definite educational quanta.

The trouble with these juveniles is that their authors are greatly interested in children and not much interested in themselves. Now, when Mark Twain wrote *Tom Sawyer* and *Huckleberry Finn* he never stopped to figure out whether his "boy psychology" was correct, or whether his story was properly adapted to a given age level. He wrote because he was passionately interested in himself, and the Mississippi River in himself, and the boy still alive in himself. Children ever since have unconsciously felt this intense reality, and that's what they've loved.

They've loved *Huckleberry Finn* even though it is over their heads, or written in old-fashioned English or dialect, or concerned with events that happened a long time ago. As a matter of fact, the child delights as much in ambiguity as he does in clarity. *Alice in Wonderland* is still an overwhelming favorite, not because it's so funny but because it's so strange.

In this connection I always think of a comment my great and good friend the late Hendrik van Loon made to me one day. Going over, for editorial purposes, one of his manuscripts intended primarily for children, I pointed out to him the large number of long, difficult words which, as I thought, youngsters would never understand. He merely said, "I put them in on purpose." I learned later what he meant: that long words tickle the fancy of children, that they like the slight atmosphere of mystery distilled by a really bang-up polysyllable.

I think also that children—just ordinary, wholesome children, not bookworms—are more sensitive to beautiful writing than is generally supposed. They'll read reams of careless prose with great enjoyment, but when they come across the real thing, they know it. I don't know how they know it, but they do. As a child my elder son was not overfond of books.

Rather than forgo an airplane flight he would willingly have
seen the Forty-second Street library vanish in flames. When
he was seven I tried the young barbarian on *The Wind in
the Willows*, and he could make nothing of it. I tried him
again a year later. He finished it with absorbed calm, clapped
the book to, and said with finality, "Now, that's what I call
well written!" The fact is that *The Wind in the Willows* was
the best-written book he had read so far, and he somehow
knew it, though he had never been given any hint to affect
his judgment.

The smooth confections the publishers turn out today are
not well written in the sense that *The Wind in the Willows*
is. They are merely correctly written. The authors in most
cases have unconsciously curbed any impulse toward style,
because style would express themselves, whereas they are
supposed to be writing for the sake of the children. If they
would forget all about the children and set down freely and
lovingly the child in themselves, they might by some glorious accident produce masterpieces. *Little Women* was not
written *for* little women or little men or little anybodies; it
was the expression of a passionate memory.

I am a firm believer in the newer methods of understanding
and handling children. But it is arguable that they have made
difficult the creation of a twentieth-century *Little Women*
or *Alice in Wonderland*. Such books are the product not of
knowledge, or even of wisdom, but of a kind of dream life,
a dreaming-back to childhood on the part of the writer.
Dream life and "child psychology" do not mix.

One of the games bibliomaniacs play in their weaker moments is the game of Century-Hencery, or literary prophecy.
It's a harmless sport, the best part of it being that there can
never be a loser. Here's how it works. You list the ten books
you believe will be most widely read and generally admired

a hundred or five hundred or a thousand years from now. Then you defend your choices. Making the unwarrantable assumption that in 2455 our civilization will still be recognizably related to that of 1955, I will now set down the ten works of literary imagination produced by the English-speaking race that I believe will be most universally alive (not merely admired in the schoolroom) five hundred years from now. Here they are, in no special order:

The Plays of William Shakespeare
Moby Dick
Gulliver's Travels
Robinson Crusoe
Alice in Wonderland
Huckleberry Finn
Little Women
Some novel of Charles Dickens, probably
  David Copperfield
Treasure Island
The Mother Goose Rhymes

It is possible that in constructing this list I have been ingenious rather than ingenuous. Whether by accident or design it reflects one of my favorite theories—that the gods tend to grant immortality to those books which, in addition to being great, are loved by children. For mark well that only two books out of the ten—Shakespeare and *Moby Dick*—cannot, generally speaking, be enjoyed by youngsters. Of the remaining eight, seven are usually ranked as children's favorites. My point is simple: as the generations pass, children's tastes change more slowly than do those of grownups. They are not affected by the ukases of critics or the whims of literary fashion. Thus Shakespeare was not universally admired by the eighteenth century and again may not be (though I'd place a small bet against that possibility) by the twenty-third. But the rhymes of Mother Goose have suffered no diminution of popularity and, being unmoved by the winds of literary doctrine, are not likely to suffer any.

This is what happens. All children who read at all are introduced at a fairly early age to, let us say, *Robinson Crusoe*. Most of them like it. Later on they meet it again in school. They are told it is literature, and its hold on their minds is re-enforced. Still later, in adult life, they may encounter it again, when they are ripe to see in it qualities not apparent to them as children. Any possible resistance to accepting *Robinson Crusoe* as a great book had been broken down years ago during their childhood. Thus *Robinson Crusoe*'s prestige remains undimmed. But a classic of greater artistic weight, such as *Paradise Lost*, does not enjoy the advantage of having been liked by readers as children. It is read by a small, select group of adults (college students) and so never passes into the consciousness of the generality. I do not mean that Milton will not be read five hundred years from now. I mean he will not be a casually accepted, generally enjoyed classic as I think *Little Women* or even *Treasure Island* (the most uncertain item, by the way, on my list) is apt to be. But remember, the book must be literature to begin with. Defoe's *Robinson Crusoe* will live, but J. R. Wyss's *The Swiss Family Robinson* is already dying.

We talk a great deal about the Greek classics. Yet what Greek classic has really penetrated among us? Not Plato surely, or any of the dramatists, but Homer and more particularly the simple, beautiful Greek myths that are read with pleasure by each generation of children. Similarly, I think Perrault and *The Three Musketeers* will outlast Proust and Stendhal, and Grimm's fairy tales still be widely read when Goethe is forgotten. If you wish to live long in the memory of men, perhaps you should not write for them at all. You should write what their children will enjoy. Or, to put it in another way, a book already has one leg on immortality's trophy when, to use Lewis Mumford's noble phrase about Van Loon's *Story of Mankind,* "the words are for children and the meanings are for men."

May I make one or two further random comments on this list? Note that three titles—*Moby Dick, Robinson Crusoe,* and *Treasure Island*—have no women characters to speak of, and several of the others depend hardly at all on romantic interest. I do not believe that love, commonly considered one of the great staples of literature, tends as a subject to have any supreme preservative value. It is Dickens' sentiment and humor, not his lovers, that attract us. It is hardly the most romantic of Shakespeare's plays that stand highest in popular esteem. And Melville, in providing his masterpiece with an all-male cast, knew what he was doing.

Finally, if I were asked to make a wild stab at the one book likely to outlast the nine others, I would name *Alice in Wonderland.* This does not mean it is the "best" book on the list, for obviously it is not. In the end the best survives but the best of the best does not necessarily survive longest. Mankind will cling to what it admires, but even more fiercely will it cling to what it loves. And what we love perhaps above all else (as Dr. Freud pointed out in other and more dismaying connections) is ourselves as children. That is why I think it quite conceivable that Lewis Carroll will be read at some remote future time when Shakespeare is no more remembered than, let us say, Plautus and Terence are today. Twenty centuries from now Shakespeare may be entirely owned and operated by scholars. But I do not see why people should not still be laughing and exclaiming over *Alice in Wonder-*

land. Among the few things resistant to the tooth of time, great fantasy is one, and great fantasy is always the special possession of children.

Not long ago, testing some of these notions, I submerged myself for an entire week in a sea of books for children. This diet of forcible reading consisted of fifty-one juveniles. In the course of seven dizzying days I was by turns Toddler, Active Child, and Older Boy and Girl. I was Fact-minded, Imaginative, Unadventurous, Bookish, Outdoor, Serious, and Family-centered.

From this experience I emerged at first filled with a sense of gratitude to author, illustrator, and publisher. The books of my childhood were far less colorful and varied than children's books today. Fewer books were written for us—one sparse month during my ninth year I subsisted entirely on Tallentyre's *Life of Voltaire* and *What Every Young Man Should Know*, which occupied a modest place behind the bookcase. The new books in those days often looked drab, and many seemed to have been composed by people five hundred years old.

Now all is changed. The fifty-one juveniles I read bristled with pretty pictures. Not one of them was "trashy." Many will interest, amuse, or improve the young reader.

But few will transport him.

Unless he is imitating his seniors, Junior does not read to kill time—the capacity for boredom is a distinction of maturity. To the child, says Arthur Ransome, "a good book . . . is an experience, something that he lives." Consider, though, how little the child actually *does* read. Librarians estimate that about five hundred books represent the *maximum* the average child can get through between seven and fourteen.

That's about seventy per year. Hence the child simply cannot afford the commonplace.

Now, several of my fifty-one examples were, without being first-rate, excellent. But the overall impression was one of high-level, conscientious, blameless, golden mediocrity.

In a great many of the books there was a tendency to view the child as a specialized animal. But the whole *point* of being a child is that he's plastic, or should be. Lear and Carroll and Stevenson understood this—they wrote for children *as* children. The books I read, however, were not for the most part written for children, just children. They were written, often with skill, for children who are presumed to be horse-minded, lumber-industry-minded, X-ray-technician-minded, weather-minded, turtle-minded, bee-minded, mining-minded, or Amalgamated-Clothing-Workers-of-America-minded.

All children, of course, have their hobbies. When I was nine I collected cigarette-box pictures of exuberantly curved ladies of the stage, all clad in tights. The collecting satisfied me; I did not lust for a book on the subject. Children may have special interests, but their major interest is the miracle of childhood itself. Being a child is in itself a profession. For this reason it is an error to assume that for every adult interest there is a corresponding juvenile form.

No, let the child breathe his own air. Render unto Caesar the things that are Caesar's, and unto the children the things that are the children's. I recall one writer who, in a violent endeavor to find a juvenile equivalent for *Hamlet*, dreamed up a story about Hamlet's three offspring (the consequences of marrying Ophelia) and how, with the help of their tutor Horatio, they defeated the villainous Fortinbras. An eleven-year-old, after finishing this stirring tale, commented, with deadly restraint, "I think it very misleading to put Hamlet and Ophelia into such a story."

Misleading indeed. Children know where they live, in a world that, as Paul Hazard in his charming study *Books, Children and Men* says, is a "universal republic." But the universality is of a special kind. It is big enough to admit another universe such as Alice's Wonderland. It is not big enough to admit the Amalgamated Clothing Workers of America. I cannot believe that thousands of grubby little hands will reach out eagerly for a book about lockouts, injunctions, and arbitration agreements. Nor do I envision a stampede of embryo journalists toward *Peter Zenger: Fighter for Freedom*. It is good for the child to know that during colonial days Peter Zenger won a case that established the principle of a free press. But that's sufficient; 242 pages about him assumes a degree of specialized interest that either does not exist or, if it exists, should be gently discouraged.

The child cannot too early learn to be a good citizen? I think this is questionable: citizenship is an adult affair. Let school and home teach the child to respect the laws and institutions of his country. For the time being that should suffice. To use the juvenile novel or biography to turn the child into an internationalist or an advocate of racial tolerance may be high-minded, but I would suggest that the child first be allowed to turn into a boy or girl. Pious Little Rollo is dead; the Good Little Citizen is replacing him. The moralistic literature of the last century tried to produce small paragons of virtue. How about our own urge to manufacture small paragons of social consciousness?

All good literature shares the same central interest—the human mind and heart. This is equally true of *Tom Jones* and *Tom Thumb*, of old King Lear and Old King Cole. The earliest storytellers for children knew this well. Here is a sentence from Perrault: "It is quite possible that the wood-cutter was more vexed than his wife, but she kept teasing him and he felt as many other people do who admire women who say the right thing, but find extremely tiresome those who never say anything *but* the right thing." Perrault deemed such a delicious insight a proper one for the consideration of the nine-year-olds of the seventeenth century. How many of our juvenile writers would dare insert a similar sentence in their books?

I admit that wisdom, humor, and imagination are not easily come by. It is easier to exploit a "subject" or work up a background than to delight the child by suddenly raising the curtain on the human heart. But a book is not as good as its subject; it is only as good as its writer.

It is with mixed respect and bewilderment that I read such productions as *Minn of the Mississippi*, written and beautifully illustrated by Holling C. Holling. It's a kind of pedagogical novel about a snapping turtle who travels downstream from the Mississippi's headwaters to New Orleans. By the time she reaches her journey's end she must surely be the best-educated turtle in turtle-history. We learn right along with her everything from Minn's scientific monicker (*Chelydra Serpentina*—she changed her name to Minn for business reasons) to the essential facts of La Salle's explorations. Perhaps there exists a multitude of youthful chelydraphiles who will be mad for Minn. But I would still prefer to place in their hands *Life on the Mississippi*. They will learn less from it. But inside themselves they will grow something new: Mark Twain.

These neat volumes describe everything—frontier life in 1782, the ways of the beaver, a country garage, the landmarks of England, the geography of Hawaii, Mexican handicrafts, and labor conditions among the coal miners of West Virginia.

From them the child can get a thousand things that an A. A.
Milne, an Andersen did not have the knowledge to supply.
Two things only he cannot get. In these pages he cannot find
himself. He cannot lose himself. Pleasant, "adapted" to the
child as such books are, they do not make even a furtive try
at producing that quick, almost fearful sense of enlargement
that comes with the tap of a cane in the courtyard of an old
inn, with the sight of a footprint on the shore, with the contemplation of a bottle labeled *Drink Me.*

I do not wish to seem captious. The average level of children's literature today is probably as high as, or higher than,
it has ever been. To call for quantities of books as good as
The Wonderful Adventures of Nils or *The Story of a Bad Boy*
or *Hans Brinker* (I purposely select works not of the first
order) would be unfair. But I do not think it unfair to point
out that the temperamental bent that generated such books
seems rare in our day; and that the writers do not appear to
want to encourage it in themselves.

There is a growing tendency among them to choose subject matter which compels them to fold the wings of their
fancy. It is hard to describe this subject matter short of saying that it does not seem to call for a writer at all. Among
my week's juveniles were a dozen brief, matter-of-fact narratives of what may very well have been actual, homely
occurrences in the life of a child—a visit to the zoo, the loss
of a tooth, a trip across the bay in a motorboat. These tiny,
carefully unpretentious, "lived-out" realistic stories are the
kind of artless yarns that twenty-five years ago the parents
themselves would make up by the yard. This parental job has
now been taken over by the professional. It is a necessary and
pleasant task, but one which should be a normal part of the
family routine, no more.

Our juvenile writers sail close to the coast; they refuse to let themselves go. They are almost *too* shrewd, they have read too much Gesell and Piaget, they are full of "age levels" and "vocabulary norms."

They have their own pet rules. Robert McCloskey, whose illustrations are delightful, says, "The most important thing is verbs—for action—and the big problem, when you get down to the very last, is to keep the pictures and the action close together." Mr. McCloskey is talking about books for very young children; yet I cannot help thinking how even these very young children will, quite fascinated, read or listen to the conversations on the raft in *Huckleberry Finn*, conversations which are scandalously verbless and even in many editions bare of any pictures whatsoever.

Speaking of pictures, I've been wondering whether they aren't *too* good. Perhaps the money and ingenuity and taste expended on them have a tendency to intimidate the mere writer, making him feel that his words are just a necessary accompaniment to the illustrations. The child is no more naturally picture-minded than he is word-minded or idea-minded or sound-minded. But if you feed him nothing but pictures or make them far more attractive than the text, he *will* become picture-minded. Soon he will begin to neglect, then overlook, at last despise words.

In my childhood the illustrations in the geography book were so wretched they drove me to the text. The pictures in one book, *The Golden Geography*, by Elsa Jane Werner, illustrated by Cornelius De Witt, are so beautiful, however, that I cannot imagine what child would ever let himself be led away from them by such seductive statements as "The countries of southeastern Europe raise tobacco, along with other crops."

Part of our trouble perhaps is rooted in the "age-level" fetish—don't make it too hard for the little dears. I am for making the little dears do some work. Soft food makes soft teeth. Write a little *above* the presumed mental level of your audience. Puzzle the child a bit, bewilder him a bit, set him guessing, groping, force him to think and feel a little above himself.

Of my fifty-one exhibits, for example, the one that seemed to me finest was *The Merry Miller*, by Rosalys Hall, illustrated by Kurt Werth. This is a gay little tale about a miller's widow who was too fat to get out of the mill which had been bought by the *new* miller. The problem is solved in a sly Gallic fashion which actually has a faint touch of the naughtiness that children love. Miss Hall breaks other rules, too. Writing for very small children, she uses such words as *dilemma, manacles, embarrassing, circumstance,* and *infuriated*. What she has really done is to write to please herself—and the result is something Perrault or Andersen might not have been unwilling to sign. I should add that *The Merry Miller* will give a real, if small, pleasure to grownups—and that, to my mind, is one of the infallible tests of a first-rate child's book. Good ones charm everybody, in different ways. Bad ones bore everybody, in the same way.

Perhaps the trouble with our writers for children is that too many of them are mesmerized by their audience. Their eyes are too respectfully fixed on the kiddies. But fine works of juvenile literature are created not so much in response to the external pull of the child in the audience as in response to the internal push of the child in the writer. Great books for children are rarer than great books for grownups for the very reason that the writer of a fine juvenile must be able to look not only *at* himself, but *back* at himself. He must be able almost at will to build up again within his imagination the child that lives forever in all of us but whose voice so few can hear.

Unless our writers for the young can re-possess the sense of wonder that the nineteenth century, for all its shortcomings, was habitually familiar with, the books they fashion may become more and more competent, skillful, morally sanitary, and ideologically blameless, but within their pages the miracle itself will not be wrought. And if it ceases to be wrought, the sense of wonder will begin to die away in our children, and if that happens, there's not much sense in their *being* children at all. They might as well be born adults and have done with it.

Mother Goose

THE QUESTION before the House, Gentlemen, is: What fictional characters so far conceived by the English-speaking peoples are most likely to be alive and kicking in the human imagination in the year 2455?

Hamlet? Huck Finn? Robinson Crusoe? Silver, whether Long John or Hi-yo? I choose a different set entirely. For their ability to survive the next half millennium I place my bets on such personages as the well-known cynophile, Mrs. Hubbard; the ingenious Jack, domestic architect; the lunatic and saltatory cow and her companions, the cat, the fiddle and the amusable dog; Gotham's trio of sapient mariners; the neurotic Porgie; the frangible Dumpty; the well-adjusted Sprats; those opposed ethical philosophers, Doctor Green and Professor Stout; the variously unfortunate Misses Muffet, Etticoat, and Peep; Banbury Cross's digitally symphonic equestrienne; and the Dee's antisocial but sanguine miller.

As by 2455 I expect to be in poor shape to make a door-to-door collection of bets, I propose to defend my thesis here and now.

Let us begin by noting that, in general, verse lasts longer than prose. Rhyme, and especially rhythm, form the benzoate of soda of letters. This in itself might mean little. It means more when you add, as you must, that these rhymes of the nursery comprise the best-known, the best-loved, and the most rapidly diffusing body of verse in the entire world.
396

In Hindustan at this moment small Hindus are chanting *Humti Dumti char gia jhat,* and confiding to each other the story of *Mafti Mai's* grisly encounter with the spider.

During the Napoleonic wars the British briefly occupied the Danish island of Anholt. Of that occupation no trace remains today, save one: diminutive, non-melancholy Danes sing what is to them a nonsense rhyme—

> *Jeck og Jill*
> *Vent op de hill*
> *Og Jell kom tombling efter.*

In fact I think I may boldly aver that, as against one inhabitant of this planet who knows how King Lear lost his kingdom, there are ten thousand who know how three kittens lost their mittens. If you seek a basic, a universal literature, incline your ear to the runes, the rhythms, the riddles of childhood.

Furthermore, may we not from the very antiquity of the rhymes argue their futurity? Even if, as the Opies point out in the magnificent annotated and illustrated collection* from which these facts are pilfered, nursery rhymes are less old than enthusiasts once thought them, still they are venerable enough. Of the 550 pieces in their Dictionary, at least one quarter and probably over one half are more than two hundred years old. About one in four, it is startling to realize, was known in the days when young Will Shakespeare walked the lanes of Stratford. Rove back to Imperial Rome: in Persius, in Horace are lullabies and doggerel that, across the chasm of two thousand years, call to us in the faint but true voice of Mother Goose—or shall we say Anser Matrona? For four centuries the frog has been setting off with his opera

---

* The Oxford Dictionary of Nursery Rhymes, edited, with an introduction, by Iona and Peter Opie.

hat to go a-wooing. The game of London Bridge, with its odd, plangent, heart-constricting tune, is linked to ghastly stories of infant sacrifice that find their dark source in the deep Middle Ages, or beyond them. And there are students of linguistics who believe the life of Humpty Dumpty to be measured in "thousands of years." Is the human race apt lightly to relinquish what it has so long treasured?

Again, consider who has preserved these rhymes for us— the arch-conservatives of the race, those savagely ritualistic creatures who listen with glittering eyes, ready to spring at your throat should you dare to change a syllable of the familiar bedtime story. Children, confident that they themselves are the only really up-to-date creatures, care not a whit for novelty or fashion; if they do, beware, for they are monsters and will turn into literary critics. Not only are their own memories inflexible as steel, but they seem to have inherited the memories of all the children who preceded them. What today's nursery loves today, tomorrow's nursery will love tomorrow. Through the procession of the generations these strange beings bind themselves together with an unbreakable chain of oral communication—the shrill immemorial chant of the street game at dusk, the fiercely put riddle at the chimney corner, the doggerel mumbled at the cribside. Yes, even though, as the Opies point out, the rhymes were not originally written for them, Mother Goose is safe enough in their clutching hands. If you wish to live forever, write perfectly for men—but see to it that the children of men love what you write. They are your life rafts. They are the eternal monasteries in which is preserved, through many a Dark Age, a vast part of what is most common in the culture of mankind.

But I will go further. In 2455 I think nursery verse will still be green and branchy because much of it, judged by high standards, is remarkable writing, proper to be read or recited

for its own intrinsic interest, its oddness, its grimness, its
humor, its satiric force, its narrative power, and its magic.

Consider its variety. Consider, if you will, the variety of
the amatory and erotic verse alone. Here is an American
version of an old favorite which, for sly truth to nature, conveyed with the utmost technical dexterity, is matchless:

> *Whistle, daughter, whistle,*
> *And I'll give you a sheep.*
> *—Mother, I'm asleep.*
>
> *Whistle, daughter, whistle,*
> *And I'll give you a cow.*
> *—Mother, I don't know how.*
>
> *Whistle, daughter, whistle,*
> *And I'll give you a man.*
> *—Mother, now I can!*

The Opies quote a Scottish version of

> *When shall we be married,*
> *Billy, my pretty lad?*

which is as gaily and naughtily erotic as anything by the
Cavalier poets. And there are other amorous nursery rhymes
—lyrical, sentimental, impertinent, absurd, even obscene.

The tenderer lullabies are familiar enough—but for knife-
like pathos, how about these six lines?

> *Bye, O my baby,*
> *When I was a lady,*
> *O then my baby didn't cry;*
> *But my baby is weeping*
> *For want of good keeping,*
> *O I fear my poor baby will die.*

Indeed there are many lullabies that seem to be soothing but
which, like the best-known of all (*Hush-a-bye, baby, on the*

tree top), are, when you ponder the words, fearsome enough.

The gamut of humor is no less wide, from almost pure nonsense to the drollery of

> *Two little dogs*
> *Sat by the fire*
> *Over a fender of coal-dust;*
> *Said one little dog*
> *To the other little dog,*
> *If you don't talk, why, I must!*

Nursery humor can be realistic to the point of the scabrous. Take the scandalous account of Elsie Marley who grew so fine that she wouldn't get up to feed the swine. Elsie was, it would appear, a real personage, and I may as well tell you, my little dears, that she was no better than she should be, if that.

(Elsie did actually exist, and a few other nursery characters can be keyed to actual events. The Opies, however, gently but firmly dispose of the fond notion that most of the rhymes are covert political satire or deal with historical personages. You will find this theory developed with a kind of genial, stubborn eccentricity in a monument of awry scholarship* I have encountered, lately reprinted twenty-one years after its first publication. From the history-ridden Mrs. Thomas one learns that Bo-peep was Mary, Queen of Scots; Simple Simon was James I; and that the cat who frightened the little mouse, the cat who was involved with the fiddle, and the cat whose coat was so warm were all Queen Elizabeth, or Good Queen Puss.)

To come back to the real Mother Goose: at times her realism is grim to the point of the shuddery. One ballad be-

---

* *The Real Personages of Mother Goose,* by Katherine Elwes Thomas.

ginning *There was a lady all skin and bone* is so macabre
that the poet Southey, hearing it as a child, would break into
tears and beg his family to stop. No, there is not the slightest
doubt, as many earnest souls have pointed out, that nursery
verse is amoral, at times even immoral. (Which is precisely
what the child's world is, of course.) Nursery rhymes deal
boldly with everything, except the whimsical-supernatural
that, it is mistakenly thought, children favor. There are few
elves or fairies in Mother Goose.

Indeed, she can be heartless, violent, bloody, mocking, and
impious. It is the recognition of this fact that has led the
versatile Frank Scully to rewrite Mother Goose so as to "de-
emphasize fear, terror and punishment and emphasize faith,
hope and charity instead." In Mr. Scully's version* the piper's
son is sent to Boys Town for moral regeneration, Mary's little
follower has become the Gentle Lamb of God, and the old
woman who lived in a shoe "had many children because she
wanted to." (And bad cess to ye, Peg Sanger!) One hopes
this sanitated version will have a gentling effect on the mop-
pets, but I have my doubts. I have seen too many of the
black-hearted brats identifying themselves enthusiastically
with the farmer's wife who performed that caudal amputa-
tion on the three blind mice.

However, it is unfair to stress only the more naturalistic
aspects of Mother Goose. What children also feel, without
quite knowing what it is they feel, is the brief but absolute
magic of many of the poems. Robert Graves has well and
truly said, "The best of the older ones are nearer to poetry
than the greater part of *The Oxford Book of English Verse.*"
G. K. Chesterton thought *Over the hills and far away* one

* *Blessed Mother Goose: Nursery Rhymes for Today's Children,* by Frank
Scully.

of the most beautiful lines in all English poetry. He must have been right for, as the scholarly Opies remind us, it has been used by Gay, Swift, Burns, Tennyson, Stevenson, and Henley. Many have felt the wild romantic feeling, the true Coleridgean thrill, in

> *How many miles to Babylon?*
> *Three score miles and ten.*
> *Can I get there by candle-light?*
> *Yes, and back again.*

or in the mysterious

> *Gray goose and gander,*
>   *Waft your wings together,*
> *And carry the good king's daughter*
>   *Over the one-strand river.*

William Blake might have written

> *Little boy, little boy, where wast thou*
>   *born?*
> *Far away in Lancashire under a*
>   *thorn,*
> *Where they sup sour milk in a ram's*
>   *horn.*

And, as others have pointed out, one of Shakespeare's clowns might well have sung

> *When I was a little boy*
>   *I had but little wit;*
> *'Tis a long time ago,*
>   *And I have no more yet;*
> *Nor ever, ever shall*
>   *Until that I die,*
> *For the longer I live*
>   *The more fool am I.*

In an Elizabethan play by William Wager (*c.* 1559) one of the characters sings a snatch of an old nursery song. When reprimanded for mouthing such doggerel, he replies, "My Mother, as I war wont in her lappe to sit she taught me these."

She taught us these. And what she taught is deathless.

The Maze in the Snow

In 1928, ONLY thirty years after the death of its author, Dr. A. S. W. Rosenbach forked out £15,400 for the original manuscript of *Alice's Adventures in Wonderland*. This was the highest price brought by any manuscript ever sold in England. The figure represents the peak point of a semireligious cult which is now leveling off, though on a high plateau.

The whole phenomenon of Carrollatry is unique in the history of English literature. Here is a mediocre mathematician, Charles Lutwidge Dodgson, who engages the attention of first-rate scientific minds: Whitehead, Russell, Eddington. Here is an orthodox deacon whose general discourse and demeanor suggest a painfully limited mind but who fascinates sophisticated intellects: Edmund Wilson, William Empson, W. H. Auden, George Orwell, Virginia Woolf. Here is a celibate Oxford don to whom nothing happened and who becomes the theme of book after book, biography after biography, essay after essay. If the children should fail in keeping him alive, the commentators will succeed.

It is easy to make fun of the Carroll cult. But cults arise out of something worth cultivating. The cultist may exaggerate. He does not invent. Hilaire Belloc, who thought that *Alice* would not survive the secure Victorian golden afternoon, has already been proved wrong. Chesterton, referring to "the implication of national loyalty" to Lewis Carroll, protested mildly but protested vainly. The tall, thin, shy cleric with the stammer, the fussy maiden aunt whose life was a caricature of Victorian propriety, who wrote serious poetry of ineffable badness, who was at ease only with little girls, who, as the real Alice recalled, "bore himself as if he had swallowed a poker"—this man-child-woman, this odd Dodo is here to stay.

Recently his legendary private diaries, not hitherto available to the public, and covering most of his life from 1855 to a month before his death, were published in two handsome, overconscientiously edited volumes.* They are quite, quite dull; a monotonous account of his proper visits to his proper relatives; of his mild, happy encounters year after year with little girl after little girl; of his armory of hobbies, particularly photography, in which field he was an early master (he seems to have invented the first self-photographing device); of his London playgoing visits; of his conventional reading; of his pottering Oxford activities as sub-librarian, mathematics lecturer, and Curator of the Common Room; of his unceasing stream of publications, some queer, some tedious, all of them interesting to the student, two of them now humanity's property.

A dull man. A fascinating man. Apparently he lived in almost complete unconsciousness of the intellectual currents of his exciting century. By profession he was a man of God and a man of mathematics. As a man of God he seems the perfect Victorian. Occasionally he suffered from doubts of his own goodness. But it would be quite true to say that he remained unshaken by the fundamental uncertainties that assailed the brainier Victorians—Huxley, Arnold, Butler. As for mathematics, he remained pretty much on a high-school-

* *The Diaries of Lewis Carroll,* now first edited and supplemented by Roger Lancelyn Green.

teacher level, quite unaware of the vast mathematical revolution that was shaking Europe in his day. In morals he
carried conformity to the point of the eccentric: "The play
is *not* a nice one, being spoiled by the regular *French* element
of making love to another man's wife." Socially he was a
curious mixture of the prim, the timorous, and the immature.
Mark Twain thought him the stillest and shyest full-grown
man he had ever met, with the exception of Joel Chandler
Harris. He was so retiring that he even hid his hands continually under a pair of gray-and-black cotton gloves.

He conceals nothing from us. His correspondence and diary
are full to weariness. He seems to have had no hidden life.
He was in the ordinary sense of the word a happy man. From
little girls he received the only kind of love he sought or
seemed to need. He wears his piety on his sleeve. A good,
kind, avuncular Victorian was the diaconal Charles Lutwidge Dodgson, known as Lewis Carroll.

And yet—

Why the curiosity about him? Why the legend? Why the
hundreds of theories to explain him and his books? Why does
the very name of Lewis Carroll make the psychoanalysts
jump and jitter? Why is he a field day for the literary critics,
the symbolic logicians, the semanticists, the mathematicians?

There is *something* there—and in the fifty-seven years since
his death we have become more and more convinced of it.
He is full of paradoxes, big ones and little ones. In the middle of a period of gigantic technical development, this fuss-
budget of genius invented dozens of useful gadgets, including Scotch tape, but never commercialized any of them to
any considerable degree. His letters to grownups are crashing bores; his letters to children are often as funny as anything in the *Alice* books. He was a model of intellectual orthodoxy and shrank from fresh ideas; yet as far back as 1856

he could write casually, "May we not then define insanity as an inability to distinguish which is the sleeping and which the waking life?" His letters and his diaries are full of sweetness and light—but *Alice,* for all its moral tone, gives any sensitive grownup the most troubling impression of the bizarre, even the morbid. The same man who disliked the "unpleasant" characters in *Wuthering Heights* created the kitchen scene in *Alice,* the Duchess, the Red Queen and the White.

He must have been, like so many eminent Victorians, a sorely divided man. Granted—but to trace the dividing lines is not so easy. Like the transformations in *Sylvie and Bruno,* they blur and waver.

Was his genius akin to lunacy, as some have thought? Did he attempt, as his ingenious biographer Florence Becker Lennon believes, to "deal with the whole of life in terms of a game" and did this lead him into an eerie, hallucinated world, represented by his boring, frightening novel *Sylvie and Bruno?* Was he a split personality? Was he a Peter Pan, refusing to grow up? Was his tender, pure affection for little girls ("They are three-fourths of my life," said the truthful Mr. Dodgson) an escape from religious doubt, or from the responsibilities of grown-up love, or from the Victorian world which he seemed to accept wholeheartedly but which oppressed him unconsciously?

And what about the Alice books? What *are* they? No one knows. They are not one thing to children and another thing to adults. They are many things to children and innumerable things to adults. Are they just nonsense, as Carroll said of his *Hunting of the Snark?* (But then he went on to say, most disturbingly, "Still . . . words mean more than we mean to express when we use them.") Is *Alice,* as Professor Harry Morgan Ayres thinks, a satire on the repressive effects of education on spontaneous childhood? Or is it a deeply Freudian book, thick with unconscious symbolism, with the fall down the rabbit hole a birth dream, and so on? Is it, as Dr. Paul Schilder believes, a wicked book, full of "oral sadistic traits of cannibalism . . . enormous anxiety . . . fear of being cut to pieces . . . severe deprivation in the sphere of food and drink"? Or is it a *roman à clef*, with the Duck in the Caucus Race being really Canon Duckworth, the Mad Hatter Gladstone, the lion Gladstone again, the Unicorn Disraeli, the Dodo Dodgson (pronounced Dodson) himself? Or is it a subtle semantic joke, or a translation into dream-world symbols of Dodgson's mathematical and logical hobbies?

All these notions, even the most lurid of them, can be and have been persuasively defended by good minds. It is unfair to dismiss them, as Alice dismissed the looking-glass court, by declaring them only a pack of cards. Of *course* Alice is a delightful fantasy and can be read merely as one. But equally of course *Hamlet* is a bloody melodrama of revenge and can be read merely as one. I do not suggest that the two works are of equal stature, only that they are of equally fruitful ambiguity.

The most interesting thing about Dodgson is how he happened to compose *Alice*. We know the circumstances. On the "golden afternoon" of July 4, 1862, Dodgson, his friend Canon Duckworth, and Dr. Liddell's three little girls went for a row up the Isis. One of the girls was named Alice. She acted as coxswain, Dodgson rowed bow, Canon Duckworth stroke. As he rowed Dodgson began to invent a tale. "I . . . sent my heroine straight down a rabbit-hole, without the least idea what was to happen afterwards. . . ." Thirty-four years later Alice Liddell recorded, "On the next day I started to pester him to write down the story for me." He did so, adding to it as he went along, publishing it three years later.

And so, on the second most important July fourth in history, during the most fateful three-mile voyage of which we have record, *Alice* was born.

These, we say, are the circumstances. But at the *process* that produced two of the most absolutely original works in the language we can only guess. We *do* guess and perhaps will never cease guessing. The game is as absorbing as any Dodgson ever contrived. As a child he once traced a maze in the snow, and of that maze his posthumous life is but a tantalizing prolongation.

Next in interest is his love for little girls. It is hard to see anything perverse in this. Today we acknowledge quite casually the existence of a large minority of oversexed people. We tend to forget that by the simple law of averages there must exist a similarly large minority of undersexed people. But they are not so visible. Most of them surrender to social conformity, get married, and cause vast amounts of silent misery. I think Carroll was undersexed, but also honest, decent, and courageous about it. His love of little girls was not a sexual release, for he didn't need any. It was a perfectly pure, proper passion of a kind more common in his day than in ours and therefore less comprehensible to us. Ruskin fell in love with a twelve-year-old girl and proposed to her when she was nubile. Swinburne was crazy about babies and toddlers. Coventry Patmore worshiped children.

Today this spontaneous *love* of children is rarer than it was in Victorian times. Instead we "understand" them, or, as we so self-revealingly say, "give them love"—which is a little different from just loving them.

Passions are fashions. The love of the child in all his innocence is today deemed "sentimental." That is one reason why our juvenile books are mediocre, while the Victorians and Edwardians produced masterpiece after masterpiece, from the pens of Carroll, Lear, George MacDonald, Kingsley, Barrie, Kipling. There is somewhere in Carroll's diaries a revealing sentence: "I fear it is true that there are no children in America." At about the same time a much more astute observer, Henry James, was making the same observation. We Americans have come to value the child's smartness, or aggressiveness, or "ability to adjust," or even his sophistication. But to value the child's *childlikeness*, his essential innocence and sweetness, is old-fashioned.

What gives the *Alice* books their varying but permanent appeal is the strange mixture in them of this deep passion for children and the child's world with an equally deep and less conscious passion for exploring the dream world, even the nightmare world, filled with guilts and fears, which is a major part of the child's life, and therefore a major part of our grown-up life.

All this has been written before, and by better pens than mine. But it cannot be said too often. The *Alice* books, for all their deceptively simple language, belong to palimpsest literature, in which text after text may be scraped off, only to reveal a new text beneath. *Hamlet* and *Moby Dick* and the works of Dostoevski are part of this palimpsest literature too. They are very great and *Alice* is very small; but they and *Alice* are of the same queer company. And, to make the game even more interesting, we know enough now about Dodgson himself to feel that he, too, is a palimpsest. Perhaps we will never have done with new readings of the thick-layered parchment that was his life.

How Pleasant To Know Mr. Lear!

I'VE BEEN reading a good deal of nonsense of late—I mean intentional, simple-simonpure nonsense, by one of the masters in the field, Edward Lear. Sixty-five years after his death, two industrious Learists have dug up some hitherto unpublished odds and ends.* I found these no better than middling dull but they had the happy effect of sending me back to a rereading of this peculiar and lovable Englishman. In his lifetime Lear did many serious things, but his life made most sense when he was being most nonsensical. His memory will be kept green—particularly by children, who are specialists in greenkeeping—by the Owl and the Pussy-Cat, the Jumblies, the Four Little Children Who Went Round the World, the Dong with a Luminous Nose, the Yonghy-Bonghy-Bo, the Pobble Who Has No Toes, Mr. and Mrs. Discobbolos, My Uncle Arly, and the leading citizens—Old Persons mostly —of Limerick Land.

The real world is continually going out-of-date; and the "realler" it is (see yesterday's paper) the more quickly it moves into the shadow of the has-been. Whatever Lear did that was of his time is dead. When he created a time and space of his own choosing, he got a handhold on immortality. Of all his contemporaries Lear venerated Tennyson most.

---

* *Teapots and Quails and Other New Nonsenses,* by Edward Lear, edited and introduced by Angus Davidson and Philip Hofer.

Yet I would wager that when the noble Lord is but an anthological memory, thousands of readers of all ages will still be greeting with delight

> *the old Man with a beard,*
> *Who said, "It is just as I feared!—*
> *Two Owls and a Hen,*
> *Four Larks and a Wren,*
> *Have all built their nests in my beard!"*

Edward Lear's life, like some of his limericks, was sad, distracted, and absurd. He was one of twenty-one children, six of whom, perhaps reluctant to face the competition, died in infancy. That under such conditions Lear should have emerged at all is a kind of miracle, as though a single ovule in a mass of caviar were to develop into an egg of distinction. Lear's stockbroker father employed his occasional non-generative moments in bankrupting himself. Accordingly, at fifteen, young Edward was already beginning to earn his bread as an artist, if of a highly specialized kind. In addition to supplying the medical profession with drawings of morbid diseases, he became a kind of zoological John Singer Sargent. He will probably rank in psittacidical history as the world's most accurate painter of parrots. He was hardly less adroit with tortoises, turtles, and terrapins.

Raised by an elder sister, most informally educated, accustomed from young manhood to support himself through the precarious patronage of the aristocracy, Lear throughout his long life never felt a solid floor beneath him. He traveled restlessly through much of southern Europe, Asia Minor, and India, undergoing unnecessary hardships and even perils, always unsure of his goal, always hesitant to put down roots.

From time to time he settled in London, but the heliotropism that ruled so many Englishmen of his period constantly

drew him south. During one of his London stays he gave
drawing lessons to Queen Victoria. Once, in admiration of
the Royal collection of miniatures at Buckingham Palace,
Lear broke out impetuously, "Oh! Where did you get all
these beautiful things?" With regal calm the Queen replied,
"I inherited them, Mr. Lear."*

Lear was a model example of a by no means rare combination: long life (he died at 76), bad health, and high
energy. From the age of seven he was a victim of the "Terrible Demon," epilepsy. A Park Avenue psychiatrist would
have loved him as a casebook demonstration. In addition to
epilepsy, poor Lear had asthma, excitable nerves, and a perfect manic-depressive pattern. He was afraid of dogs and, a
sinister sign, they didn't like him either. His sight was bad, he
had bronchitis, and in his latter years a heart weakness.
Brought up among ten sisters, which is enough to unfit any
man for life, he never married. There is, however, no indication of any abnormality in his sex habits, unless you care to
count the fact that from the evidence he just didn't have any.
Following a fever he lost most of his head-hair, compensating
for it by a Victorian jungle of beard and whiskers. At forty-
one—so lively was his sympathy for children—he cut two new
teeth. No one has described Lear better than he himself, in
his sad-funny Self-Portrait:

> *How pleasant to know Mr. Lear!*
> *Who has written such volumes of*
> *stuff!*
> *Some think him ill-tempered and*
> *queer,*
> *But a few think him pleasant*
> *enough.*

---

* For this anecdote, as indeed for most of the facts about Lear's life, I am
indebted to Angus Davidson's workmanlike biography *Edward Lear.*

His mind is concrete and fastidious,
His nose is remarkably big;
His visage is more or less hideous,
His beard it resembles a wig.

. . . .

He has many friends, laymen and
clerical;
Old Foss is the name of his cat;
His body is perfectly spherical,
He weareth a runcible hat.

Lear was one of those unquiet souls the Victorian era produced in wholesale quantities, his inner turmoil and desperation overlaid by an outer orthodoxy of conduct imposed upon him by the conventions of his time. The most respected and respectable Englishmen of the period frequently exhibit this paradox—Tennyson himself, the arch-Victorian, had a frantic streak in him a mile wide. Lewis Carroll carried primness to the point of oddity. As for poor Lear, his fundamental disease was loneliness arising from the impossibility of ever receiving as much love as he was willing to lavish. This nursery god who charmed thousands with his gay nonsense and who fascinated children ("I knew he was 'safe,'" said one of them years later) was the same creature who could make diary entries such as "Woke to impatience, blindness and misery, incapable of deciding whether life can be cured or cursed." His letters—he sometimes wrote thirty-five before breakfast —are often bubbling over with his characteristic nonsense, but an underlying despair reveals itself again and again: "If you are absolutely alone in the world & likely to be so, then move about continually & never stand still." Or again: "At present I am doing little, but dimly walking along the dusty twilight lanes of incomprehensible life."

Lear wanted from the world something it cannot give, perennial childhood. From this sprang his charm, but also his melancholy. One must look behind the mock-Cockney jocularity for the wistfulness hidden in his vision of Utopia: to sit "under a lotus tree, a eating of ice creams and pelican pie, with our feet in a hazure coloured stream with the birds and beasts of Paradise a sporting around us."

He knew "everybody," particularly the well connected, for he seems to have had the double charm of the child and the entertainer. Yet, though his friends remained loyal and even affectionate, they never seem to have been adequate to the love demands he almost apologetically made upon them. It is probable that the only creatures who really returned his love were his Albanian servant, Georgio Kokali, and his cat Old Foss, who lived to be seventeen, predeceased Lear by a few months, and of whom he has left an affectionate pictorial record. At times Lear must have felt himself as abandoned as his great namesake; and perhaps saved himself from madness only by his ability to play his own Fool.

This melancholy Englishman with the odd nose, the out-sized spectacles, the untidy costume, looking like a gigantic near-sighted molting wren, racked with a dozen diseases, clouded by a mental anguish he was unable to account for, was among the most feverishly productive artists that ever lived. During the decades he spent poking about the most desolate corners of the Balkans, the Near East, Italy, and India, he never—one could almost say never for a moment—ceased turning out, with fabulous mechanical dexterity, a steady stream of topographical landscapes, in black-and-white, water color, and oils. We do not know how many of these are in existence, but we may get an idea of his industry from the fact that during one not especially energetic winter he completed one thousand drawings. At his death he left over ten thousand water colors alone to his friend Franklin Lushington.

The bad taste of his period was not bad enough to enable him to dispose profitably of this avalanche of art. Nor has he fared any better posthumously. Committed to the literal, he was one of the army of artists fated to die at the click of the first camera. A great geologist of the period said that he could from Lear's oils always tell the geology of the country; and another friend, Henry Strachey, himself a painter, remarked, "One is sometimes tempted to think that when Lear painted an olive tree near at hand against the sky he counted the leaves."

No one knows how many tens of thousands of the productions of this self-styled "Globular foolish Topographer" molded in dusty stacks and portfolios in the dim attics and unvisited storerooms of a hundred English country houses, mutely recording a life which it is ungenerous to call misspent but which does seem directionless.

But, of course, it wasn't at all directionless, though it may have seemed so to the man who lived it. We open any of the Nonsense Books (the first appeared in 1846, the last in 1895) and we are struck at once with the conviction that these comic drawings could have been done only by a genius. All the imagination—and I would even say sense of design—that Lear conscientiously excluded from his "real" work flowed freely into these hundreds of absurdities, each one not only a small masterpiece of humor but a perfect example of economy of line.

These drawings plus his nonsense limericks, songs, stories, alphabets, recipes, botany, etc., have for over a hundred years captivated the English-speaking world. They have caused Lear's professional career to be completely forgotten.

As for this nonsense, it is hard to write about it (or about any kind of nonsense) without sounding solemn. The most conventional of the prescribed solemnities is that put in words by Santayana: "The logic of nonsense has a subtle charm only because it can so easily be turned into common sense." The poet-critic W. H. Auden, who has himself written some beautiful nonsense, believes that "the writing of nonsense poetry which appeals to the unconscious . . . was an attempt to find a world where the divisions of class, sex, occupation did not operate." This statement I find more persuasive than Santayana's, which it would seem in a way to contradict.

A learned lady named Elizabeth Sewell has written a whole book* on nonsense which shows how serious the study of nonsense can be if you can only contrive to prevent laughter from percolating into it. Miss Sewell regards nonsense as "a structure held together by valid mental relations," conceives it as "much nearer logic than dream" and as a kind of complex game played, as with chess, in accordance with rigid rules.

My own notion is even more solemn than any of the foregoing and probably less tenable. Nonsense prose and verse are the comic spirit's organized defiance of experience. Thus surrealist poetry, while it does not make much sense, is not nonsense, for its practitioners are barren of the comic spirit. Gertrude Stein, whose spirit was as far from comedy as possible, wrote absurdities that defied ordinary experience—but she did not write nonsense. Germans cannot write nonsense because the comic spirit has not as yet been domiciled among them. But they can write fantasies and nightmares.

Nonsense flourished briefly in England and to a lesser ex-

* *The Field of Nonsense,* by Elizabeth Sewell.

tent in the United States during the latter half of the nineteenth century and the first quarter of the twentieth. Its two
greatest practitioners are Lear and Lewis Carroll, its lesser
ones Belloc, Chesterton, Kenneth Grahame occasionally, and
Edith Sitwell.

It was during this period that the pressure of "normal"
experience became just sufficiently intense to cause these fine
comic artists to rebel against it by writing nonsense. In our
own time the pressure has gone beyond this point of intensity,
so that the comic spirit is overwhelmed and cannot operate
on the nonsense level. The defiance of experience takes the
form of hallucination, as in Franz Kafka, or bitter satire.

The central note of Lear's nonsense (and Carroll's too) is
rebellion, even subversion. All of Lear's songs are songs of
escape. Many of the limericks are too:

> *There was an Old Person of Ischia,*
> *Whose conduct grew friskier and*
> > *friskier;*
> *He danced hornpipes and jigs,*
> *And ate thousands of figs,*
> *That lively old Person of Ischia.*

The Ischian is Lear's expression of impatience with the re-
straints normal experience imposes on us. The Ischian conduct is organized defiance, but a defiance that is clearly not
intended to be taken seriously or to lead to action on the part
of the reader. (In such a case Lear would have been writing
satire.) Nonsense is harmless; its appeal is not to the strongly
reasoning mind, but merely to that deep fund of impatient
emotion in us which is always, no matter how censored or
throttled, craving to upset routine, defy the rules, and escape
from the dull wisdom of our superiors. Here lies its great
appeal to children; and here also lies its appeal to the children concealed within the grownups. The greatest men—in

fact *especially* the greatest—feel this appeal precisely because their lives are spent in organizing experience, in subduing the mad stuff of living to orderly forms. Lincoln loved nonsense, he escaped through it. William Pitt put it profoundly: "Don't tell me of a man's being able to talk sense; everyone can talk sense. Can he talk nonsense?"

But the comic spirit is not irresponsible. It is wise and balanced; it knows that defiance of reality often entails punishment. (Only the genuine lunatic escapes completely.) Accordingly most of Lear's limericks are the product of a tension between his gleeful try at kicking over the traces and his rueful knowledge that it can't really be done. The typical Lear limerick is both funny and catastrophic, as the finest comedies somehow involve someone's discomfiture.

> *There was an Old Man with a gong,*
> *Who bumped at it all the day long;*
>   *But they called out, 'O Law!*
>   *You're a horrid old bore!'*
> *So they smashed that Old Man*
>   *with a gong.*

All thoughtful admirers of Lear agree that while he is funny, he is seldom *purely* funny. There is almost always an undertone either of punishment (*Alice in Wonderland*, too, is full of it) or of sadness. The punishment is not a "real" punishment, but an absurd one; therefore it does not make us uncomfortable; but it is there all the same.

> *There was an Old Man on some*
>   *rocks,*
> *Who shut his Wife up in a box,*
>   *When she said, 'Let me out,'*
>   *He exclaimed, 'Without doubt,*
> *You will pass all your life in that*
>   *box.'*

This is the story of Bluebeard passed through the prism of the comic spirit.

The sadness is more subtle.

> *O my agèd Uncle Arly!*
> *Sitting on a heap of Barley*
>   *Thro' the silent hours of night,—*
> *Close beside a leafy thicket:—*
> *On his nose there was a Cricket,—*
> *In his hat a Railway-Ticket;—*
>   *(But his shoes were far too tight.)*

Uncle Arly has a double effect on us. An obviously unconventional person, he for a split second releases us from the thralldom of the conventional; but at the same time he is pathetic, as all desperate nonconformists are, and we feel—the tight shoes strike the dread note of disaster—that he will, poor dear chap, come to no good end.

In which case he will be no worse off than this theory of nonsense.

Assortment

Fanfare for Fireworks, Fawkes, and the Fifth

No warmth, no cheerfulness, no healthful ease—
No comfortable feel in any member—
No shade, no shine, no butterflies, no bees,
No fruits, no flowers, no leaves, no birds,
No-vember!

AND, SAY I, no fair. For the poet Thomas Hood chooses not to recall "the Fifth of November, Gunpowder, treason and plot," whereas to my mind Guy Fawkes has made the eleventh month a perennial pretext for celebration. November 5, 1605, of course marks the day on which he failed to administer a hotfoot to Parliament, not to mention James I. But, though he started his post-gibbet career as a villain, Fawkes has, for all his explosive temperament (or rather because of it), turned out to be a pretty good Guy. More than any other person he has, through the celebrants of his Day, been responsible for the spread, starting in England, of the art of pyrotechny. Guy Fawkes means fireworks. As he must rank as the patron saint of one of the few human inventions that please everybody, I calendar November, even apart from Thanksgiving and Election Day, as a jubilee month. American firework-buffs, in no peril of forgetting the Fourth, may as properly remember the Fifth.

I cannot recollect a time when I did not love fireworks. When I was three, my elder brother, all a-tremble for my inflammability, placed in my hand and lit a "sparkler." That was an Independence Day indeed, for I was suddenly made free of a new world. The stars blooming from the sparkler have remained fixed. From that moment the smell of punk was as the odors of Heaven.

Even today I cannot regard without a slight vibration of awe those squat, unquenchable pots of fire set out as nightly danger signals along roads under repair. They seem to have intruded into the world of steam rollers and asphalt from another time, thicker with romance. They take one back to the fire festivals of the Druids, or to the serial mountaintop beacons flashing to Argos the news of Troy's far-off fiery fall.

Fireworks comprise fire's loveliest mutation; and, if so, neon lights must be its ugliest. A certain candescent splendor once gleamed along New York's Great White Way. Today, with its flickering neon signs, like so much palsy and St. Vitus's dance rendered in raw color, it is a vulgar Hell through which drift the livid, hectic or chlorotic faces of Manhattan's restless damned. G. K. Chesterton's comment—that Times Square at night would seem an exquisite fairyland to anyone who couldn't read—no longer holds true even for morons.

But fireworks are a fairyland for all. It is true that great displays are not so easily come by as they were twenty-five or fifty years ago. Far from our brittle, knowing era are those gorgeous pyrotechnical naïveties of Victoria's time, with its set pieces, its "Mt. Etna," its "Forge of Vulcan," its "Battle of Waterloo," its fire portraits sixty feet high. Will our self-styled age of wonders ever witness anything as wondrous as New York's Columbian Celebration in 1892, when, on October 10, a lambent Niagara fell along the whole length of the central span of Brooklyn Bridge, setting the East River, if not the Thames, on fire, bringing delight to the watchers on a hundred thousand rooftops? And we are distant indeed from fireworks' greatest days in the reign of the Sun King and his great-grandson, when fabulous displays, both aquatic and aerial, were given at Versailles, sometimes for five successive nights.

On the other hand we do not, as they did in eighteenth-century London's pleasure gardens, turn loose bulls with flaming fireworks fastened to their bodies. Nor do we admire the spectacle of "living fireworks"—pyrophores clad in asbestos suits, one of the more dismaying novelties of the late nineteenth century in England. Let us be fair to our own age. Not yet are our revels ended. For example, among the festivities marking the coronation of George VI was a simultaneous flight of one hundred thousand rockets from the decks of the ships of the fleet drawn up at Spithead. This must have been the greatest flight of rockets in the history of pyrotechny. (In passing, if you collect nouns of assembly, it's a *flight* of rockets, a *salvo* of shells, and a *battery* of roman candles.)

If alchemy is chemistry's father, it owns in pyrotechny a wayward but joyous grandson. Base matters—saltpeter, sulphur, charcoal, iron filings, shellac, gum, and a few cheap chemicals—are transmuted not into gold but into something lovelier by far, colored light moving in controlled patterns. The pyrotechnist is a dynamic painter, with all space as his dark canvas. It is easy to credit the well-attested tradition that both Da Vinci and Michelangelo staged fireworks displays. Callot, Daumier, and Degas, Rowlandson, Hiroshige, and Winslow Homer are among the artists who have been drawn to the fireworks theme.

The pyrotechnist seems almost to confute the law that nothing can come of nothing. From these trivial metal salts and particles of magnesium a whole ephemeral cosmos may flower, with its own astronomy, its own sun systems and shooting stars and wild-haired comets, its own Auroras to dazzle any latitude. A dream landscape gleams upon the sight, with showers and storms, fountains, trees, and cascades, chariots of fire and bows of burning gold. Yet a flashing second ago this weird green was but a little acetate of copper, this awful red a bit of strontium, this pure, triumphant blue mere copper, these wild rains of flame and tempests of sparks a heap of iron filings.

For two thousand years—Chinese pyrotechny is quite probably that old—such bursts of enchantment have drawn from the throats of millions a universal "Aah-h!"—partly a protracted note of rapture and partly a *diminuendo* sigh of sorrow for beauty that must die. Kings like Louis XV, queens like Elizabeth I were lovers of fireworks. The fireworks that in 1856 signalized the coronation of Tsar Alexander II covered fifty acres.

Children unendingly have loved them: Chinese children watching the wonderful geometry of "the Drum," a glowing lattice of colored lanterns; Japanese children open-mouthed at the formal, almost military precision of their native aerial fireworks; our own children, with fearful joy flourishing their roman candles, setting off their Catherine wheels and serpents, their "flowerpots" and "volcanoes." The poet Robert Hillyer has written beautifully about the old-fashioned Fourth in verses ending with a dying fall:

> *I will but say I loved the old Fourth dearly*
> *That threatened my survival each July;*
> *But now it fades, and I remember merely*
> *One bright balloon adrift in evening sky.*

The appeal of fireworks is partly a matter of tradition. For at least four centuries, beginning in Italy and spreading quickly to the rest of the Continent and England, that controlled triumph over darkness which is fireworks has been accepted as a high expression of man's sense of holiday. Partly the appeal is crypto-military: these radiant flares are to real explosives what lead soldiers are to real ones, the assault on heaven's dark vault is a kind of toy war. Perhaps too there is the human delight in splendid waste, the using up of matter for the purpose of joy. Add now the thrill of lighting the fuse and thus magically producing action at a distance. Is there one of us who has not clamored, "Let *me* light it!"? In Paris, in 1749, during a fireworks celebration of the peace treaty of Aix-la-Chapelle, groups of French and Italians fought savagely for the privilege of lighting the fuse first. Both parties lit it together, the entire display was accidentally set off, forty were killed and nearly three hundred wounded.

Doubtless the magnetism of fire itself accounts in part for the almost unexplainable pleasure of fireworks. We are all unburnt children; fire draws us as mystically as does the sea. Pyromania is more widespread than we dare admit. It may reach forms as intense as the fabled suicide by fireworks of the Greek philosopher Empedocles who was supposed to have thrown himself into the crater of Mt. Etna—a dire warning to those mischief-makers who violate a safe and sane Fourth.

Yet back of all this lies the deep appeal of that "excellent beauty," in old Bacon's phrase, that "hath some strangeness in the proportion," an unearthly wonder making all ages one, conferring the fleeting immortality of self-forgetfulness.

Whenever I think of fireworks three night pieces begin to glow in my memory.

The first goes back to 1912, when I was eight. The scene is the beach at Revere, Massachusetts, then largely a summer

resort. It is the night of July 4th. On the sands a deep water
tank has been erected and just back of it a platform sixty
feet high. Up an incline, to slow music, shining in starlight,
steps a magnificent white stallion. Reaching the high platform he freezes for a moment to an alabaster statue. Then
fireworks, mounted along the sides and top of the wooden
structure, burst into myriad spears and pennons of light,
framing the gleaming body of the brave horse as he dives
into the tank sixty feet below.

The second memory is shared by many: the uneasy summer of 1939, at the New York World's Fair, with its fabulous
pyrotechny over the serene lagoon, mirroring strange moons
and meteors night after night as we looked on, trying not to
vision in this explosion of beauty that greater explosion we
knew would soon shake our whole world.

My last memory is recent. A few summers ago I was in-
vited to be one of several speakers at the Aspen Institute for
Humanistic Studies, in Colorado. I suppose they needed a
kind of court jester—at any rate my colleagues were all grave
scholars, presidents of universities, philosophers with their
minds fixed on eternal truths. To my notion, however, among
these eternal truths were fireworks. During the day of July
4th I furtively purchased a staggering number of roman
candles, sky-rockets, pinwheels, sparklers, and similar immortal perishables. In the evening, my heart faint within me,
I asked my dignified associates to a fireworks party. My
doubts proved unnecessary. Within five minutes a dozen middle-aged or elderly scholars had turned into lunatic pyro-
philes. In an unphilosophical frenzy they set off the vast
assortment, endangering their own valuable lives in the
process, fiery-eyed with enthusiasm, the great issues of life
and death forgotten amid the pleasures of pyrotechny.

Three nights of fireworks: the first a now lost part of the Age of Innocence; the second belonging to the Decade of Fear; the last the tiniest of tiny candles throwing its beams forward into a naughty but not hopeless world.

Guy Fawkes, hail!

Fadiman's Law of Optimum Improvement

Two SCRAMBLED eggs was what I ordered from the pleasant-faced drug-store counterman.

"On buttered toast," he declared firmly. "White, rye, gluten. Marmalade or jam."

"Just two scrambled eggs," I muttered.

He eyed me with suspicion. A pause. Then, "Potatoes on the side," he stated.

"Just two scrambled eggs."

Another pause. "Nothing on the side?"

Down but still twitching, I said, "Eggs."

"Coffee now or later?"

"No coffee. Eggs."

Lost in misgivings, he prepared the eggs and was about to crown them with a generous bouquet of parsley, when I quavered, "Just the eggs—no parsley."

The eggs were fine. Asking for salt and pepper helped to patch things up a little, but I know I left the counter under a cloud.

Man, boy, and Master of Ceremonies, I have worked in radio and television for over fifteen years. During this period —such is the public's good sense—I have drawn weighable fan mail only once. That was when, through the courtesy of an obliging network, I explained the difficulty I had always

430

met in getting a ham sandwich. By a ham sandwich I meant a ham sandwich—a slice of ham between two pieces of buttered bread, minus lettuce, parsley, olives, pickles, carrots, shredded cabbage, mayonnaise, whipped cream. My open confession attracted many heartfelt letters, all from males.

"Man wants but little here below," the poet Goldsmith tells us. But try to get it. Try to get potatoes without parsley. A Martini without the olive. An Old-Fashioned or an ice-cream sundae without the cherry. Soft-collar shirts laundered without starch in the collar. A jacket pressed without creases in the sleeves. A cigarette box without a horse's head on it. A bottle of pills without an almost unremovable wad of cotton below the stopper. Cocktail napkins without floral curlicues. A baby's crib in a solid color (not pink or blue) without cherubs or roses stamped on the headboard.

Try, just try, to pay a bill without going through a forest of Stuffers and Fillers. The other day I opened an envelope from a New York department store with which my wife is at present conducting a fervent romance. After seventeen minutes passed in investigating the contents of the envelope, I succeeded in unearthing a bill for $17.60.

You may well ask why it took seventeen minutes to find the bill. I may well tell you. Along with the bill were eleven enclosures of varying sizes. They were all beautifully written and expensively illustrated, these stuffers were; and, if I only had had the time or were in jail or quarantine, I could have spent an exciting hour and a half reading them.

One pleaded with me to buy the latest patent moth-killer. Another directed my attention to bras in heavenly tissue-skin nylon. Another offered me my very own printed airmail stationery. Another pressed upon me the virtues of an electric shoeshine boy (AC only). Another made it clear that life was dust and ashes without a Koolfoam airy cellular latex pillow.

Another urged an automatic snoozing chair. Still another tantalized me with the possibility of owning a complete flower master-kit, containing more than a hundred items for arranging flowers.

A man who gets a bill wants to be able to remove it at once from its envelope and either pay it or invent some excuse for not paying it. He does not want to receive at the same time a complete inventory of the store's merchandise. Three times out of four it is virtually impossible to find the bill without the help of two secretaries. By the time it is found the debtor is bewildered to the point of fury.

In our kitchen we have a garbage-can. A pedal is attached to its base. As you step on the pedal, the lid flies up, you throw in the disposables with one hand, the other hand being completely free to play the piano. That's the theory. In practice the foot slips off the pedal and you find yourself guiltily lifting the lid with your crude bare hands. Or it partially slips off the pedal and the lid opens shyly, just wide enough to admit a postcard. Or it works perfectly, but, the can being empty, the lid bangs up with enough power to send the entire contraption skidding along the floor, and enough clatter to wake up the dramatic critics at the first night of an Ibsen revival.

A bottle of ink used to be a bottle of ink. You filled your pen by dipping it into the bottle. Today my ink bottle comes equipped with a small shallow trough or well built on to the upper part of the inside of the bottle. This trough is for the ink—the bottle itself has been demoted into a mere storehouse. To fill the trough you tip the full bottle, thus getting the contents over anything receptive to ink. The trough full, you now unscrew the ink-drenched lip and dip your pen into the well. As it is shallow you bang your point against the bottom. A good penpoint will survive about fifty such bangs. Three new pens to one bottle of ink is par for the course. The ink itself, by the way, is excellent.

At one time a man could ask for razor blades and get them. This is becoming increasingly difficult. My favorite blades— splendid, keen chaps—no longer come loose in a small packet. They are nested in a slotted receptacle in such a manner that if you exert just the right amount of thumb pressure on the top blade you can slide it out of the slot. The occasions when I have done this are noted in my diary. I might add that the old three-piece razor will soon be one with the American buffalo. Razors are now one-piece. They boast an ingenious system of screws and movable clamps which succeed in making the razor uncleanable, the blade loose, and the balance in the hand an uncertain quantity.

Books used to come wrapped in a piece of paper tied up with a piece of cord. In no time you could be reading the book. Today they arrive in cardboard iron maidens, suitable to the transportation of safes or pianos, without any visible weak point. Or they come swaddled in thick bags stapled at one end. The ingenious company that manufactures these bags cites their virtues: they are protective, time and labor saving, economical, space saving, simple and clean. Possibly. But they are not openable. Sometimes you can undo the staples without much loss of blood, but if you make the slightest wrong move, you tear the bag. Out flies a bushel of ancient furry shredded gray paper, the perfect stand-in for mouse dirt. This distributes itself impartially over floor, walls, and your throat and nasal passages.

Admitting without argument that I belong to that oppressed majority who are all thumbs, I would suggest that the real trouble lies elsewhere. The fact is that we are becoming victims of our surplusage and—to use a nasty seven-letter word—our know-how. In the field of prepared food and drink we cannot let well enough alone; in the field of gadgets the same thing is true. Our native ingenuity is so restless that the potentialities for change lying within the gadget begin to dominate our imaginations, drowning out any sense of that perfectly proper *resistance* to change lying within every human being. The man who falls in love with the gadget has fallen out of love with his own humanity. By fooling around too much with our materials we can outsmart ourselves. Remember the fountain pen that wrote under water. Nothing fails like excess.

The car with the automatic shift is doubtless a better car. The question is whether the subnormal who can now drive an automobile is a better man. A super-speed highway is a better highway, but its users are slightly worse humans, because super-highway travel, with no scenery, few curves, no obstacles, is so dull as to be a kind of prison in motion. Better to watch a cow from a canal-boat than the Andes from the air.

Take bread. Mass-produced bread—or rather its pallid, sectioned ghost, hardly to be distinguished from the cellophane in which the neat slices are wrapped—is doubtless more convenient to handle; but eat enough of it and you will lose one of the oldest and most precious of human talents—the taste for the staff of life.

To relieve the over-familiarity of this doubtlessly reactionary viewpoint I think I had better refer to Aristotle. Aristotle tells us: "Moral virtue . . . is a mean between two vices, the one involving excess, the other deficiency," and, as an example, he remarks, "With regard to the giving and taking of money the mean is liberality, the excess and the defect prodigality and stinginess."

Let us now set beside Aristotle's Doctrine of the Mean another doctrine, hereafter to be known as Fadiman's Law of Optimum Improvement. I am persuaded that in the realm of objects, as well as in the realm of ethics, there can be an excess of refinement as well as a defect of crudity. It is my further conviction that a proper technological society is not the one capable of endlessly improving its artifacts, but the one able to see at what point it is best, from the point of view of the whole human being (and indeed of the whole human race), to stop the improvement.

When John Montagu, fourth Earl of Sandwich, invented the comestible named after him (he once spent twenty-four hours at the gaming table living on beef sandwiches) he placed mankind in his debt, and obeyed the doctrine of the mean. When some meddler, not satisfied with this perfect contrivance, "improved" it with lettuce, tomatoes, and other vitamin-reeking horrors, he erred in the direction of excess.

The old-fashioned kitchen was defective. The modern kitchen, with its stainless-steel double sink, its freezer, its refrigerator, is a joy, the perfect mean, improvement at its optimum. Fill it with all the "labor-saving" devices, from egg-slicers to carrot-curlers, and you have an excess, a frantic inferno of machinery.

I am not urging a return to the spinning wheel. I am only suggesting that many objects, from food to machinery, are subject to an invisible and overlooked law of maximum complication and development. Nature has wisely seen to it that human beings generally stop short at seven feet. With respect to things we must assume the role of Nature.

When I think of my own odd trade of mass communication I find myself lost in admiration before the vast technical improvements of the last thirty years, and at the same time troubled by an uneasy sense that each such improvement brings, along with its concrete benefits, some less concrete losses.

When a performer shifts from the stage to the radio microphone he says good-by to certain possibilities, among them visibility and mobility. He becomes the servant of a metal neck surmounted by a metal ear. When he transfers to the television studio he regains some visibility—but his mobility is further reduced. He has now become the servant of *two* pieces of machinery. In certain ways the camera allows him to create new effects; in other ways it circumscribes him in accordance with the unchangeable laws of its own nature. There's a television gadget called a "mixer" which permits any collection of small objects to be photographed by a special camera in such a way that they seem to comprise a full-size natural background for the actor or singer. This makes many wonderful effects possible—but the performer is even further circumscribed in his movements: any deviation outside a prescribed area will blur the image. Eventually color television will look magnificent—to the spectator. The actor, however, will be forced to wear clothes of a particular color, to be made up in a specific way, etc.

Each of these apparently petty progressive limitations places a greater and greater distance between the personality of the performer and the performance itself. Not that the performance is uninteresting, but that its interest in part depends on the efficiency of a battery of machines. Perhaps even in the field of communication, then, works some subtle limiting law of optimum improvement.

The Sermon on the Mount, produced without benefit of even the crudest studio facilities, has since its première constantly enjoyed a high rating. How much would have been lost, how much gained, had it been properly produced over a coast-to-coast television network, backed by full orchestra and electric organ?

Plain Thoughts on Fancy Language

Not long ago I bookwormed my way into a radio program that involved talking about a Greek classic. The small stint over, one of my associates, an eminent scholar, remarked, "A pleasant half hour," and then with a grin added, "Nice to make a fast buck, too."

Later I found myself pondering his use of a phrase that would surely have floored Plato. Scholarship and the "fast buck" are not natural bedfellows. Perhaps, I figured, the guys-and-dolls lingo functioned as a ladder, enabling the professor to scale the walls of the academy and at least wave his mortarboard at the outside "practical" world. Might it not help to armor him, if not against being naïve, at least against being thought so?

But no. On further reflection I concluded that the professor might have thrown the phrase around casually at the Faculty Club. Would this have been possible twenty-five years ago? Probably not. Fifty years ago? Surely not. Today, however, the once stout barrier between "correct" and colloquial speech has thinned to a membrane of gossamer. The withering away of class distinctions, the incessant pressures of mass communication, and in particular the vast increase of travel —all tend to spread the vernacular. Fresher, more pictur-

esque than stiff-collar English, the experimental phrase, obeying a kind of linguistic Gresham's Law, often drives out the
established one, only to become in its turn standard speech.
My professor, then, was merely using a phrase that might
soon be accepted as regulation American. The same unify-
ing influences that act upon the rest of us were at work upon
him. Democracy is indivisible: it pervades the field of speech
as it does that of politics—or, as my classical friend might
have put it, it works speech-wise like it does politics-wise.

And on the whole the results have been fine. We view
language as we view matter, as something to be manipulated
into new, exciting, useful shapes. All of us are Yankee tinkers
of words, our joint creation being a popular speech of admirable force and color.

But this national talent will sometimes go hog-wild, as the
child's exuberance, unchecked, may flare into hysteria. It's
fun to play with words—but not at the cost of forgetting that
their job still remains that of clear communication. Philip
Wylie's *momism* is a coinage of genius. It points sharply and
humorously to a complex idea. *Stripteuse* and *cinemactress*
are less happy inventions, for they seem to call attention to
themselves rather than to the objects they denote. They are
verbal show-offs, or perhaps more like jokes that amuse only
at the first telling.

In his stimulating *Words and Ways of American English*
Thomas Pyles writes: "What is fittest in language has a way
of surviving, as the admirable *o.k., the real McCoy, highbrow,
crook, lengthy, haywire, panhandle, roughneck, Annie Oak-
ley,* and *bawl out* . . . have done. What is graceless or fraudulent or ponderously 'cute' . . . ekes out a banal and colorless
existence among the silly, the sentimental, and the addle-
pated. . . ."

You and I have set working thousands of useful little inventions, such as *baby-sitter, soap opera, build-up.* But we have also, by dint of thoughtless and uncritical parroting, put in circulation many a word or phrase that is "graceless or fraudulent or ponderously 'cute'."

Of these three adjectives the most meaningful is "fraudulent." Correctness, of course, is a schoolmarm's hallucination; there are more double negatives in Shakespeare and Chaucer than on New York's Tenth Avenue. Departures from standard literary English are neither "right" nor "wrong"; but they may be honest or dishonest. The firm-lipped executive sets his jaw and barks, "I want you to hit that line—and *hit it hard!*" The alert sales representative (*salesman,* except in retail stores, has gone the way of *drummer*) sets *his* jaw, shoulders his fountain pen and is off to the wars with a clipped *"Roger!"* Here the lingo of football field or airfield, however proper in its original setting, breaks through the frosted glass of the business office only at the cost of a tiny twisting of reality. The fraudulence of feeling may be slight. But it is there.

Like any American who listens to many other Americans, I habitually pick up, along with some negotiable new word-currency, a certain amount of lightweight coin. In some cases I can detect the dishonesty; more often I cannot, until the same coin has come around again several times. Here's a little list which we may divide into a few convenient categories, the first being

Sheep-Talk: Sheep-talk flows from a fear of using garden-variety English as against the latest fashionable substitute (journalese: *ersatz*) catch-phrase. It is unselective, unthinking follow-the-leader. When I ask for scotch-on-the-rocks instead of scotch-with-ice, I am talking sheep. A good metaphor illuminates the object compared; here the metaphor, by calling pleased attention to itself, obscures it. It is so *knowing*.

I am talking sheep when every minor verbal encounter becomes a *hassle*. (By the way, what's its origin—*haggle* + *tussle*?) I am talking sheep when I over-exercise such trumpery jocosities as *unlaxed, what gives?, big deal, wha hoppen?, I've got news for you*, and *oh brother!* I am talking sheep when, following the modish journalistic bellwether, I delight in *balding* and *know-how* and *look-see*. Is *from where I sit* any brisker than *from my standpoint*? (The latter, is, of course, precisely the same figure of speech, now regaining novelty as its competitor becomes frayed from much handling.)

The Enfeebling Intensifier: The girl who can't say No has been replaced by the man who can't say Yes. There can be no objection to the handy *o.k.*, or even to the richly varied *y-p* series: *yap, yahp, yep, yip, yop*, and *yup*. These are all sound, honest American. Less honest, however, is the current rash of questionably emphatic surrogates for the obsolescent *yes*. These include the jerky-brisk *definitely!*, the fake-commercial *it's a deal*, the tiresomely bright-eyed *you can say that again!*, the effusive *I know just what you mean*, and the genteel-epicene *you're so right!*

A poor relation of these enfeebling intensifiers is *period!*, pronounced at the end of a sentence to mark the speaker's feeling that he has said something peculiarly decisive. Its habitual use points to an underlying uncertainty on the user's part. It's like a man who bellows. Fortunately this one has been kidded almost to death.

Other enfeebling intensifiers that enjoy a high degree of

dispensability include: *frankly, candidly, basically,* and their numerous kin; *check into* for *check; too,* as in "I didn't make too much progress," where the speaker simply means that he didn't make much progress; and *personally,* as in "I personally found it very educational." It's hard to figure out why *personally* is so epidemic. We seem to be as wary of the unaided perpendicular pronoun as we are of the unclothed affirmative. The addition of *personally* does not remove from *I* its presumed flavor of egotism. It merely weakens the word and thickens the sentence.

The Learned Vulgarism: This is not peculiar to our day. Whenever people are short on ideas they tend to use long words. But this disease has attacked us in a rather special form, mainly as a consequence of the over-hasty current popularization of science. The use of the learned vulgarism is an attempt to bridge the gap between our brash confidence that science is basic to our lives and our unadmitted fear that it is closed to our understandings. The savage believes that to name an object gives him a certain control over it. Similarly we gain assurance when we use *allergy* for dislike, *schizophrenia* for mental eccentricities of varying types, *nostalgia* for yearning, *philosophy* for virtually any notion or opinion or slant, *psychology* for any insight into a mental process, *complex* to denote a strong interest or concern, *compulsive* for what is merely habitual, etc.

Writers with an imperfect scientific education, such as myself, are much given to the learned vulgarism.

Baby-Talk . . . Let's, as we say, face it: the bathroom and washroom have disappeared. They are occasionally brought to mind by such purified avatars as *powder room, smoking room,* and *lounge.* (In one restaurant a door marked *Lounge* was flanked by one marked *Cocktail Lounge,* a juxtaposition calculated to stump even the experts.) But in certain circles the b---r--m has been given the Lilliput treatment. It is coyly referred to as the *little boys'* or *little girls' room.* This reversion to the nursery is becoming quite marked in our popular speech. I understand that Miss Greer Garson and her well-fixed husband affectionately exchange frequent gifts, such as Texas counties, and that they call these *prezzies.* A minor subdivision of American baby-talk is *Menu Goo-Goo.* A certain modest but excellent restaurant I frequent lists "Crunchy Corn" and "Crispy Salad," like a mother feeding babykins "lovely, 'licious mush."

Let's watch our little tongues, kiddies.

Madison Avenue English: Variety, the show-business trade paper that has been responsible for a host of brilliant and permanent additions to the vernacular, once printed a few parody-paragraphs of this interesting dialect, asserting them to be the text of a memorandum passed around at one of the major television networks:

> You will recall that we've been firming up this problem for some time, and just in the nature of pitching up a few mashie shots to see if we come near the green, I'd like to express these angles:
>
> First, I think we should take a reading of the whole general situation to see if it is being spitballed correctly so that we can eventually wham it through for approval or disapproval as the case might be. In other words we've got to live with this for a long time, and there are certain rock bottom slants which we will have to try on for size.
>
> Since this situation hits us where we live, and since it has to be geared in before we hit the stretch it is only logical that we throw in a few cross-bucks before we take it off tackle. I can't help feeling that we're all soft as a grape at this stage of the game, and unless we want to get caught with our meta-

phors down, we'd better get the egg off our faces and the cablestitch sweaters off our teeth.

In other words, we might get caught off first base, and the whole thing might go over like a lead balloon. So let me urge that we all kick this around and put on our creative thinking caps so that all of us will profit in the final wrap-up.

It is an open secret that of late businessmen (that is, *some* businessmen) have been making heavy weather of the problem of communication. Their difficulties have been well analyzed (broken down) in *Is Anybody Listening?*, by William H. Whyte, Jr., and the Editors of Fortune. What Mr. Whyte calls "shirtsleeve English" and "reverse gobbledegook" is the business world's gift to our language, and one which seems to be getting a warm general reception. It is a rich hash of metaphors drawn from sport (largely football), technology, run-of-the-mine clichés, the columns of our more frenzied newspapers, and the jargon of "social scientists" and "social engineers."

Mr. Whyte believes that Madison Avenue English does certain jobs for its user. It enables the speaker to conceal the fact that he has nothing to say—but to conceal it with dynamic emphasis. It also imparts to him "an appearance of savviness, cooniness, and general know-how." Finally, it is a soul-satisfying rebellion against what the businessman calls gobbledegook, or bureaucratic English. Somehow he feels that shirtsleeve English is more "down to earth" than either formal business language or casual conventional language.

I have a small theory of my own which has at least the merit of being a bit less hard on the kicked-around businessman. Madison Avenue English is aggressive, independent-as-a-hog-on-ice, free-swinging, and folksy. But does it reflect the business atmosphere that has actually prevailed since the onset of the New Deal? Hardly. The poor businessman is bedeviled with regulations, hounded with forms, beset by unions, attacked by journalists, and upper-cutted by taxes. In most cases he has long since ceased to be a completely free enterpriser.

I would suggest that the free-wheeling metaphors of Madison Avenue English are his imaginative compensation for the lack of freedom imposed on him by the hard world of fact. His natural aggressiveness hemmed in by a thousand gags and binders, he releases himself in punchy tropes, thick with the heady, lusty, sanguinary atmosphere of the football stadium. His business may be fettered but his prose rides free. His paragraphs buccaneer for him.

Now I see no reason why the businessman should be denied his private language any more than I see any reason, for example, why the super-highbrow literary critic should be denied his. Both jargons bear little relation to cleanly English, it is true; but both supply their users with some deeply based, badly needed personal solace. The question that interests us is, Does the public speech stand to gain by importations from these private tongues? While there is little danger of the literary lingo seeping into our current language, there is considerable danger that Madison Avenue English may do so, mainly because the businessman, for all the javelins hurled at his head, commands more social prestige in our country than any other group except the military. Well, if Executive English should really begin to take hold generally, I do not believe that it would greatly enrich our lively tongue. Synthetic, its "punch" a delusion, its sources dubious, this new jargon would seem to illustrate a statement quoted by Mr. Pyles and made as far back as 1838 by James Fenimore Cooper: "The common faults of American language are an ambition of effects, a want of simplicity, and a turgid abuse of terms."

Of course I'm just thinking out loud, fellers, but that's the pitch. 'Bye now. Be good.

A Period Sample: Three
Reviews of John O'Hara

From May 27, 1933, to November 20, 1943, I had the luck to be employed as a book-reviewer by one of the best magazines ever published in the English language, the *New Yorker*. People seemed to find the reviews interesting. That was not because the writing was good and not because they were particularly sound. But I had two factors on my side. I was young enough and brash enough to say exactly what I thought, minus the mellow qualifying that comes with age; and I was so passionately interested in current letters that I persisted in making my meaning, however unimportant, clear even at the cost of elegance or subtlety.

Even in those days, but far more so in the decade or so before my time, book-reviewing had a lively, vascular quality. It has been replaced by greater gravity, deeper scholarship perhaps, more judgmatical caution. In the process it has both gained and lost something.

I wanted to include in this book, not so much for the general reader as for the special student of this minor art, a few reviews that would transmit a little of the puckery flavor of the period. To this end I went through my *New Yorker* output, squirming. Every working journalist who has been fool enough to keep a scrapbook and later on to reread the stuff knows that feeling of general humiliation relieved intermit-

446

tently by voluptuous pleasure at recognizing a good phrase or fortunately sound judgment.

Finally I chose the three subjoined reviews of three books by the brilliantly talented and still wayward John O'Hara. These pieces are neither very good nor, I believe, very bad. They are eminently characteristic of the period, as the books themselves were, and I include them mainly for that reason. Like a popular song or a half-recollected slang phrase, they bring something back. That's about all.

The first dealt with Mr. O'Hara's bombshell, *Appointment in Samarra,* and appeared on September 1, 1934.

Any novel like John O'Hara's *Appointment in Samarra* has, among other virtues, that of being able to terrorize reviewers. Recommend it, and the job's done. It holds out hardly a peg upon which to hang the old clothes of critical comment. Just about the most readable novel within miles, its meaning lies in that readability, and stops there. Here, at last, is the ripe fruit of the nonspeculative, perceptive American newspaper-man mind. A precise and conscious talent devotes itself to a tale from which is extracted all possible point, even the point of pointlessness. For, though there is no faith here in anything, there is also no faith in nothing. The suicide of Julian English (which by this time you should know all about) is no gesture of denial, or even of rebellion. It is tragedy in a vacuum, the tic of a young man who has had a couple of hard days and too much hard liquor.

Here, Mr. O'Hara seems to be saying, is a story about a group of people living in the anthracite town of Gibbsville, Pa. I present you with a racketeer, a bootlegger, a roadhouse wench, a decent middle-class couple, a collection of success-ful young businessmen and their wives. They have no meaning, they do not make up a social whole, their mutual connections are accidental. I shall describe these accidental connections, sketch briefly, sharply, the biographies of these people, trace their behavior during a given forty-eight hours of stress. I give you the surface of Gibbsville. He who gives the surface gives all. If you can find any meaning in the life and death of Julian English, auto salesman, you're welcome to it. Wrap it up, take it home, give it to the kiddies to play with.

Thus Mr. O'Hara is uncannily exact in his differentiation of Morgan, Harjes girls and American Express girls, Bryn Mawr and Smith women; he knows to a nicety just what social gestures a two-fifty (filet mignon) country-club dinner dance entails; he can draw you a map of Gibbsville's social strata, from petty tycoons to poolroom hangers-on, with the proper shading for every tiny snobbery; he has been behind the living-room divan with camera and dictaphone, coolly recording the amorous hesitations and consummations of young bond salesmen and small-town débutantes; he knows with the sureness of instinct everything about automobiles, victrola records, what upper middle-class Americans drink, roadhouses, hangovers, locker-room arguments—period stuff, the décor of country-club civilization. But about all these things he deliberately has no ideas. To have ideas and emotions about them, to rise into that extra dimension within which an *Of Human Bondage* lives its life is to blur his particular effect, which is to produce no effect at all. It is the aim of this new school (James Cain and Dashiell Hammett belong there, too) merely to interest, but to interest so intensely, and with such art, that its work cannot be classed as mere entertainment.

A few years ago we used to think half-baked ideas about life sentimental. Today, Mr. O'Hara and his School of Hard Eyes apparently believe that any ideas at all are a bit on the soft side. If the point isn't clear, compare *Appointment in Samarra* with *This Side of Paradise* and *The Great Gatsby*, two novels of a dead epoch dealing fundamentally with O'Hara's social material. The difference may be put crudely: Fitzgerald didn't quite know what it was all about, but wondered, and his wonder gave his novels their quality. O'Hara has stopped wondering.

To convey his sense of life's chill meaninglessness (warmed only by the incidence of clean moments of sexual lust), O'Hara has worked out a style of admirable colloquial force and precision, with machine-turned dialogue, barren of color, but never hardboiled in any phony way. It is a style whose perfection is perhaps its weakness; it impresses us as real because it is so exquisitely contemporary. The opposite of euphuism, it will in ten years be as strange to us as are the pages of John Lyly. *Appointment in Samarra*, bare, undecorative, without a single flourish, is yet, in a way, a period novel. A decade hence, it is something we will want to look up. Today it is something we cannot lay down.

That was about twenty years ago. The reader may decide for himself, with all the hindsight in the world at his disposal, just how far beside the mark these judgments have turned out to be.

A year later came *Butterfield 8*. I called my little piece— in those days readers liked that sort of punning and the reviewer was not demeaned by it—"Disappointment in O'Hara." Today I regret the easy joke, for it may have unnecessarily irritated the author, which was hardly my purpose.

John O'Hara's second novel, *Butterfield 8*, may have been suggested by the Starr Faithfull case. So Dame Rumor has it, and, for all of me, the Dame may keep it. I can't see that it makes any difference. To take pleasure in sniffing out the originals in *romans à clef* is to confess a certain lack of interest in the novels themselves. Mr. O'Hara is a writer, not a rebus, and his story exists to be read, not deciphered. The people in *Butterfield 8* may be consistently unsteady, but their creator, at any rate, can stand on his own feet.

Butterfield 8 is almost, if not quite, as easy to read as *Appointment in Samarra*. The photographic eye is brighter, the phonographic ear sharper than before. The dialogue is still slicker, the pace still quicker, the plot still thicker, the main interest of the characters still liquor. New York (a few blocks of it—hence the title) at the zenith of the speak-easy era is caught and pinned to the mat with incomparable deftness. Mr. O'Hara can handle seduction scenes, all varieties, with a casualness that does not necessarily indicate cynicism. He knows exactly who was apt to be in a given speak-easy on a given afternoon in 1931. He can tell you the difference (and make it, for twenty seconds, sound important) between John Held people and F. Scott Fitzgerald people. He knows that at theater time of a certain day Fifty-second Street between Fifth and Sixth Avenues could be full of Lincoln town cars. He can reproduce like nobody's business the predinner cocktail yak-yak of a quartet of Butterfielders. He will show a mother and daughter having a cozy, technical chat about clothes, and make it sound genuine. He knows how a Junior Leaguer will talk to her best girl friend when breaking the news of her engagement. He is an expert on the Petronian New York of 1931, its benders, college boys, dinner parties, light ladies, assignation houses, adulteries, popular songs, jazz bands, specific vernacular, class, race, college, and fraternity distinctions, costumes, amusements, gangster hide-outs, snobbisms, alcoholic despairs, chaise-longue sensualities, rackets, speak-easies from the Village to Harlem, tastes in food and liquor, good jokes and bad manners. People are going to quarrel about Mr. O'Hara, but all are bound to agree that he has written a historical novel which, though it is about things and people that happened only four years ago, is letter-perfect in its atmosphere and detail, just as *The Cloister and the Hearth* is, or *The Last Days of Pompeii*. For recall value, *Butterfield 8* rates high.

The story concerns a high-grade nymph named Gloria

Wandrous. Corrupted in childhood by two middle-aged lechers, she thenceforward devotes herself to rye, despair, and venery in about equal proportions. At twenty-two she knows all about males, but perhaps not very much about men; knows how to have a high time, but not how to enjoy herself; and has as much bitter wisdom as can be garnered from intimate observation of Yale sophomores, brokers on semi-annual benders, barflies in dinner jackets, degenerate college professors, Westchester débutantes, and Gotham celebrities whose fame lives and dies with Mr. Winchell. She sounds very much like some kind of Symbol or other, though Mr. O'Hara would deny it.

Gloria, in between times, has a real and pathetically non-carnal friendship with Eddie Brunner. This is about the biggest thing in her life until Weston Liggett, who is in his forties and means business, comes along. Their affair starts at high temperature and then zigzags jaggedly because Gloria's various neuroses prevent her from making up her mind. Liggett's mind, however—what there is of it—is made up. He leaves wife and children to pursue Gloria. On the deck of a New York-to-Boston passenger steamer they meet. Gloria is almost ready to capitulate and give real life (home, husband, children) a chance. Then there's an accident; she falls overboard and is churned to death by the side wheel of the boat. The book ends with all the pointlessness and lunatic horror of a tabloid tragedy.

Sydney Smith once remarked of a young lady that she was practically perfect, her only fault being that she was intolerable. Similarly, Mr. O'Hara's book seems to me a dazzling performance, my single objection being that I have not the slightest interest in any of his people. Mr. O'Hara thinks they have meaning—or at least they excite him—and perhaps others will feel the same way. Everything is done for them that brilliant and deadly precise writing can do, but I can't help seeing them either as animated puppets or as juveniles who should be sent to a good school. Everything about them—their adulteries, their conversations, their lusts, their yearnings—seems so small that one wonders how Mr. O'Hara, generously gifted, intelligent, witty, can possibly care to spend so much of his time with them.

I still believe that the path he so brilliantly struck out for himself in *Appointment in Samarra* is bound to end in a blind alley, and I think *Butterfield 8* proves it. The fact remains that he is superior to his material. He's far too good a novelist to waste his energy (no matter how spectacularly, how cleverly he wastes it) on a basically meaningless and sensational story. As entertainment, *Butterfield 8* will and should lead the fiction field for some months to come. But Mr. O'Hara, as many single passages in his book demonstrate, is far more than an entertainer. My guess is that *Butterfield 8* is an interlude. Why not let Jean Harlow have it, Mr. O'Hara, and start a fresh page?

In March of 1938 along came *Hope of Heaven* and I fear I didn't like that any better. Here's how a high-grade novelist of the hard-boiled school struck a medium-grade reviewer of the medium-boiled school in the free-swinging Thirties.

It looks as though John O'Hara were going to go his own bitter way and bad cess to anyone who tries to stop him. The latest exhibit in what may be called the Sourpuss School of American Literature is *Hope of Heaven*. In this thirty-five-thousand-word novelette the hero makes a thousand Hollywood dollars a week, is quite a hand (bit rough, though) with the girls, and calls waitresses by their first names. You'd think he'd be pretty complacent, but actually he is sore as a pup about everything and is always ordering, in the grimmest way you can imagine, corned-beef hash with poached egg. His attitude toward life, as the heroine says, is "To hell with it." Now, just why Malloy (that's his name) should be so long in the face and so ready to growl "Wanna make sump'm otta-vit?" whenever any other male comes along is not made clear.

You've got to accept Mr. O'Hara's glowering heroes as given.

Hope of Heaven has to do with Mr. Malloy's love affair with Peggy Henderson; the manner in which her smooth, rascally father disturbs their relationship; the tragedy which finally breaks it up; and a fellow named Miller, who has forged some traveler's checks and whom Malloy, for no assignable reason, protects from the law. Just what the whole Miller episode has to do with the story is not clear to me. It functions, to be sure, as a pretext for getting the elder Henderson to Hollywood, but that's rather thin. Put it down to Mr. O'Hara's liking for melodrama and for shady characters, and let it go.

You might not think it, but for some things I admire Mr. O'Hara as much as I do almost any American writer of his generation. I admire, for instance, his unrelaxing control over the curt rhythms and idioms of our common speech; his capacity for rendering bibulous-erotic dialogue; his remarkable talent for drawing certain minor characters—there's an epicene young man in the book who is Something; and his gift for rapid, economical narrative. But it seems to me that all these talents ask for approval separately, as clever tricks. They are used in the service of an absurd story whose major characters need a good grade-school education, whose construction does not bear examination, and whose tone of pessimistic irony reminds one of those to-hell-with-the-universe orgies we all indulge in during our youth. Mr. O'Hara can write like a streak, but he just won't think, or at any rate he won't think in his novels. The result is that though, as a consequence of his dexterous manipulation of pace and suspense, we are genuinely interested in how *Hope of Heaven* is going to turn out as a story, we don't give a damn about how the characters are going to turn out as people. It isn't that they have no stature—Madame Bovary has no stature—but that they are not studied deeply enough in their very limitations.

A minor matter: the book is full of that pseudo-portentous detail which was so effective ten years ago but has become shiny with wear of late. You know the sort of thing: "I put on a new brown double-breasted suit and a blue shirt and brown foulard tie and an old pair of brown Scotch grain brogues." I say this is spinach. Let others write ads for Brooks Brothers, Mr. O'Hara; you go ahead and be a novelist.

Still, better read *Hope of Heaven*. It's got some fine things in it, the talent is there, the skill is there. Maybe it's something Mr. O'Hara tossed off as a prelude to tackling a real novel. One prefers to assume that. Otherwise we must conclude that there has been no growth since the brilliant *Appointment in Samarra*. Otherwise we must conclude that a truculent, self-pitying futilitarianism really represents Mr. O'Hara's view of humanity. I do not care to believe this.

The Wolfe at the Door

THERE THEY were, two dark wandering atoms.

Uncle Habbakuk, one of the legendary, far-wandering Gants, and full of their dark, illimitable madness, was of but average stature, being only eight or nine feet high. He lifted his fork from one of hs characteristic disgusting, unsavory, and nauseating messes. It consisted of old iron filings, chopped twine, oats, and clippings *hachis* from the *Times* classified ads section. With his hard, bony fore-finger he prodded Aunt Liz. Ceaselessly he prodded her, hungrily, savagely. But she gave no sign. She was lost (Oh lost! lost! who shall point out the path?) in a dream of time.

"Phuh! Phuh!" howled Uncle Habbakuk, the goat-cry welling up like a madness out of the vine of his throat. "Phuh! Phuh! Ow—ooh! *Beep!*"

Uncle Habbakuk, with demonic, fore-fingered energy, continued to lift up his idiotic, wordless and exultant howl. It was monstrous, yet somehow lovely, not to say fated, this gaunt confrontation of these two lonely atoms. . . . How strange and full of mystery life is! One passes another in the street, or a face flashes past as the great huge train-projectiles of America hurtle by, in all their thrill and menace, over the old brown earth, and the soul fills with sadness and irrecoverable memories. Why is this? Is it because we are the sons of

455

our fathers and the nieces and nephews of our aunts and uncles?

Who will answer our questions, satisfy our furious impatience, allay our elemental desires, soothe our tormented unrest, and check our heavy baggage? Who?

"Beep!" barked Uncle Habbakuk in his coruscating and indefinite way. "What is man that thou—*whah!*—art mindful of him?"

"Whoo-oop," chirped and sniggled Aunt Liz. Sly and enigmatic, she picked up a morsel of bread and hurled it savagely upon the table, with a gesture old as time itself, and secret with the secretiveness of a thousand secretive, lovely and mysterious women, all secret. Then she relapsed into her dream of time. She was entranced in one of her brooding and incalculable states—(O the States, O Alabama, Arizona, Arkansas, and California; O Colorado, Connecticut, Delaware, and Florida; O Georgia, Idaho, Illinois, and Indiana; O Iowa, Kansas, Kentucky, and Louisiana; O Maine, Maryland, Massachusetts, and Michigan; O Minnesota, Mississippi, Missouri, and Montana; O Nebraska, Nevada, New Hampshire, and New Jersey; O New Mexico, New York, North Carolina, and North Dakota; O Ohio, Oklahoma, Oregon, and Pennsylvania; O Rhode Island, South Carolina, South Dakota, and Tennessee; O Texas, Utah, Vermont, and Virginia; O Washington, West Virginia, Wisconsin, and Wyoming; and O! O! the District of Columbia!)

At this very moment, so pregnant and prescient with the huge warp of fate and chance, the dark, terrific weaving of the threads of time and destiny, there was heard one of the loveliest and most haunting of all sounds, to echo in the ears of Americans forever, surging in the adyts of their souls and drumming in the conduits of their blood. The doorbell tinkled.

"A moment's—*beep!*—peace for all of us before we die," snarled, bellowed, and croaked gaunt Uncle Habbakuk, prodding himself violently in the midriff with his hard bony fore-finger. "Give the goat-cry!"

"Phuh-phuh! Ow-ooh! *Beep!*" came the goat-cry from without, and Aunt Liz opened the door. It was he, the youth, of the tribe of the Gants, eleven feet, eight inches high, with slabsided cheeks, high, white, integrated forehead, long, savage, naked-looking ears, thirty-two teeth, and that strange, familiar, native, alien expression common to all the Gants, wandering forever and the earth again. It was the youth, but no less was it Jason and Faustus and Antaeus and Kronos and Telemachus and Synopsis and all those shining young heroes who have hungered amid the *Gewirr* of life and sought their fathers in the congeries of the compacted habitations of man, hot for the alexin of our cure and amorous of the unknown river and a thousand furious streets.

With a loose and powerful gesture Uncle Habbakuk, in frenzied despair, luminous hope, and frantic entreaty, welcomed the youth, snuffling.

"Where have you *been*, youth? Have you touched, tasted, heard, *and seen everything?* Have you *smelt everything?* Have you come from out the *wilderness*, the buried past, the lost *America?* Are you bringing up Father out of the *River?* Have you done any delicate *diving* for the *Greeks?* Have you embraced *life* and *devoured* it? Tell me! Open the adyts of your soul. Beep."

"Beep," chirped the youth somberly. "I have been making mad journeys, peril-fraught and passion-laden, on the Hud-

son River Day Line, watching my lost, million-visaged
brothers and sisters. I have been lying in my upper berth
above good-looking women in the lower berth on a thous-
and train-wanderings. They were all of them tall and sensual-
looking Jewesses, proud, potent, amber, dark, and enigmatic.
I always felt they would not rebuff me if I spoke to them,
but yet I did not speak. Later on, however, I wondered
about their lives. Yet I have been with a thousand women,
their amber thighs spread amorously in bright golden hay.

"Pent in my dark soul I have sought in many countries
my heart's hope and my father's land, the lost but un-
forgotten half of my own soul. In the fierce, splendid,
strange and secret North have I sought; and, on the other
hand, in the secret, strange, splendid and fierce South.
In the fatal web of the City strangely and bitterly have
I savored the strange and bitter miracle of life and wondered darkly at the dark wonder of man's destiny. Amid
this phantasmagoric chaos, in a thousand little sleeping
towns built across the land (O my America! O my!) I have
pursued my soul's desire, looking for a stone, a leaf, a door
we never found, feeling my Faustian life intolerably in my
entrails. I have quivered a thousand times in sensual terror
and ecstatic joy as the 5:07 pulled in. I have felt a wild and
mournful sorrow at the thought, the wonderful thought,
that everything I have seen and known (and have I not
known and seen all that is to be seen and known upon this
dark, brooding continent?) has come out of my own life, is
indeed I, or me, the youth eternal, many-visaged and many-
volumed.

"Whatever it may be, I have sought it through my kalei-
doscopic days and velvet-and-duvetyn-breasted nights, and
in my dark, illimitable madness, in my insatiate and huge

unrest, in my appalling and obscene fancies, in my haunting and lonely memories (for we are all lonely), in my grotesque, abominable and frenzied prodigalities, I have always cried aloud—"

"Whoo-oops," gargled, snorted, and snuffled Aunt Liz from out her dream of time.

"What is it that we know so well and cannot speak?" continued the youth, striding a thousand strides across a hundred floors. "What is it that we speak so well and cannot know? Why this ceaseless pullulation stirring in my branching veins, not to be stilled even by the white small bite and tigerish clasp of secret women, of whom I have had one thousand in round figures? Whence the savagery, the hunger and the fear? I have sought the answer in four hundred and twelve libraries, including the Mercantile, the 42nd Street Public, the Muhlenberg Branch, and the Brooklyn—ah, Brooklyn, vast, mysterious, and never-to-be-forgotten Brooklyn and its congeries of swarming, unfathomable life, O Brooklyn! I have read in ten years at least twenty thousand books, devouring them twelve hours a day, no holidays, four hundred pages to a book, or in other words,—and I am furiously fond of other words— I have read thirty-three pages a minute, or a page every two seconds. Yet during this very same period I managed with ease to prowl ten thousand wintry, barren, and accursed streets, to lie with one thousand women, and take any number of train-trips. (Oh! the dark earth stroking forever past the huge projectile!) This is it to be a Gant! Questing my destiny lying ever before me, I have been life's beauty-drunken lover, and kept women and notebooks in a hundred cities, yet have I never found the door or turned the knob or slipped the bolt or torn off the leaf or crossed the road or climbed the fence. I have seen fury riding in the mountains, but who will show me the door?"

"Phuh! Phuh!" howled Uncle Habbakuk from out his illimitable loneliness; and "Whoo-oop!" came from Aunt Liz, lost in her dream of time. Both lost, all lost, lost forever, forever lost.

How to Attract the Attention
of a Schrafft's Hostess

Before setting down one or two methods which the writer has found practical, it may be helpful to explain how Schrafft's hostesses are selected. There are four basic tests. The applicant must secure a passing grade in Extension, Chin Inclination, Eye-Glazing, and Automatic Ear-Muffling.

Extension. The applicant must be sufficiently tall so that it will not be feasible for her to notice, without bending, the signal of any seated guest, male or female, of ordinary size.

Chin Inclination. Let us assume that the common or non-hostess chin is normally held out from the vertical line of the neck roughly at a right angle. Looking up from Thirty-fourth Street to the Empire State tower, one enlarges this angle considerably, approaching as a limit 180°, or a straight angle. The would-be hostess must either possess naturally or be able at will to assume a Chin Inclination striking a mean between these two angles—or, in other words, 135°, measured against the neckline. It is hardly necessary to point out the reason for this. I, for example, am five feet eight and three-quarters inches tall—about the stature of an average American male. Let us imagine that, wishing to attract the attention of a passing hostess, I suddenly rise from my seat directly in her path and look square into what I assume (as

461

she is apt to be about my own height) will turn out to be her eyes. A 90° Chin Inclination would be fatal. She is sure to see me. But consider the 135° Chin Inclination. If I am not six feet one or over, I cannot meet the hostess's eye unless I have made an appointment in advance. Hence, she does not see me, performs that dreamy and graceful sidestep characteristic of her profession, and is off.

However, fully to protect the hostess against being successfully accosted or signaled by a guest, two other safeguards are called into play. The first is the *Eye Glaze*. This physiological talent is used whenever, through ill chance, the glances of the hostess and the patron actually meet. Exactly at the split second of intersection, a sort of semi-opaque film is drawn over the eyes of the hostess and she undulates by.

It is at this point that the average or amateur guest will tend to utter some such salutation as "Miss," in accents ranging from an intimidated mutter to a strong clarion cry. Should the diner thus call out, the hostess reacts with another specialized physiological characteristic—the *Automatic Ear-Muffle*, which requires no further description.

The applicant who passes these four tests—Extension, Chin Inclination, Eye-Glazing, and Automatic Ear-Muffling —becomes a Schrafft's hostess and is ready to non-observe patrons professionally.

What is to be done? First, it is important not to be discouraged. The number of Schrafft patrons who have successfully attracted the attention of a hostess is, despite the strength of the opposing forces, relatively large and, in my considered opinion, increasing. Indeed, I know of a case in which a patron suddenly held up his index finger, caught a hostess completely off guard before she had time to adjust

Chin Inclination or Eye Glaze, and actually got her attention without more ado. This is known as a hostess-in-one.

I submit herewith a few sample suggestions. Each has been personally tested; none is infallible; all have proved successful at least once.

First, the elements. Tripping up a passing hostess is not good form. It has been done. I have done it myself, though only when wearing tennis shoes. But I do not advise it as a general mode of attack, for the entire maneuver is apt to be misunderstood by your fellow-diners, as well as by the management. A light kick on the shins, apparently accidental, as your hostess goes by, is excusable and often effective, though the average hostess shin tends to the osseous and must be approached with caution. Never, of course, pinch a hostess.

The sudden assumption of a grotesque mask as the hostess floats by, the wearing of luminous paint, and the use of various noise-producing machines, such as rattles, whistles, small cap pistols, and bull-roarers—all these have their points, but are tainted with a fatal defect. They are *outré*, hence easily remembered. Your competent hostess may stop once at the sight of a cut-out pumpkin quickly adjusted over the patron's face, but she will never do so again. Once conditioned to such obvious signals, she is as remote and unseizable as ever.

Nor is there much use in requesting your waitress to ask your hostess to stop by for a moment. A well-seasoned hostess pays no more attention to a waitress than to a patron. But a hostess—and this is her Achilles' heel—will gladly notice *another* hostess. In fact, hostesses are abnormally gregarious. At almost any time, but particularly during the height of the luncheon and dinner hours, a small, compact knot of hostesses may be observed in some inaccessible corner of the restaurant, busily devising plans for rendering the service in

Schrafft's more homey. The existence of such hostess coveys provides the alert diner with, if I may be jocular, an attractive weapon. I call it the Divided Family Shift. If you are dining with your wife, place her at a table at one end of the dining room; yourself you place at the opposite end of the room, along the diagonal. This makes it impossible, of course, for you to dine with your wife and lays your behavior open to a certain amount of misinterpretation in case the two of you are noted by a friend; but omelets cannot be made without breaking eggs. Now wait until all the hostesses are congregated in or near your wife's corner. She is watching you. You pass her some simple, previously agreed upon signal. At once she tries to catch the attention of the hostesses conferring near her table. They, of course, obey an automatic tropism. They move rapidly in a body in such a manner as to get as far away as possible from your wife's signal. This, naturally, takes them in *your* direction. As they pass by, you get into action. You still have their individual resistances to overcome, but your chance of actually attracting their attention is multiplied by the number of hostesses. I have tried the Divided Family Shift many times, with an average to date of .250. I consider this quite decent.

The simplest of my methods, requiring no apparatus in the way of a wife, is the Contrary Act. Be oblivious of the entire world of Shattuck. Pay no attention to the waitress when she brings you anything. Bury your nose in your Southern Bisque. With calculated abstraction allow your free hand to dabble gently in the butter. Within three minutes you will have a hostess at your side and a "Something you wanted?" dropped in your ear. And you have her—for the joke is that you *do* want something. During those years when I was first sowing my wild tables d'hôte, I spent many enjoyable moments watching the startled expression on a hostess's face as she fell like a perfect *fool* for the Contrary Act.

During this early period, too, I often resorted to the use of a small sign reading "Miss!" which I attached to a stick and raised above hostess-eye-level at a favorable moment. Napkin-flapping, hitting the tumbler with a knife, finger-snapping, or even dropping your chicken patty on the floor are all methods of a similar type. They are elementary but frequently successful in the case of an inexperienced and incompetent hostess, or one who has been poorly trained and really should have been a waitress.

My favorite tactic, however, is the Small Boy Decoy. To work this successfully, you are obliged to own a Small Boy, as I do (though he is rapidly growing too large for effective manipulation), and he must be a constant accessory whenever you eat at Schrafft's. The Small Boy Decoy method is based on my observation that a Schrafft's hostess, while paying no attention to the most frantic adult, will, upon noticing that a Small Boy is one of the party (a Small Girl will do in a pinch, but a Boy is the thing), at once bend over, smile, coo, be gracious, and offer him a plate of pink mints. At this point you have your hostess at an obvious disadvantage; she is bent over—Chin Angle gone, Eye Glaze forgotten, Muffle cut out. You address your request to her, and the thing is done. The Small Boy, once his work is over, may be stuffed under the table, together with the mints, and forgotten until you wish to attract the attention of the hostess again, at which point he is reproduced. A fairly tough Small Boy will last you a dozen meals before wearing out.

Some Passing Remarks on Some Passing Remarks

ONE OF my hobbies is the collecting of deathbed utterances. I consider this pastime thoroughly healthy-minded. Philately seems far less defensible. A stamp is issued by a faceless government office with which our personal connection is slight. A good passing remark, as we may call it, is issued by an interesting human being taking a final journey we are all scheduled to make. True, a stamp's value may increase, but a great curtain line's value is vast to begin with. Into it a man may pack the meat, the very pemmican of his character. He may say what he truly thinks or—just as revealing—what he would like us to think he thinks. In short, I collect deathbed statements for the life that is in them.

To all is granted the experience of dying, to none the experience of death. We may watch the candle as it gutters but never as it goes out. My file of final bulletins therefore tells us nothing about the exact moment of extinction but much, I think, about the highly charged period just before that moment.

Some of the bulletins, of course, are too deliciously pat to be trustworthy—Voltaire's for example. As his bedside lamp flared up he is *supposed* to have said, "The flames *already*?" Of all these communications, however, I find least satisfactory those that have been patently worked up against that
466

experience in our lives for which we have more time to prepare than any other. I fear we must put down as too well-rehearsed Heinrich Heine's farewell frivolity: "God will pardon me—it's His profession." So, too, is Madame Roland's "O Liberty! Liberty! How many crimes are committed in thy name!" Lope de Vega, that prodigy of nature, survived the writing of some two thousand plays, and in his last hour issued the following full-dress solemnity: "True glory is in virtue. Ah, I would willingly give all the applause I have received, to have performed one good action more." This is too goody-goody to be true. Such a last-minute attempt to bribe the fair opinion of posterity seems counterfeit. Similarly pompous is the final remark of Laplace: "What we know is not much; what we do not know is immense."

To die like a saint one must have lived like a saint. In one of the most beautiful sentences ever uttered *in extremis* the great philosopher Plotinus, dying in A.D. 270, said: "Now I shall endeavor to make that which is divine in me rise up to that which is divine in the universe." But to get away (if I may so put it) with such magnificent rhetoric one must be a Plotinus.

Joseph Addison, the essayist whose *Spectator* Papers millions of school children have carefully learned to avoid reading, was a good man but a stuffy one. The stuffing still clings to his last utterance: "See in what peace a Christian can die." A good many famous men have, like Addison, been the last to congratulate themselves. For self-esteem, however, Addison pales before Auguste Comte, the French Positivist philosopher who, just before expiring, made his last positive statement. "What an irreparable loss!" sighed Comte.

On the other hand self-disregard has marked many concluding hours. Old Crome, the English landscape painter, died with the name of Hobbema, another painter, on his lips.

Gainsborough died saying cheerfully, "We are all going to Heaven, and Vandyke is of the company." Charles II, the perfect cavalier to the end, died with Nell Gwyn's name on his lips. ("Don't let poor Nellie starve.") The most moving example on record, not merely of self-disregard but of the most exquisite consideration for others, is that of Lawrence Oates, a member of the tragic Scott Antarctic expedition of 1912. Aware that he was dying, unwilling to handicap his comrades who were in almost equally grievous case, he remarked quietly, "I am just going outside and may be some time." Then he left the tent, walked out into the blizzard, and was never seen again.

Of all the valedictory notes that of nobility is the most perilous to strike. As we see in Lope de Vega's case the phrasing betrays even the slightest falsity of touch. "Perhaps the sentence gives you more alarm than it does me," said Giordano Bruno, condemned to the flames, to his Inquisitor. This sounds and is genuine; for Bruno was telling the truth not only about himself, but about something bigger than himself, man's passion to be free.

No less noble, if more eloquent, are the last words of the martyred Latimer to his fellow-martyr Ridley, as the flames began to rise about them: "Be of good comfort, Master Ridley, and play the man. We shall this day light such a candle, by God's grace, in England, as I trust shall never be put out."

Grim wit lies in the words; a lighter-hearted humor shines in the final utterances of Sir Walter Raleigh as he was led to the block. Feeling the edge of the axe, he commented, " 'Tis a sharp remedy, but a sure one for all ills." When asked how he wished to place his head on the block, he replied, "So the heart be right, 'tis no matter which way the head lies."

The gallant behavior of Raleigh is matched by that of the

great-hearted Sir Thomas More, sent to the Tower by his King in 1534. As he ascended the rickety scaffold, he turned to the attendant with the words, "I pray you, Master Lieutenant, see me safe up, and for my coming down let me shift for myself." On the block he drew his beard aside, saying, "This hath not offended the King."

Last-minute nobility may be entirely secular. The concluding words of the free-thinking feminist Mary Wollstonecraft were addressed to her husband, anxiously awaiting some sign of grace: "I know what you are thinking of, but I have nothing to communicate on the subject of religion." Such indefatigable strong-mindedness has its humorous as well as its heroic aspect. In a related but wittier vein are Thoreau's well-known final comments. Asked whether he had made his peace with God, he replied mildly that he was not aware they had ever quarreled. Reference being made to a hereafter, he remarked, "One world at a time." His ultimate words, however, uttered as his mind began to fog, have about them the wistfulness of a dream. "Moose . . . Indians. . . . " whispered the author of *Walden*, and died. This has a kind of incoherent poetry, just as Stonewall Jackson's variously quoted final sentence (from which Ernest Hemingway may have derived the title of one of his novels) has a perfected poetry: "Let us go over the river, and sit in the shade of the trees."

Nobility is perhaps not quite the word for the way in which certain aristocrats, particularly the French, have faced the finish. In 1567 the aged Constable de Montmorency, receiving a mortal wound on the field of battle, waved off assistance with "I have not lived eighty years without learning how to stand dying for a quarter of an hour." Admirable arrogance, this; and even more admirably arrogant, Philippe

Égalité's curt command in 1793 to the executioner who was about to remove his boots: "Tush, they will come off better after. Let us have done."

Thus the French manner. The English is rather different, with less *panache* and more phlegm, though everyone remembers Nelson's magnificently theatrical "Kiss me, Hardy." The great economist Adam Smith looked around at his mourning friends and remarked, "I believe we must adjourn the meeting to some other place." Even more characteristically British is the last recorded statement of George III's Lord Chancellor, Edward Thurlow: "I'll be shot if I don't believe I'm dying." But the most wonderfully British farewell utterance of all is preserved for us in the *Notebooks* of Samuel Butler. He mentions a New Zealander named Wright who, visited by a friend in his last hours, said casually, "Be pleased to leave the room. I want to die." The friend did so, and so did Mr. Wright. Butler's own last words, addressed to his valet, were, "Have you brought the checkbook, Alfred?"

The seventeenth-century English poet, Sir William Davenant, apologizing for his inability to finish a heroic poem on which he had been working, said gracefully, "I shall ask leave to desist, when I am interrupted by so great an experiment as dying." Lord Chesterfield's last remark was as urbane as his entire life. Indicating one of his bedside visitors, he said politely, "Give Dayrolles a chair." Such understatement runs through many of the curtain lines of Englishmen.

Some curtain lines have the quality of heartbreak, like O. Henry's echo of a current popular song: "Turn up the lights, I don't want to go home in the dark." To me Grover Cleveland's "I have tried so hard to do the right" has this quality. The famous naturalist John Burroughs was homeward bound on a train from California when death overtook him. The pathos of his last utterance was unconscious: "How far are we from home?" Most touching of all is the last moment of Evariste Galois, the Chatterton of mathematics, one of the greatest mathematicians of the nineteenth century. Shot through the intestines as the result of an idiotic duel, he said to his sobbing younger brother: "Don't cry. I need all my courage to die at twenty."

The curtain speeches of scientists, however, are usually more detached. The noted English surgeon, Joseph Henry Green, passed away in 1863. Just before the end he looked at his doctor, pointed to his heart, said "Congestion," then counted his own pulse, remarked, "Stopped," and died. The great eighteenth-century Swiss anatomist Albrecht von Haller followed much the same procedure, his last words being "The artery ceases to beat." DeLagny, the French mathematician, was quite unable to recognize the faces of his friends, but, asked by one of them, "What is the square of 12?" promptly replied, "144," thus expiring with an immortal truth upon his lips.

In his *Urne-Buriall* Sir Thomas Browne comments, with masterly understatement, "The long habit of living indisposeth us for dying." This may be so; yet it is surprising how many curtain lines have been witty or humorous or even cheerful.

In some cases the humor may have been unintentional. W. H. Vanderbilt (this is the gem of my collection) died worth about $200,000,000. His closing message: "I have had no real gratification or enjoyment of any sort more than my neighbor on the next block who is worth only half a million." The German philosopher Hegel's final reflection was "Only one man ever understood me." A pause. "And he didn't understand me." Frederick the Great's father, Frederick William I, probably saw nothing funny in his last remark. The attending man of God, quoting from Job, intoned, "Naked came I out of my mother's womb, and naked shall I return thither." The king—the Prussian cannot change his spots—interposed, "No, not quite naked, I shall have my uniform on."

Of witty closing remarks we have hundreds. There is the little dialogue (originally in French) between the dying Queen Caroline and her husband, George II. When she urged him to remarry after her death he said with noble renunciation, "No, I shall have mistresses." To which the Queen replied, "Ah! mon Dieu! That needn't stop you." There is Oscar Wilde calling for champagne, saying, "I am dying, as I have lived, beyond my means." There is Alexander Pope's statement to his doctor: "I am dying, sir, of a hundred good symptoms." There is Viscount Palmerston's "Die, my dear Doctor? That's the *last* thing I shall do." There is Disraeli, replying to the suggestion that Queen Victoria attend his deathbed: "Why should I see her? She will only want to give a message to Albert." One hundred per cent Hollywood is the similar near-the-end quotation of Barney Dean: "Anybody got any messages for Jolson?" Most charming in its wit is the centenarian Fontenelle's smiling reply to a question from his physician: "I feel nothing except a certain difficulty in continuing to exist."

Occasionally a last line will become immortal because it is so exquisitely irrelevant and ill-suited to the dimensions of the moment. William Pitt (the Younger) is supposed by pious historians to have uttered one of several variations on the "My country! Oh, my country!" theme. What he probably said, however, was: "I think I could eat one of Bellamy's pies."

One of my favorites is not exactly a simon-pure curtain line, but is too delightful to keep locked up in my collection case. It is said of Henry James that during his very last days he was visited by a friend, Sir Edmund Gosse, who came to inform him that James had just received the Order of Merit. The face of the dying novelist showed no sign of having understood a word of the message. Gosse tiptoed out. Then James opened his eyes and said, "Nurse, take away the candle and spare my blushes."

Somewhere the English detective-story writer Dorothy Sayers remarks: "Death seems to provide the minds of the Anglo-Saxon race with a greater fund of innocent amusement than any other single subject." There is much truth in this. At any rate, I hope I will not be thought ghoulish if I confess that I have frequently diverted myself by trying to invent appropriate closing remarks for the notables of our own time. Here, for instance, is the best I can do for Sam Gold-wyn: "I never thought I'd live to see this day."

Many of us, perhaps, in our secret moments, imagine the perfect curtain line that we would like to be remembered by. In my own case, to my great annoyance, the line I would like to leave behind was uttered many years ago by that great lady, Mary Wortley Montagu. It seems to me the perfect deathbed remark. "It has all been very interesting," said Lady Mary.

About the Author

CLIFTON FADIMAN was born in New York City in 1904, and graduated from Columbia University in 1925. In the half century just completed Mr. Fadiman has been a translator, a teacher, an advisor to Samuel Goldwyn, editor of Simon and Schuster, lecturer, and book review editor of *The New Yorker*. During these years writing—and editing such books as *Reading I've Liked, The Short Stories of Henry James*, and other books and anthologies—played a concurrent part, as this book gives evidence; and radio and TV chores grew into a memorable ten years as host of *Information Please*, M. C. of *This Is Show Business*, and conductor of the popular NBC radio series *Conversation*. Mr. Fadiman, a member of the Board of Judges of the Book-of-the-Month Club, an essayist for *Holiday* magazine, keeps a busy schedule as a platform reader across the country.